Hunting the Unicorn

To John

With great appreciation for
your work in Long Creudon
and in honor of Ruth Pitter,
who for many years was a
faithful member of this
parish —

With all best wishes and
to the glory of God —

Don W. King

Ruth Pitter standing on a piling, looking off into the distance. Courtesy of Mary-Lou Legg.

Hunting the Unicorn

A Critical Biography of Ruth Pitter

DON W. KING

The Kent State University Press
Kent, Ohio

Library of Congress Catalog Card Number 2008001511
ISBN 978-0-87338-947-1
Manufactured in the United States of America

Library of Congress Cataloging-in-Publication Data
King, Don W., 1951–
Hunting the unicorn : a critical biography of Ruth Pitter / Don W. King
p.   cm.
Includes bibliographical references and index.
ISBN 978-0-87338-947-1 (hardcover : alk. paper) ∞
1. Pitter, Ruth, 1897–1992. 2. Poets, English—20th century—Biography. I. Title.
PR6031.17Z75 2008
821'.912—dc22
[B]   2008001511

British Library Cataloging-in-Publication data are available.

12 11 10 09 08   5 4 3 2 1

To Bethany, Rebecca, Nathan, and Joanna

Contents

Acknowledgments — ix

Permissions — xi

Introduction — xiii

1 The Growth of a Poet, 1897–1920 — 1

2 Artisan Poet, 1921–1931 — 24

3 Critical Acclaim, 1932–1937 — 52

4 War Watches, 1938–1941 — 84

5 Crossing Over, 1942–1946 — 112

6 Friendship with C. S. Lewis, 1947–1949 — 141

7 Lurking in the Undergrowth, 1950–1953 — 162

8 Unexpected Turns, 1954–1955 — 195

9 Public Figure, 1956–1966 — 222

10 Flickering Fires, 1967–1992 — 250

Notes — 275

Bibliography — 319

Index — 335

Acknowledgments

This book began with a conversation and a mystery. When I was doing research for what eventually became C. S. *Lewis, Poet: The Impulse of His Poetic Legacy* (Kent State University Press, 2001), I spent many hours in Oxford at the Bodleian Library. One day while we were conversing, Judith Priestman, curator of the Bodleian's literary manuscripts, told me that a biography of Ruth Pitter was long overdue. She pointed out that while feminist criticism had rehabilitated the work of many seventeenth-, eighteenth-, and nineteenth-century female poets, those of the twentieth century had remained largely neglected, conspicuously so in the case of Pitter, the first woman to win the Queen's Gold Medal for Poetry. Priestman argued Pitter was worth writing about on those grounds alone. I made a mental note of her point and decided to explore the possibility of writing a critical biography of Pitter after I finished C. S. *Lewis, Poet*.

This decision was affirmed days later when I came across correspondence between Lewis and Pitter about her admiration for *Perelandra*, the second book in his Ransom trilogy. Pitter had been so taken with the ending of *Perelandra* that she asked Lewis if she might compose poetic transcriptions of the final pages as a mnemonic. He readily agreed, although he joked that he did not see why she wanted to waste her poetry on his prose. In subsequent letters between them I learned that she had done the poetic transcriptions. Since her transcriptions supported my essential contention in C. S. *Lewis, Poet*—that Lewis's best poetry is found in his prose—I began a dogged search for the transcriptions. I wrote the Lewis estate, but they did not know where Pitter's papers were located. I wrote Pitter's publisher with similar results. I was stumped by the mystery. So when I returned to the Bodleian the following summer, I decided to ask if the library held Pitter's papers. To my delight, I learned that her papers were indeed held by the Bodleian.

My happiness was short lived. When I asked if I could review her papers, I was told I could not. Why, I asked. Because, I was told, Pitter's papers had not been cataloged. When I explained why it was so important for me to look at her papers (of which there were at that time thirty-six boxes), I was given limited access to her papers. Since I was certain the transcriptions were in spiral notebooks, I soon limited my search to three boxes. At the same time, my time at the

Bodleian was almost over, and I had a plane to catch. On the last afternoon of my visit and in the next-to-last notebook of the last box, I struck the equivalent of research oil—there were the transcriptions. Solving this mystery confirmed my interest in and appreciation for Ruth Pitter, and so this book was born.

I have many people to thank. In addition to giving me the initial push, Dr. Priestman has been a faithful supporter in all my efforts, as has her colleague Colin Harris, reader services librarian and superintendent of the Modern Papers and John Johnson Reading Room. Also of great assistance has been Jeff Walden, archives researcher at the BBC Written Archives Centre, Caversham Park, Reading. Elizabeth Pearson, the library director at Montreat College, and her staff have been endlessly patient and helpful in securing materials. I am grateful as well to the staff at the Marion E. Wade Center, particularly Christopher W. Mitchell and Marjorie Mead, who encouraged my research and made me comfortable during my many visits to the Wade Center. I am most thankful to have made a delightful new friend in Mark Pitter, Pitter's nephew and literary executor; Mark has been ever helpful and encouraging, and I have fond memories of many visits to his home in Ludlow. I am grateful to the C. S. Lewis Society of Oxford for inviting me to speak on Pitter and for their helpful criticism, and I thank also the C. S. Lewis Foundation for permitting me to lead a two-week seminar in the summer of 2004 at the Kilns, where I floated drafts of my chapters with the students in attendance.

I owe debts of gratitude to Dan Struble, president of Montreat College, for granting me a sabbatical to work on this book, and the Appalachian College Association for awarding me two summer research grants. Thanks are due as well to my student research assistants Lee Shirk, Jennifer Philips, and Ashli Roland. I have also been encouraged and urged on by many of Pitter's admirers, including Thomas McKean, Ian Timpany, Kerry Montgomery, Peter Dickinson, Morar Randolph, Mary Thomas, Ann Soutter, Walter Hooper, Joe Christopher, John Adams, Salwa Koddham, Laura Cecil, and Michael Morrey. I am also grateful to Kim McMurtry, who read and edited the manuscript. I am most appreciative of the excellent editorial advice of the Kent State University Press, especially my editors, Mary D. Young and Joanna Hildebrand Craig. Finally, I owe my wife, Jeanine, a great debt since I spent so many hours away from her while working on this book; while Ruth Pitter was never really my mistress, at times I am sure my wife wondered why I spent so much time with "that woman"!

Permissions

All copyrighted material by Ruth Pitter is used by permission of Mark Pitter. Unless otherwise indicated, all letters, both to and from Pitter, other material about her life, her manuscript notebooks, and her unpublished poems are available in her uncataloged papers in the New Bodleian Library, University of Oxford. Used by permission. Pitter's Journal recollection of her correspondence with C. S. Lewis is also in the Bodleian Library, MS. Eng. lett. c. 220/3 and c. 220/5. Used by permission.

The Oral History Interview with Pitter, conducted by Lyle W. Dorsett on July 23, 1985, © The Marion E. Wade Center, Wheaton College, Wheaton, Illinois, is used by permission.

Unless otherwise indicated, transcripts of all BBC radio and television broadcasts in which Pitter appeared and all her letters to the BBC are available in the BBC Written Archives Centre, Caversham Park, Reading, England. Used by permission.

Appearing in this volume is adapted material originally published in the following articles: "The Poetry of Prose: C. S. Lewis, Ruth Pitter, and *Perelandra*." *Christianity and Literature* 49 (Spring 2000): 331–56; "Quorum Porum: The Literary Cats of T. S. Eliot, Ruth Pitter, and Dorothy L. Sayers." *Seven: An Anglo-American Literary Review* 18 (2001): 25–45; "The Anatomy of a Friendship: The Correspondence of Ruth Pitter and C. S. Lewis, 1946–1962." *Mythlore* 24 (Summer 2003): 2–24; "Silent Music: The Letters of Ruth Pitter." *Bulletin of the New York C. S. Lewis Society* 35 (Spring 2004): 1–15; "The Religious Poetry of Ruth Pitter." *Christianity and Literature* 54 (Summer 2005): 521–62; and "Fire and Ice: C. S. Lewis and the Love Poetry of Joy Davidman and Ruth Pitter." *Seven: An Anglo-American Literary Review* 22 (2005): 60–88.

Excerpts from *Books, Broadcasts, and War, 1931–1949*, vol. 2 of C. S. Lewis, *Collected Letters*. Ed. Walter Hooper (London: HarperCollins, 2004) and *Narnia, Cambridge, and Joy, 1950–1963*, vol. 3 of C. S. Lewis, *Collected Letters*. Ed. Walter Hooper (London: HarperCollins, 2006) used by permission of C. S. Lewis Pte. Ltd. All references from *Letter to a Comrade* are used by permission of David and Douglas Gresham.

Excerpts from letters from Ruth Pitter to Walter Hooper are from the Walter McGehee Hooper Papers #4236, Southern Historical Collection, Wilson Library, and are reprinted with permission of the University of North Carolina at Chapel Hill.

Excerpts from letters from Ruth Pitter to Hilaire Belloc are reprinted with permission of John J. Burns Library, Boston College or University Archives, John J. Burns Library, Boston College.

Excerpts from letters from Ruth Pitter to David Cecil are reprinted with permission of the David Cecil estate.

Excerpts from letters from Ruth Pitter to Mary Cooley are reprinted with permission from Mary E. Cooley Papers, Special Collections Library, University of Michigan.

Excerpts of letters from Ruth Pitter to Lawrence Lee are from the Papers of the *Virginia Quarterly Review*, MSS 292-a, Special Collections, and are used by the permission of the University of Virginia Library.

Excerpts of letters from Ruth Pitter to Herbert Palmer are used by permission of The Harry Ransom Humanities Research Center, University of Texas at Austin.

Excerpts of letters from Ruth Pitter to Nettie Palmer are from Palmer Papers, MS 1174, and are used by permission of the National Library of Australia.

Excerpts of letters from Ruth Pitter to Arthur Russell are from Ruth Pitter Letters, Add. 70721, and are used by permission of the British Library.

Excerpts of letters from Ruth Pitter to Stephen Tennant are either privately held by Ann Soutter (used by permission) or are from Stephen Tennant Papers, 1929–1977, Cage 643, Manuscripts Archives and Special Collections, and are used by permission of Washington State University, Pullman, Washington.

Excerpts of letters from Ruth Pitter to Theodore Maynard are from The Theodore Maynard Papers, Special Collections Division, and are reprinted with permission of Georgetown University Library.

All biblical references are to the King James Version.

Introduction

Although Ruth Pitter (1897–1992) is not well-known, her credentials as a poet are extensive, and in England from the mid-1930s to the mid-1970s she maintained a modest yet loyal readership. In total she produced seventeen volumes of new and collected verse. Her *A Trophy of Arms* (1936) won the Hawthornden Prize for Poetry in 1937, and in 1954 she was awarded the William E. Heinemann Award for *The Ermine* (1953). Most notably, perhaps, she became the first woman to receive the Queen's Gold Medal for Poetry in 1955; this unprecedented event merited a personal audience with the queen. Furthermore, from 1946 to 1972 she was often a guest on BBC radio programs, and from 1956 to 1960 she appeared regularly on the BBC's *The Brains Trust*, one of the first television talk programs. In 1974 the Royal Society of Literature elected her to its highest honor, a companion of literature, and in 1979 she received her last national award when she was appointed a commander of the British Empire.[1]

However, little critical work has been done on Pitter. There is no biography, no book-length evaluation of her work, and no critical edition of her poetry. Accordingly, *Hunting the Unicorn* is a first step in correcting this critical oversight, providing both a biographical overview of Pitter's life and detailed discussions of her important volumes of verse. Pitter's poetic impulse, the desire "to express something of the secret meanings which haunt life and language,"[2] marks her as an important voice of twentieth-century British poetry. Yet because she was never associated with a literary group or movement, and in spite of the many poets and writers who admired her work, she has not attracted widespread critical notice. Pitter, in contrast to the modernist poets T. S. Eliot, Ezra Pound, and W. H. Auden, was a traditional poet in the line of Thomas Hardy, A. E. Housman, W. B. Yeats, and Philip Larkin. She rarely experimented with meter or verse form, nor did she explore modernist themes or offer critiques of modern English society. Instead she worked with familiar meters and verse forms, and the essential subject of her poetry is the human condition. For example, in "The Bridge," from *The Bridge*, written during the height of World War II while she was living in a heavily bombed area of London, she asked: "Where is the truth that will inform my sorrow?" Her decision to take a job in a munitions factory and leave her life as an artisan was played out daily as Pitter crossed the Battersea

Bridge, leaving behind her Chelsea studio. However, rather than sink into despair at this prospect, Pitter embraced the unknown, thus affirming the resiliency of the human condition:

> O truth, is it death over the river,
> Or is it life, new life in a land of summer?
> The mind is an empty vessel, a shape of sorrow,
> Fill it with life or death, for it is hollow,
> Dark wine or bright, fill it, let us go over.
> Let me go find my truth, over the river.

Pitter's reluctance to alter her voice and follow in the modernist line explains in part why critics have overlooked her poetry. She was not trendy, avant garde, or impenetrable. As a result, for many years she labored at her craft "in comparative but wholly unjustified obscurity."[3] Moreover, when significant literary success came, critical recognition of her achievements was muted. I believe the failure to bring a critical perspective to her life and work is a serious aesthetic, intellectual, and literary oversight. The intensity and passion yet controlled insight into the human condition reflected in her poetry merit sustained scholarly attention and broad exposure. Accordingly, Hunting the Unicorn is for both scholars and general readers: for the former so that they may place Pitter into the overall context of twentieth-century British poetry, and for the latter so that they may read about a modest, hard-working woman who witnessed the world through the lens of a gifted poet.

That said, if this were a different book, it might begin: "Once upon a time in a mysterious, dark forest, there lived a misty-eyed young girl living in a magical cottage. . . ." Indeed, any study of Pitter must take as its starting point her deeply felt sense of place. In particular, the Hainault Forest in Essex, an ancient grove of oak, chestnut, beech, and elder on the outskirts of greater London, was a much beloved spot for the young Pitter. Though reduced somewhat in size in the hundred-plus years since Pitter's birth, this tract of forest is still largely intact, preserved by the Woodland Trust. Within five miles of the London suburb of Ilford, where Pitter grew up, Hainault Forest was a favorite place for family walks and day trips. When a small cottage became available for rent, Pitter and her siblings, Olive and Geoffrey, begged their parents to rent it, renouncing any future holiday visits to the seaside.

In 1914 the cottage was rented, and Pitter's delight was unbounded. Weekends and summer holidays were now consumed by visits to the cottage, and it became the family's second home. Free to wander in the forest, Pitter developed an acute eye for the natural objects she encountered. The symbolic power of the cottage and the forest finds outlet, however, not in her early poems; instead,

later in life, especially as she is developing her mature poetic voice in A Mad
Lady's Garland, she returns imaginatively to the cottage and the forest in dozens of poems. It becomes a "spot in time" that sustains and nurtures her poetic
sensibilities for the rest of her life. While some of her poems reflect an eye for
minute natural detail, many others resonate with mystical reflections on the relationship between humankind and nature as well as thoughtful musings on the
human condition. While it would be an exaggeration to say that every poem
she writes after A Mad Lady's Garland is influenced by her experiences in the
cottage, it is certainly accurate to say that Hainault Forest is the most dynamic
and pervasive force powering her fertile imagination.

    At the same time, the story of Ruth Pitter is not a fairy tale. On the contrary,
although she was brought up by loving parents and enjoyed an almost idyllic
childhood, she did not enjoy her early schools, and whatever hopes she may
have entertained about a university education were dashed by World War I.
Later she worked as an artisan, doing decorative painting and even opening her
own business, Deane and Forester, with her friend Kathleen O'Hara in 1930.
Years of hard work were ironically repaid when the business failed because of the
shortages brought on by World War II. In addition, in spite of Pitter's critical success as a poet, her volumes of poetry sold modestly; as she herself admitted, she
never could have survived on profits from her writing. Furthermore, while Pitter
enjoyed several romantic dalliances in the 1930s during her Bohemian days in
Chelsea, where she and O'Hara ran their business, she never married. After 1953
she and O'Hara retired to the village of Long Crendon near Oxford, and while
she enjoyed visits from Lord David Cecil, C. S. Lewis, and Owen Barfield, she
continued her work as an artisan and relied upon a good deal of work from BBC
radio and television to make ends meet. After O'Hara died in 1973, Pitter faded
a bit from public view, although she remained active in the events of her church
parish. Blind in the last years of her life, she died February 29, 1992.

    In approaching this study, I have organized each chapter around the impor-
tant people, events, and publications in the years covered. Accordingly, chapter
1, "The Growth of a Poet (1897–1920)," considers Pitter's early development
as a poet with particular attention to how A. R. Orage, editor of the socialist
weekly the New Age, helped launch and nurture her poetic career. Central
to this chapter is an exploration of her earliest published poems, culminating
in a discussion of First Poems (1920). Chapter 2, "Artisan Poet (1921–1931),"
explores Pitter's experiences in Chelsea as a hard-working artisan and how she
labors to write verse in the few free moments she can snatch. In addition, it
examines how Hilaire Belloc's befriending of Pitter contributes to her poetic
success in publishing First and Second Poems (1927) and Persephone in Hades
(1931), Pitter's only sustained attempt at narrative verse. Chapter 3, "Critical
Acclaim (1932–1937)," offers close studies of A Mad Lady's Garland (1934),

the satiric transitional volume in her development of a clear, distinct, mature poetic voice, and A *Trophy of Arms* (1936), winner of the Hawthornden Prize, the breakthrough volume that would bring her sustained literary attention.

Chapter 4, "War Watches (1938–1941)," discusses her developing relationship with literary critic Lord David Cecil, her experiences in London during the early days of the blitz, her mystical *A Spirit Watches* (1939), and her comic *The Rude Potato* (1941). Chapter 5, "Crossing Over (1942–1946)," investigates how World War II affects Pitter's professional and poetic life, especially as she sees her business gradually dry up and is forced to begin working in a wartime munitions factory. Yet during this time she produces *The Bridge* (1945), her most powerfully disturbing volume of verse. Chapter 6, "Friendship with C. S. Lewis (1947–1949)," explores in detail the genesis of her friendship with Lewis; another comic volume, *On Cats* (1947), is also discussed. Chapter 7, "Lurking in the Undergrowth (1950–1953)," continues exploring Pitter's friendship with Lewis as well as her move from London for the leisurely fields of Long Crendon. Most importantly, however, this chapter explores the pinnacle of Pitter's poetic success in *The Ermine* (1953), a volume reflecting both her deft technical expertise as well as her movement toward Christianity.

Chapter 8, "Unexpected Turns (1954–1955)," continues the story of Pitter's relationship with Lewis, highlighting in particular Joy Gresham's impact on Pitter and Lewis's relationship; in addition, I explore in some detail the love poetry of both women, suggesting how this poetry sheds light on why Lewis eventually married Gresham. I also chronicle how Pitter achieves unexpected public prominence, in part because of her achievement of the Queen's Gold Medal for Poetry in 1955. Chapter 9, "Public Figure (1956–1966)," follows up on her years in the public eye, especially her work on BBC radio and television. She appeared often on a variety of BBC radio programs such as *Woman's Hour,* and as a frequent panelist on the BBC television program *The Brains Trust,* where Pitter's thoughtful comments on the wide range of issues discussed made her a favorite among viewers. Moreover, her muted but still powerful poetic voice calls out again with the appearance of *Still by Choice* (1966). Chapter 10, "Flickering Fires (1967–1992)," traces her years of retirement and discusses not only several collected editions of her poetry and her new volume, *End of Drought* (1975), but also her efforts at writing religious drama for her parish church in Long Crendon. The final portion of the chapter shows that her mind remains sharp as she corresponds with her many admirers, and that until the very end she writes poetry, culminating in her last new volume of poetry, *A Heaven to Find* (1987).

At her death in 1992 one critic wrote: "She came to enjoy perhaps the highest reputation of any living English woman poet of her century."[4] It is time that her work is afforded the recognition it merits. More than anything else I believe the key to understanding Pitter's life and work is found in her essay "We Cannot

Take Less," which eventually aired as a BBC radio address under Pitter's title "Hunting the Unicorn":

> I was sitting in front of a cottage door, one day in spring, long ago; a few bushes and flowers round me, a bird gathering nesting-material, the trees of the forest at a little distance. A poor place—nothing glamorous about it . . . [when] suddenly everything assumed a different aspect—no, its true aspect. For a moment, it seemed to me, the truth appeared in its overwhelming splendour. The secret was out, the explanation given. Something that had seemed like total freedom, total power, total bliss—a good with no bad as its opposite—an absolute that had no opposite—this thing, so unlike our feeble nature, had suddenly cut across one's life—and vanished. . . . What *is* this thing? . . . Is it—could it be, after all—a hint of something more real than this life—a message from reality—perhaps a particle of reality itself? If so, no wonder we hunt it so unceasingly, and never stop desiring and pining for it.[5]

Ruth Pitter's poetry often takes us to hidden places—to the secret things of life, to the things just beyond the material, to the very meaning of life. Many times we catch glimpses of the hidden treasure. If human life is lived behind a veil faintly obscuring reality, Pitter's poems often lift the edge of the veil. In her hunt for the unicorn, many of us join the pursuit, because, like Pitter, we cannot take less.

Unless otherwise indicated, all letters—both to and from Ruth Pitter—other material about her life, her manuscript notebooks, and her unpublished poems are available in her uncataloged papers in the New Bodleian Library at the University of Oxford.

ONE

The Growth of a Poet,

1897–1920

Ruth Pitter was born November 7, 1897. The doctor who delivered her looked at his watch immediately afterward and said, "12, noon, exactly. Too late for church, but in excellent time for dinner." The terraced East End house at 1 Meath Road, Ilford, Essex, stands, indistinguishable from all the others, just a short walk from the Ilford railway station. Born near the end of Queen Victoria's reign, Pitter lived her early life under the benevolent shadow of the queen. World War I was still almost twenty years away, and while the Boer War excited much enthusiasm from 1899 to 1902, Pitter's childhood was largely free of political or military threat. Much of life was imbued with the still vigorous though dimming spirit of the queen. While the Industrial Revolution had taken place over a hundred years before and the rush of late nineteenth- and early twentieth-century technology had made a tremendous impact on English life, Ilford was still something of a backwater. Indeed, Pitter filtered much of her early life through the lens of living in direct contact with the English countryside.

At the same time, there were pressing economic concerns. Although the atom was still unsplit, the spirit of free trade and competition and the lack of a social welfare system meant that hundreds of thousands of Londoners lived in uncertainty. Each man had to provide for his family; failure to do so meant poverty, homelessness, and near starvation. There was no minimum wage, no unemployment pay, no free medical service, and no state or company retirement plan. For the respectable middle class, with almost nothing to fall back on, the fear of not being able to make ends meet was a perpetual worry. Even with regular work, a man could earn only enough income for the essentials; saving for a rainy day was almost impossible. Decent food, clothing, and shelter were all most families could hope for. Early on Pitter learned from her parents the signature tune of her time and class: "We can't afford it." Anxieties about food and clothing were so commonplace that Pitter's early life was tinged by melancholy; she learned as a young child that if one did not look after oneself and one's family, no one else would.

Her father, George Pitter (1862–1926), was born in nearby Bromley-by-Bow, and after his education at Culham College near Abingdon, he was employed by the London County Council as an assistant elementary teacher to poor and educationally disadvantaged children. A man committed to socialist ideas and causes, he lived out his principles through his devotion to teaching the children of lower-working-class families in Ilford. Quiet, self-contained, and detached, he had a rough-hewn physical handsomeness augmented by his big head of curly brown hair. Ruth's mother, Louisa Rosamund Pitter, née Murrell (1870–1941), was a formidable woman. Louisa's mother had been a boarder in a convent and was never visited by her parents; for this reason, she assumed she was illegitimate. Married to a master cabinetmaker who died young, Louisa's mother experienced a hard life. Her married life was unhappy and the births of her eleven children were often punctuated by attempts at self-induced abortion when she would throw herself down stairs. Because Louisa was one of the older children, she had to care for the younger ones, a task she did not relish. In order to be relieved of the responsibility of being nurse to one of her baby brothers or sisters, Louisa would take the child down into the scullery, take off its clothes, and make it sit bare bottomed on the cold, damp stone floor. When the child inevitably began crying, Ruth's grandmother would say, "Baby always cries with you. Give it to Alice [her sister] to nurse."

This hardened spirit could have proved dangerous when Louisa gave birth herself. In fact, after Ruth was born, Louisa, lacking any help and forced to get on as best she could, initially suffered from postnatal depression. For the first three weeks after the birth, all Louisa wanted was for someone to come and take Ruth away. But soon her maternal instinct was awakened, and Louisa decided she liked her new daughter very much. When Louisa went into labor with her second child, Olive, George was in a quandary, not knowing what to do with Ruth. Because he could not leave a two-year-old alone, he grabbed her, heaved her onto his shoulders, and ran out into a violent thunderstorm to get the doctor. As they plodded through the pouring rain, every time the thunder clapped, Ruth exclaimed, "Do it again, God!" Fortunately, all went well and Olive's birth in 1899 was an easy one; a third child, Geoffrey, followed in 1902.

Pitter's greatest early fortune was her parents because they worked selflessly to provide for her, Olive, and Geoffrey. While worries about money were constant, food was very cheap and the quality was high. For instance, imported fruit was plentiful, and Pitter's early love for luscious fruit is reflected later on in her gardening and poetry. Furthermore, Louisa worked hard to keep her children sensibly and comfortably clothed—knitting and sewing for them as well as earning money at odd jobs until she returned to teaching after Geoffrey started school. She also saw to it that their shoes were made to measure, relying on the services of an old crippled cobbler who lived nearby, and the shoes lasted an incredibly long time. Even when both parents were teaching, their combined monthly salaries barely made ends meet; often there was not one shilling left over. In spite of this, Louisa was above niggling economies. On more than one occasion she treated her family to a tin of tasty peaches she ought not to have purchased.

Although they had been educated as teachers at Anglican training colleges, George and Louisa were not devout. After having taught in the impoverished East End school all week, and perhaps furious at the poverty, dirt, and substandard housing they knew their students were mired in, the Pitters failed to see the connection between their own experience and the message of the church. At the same time, they did send their children to Sunday school, less perhaps because they cherished biblical training for their children and more because they needed to sleep in. Indeed, they told the children they could choose which Sunday school to attend. The three, probably at Ruth's direction, steered clear of the Roman Catholic Sunday school and attended a Wesleyan one instead because it had the best refreshments. Ruth was moved by a great placard there that depicted a glass of red wine and the text, "Look not thou upon the wine when it is red, when it giveth its colour in the cup, when it moveth itself aright" (Prov. 23:31). Her conclusion was that red wine was unwholesome but white wine was perfectly sound. Similarly, she learned her prayers imperfectly, substituting for "Almighty God" the phrase "Fortnightly God."

As an elementary school teacher, Louisa was well qualified, skilled, and experienced. In addition to the money she earned for her family, teaching gave her the interest and dignity of a professional life; moreover, she was a friend to the very poorest children she taught. She never complained about them, even though some were undoubtedly rough around the edges. As a firm disciplinarian, she took them all in stride. Her compassion for these disadvantaged children made her a passionate advocate whenever their welfare was in question. With a hard day behind her, she sometimes had little energy left for her own children. So, while the money she earned was necessary, weekdays during term were times when the three children were not closely attended to by their mother. To counter this, for a time one of Louisa's younger sisters, Kitty, came to care for the three children during the week. To Ruth, Aunt Kitty was an exotic, especially because she had imbibed completely the art nouveau movement. Everything she did was touched with magic—her workbag was a mysterious satchel and must be left alone, and her room had an uncanny, forbidden air. On one occasion Ruth and Olive accidentally broke Kitty's tiny Japanese teapot; Kitty held an inquest, putting out her hand for the broken pieces. Then she put her hand behind her. Looking solemn, she brought her hand forward again, now holding the unbroken teapot in it. For Ruth and Olive it was a mystifying but thrilling incident.

The family loved their Saturdays. With the week over, they awakened to the fact that no one had to go to school that day; if it was fine, they would plan a day trip, and during these times together the family felt most content. A favorite place was the Hainault Forest five miles away. While his children chattered excitedly about the flowers and birds they saw, George's nearsightedness prevented him from entering into their conversations. To their questions, he often said he did not know the answer or would simply refuse to speculate. Their favorite games included versions of the Swiss Family Robinson and Robin Hood. One of their own inventions was a game founded on the idea of one of them being the monarch of the world, owning everything and everybody. Of particular focus in this game were twelve castles filled with gold and jewels. Ruth always assumed the part of absolute monarch. She would cast her sister as a gentle creature who was allowed to put in a few timid words as a mother, aunt, or some other harmless relative. Geoffrey she normally made a small but smart dog, full of amusing tricks.

Ruth's early precocious spirit was revealed in several episodes. Until she was eight or so, her parents loaned her out to neighbors for parties when a child's entertainment might offset an otherwise dour event. Because she was so exuberant and energetic, she would turn cartwheels spontaneously out of sheer enthusiasm; so she was always sure she had on clean knickers. In another instance, probably in 1908, she wrote a letter to a local newspaper about the family dog:

Our pet is a little black dog. He is rather "freaky" in some places. He has one tooth that he does not want; it sticks out and makes him look "warlike." (No, I will not call it "formidable." My reason for this is that he is *not* formidable—far from it!) His left hind foot is graced by two spurs; the right one goes without. He is six inches longer than he ought to be, and one ear always looks dejected, and will not stand up. Perhaps he was behind when features, limbs, etc., were dealt out, and had to be content with what he could get! His proper name is "Nelson"; but he has been called by many others. He appreciates music; for, with his nose tilted towards the skies, he always endeavors to accompany one, especially with the violin, or vocal music. It is strange that his best musical efforts are brought into play when the doleful strains of "Oh where, oh where is my little dog gone?" are wailed out of a violin. I suppose he thinks he is lost. Very likely he says rude things to big dogs, for they always dust the pavement with him. I have never seen a more abject dog. He will not cringe before a stranger, but under the upraised hand of one he knows he will grovel in exquisite humility. He often gets on the table when it is set for tea, and steals the milk and sugar. He does not relish the presence of visitors. He will nip their calves or hang on their dresses. Once we failed to receive our morning correspondence, but next morning we received a double lot, which included the previous day's letters. These were all neatly written across with the words, "Dog loose."

The dry wit of this letter suggests a lithe mind and winsome spirit as well as delight in a good joke and buoyant self-confidence. Indeed, in spite of the real economic threats hanging over her family, Pitter's early life suggests a happy family unburdened by angst and self-pity.

The family certainly enjoyed the luxury of an infrequent holiday. On one excursion the family booked a train from Liverpool Station and nestled down comfortably in their seats. After a short while the train came to a junction at Crewe and an enormous woman with babies and bundles squeezed in. Seeing her plight, Pitter's mother ordered Ruth, Olive, and Geoffrey out of their seats and into the corridor. Although the three children were incensed at what they perceived to be a violation of justice—they were there first and were so enjoying their comfortable seats—they knew they could not protest to their mother. She would only say, "It's an order." Unlike her husband, who was rather tender and vulnerable, Louisa was firm and determined. She used to tell Ruth, "You are too like your father—bowled over by the first whiff of grapeshot."

Ruth's earliest effort to write a poem shows her innate love of language. After visiting an old derelict windmill, she felt the sensation of a poem "coming," and she likened it to the feeling one gets after being struck on the nose. The paradox of this old windmill—that it had once been so busy and productive but was now deserted and decaying—moved her to write this line: "The old mill stands with broken shaft and bulrushes all about." While she never finished the poem, the sudden overwhelming sensation that a poem was coming set the pattern for the genesis of almost every poem she wrote thereafter.[1] From her youth, a poem was like a physical encounter, often making her shiver and weep mysteriously. Her parents reinforced her early love for poetry. While their tastes in poetry were simple, characterized by an almost religious devotion to Francis Palgrave's *The Golden Treasury*, an anthology of traditional English verse, they nonetheless imprinted upon their children a profound love for poetry.[2] As teachers they never stopped teaching, so their children were regularly assigned poems to learn and then recite; a successful recitation usually resulted in a sixpence reward. During one poetry audition, Geoffrey, anxious and ambitious to please, attempted a piece he really did not understand; instead of beginning a stanza of Robert Herrick's "Corinna's Going A-Maying" with "Come, my Corinna, come," he bawled instead, "Come, my gorilla, come." Such mistakes aside, her experiences repeatedly reading *The Golden Treasury* and memorizing these poems stayed with Ruth throughout her life and brought a good deal of comfort to her.[3] She claimed this early discipline made her poetic memory "wax to receive and marble to retain," and this served her well later; after she went blind in the years just prior to her death, she often comforted herself by reciting favorite poems by Shakespeare, Milton, Wordsworth, and Tennyson.

Pitter's early love of language also led to mischief on occasion. After she started attending Downshall Elementary, the local elementary school in Ilford, in 1903, she was exposed to earthy slang, some of it quite obscene. She was fascinated by rude words more than anything else for a time. One day she came home for her midday meal (at this time there were no school lunches), pulled Olive aside, and told her she had something important to tell her. With Olive waiting in expectant excitement, Ruth said, "Bum!" Olive shrieked with delighted laughter, although, like Ruth, she did not know what the word really meant; the attraction for both girls was its forbidden quality.

Her experiences at Downshall Elementary outside class were rarely pleasant. Ruth was protective of Olive and early on acted as a substitute mother. After Olive began school, Ruth worried about her because she was small of stature. Having experienced herself the bullies of her own day, Ruth would often be in torment if she could not find her sister to see her home safely. Thrown together with hundreds of other children, many of them undisciplined and unruly, Ruth often found school life to be a matter of survival. Yet her pluck served her well. One day on her train trip back home from school, a boy swept into the railway coach where she and her girlfriends were sitting. Seeing a chance to bully them, the boy threw himself into them, knocking them down like bowling pins. Outraged, Pitter took up her fully loaded book bag and flogged the bully, eventually driving him from the coach. Later that day as her father was returning from school on the same train, the conductor tapped him on the shoulder and quipped, "Your daughter has a mighty swing!" On another occasion a different bully tormented Pitter and her girlfriends by pulling their hair so hard that they fell down on their backs. Enraged, she punched the bully on the chin. While her father may have secretly approved of her action, he did make her apologize to the boy and his parents. However, the next time she saw the bully, she threw him and his bike into a brook. Clearly Pitter was afraid of the enormous mob of unruly children that roamed the Downshall school, especially the rougher boys, and so she defended herself in order to survive. Worse perhaps than the physical menace, however, was the damage to her budding dignity; it was this that led at least in part to her rage. Years later she recalled these events with such vividness that she slammed her fist on the table and exclaimed, "It was a stinking bad bit of business!"

As she neared her twelfth birthday in 1909, she began attending the Coborn School for Girls in Bow, where she remained until 1915.[4] While it was a charity school (supported by private donations and foundations), it was a very good one. Pitter's parents paid fees for her to attend the school since their combined salaries did not allow them to qualify for assistance. Her teachers were superb, and Pitter's love of language was nurtured by an excellent Latin mistress. She was fascinated by Ovid's *Metamorphoses* and the myth of Persephone; the story of Hades coming up through a sudden split in the ground and carrying off the spring goddess to the underworld lived vividly in her imagination all her life. In fact, this story was the source later of her only narrative poem, *Persephone in Hades* (1931). Her exposure to Latin at the Coborn School was something she treasured, and later in life she frequently spiced her letters with Latin words and phrases.

However, Hainault Forest was the primary catalyst to Pitter's imaginative life. The unfolding of the seasons there was an endless folktale.[5] When in the forest, she moved in a hush, looking, listening, waiting for the next wonderful event. Here she could wander alone in the forest, free and enchanted. Once her parents agreed to rent a cottage there in the spring of 1914, Pitter visited at every chance, living there full-time for weeks during the school holidays. A tiny, old, long-uninhabited rambling shack, the damp low dwelling was discovered during one of their long walks in the wood. This cottage came to be her oasis. On one side were meadows, and on the other, forest. One side was gay with sunshine, filled with lark songs and buttercups; the other side was dim, hushed, dreamlike. Whenever she approached the cottage, she would not barge right up to it. Instead, she would hover around it in the fringe of the woods and "peer through the branches—low hornbeam boughs hung with fresh, crumbling green catkins, and new, translucent, sharply pleated little leaves." Through this lovely veil she would gaze "in a trance of felicity as happy as she would ever be."

A close inspection of the cottage would leave the viewer wondering about Pitter's deep affection for it. Only part of it was visible—a dilapidated brick chimney; a sweep of low, weathered, and lichen-covered tiles on the roof; a glimpse of the upper half of two dim little windows; and a bit of shabbily plastered wall. The rest was hidden, "engulfed in great over-arching sprays of hawthorn hedge in bloom, fierce brambles, and groves of cow parsley" almost as tall as the little house itself. Yet it snuggled well down into the warm, welcoming weeds, "almost whispering, 'As I've served faithfully as a dwelling for hundreds of years, I've earned a nice lay down.'" The two sleepy windows, "like half shut eyes, gave the cottage the appearance of the after dinner forty winks of some aged person who has worked very hard in her time, now enjoying a comfortable haven at last."

Most importantly, the essentials were there. After a bit of plastering, a few new bricks, a coat of whitewash, and a replaced floorboard or two, the family was installed by Midsummer Day. George had already cleared and planted a large area for a garden. Cultivating a patch of garden in this wilderness was not easy—brambles and briars fighting to overwhelm it, weed seeds blowing in on every puff of wind, jays and pigeons eating at the peas, smaller birds pecking out buds, and greenflies, caterpillars, and other pests moving in from the neglected hedgerows nearby made his task a difficult challenge. But by the time they moved in, crops were already showing; soon they were enjoying great frilly three-pound lettuces as well as new potatoes. Pitter owed her lifelong love of gardening to her father. He used his children to help him weed his garden, but sometimes he would delight them with his special knowledge. One favorite plant grew in a little hollow; after it reached one foot in height, he lit a match above it, there was a small explosion, and the flame went out.[6]

They brought five rudimentary beds into the cottage, a table of sorts, six cheap rush chairs, some cookware and serving pieces, and little curtains for the windows. Her parents did have to endure the gentle scolding of friends over what they saw as a rash luxury (these same friends, nonetheless, enjoyed coming for tea), needlessly worrying that such extravagance would "put ideas in the children's heads." However, the only "ideas" Ruth found were blessed ones that sweetened the rest of her life. Ruth especially loved the Sunday evenings in the summer when she did not have to return to town. Often she would walk the mile to the nearest road just for the luxury of seeing the last bus go without her. Too happy to speak, she would turn back into the cloistered twilight peace of the woods to experience the delicate mysteries of darkness and moonrise, flower scents, and nightingales.

She would slowly return to the cottage, having "crossed the gentle brook, already veiled with chilly mist, and approach the low door, night falling rapidly." Nights in the cottage were thrilling. As darkness fell, she felt as if she had moved suddenly backward in time. Here she was experiencing night in the woods as it had been for untold centuries: no paved streets, no streetlights, no honking cabs or grinding lorries. As darkness came into its own, owls and foxes would cry out. Pitter loved to huddle in close, shut the door, sip a hot drink, and slip into bed quickly. The sense of keeping close while the things "out there in the night" enjoyed their own devices was delightful to the young teenager. Yet often her excitement woke her, and she would kneel on her creaking little bed and peer out the tiny window. A full moon powdered the landscape while two nightingales throbbed their hearts out. Magical odors breathed from the earth, wafted from the trees, and billowed from thousands of flowers. She could see dots of dim phosphorescent light flicker in the woods and wondered about ghosts, fairies, and enchanted princesses. While her conscious mind knew their existence was unlikely, she easily imagined them, half-believing in all of them. She felt she was sharing the last remnants of the childhood of the world, and she yearned deeply after it with the longing one feels for something lovely that is perishing from the earth. Eventually she would fall asleep and dream of a vanishing trail of magic.

In the morning she would awaken at first light, tumble out of bed, wash in the brook, and hover eagerly around the old fireplace "while the kettle sang and the bacon sizzled." A few simple chores completed, she would head out into the fields and woods, collecting firewood, looking for birds' nests, picking wild orchids, or carrying water from the spring with yoke and pails. Sometimes she would go to the nearby Elizabethan farmhouse to fetch milk, lugging the big tin can through less familiar groves and glades, skirting a fascinating boggy patch of ground where silver birches stood elegantly above swatches of yellow sphagnum moss and dwarf willow. Moving to the back of the farmhouse and into the dark, cold dairy, she would collect the rich milk, not yet an hour from the cow. Back in the cottage, she enjoyed a cup of strong tea perfectly complemented by the creamy milk.

On the occasions when the children preceded their mother to the cottage, Olive and Geoffrey took it as a sacred duty to go as far as they could to meet her and take her shopping load while Ruth stayed in the cottage, keeping the kettle on the boil with a twig placed on the fire here and there, one eye out the door, ready to fill the teapot as soon as the little convoy crossed the brook. This was a tremendous relief for Louisa, who had been the primary force behind acquiring the cottage. She determined the family should rent the hut, come what may. Accordingly, she went out and earned the extra money. And she remained behind, doing the shopping, while the children went on ahead earlier in the day. After lunch mother and children would hike the woods or visit the weekly cattle market at the ancient village nearby. Animals slowly driven in on the hoof, produce gathered that morning from local farms and gardens, and bread, cakes, and pies baked on the spot filled the market with rich sights, sounds, and smells. Ruth particularly enjoyed looking at the women in voluminous skirts and petticoats, with thick nailed boots and faded straw hats tied on with bright-red handkerchiefs. Men wore fustian, corduroy, and gaiters and carried sticks or whips as they crowded around one another amidst a jumble of dogs and horses. The rich odors of great roast beef or mutton dinners floated through the air, and she could glimpse inside the cool, beery taprooms with sawdust-covered floors. The vividness of these memories was later captured in her poem "Romford Market":

With human bellow, bovine blare,
Glittering trumpery, gaudy ware,
The life of Romford market-square
Set all our pulses pounding:
The gypsy drover with his stick,
The huckster with his hoary trick,

The pork with fat a good foot thick
And sausages abounding:

Stalls of apples, stacks of cake,
Piles of kippers, haddocks, hake,
Great slabs of toffee that men make,
Which urchins eye and pray for:
Divine abundance! Glorious day!
We stayed as long as we could stay,
Then upped our loads and went our way
With all that we could pay for.

And homeward bound by Clockhouse Lane
We jabbered of our golden gain,
And not in our too usual vein
Of rancorous dissension;
Here is the little onion-hoe
We bought that day so long ago;
Worn down—but so are one or two
More things that I could mention.

Threading the silent, mist bedewed
And darkening thicks of Hainault Wood,
We reached that cottage, low and rude,
Which was so dear a dwelling;
By the black yew, solemn and still,
Under the brow of Crabtree Hill;
Ah, dear it was, and ever will
Be dear beyond all telling.

Dry hornbeam-twigs roared up in flame,
The kettle quivered to the same;
When home the weary parents came
The sausages were frying;
The tea was brewed, the toast was brown—
We chattered of our day in town;
Outside the leaves went whispering down,
And autumn owls were crying.

Our market day was done. But we
Enshrine it still in memory,

For it was passed in perfect glee,
By youth and health begotten:
My Romford on the Essex plain,
My upland woods! While you remain
One humble jewel we retain
One day is unforgotten.[7]

After the market the little troop passed by the great water mill on the cool
river, its banks and edges filled with yellow iris and lilies. Inside the mill "the air
was dim with flour and ringing with an endless Wagnerian song—a throbbing,
humming, beating roar, made up of the pouring, plunging, thundering water
noises, the deep groan of the great wheel, echoing shouts and tramplings, the
hoist shrieking, and the whole vast, resilient timber structure acting as a sounding board." They stood there, rested and refreshed, watching the water "hurtle
out from the wheel and leap away in rioting white masses to the boiling pool
below." From that cavernous coolness, they looked out across the shimmering,
heaving water to the dark soaring masses of lofty elms, alders, and horse chest-
nuts and "traced the low line of hills, turquoise gray with heat" and caught,
"quick as lightning, a flash of intense tropical blue as a kingfisher darted down
then up again like an electrical discharge."

As they returned to the cottage, Ruth most enjoyed the silent spots. One
field of red clover was a favorite—an "unbroken mass of rosy purple all along
the horizon." In addition to the feast to her eyes, she breathed in with delight the rich scent—it smelled of honey, a rich clover honey, and even gave
hints of newly baked bread. The sheer abundance of the smell "suggested a fairy
godmother's kindness and blessing." It was something she would never forget,
a memory from which she would draw strength later in life when things were
grim and bleak. The red clover field was "a store of sweetness" that nothing
destroyed. Down the deep little lane, they moved where "the steep banks, tall
foxgloves, and riotous honeysuckle" hemmed in the narrow road, shutting out
the breezes until "they felt they were in a glasshouse." Then another rich scent
reached them, stronger than hay or honeysuckle—"a carpet of gemlike wild
strawberry plants, with their perfect little flowers still lingering amid the beautiful, flushed leaves, and the dark crimson fruit ready to drop with ripeness." In
a later poem, "The Strawberry Plant," Ruth celebrated her affection for this
plant; its simple beauty always stimulated her imagination.[8] Other plants and
flowers crowded around them as they passed down the lane—cornstalks, heath,
harebell, and yellow toadflax. Back at the cottage, they collapsed in contented
joy, their minds filled with the English countryside the entire family so loved.
Dreamlike stories floated up between the children, with one starting an idea
or incident, and another taking it up and giving it a new direction. With a

common stock of experience, and speaking a family language, they were of one mind. They only had to pause and remember.

Pitter's experiences at the cottage in Hainault Forest stamped an indelible mark on her; the natural environment—plants, animals, earth, sky, and water— dominates her best poetry, suggesting a deep union and mystical connection with the world around her. Furthermore, she saw the interconnectedness of things; each slice of bread or pint of milk, every apple or potato or lettuce, should be valued not only because it was a gift from God but also because someone had the foresight to work hard to produce it. She and her father used to hike the trails and byways of Hainault Forest. Often they would take a break from a hot afternoon by popping into a pub. Once George left Ruth outside a local pub, intending to heft a quick one. However, he soon became embroiled in political discussion and only several hours later emerged from the pub, seemingly unaware that he had left his daughter alone and thirsty. On another occasion the two of them were repairing a section of the cottage. As it was a very warm day, they were drinking beer and enjoying the work. Her father looked across the way and saw a neighbor approaching. "It's old Maybrook and he'll be wanting tea," George worried, since they knew the neighbor was not a beer drinker. Ruth wanted to dash off to the nearby well for fresh water, but her father said they would have to make do with water from the rain barrel, even though the inside of the barrel had just recently been tarred. Hoping for the best, they served Maybrook the tea. He sipped it appreciatively and said, "Fine tea this—I do like the taste of tar in a good tea."[9]

Often the Pitters were joined for forest walks by friends. The Pattersons, especially the father and son, were frequent guests. At twelve years old, Ruth developed a girlish crush on Mr. Patterson, hero-worshipping his clean-shaven face, his handsome profile, and his good figure. In addition, he was a snappy dresser, particularly when he wore his Harris tweed suit: "I knew all about Harris tweeds. They were excitingly rough and shaggy, with a magical scent of peat about them. They embodied the spirit of the great out-of-doors, and carried manly charm in every fibre. In the fiction magazines, it was too lovely when the little woman could break down at last and bury her tear-stained face in the Harris tweed lapels, while the Harris tweed arms went round her. Eager to catch the least whiff of the peaty perfume, I would sniff in Mr. Paterson's wake like a hungry dog, as I tagged along behind with the other children." Several years later in early spring when Ruth had a half day off from school, they accidentally met and decided to have a picnic in Hainault Forest. She delighted in the afternoon with her hero all to herself since "the early sunshine brought out the tweed-scent, and I was in heaven." Her delight was shattered that evening when she told her mother; Louisa screamed at her, "Never dare to do such a thing again. We don't want your name dragged through the divorce court!" In an instant Pitter matured five years.[10]

This one instance aside, Pitter's days in Hainault Forest were largely idyllic. But they did not last, as war clouds soon swept across Europe. When World War I began, Pitter had matriculated to the intermediate arts curriculum at London University. However, she soon left, and on her eighteenth birthday, November 7, 1915, she became a temporary junior clerk in the income tax department of the War Office. Because the ledgers were so heavy, she often dropped them and won the nickname "Crash." The work was monotonous and she developed serious health problems, including boils; as a result, she left in the spring of 1917. Upon her departure, on Primrose Day, April 19, 1917, her boss, Mr. Trantham, wrote her a letter complimenting her singing voice and sent her a three-volume set of contemporary French verse. On the same day she received a signed card from her colleagues noting their own part in the gift and wishing her the best in the future.

Following a vague desire to be an artist, perhaps motivated by her early efforts at watercolors and pen-and-ink drawings, she answered an ad in the magazine *The Studio* to work as an artist and moved to the Suffolk coast at the village of Walberswick. There she worked for Mildred Jennings and her sister-in-law, Marie-Rose Jennings, who operated a decorative furniture business, the Walberswick Peasant Pottery Company.[11] The mission of the company was "to produce furniture which in proportions, colour and style will suit as exactly as possible the person and the room it is intended for."[12] At first she lived with the family and received her room and board as her wage. However, after she became more proficient in her painting, she received a small wage as well. More importantly, Pitter was able to work on her poetry in the evenings and weekends, and for the first time she came into direct contact with other artists. Mildred Jennings was a talented painter of some merit, and her husband, Frank, was an able architect whose tastes tended toward the Gothic. From the Jenningses she was first exposed to the workings of the aesthetic conscience, particularly the sense that artistic work should not be done hurriedly. The sense that her own poetry could be made better through continuous effort was new to Pitter; heretofore she had been content to produce whatever poems came her way, but few of these early efforts are memorable today. It was only later that she internalized her creative energy and allowed it to touch her fertile imagination; when this happened, she wrote powerful poems. However, between 1916 and 1919 she was just beginning this process. As World War I came to a close, the Jenningses expanded their business and opened a second shop in London at 12 Holland Street, Kensington.

Few letters survive from Pitter's parents during this period. However, both wrote her prior to her twenty-first birthday. Louisa, who was normally reticent, writes:

What can I say to you for tomorrow? Your 21st birthday and *me* not there—ow. Why did you ever go for to leave your own Dinah who lub you honey? Well—the frock is finished and frucked. I have made you a cake & meant to ice it but sugar failed at the last moment. I hope the frock fits & is a success. I sewed a little love into every stitch & when you wear it you will know. . . . Dear one I am very tired & I think I can write nothing worth sending tonight. I wanted to compose a real nice letter for your birthday but I cannot. I can only love you same as ever. All I can add is that you, my dear one, have made my married life worth while. What greater praise can I give you? All these horrid years that stretch away behind me like slain beasts of prey I would live again for my Ruth—think of it dear and know that your mother blesses the day you were born. I won't even say God bless you for He has blessed you and you shall be blessed. My dear happy child, be happy on your birthday. I shall not have the fun, but I shall have a quiet happiness all my own thinking of you. Kindest regards to the [Jenningses] and all my love on the day to you my blessed Damosel and through the ages always. (Nov. 5, 1918)

Louisa's admission about the difficulty of her married life is intriguing. We know she had not enjoyed caring for her younger siblings, so perhaps she was reflecting back on having to bear the burden as a mother that she had resisted as a child. However, her reference to the "horrid years that stretch away behind me like slain beasts of prey" suggests a darker disappointment. Had her labor to support her family blunted her zeal for life? Had marriage killed her hopes for a successful teaching career? Had her affection for George been dulled by the years of monotonous routine? Had the oppressive years of World War I and the sense that civilization was on the brink of collapse worn down her spirit? In all likelihood each of these contributed to produce a letter that, although meant to encourage her daughter, ironically may have discouraged her since it was overshadowed by the confession that Louisa's own life masked a profound sadness verging on despair.

The tone of George's best-wishes letter on the occasion of her twenty-first birthday stands in stark contrast to Louisa's:

Accept my heartiest congratulations on reaching your 21st birthday. May health, success, and happiness ever await you. I enclose a pound note for a birthday present. I could not buy you anything, as I had not the remotest idea of what you would like, & was afraid I might send you something you did not want. I am glad you are able to receive Olive & [your aunt] Kit[ty]. They both deserve a holiday. I hope you will be able to persuade your mother to come down to Walberswick for a week at Easter. I feel she needs a holiday very much. I hear you are going to have a long holiday at Christmas. That is good news indeed. With best love. (Nov. 5)

Reserved in tone, George's letter could just as easily have been intended for an acquaintance or student. Typical of most men, he sends money, ostensibly because he feared making a poor gift selection, but most probably because he did not have the time or energy to look for something uniquely appropriate for his daughter. In addition, his desire for Ruth to convince Louisa to visit at Easter is odd for a birthday congratulations letter. On one hand, perhaps his sentiment suggests a loving husband sincerely worried about his wife's sadness; on the other, perhaps he wants her to get away so he can be spared her gloomy countenance and critical spirit. Whatever the exact nature of the relationship between George and Louisa was at this time, Pitter herself may not have known.

Pitter's romantic yearnings during her adolescence are hard to gauge. Later in life she recalls that at this time she was attracted to yellow curls reaching almost to the shoulders of one blue-eyed neighbor. Fantasizing in the tradition of a fairy tale, she imagined him her Prince Charming.[13] Yet she never spoke to this boy because she knew he did not care for her and never would. Other girls' brothers, distant figures of royalty, artists (with floppy ties and hats), and even wartime heroes became the revolving objects of her romantic longings; she would create a beautiful myth about herself, look around for a likely victim, and then imagine he might subscribe to the myth and help her carry out her private fantasies. But when the fantasy touched reality, the rather well-behaved boy with white silk stockings could not fill the vacant throne she had built for him. Instead, he "twigged her infatuation" and made fun of her.

Yet she writes several poems hinting at her romantic longings. A number of these poems revolve around a brief relationship with a young man she never names. The relationship was on again, off again, and Pitter took the job with the Jenningses, in part, in order to get away from this young man. She relates: "I had a sweetheart . . . [but] we never seemed to come to any conclusion . . . with this sweethearting about all over the place. . . . And besides, he was a Roman Catholic, and that's one thing I couldn't take, so I thought it would be a decisive thing to get this job at a distance, and this would put an end to this rather futile sort of courtship." While this may have been an unsuccessful relationship, in a series of poems published from 1917 to 1920 she offers fleeting insights into her desire for love. In "The Poor Poet" she laments:

> The sparrow hath his mate
> And is not desolate:
> The flower, complete unto herself,
> Never pursues a wraithy elf:
> O black-eyed Melancholy,
> I never shall be wed![14]

Little could Pitter have known at the time how prophetic was the last line. Her emotional longings also come through in "Song" when she writes ironic lines like, "The end of true love is to sit and mourn," "The end of true love is to lie and weep," and "The end of true love is a sorry end," culminating in: "Love's is a life not any leech may save; / So, since he's fair, / And thou must full soon lay him in his grave, / Be love thy care."[15]

In "The Consummation" her wistful longings for love are also evident: "Looks royal, songs for heaven meet, / Thou wishest, thinking on his worth / Whose faintest image is more sweet / Than all thy dearest loves on earth."[16] Yet she realizes her longings are likely to be unrequited: "Thou art foredone, thine heart is rent / To praise who hath not fear nor shame, / Yet when thine utmost life is spent / Thou hast not even said his name." In "My Love's Cold" she tries to describe a broken heart but stumbles with lines like "O my Love's cold on the green hill, / O my Love sleepeth under a stone! / Of my Love that did no ill / Womanly I make my moan; / I am dead since my Love's gone."[17] Rather than feeling the young girl's maudlin anguish, we find these overwritten lines embarrassing. Pitter's adolescent longings were painted fantasies, delicate bubbles unable to withstand the disappointing reality of the young men she actually encountered.

Early Verse

Pitter was a prolific writer of verse as a young person. Her earliest surviving work, probably composed between 1903 and 1905 and written in crayon by the hand of a child of no more than eight, are three short chapbooks about the importance of obeying mother, finding true love, and honeysuckle fairies.[18] An examination of her manuscript notebooks from between 1903 and 1912 reveals she composed over thirty poems; between 1913 and 1915 forty poems; and between 1916 and 1920 ninety-six. This leap in verse production was not simply the result of growing up; it was primarily due to her almost single-minded devotion to writing poetry.

Pitter was fortunate, although some might argue the contrary, to secure early on an advocate, A. R. Orage, editor of the *New Age*, who published many of her early poems.[19] George Pitter and Orage had been fellow students at Culham College; when George discovered his daughter's precocious gifts as a poet, he contacted Orage and sent him one of Ruth's earliest efforts at verse. On May 5, 1911, Orage writes: "Dear Miss Ruth Pitter, I shall be very pleased to publish your graceful lines in *New Age*. They are charming, and I hope you will always live in this pure & saintly spirit." The poem, "Field Grasses," was her first published poem, a heady event for someone only thirteen years old.

Purple and brown are they,
Purple and brown,
Yellow and silver-grey,
Clothing the down.
Dancing and nodding wise,
Gravely they go:
Bow to the wide blue skies,
Stately and slow,
Purple and brown are they,
Purple and brown,
All little ladies gay,
Treading the down.[20]

The lines of dactylic dimeter with the even-numbered lines severely truncated, the simple rhymes and easy rhythm, the visually concrete refrain "purple and brown," and the occasional use of alliteration illustrate Pitter's effort as a crafts-man. Although not profound, this poem is an earnest effort to freeze-frame a natural scene; it is a workmanlike effort for a thirteen-year-old. Pitter's prosody throughout this period is characterized by traditional figurative language (pre-dictable similes and metaphors in particular); alliteration; iambic tetrameter or pentameter; rhyming couplets, lines of alternate rhyme, or an infrequent tercet; simple diction; monosyllabic words; easy, rhythmic cadence; and little experi-mentation with stanza forms except for the occasional rondeau.[21]

In subsequent letters to George, Orage takes an active interest in Ruth's poetry. On July 5, 1911, he arranges for a meeting between the two men so they can "have a big talk about Ruth's work of which I think the promise is considerable. Do you happen to have a photograph of her that you could bring without vexing her?" Orage is clearly taken by Ruth's verse, writing her father at one point: "Your Ruth is a little diamond" (Jan. 8, 1912). However, in spite of his admiration for Ruth, Orage was not above offering criticism. On April 15, 1912, he writes: "We all like Ruth's new poems very much. . . . [But] would the young lady deign to change a single word in the 'Song'? Verse 1, line 3: amorous kissed. The attribution of human emotion, & this one in particular, to natural objects is fancy not imagination. Do ask Ruth if she will find the right word to take its place. Then I shall publish it at once."[22] Seeing Ruth as his protégée, Orage writes George with additional encouragement: "The photograph of Ruth has delighted us all. What a *powerful* character! . . . Ruth should mow down some [great?] work before very long. We are all very charmed & proud of her. One of these days I hope she will be able to be brought to town for a little tour & inspection; she will see & feel then how much work awaits her. Meantime, singing [writing verse], pure singing, & lots of *classical* reading" (May 21).

Yet after meeting Ruth, Orage writes her father a letter that is curiously am-
bivalent about her potential:

> I'd much rather have talked than written on the subject of Ruth. It is
> so difficult to recall a written word, even though it should have been
> meant tentatively. But you are not to conclude that I was disappointed in
> Ruth. Far from it. She was even more beautiful than her poems. On the
> other hand, I was & am grieved beyond words to reflect about her most
> probable future; for I see nothing for it but a progressive dimming of her
> spiritual powers & their final extinction in good prose. What influences
> are conducing to this I can in part speculate, but, so far as I can see, they
> are irremediable. None of us can do anything, I fear, but watch the light
> fail. I am not surprised to hear she has written nothing since the exquisite
> "Fairy-Gold," though I could weep for it![23] I shall be surprised if she writes
> again for perhaps years & more. Now, my dear Mr. Pitter, you will perhaps
> understand why I have not felt disposed to intrude my opinions on you.
> But, thank God, my opinion may be wrong. (Dec. 28)

Why Orage writes this dark prediction is unclear. Perhaps he says this to pique her
into writing more poetry as he senses a falling off in both the quality and quantity
of her poetry sent to him between May and December of 1912; whatever the case,
none of her poems appeared in the New Age from July 1912 to June 1914. Notwithstanding this brief gap, from 1911 to 1920 Orage published eighty-five of her
poems in the New Age.[24] Indeed, by the spring of 1914 he is writing George with
renewed enthusiasm: "I'm delighted to hear that Ruth is singing [writing poetry]
again. I was afraid her voice would not return until she was past twenty-one! . . . I
like the Rondeau very much. . . . May I publish it?" (April 9, 1914).[25]

In spite of Orage's enthusiasm for Pitter's early poetry, on balance it is not
very good. Another way to put this is that she writes competent verse, but rarely
does she write a powerful poem. Typical of Georgian verse, most of her efforts
are vapid, abstract, detached, and impersonal. The weaknesses are legion. For
instance, Pitter effects archaic spellings, as in these lines from "Fairy-Gold": "I
have a brother clepëd Fairy-Gold, / Who dwelleth not in housen nor with men."[26]
"Clepëd," "dwelleth," and "housen" illustrate the inordinate influence of The
Golden Treasury upon her early poetry. Also bothersome is her frequent use of the
archaic second person "thou," "thee," "thine," and "ye." On occasion a poem, for
example, "To the People," suggests her knowledge of the wider world: "Are ye
not in captive thrall, / Bondmen, body, mind and soul, / Slaves and drudges one
and all, / Work your only goal?"[27] Most, however, are childlike, celebrating peace,
happiness, and contentment. "A Song of a Child's Happiness" is representative:

I am singing from my heart,
Let me now my muse impart:
Trumpet, be thou still; and lute
To my music be thou mute.

Golden dream and silver sleep
Make my slumbers calm and deep;
All my lifetime God doth bless,
So sing I of happiness.

Fancy peoples plain to me,
Meadow down and hilltop tree;
Wraiths and elves and ladies fair
Fancy places for me there.

Ev'ry thicket, blossom-strewn,
Mantled with the cloak of June,
Harbours fairies day and night,
Puck, and gnome, and flower-sprite.

Even pixy men for me
Live again upon the lea;
These I own, and nothing less,
So sing I of happiness.[28]

This poem also demonstrates Pitter's immature fascination with fairies and elves; later in life she critiques herself for this early appetite for the supernatural, claiming that she believed in fairies until she was eighteen.

In addition, too many poems employ abstract rather than concrete description, as in the opening lines of "Spring (Rondeau)": "From Winter's rule now comes the sky, / From wind, from coldness, and from rain, / And by the sun is clothed again / In clear and comely broidery."[29] When she does attempt more concrete imagery, the effect is stylized:

The Earth draws off her robe of broidered flowers,
And in green kirtle standeth for a space
Ere she doth wrap her for the slumberous hours
In her white shift of mist, and veils her face:
She standeth in her kirtle green, and saith
Her evening prayer, whose incense is her breath.[30]

This passage does not have the effect of placing us in the natural environment where we might imaginatively experience the setting; instead, we feel as if she is describing images she has observed on an inexpensive piece of pottery. For the most part, her early verse does not convey human experiences with convincing imaginative intensity. For example, almost never do we hear a voice that is self-reflective, informed, or contemplative. Instead a detached, impersonal voice appears even in lines meant to be moving, as in the ending of "Prayer for a Fair People": "Now have I ended all my plaint, / Now have I made thee all my prayer, / And the last incense, thin and faint, / Smokes upward from mine altar stair."[31] Rather than displaying genuine passion or heartfelt spiritual anguish, these lines are stylized, impersonal, and unconvincing. She keeps real emotion at arm's length; she plays it safe.

Even in poems where we might expect a more genuine, personal voice, Pitter remains distant. For instance, when Pitter does write about World War I—and this is rare—she is unable to help us feel the utter waste and futility of that conflagration. "Song, Grieve No More" could be about the death of any person at any time: "Grieve no more for the silent dead, / They are fled from the earth."[32] Comparing them to the well-worn image of dead leaves "gone far from our ken," she does little to help us care about the dead. Instead, she ends the poem by offering cold comfort: "Dry thy tears, and grieve thou not: / Think no more upon troubled men." Her imperatives to buck up and to stifle grief ring hollow at best and are insensitive at worst. This emotional detachment is highlighted as well in "Whom We Have Buried":

> Whom we have buried,
> We do not wholly cast away.
> The bones of the wise dead
> Feel our swift feet over their clay,
> And their patient hands do keep
> > Night and day
> On their hollow breasts in sleep.[33]

She is somewhat better in "Silence Shall Cover Thee": "Silence shall cover thee; the dark / Shall wrap thee from the curious sun; / Thy monuments of sorrow stark / Weather and crumble one by one."[34] These lines picturing a desolate, weather-worn graveyard evoke a genuine sense of human waste. "Of the Damned" also strikes an ominous chord:

> I hear the lost their torment tell
> Now am I cherishèd of none;
> I see the naked bones of hell

I fear: and yet I know 'tis well
That in the ash, and rain of stone,
I hear the lost their torment tell.[35]

But can the following lines from "The Debtor" be anything but insincere moral-izing—unfeeling and unmoving? "When I am dead, then shall Remorse most vile / From eating of mine heart ychasèd [sic] be, / And Covetise shall leave mine eyes the while, / Where she in former time lurked loweringly."[36] Even in 1919 such a poem must have sounded false, especially in contrast to the war poetry of Wilfred Owen and Siegfried Sassoon. These problems with voice—af-fected rather than natural, artificial rather than genuine, distant rather than personal—suggest Pitter's inability at this time in her life to integrate her emo-tional life into her poetry. Rather than plumb the depths of her emotions, she blocks access to her inner life. Accordingly, she too often relies upon a familiar, tired Georgian persona that skates on the surface of things, content with shal-low, unconvincing musings.

The early poems that do hint at her genuine gifts as a poet celebrate natural objects. For example, "The Oak Tree" concerns the ancient wisdom and peace of a noble forest sentinel:

At the golden door
Of thine own glade the silent sunbeams pour:
And thou look'st out across the hazy plain
From the cool greenness of thy quiet throne:
Where is the biting winter? Neither pain
Nor vain regrets in thy deep heart remain:
Nor dost thou count the weary drooping years
In slow and miserly cycle, one by one.[37]

Here she effectively captures a snapshot-like vision of a towering oak whose relative permanence contrasts sharply with human frailty; that the oak remains untouched by human misery and decay is something she longs to emulate. In "The Swan" we see movement toward concrete imagery: "With his red beak and marble plume, / Uttering his wild, his pulsant cry, / The Swan into the wild did fly." [38] In Pitter's later verse, birds are important, often functioning as emblems of spiritual, poetic, or mystical reality. Here she anticipates such poems in the final lines: "Into the fiery dawn rode he, / And many a burning cherubim / That knoweth the face of the Most High, / In godlike flight did go with him." Inspired perhaps by Hainault Forest, "The Promised Rest" explores Pitter's search for refuge: "Yea, thou shalt have thy peace, thy calm delight, / Dim sanctuary, thy canopy of leaves."[39] Hidden in the dark warmth of the forest,

Pitter reflects on her many retreats into the Hainault and its delights: "The light web that the summer starlight weaves / And the wild wayfaring of waters bright, / And songs of husbandmen among the sheaves: / Thus may thou be with many glories dight: / Thus sit and sing under thy forest eaves." Similarly, "Alone" concerns the forest and connects to her longing for solitude:

> Along the west way of the wood
> When light doth gild its floor,
> My spirit saith "O solitude!"
> And shuts her chamber door:
>
> And doth a solemn silence keep;
> I think that she doth pray,
> But whether she doth smile or weep
> I may not know nor say.[40]

These two stanzas anticipate more mature poems like "For Sleep, or Death" and "Call Not to Me" from A Trophy of Arms (1936), and "The Bridge" from The Bridge (1945).

Pitter's single-minded commitment to writing verse culminated in the publication of her first volume of poems in 1920, First Poems. While the majority of the poems had already been published in the New Age, fourteen had not.[41] Not surprisingly, one of the most favorable reviews appeared in the New Age. Citing as strengths her "individual vocabulary, consisting almost of an anthology of 'fairy' words; a spiral or trailing rhythm like that of a vine; simple subtlety; and a never-failing sense of style, even in the most apparently incongruous passages," the reviewer also identifies her poems as revealing "a pre-occupation, or, perhaps, a re-occupation with fairy morality, distant and distinct from human morality."[42] Yet rather than discuss how such an emphasis actually distances Pitter from her readers, the anonymous reviewer, somewhat prophetically, states: "[In her poems] the pitch of the contemplation is not, as yet, very exalted, being rarely above such subjects as grief and death and change; it will in all probability rise." In addition to First Poems, during 1920 she published another thirty poems in the New Age, marking this year as a high-water mark for productivity. While it is doubtful Orage had the requisite critical gifts necessary to sharpen Pitter's muse, his willingness to publish her frequently provided a public forum for her verse. In addition, when we consider he also published poets like AE (George Russell), Hilaire Belloc, G. K. Chesterton, John Galsworthy, Katherine Mansfield, Edith Nesbit, Ezra Pound, Siegfried Sassoon, and Louis Untermeyer, often in the same issues with Pitter's verse, his contribution to Pitter's development as a poet cannot be underestimated. For Pitter it was undoubtedly encouraging to appear in print alongside such poets.

Pitter's early verse only hints at her later success as a poet. Although she frequently employs diction reminiscent of John Keats and William Blake, perhaps gleaned from their poems that appear in *The Golden Treasury*, Pitter is hampered by the lack of a distinct voice, archaic diction, imprecise imagery, reluctance to explore her emotional life, and lapses into reveries about fairies; that she later becomes an effective poet cannot be predicted from these early efforts, making her later success all the more remarkable. Perhaps the best way to think of these early efforts is as those of an apprentice poet. She pursues her muse tirelessly and is incredibly prolific, if not inspired. Her passion for poetry drives her to do the one thing a young writer can ill afford to neglect to do: write, write, and write some more. As we explore the next period of her life, we will see how she begins to transcend her poetic limitations and to move to the verge of literary success.

TWO

Artisan Poet,

1921–1931

A critical turning point in Pitter's personal life occurred when Mildred and Marie-Rose Jennings decided in 1919 to move the center of operations of the Walberswick Peasant Pottery Company to London. The Jenningses set up a workshop at 20 Portobello Road and a showroom at 12 Holland Street, Kensington; Pitter briefly moved to the Portobello Road address as well. In the autumn she met Kathleen M. O'Hara, who had been hired by the Jenningses as a part-time secretary and painter. In recalling this meeting, O'Hara writes:

> I shall always remember my first day . . . [when] Ruth, whom I had not hitherto met, opened the door to my knock. She was wearing a most unbecoming khaki coloured woolen jumper and also had a cold in the head, which lasted some months. We no sooner met than we belonged to each other. There was that complete understanding . . . founded, I think, on the fact that each would trust the other to the last ditch and the last halfpenny—a state of affairs which, I flatter myself, is of the utmost rarity among our sex, and indeed anywhere. Another, and important factor, is that we have the same notion of what constitutes a good joke, of the kind that lurks round the cockles of the heart and occasionally gives a violent tickle.

Painting above the shop, Pitter and O'Hara spent countless hours working together and developing a friendship. Because the two rooms Pitter was renting at this time were small, stuffy, airless, and without amenities, in 1920 O'Hara arranged for Pitter to move to a flat near her at 28 Mall Chambers, Kensington. This proved convenient, since not only did Pitter now have more comfortable quarters, but she and O'Hara were able to alternate evening meals at each other's flats; in addition, Pitter soon invited O'Hara for regular visits to the cottage in Hainault Forest.

This move was fortuitous as well since the two women found themselves living near the flat of the parents of Eric Blair; they soon befriended Blair and over the years witnessed his growth as a writer, culminating in his worldwide acclaim later as the writer George Orwell.[1] In an interview Pitter recalls her first experiences with Orwell:

I first saw Orwell, or Eric Blair, to give him his real name, in 1920. He was then about 17. A young woman who worked with me knew his parents; they were neighbours of hers in the block of flats where she lived in the Notting Hill Gate district of London. Orwell's elder sister and her husband also had a flat there for a time, and I suppose they had asked my friend and me to supper. The outer doors of the flats opened almost directly into the sitting-rooms. So the moment our hostess let us in I saw a tall youth, with hair the colour of hay and a brown tweed suit, standing at a table by the window, cleaning a sporting gun. There was something arresting in the way he looked up. His eyes were blue and rather formidable, and an exact pair—most people's eyes are not. His sight was very keen, as I learned afterwards. He was, of course, still at school, and I can't remember if I saw him again before he joined the Burma police. But the idea of Orwell as an interesting person was indelibly stamped on my mind.

As we all know, he left the Burma police after about five years' service. To my surprise, I had a letter from him at this time, asking if I remembered him. He wanted us to find him a cheap lodging. We found a bedroom in a poor street, next door to a house our employers used as an arts and crafts workshop. I have a clear picture in my mind of Orwell lugging some heavy suitcases into our workshop house; no doubt to sort out the contents more easily than he could have done in the cramped bedroom next door. He was now a very tall man; he had the same rather formidable, perhaps defensive, look; and the very wide *terai* hat he was still wearing made him look still more imposing. He was far from well, even then. I don't think the tropics suited him, but I think he was also sick with rage. He was convinced that we had no business to be in Burma, no right to dominate other nations. He would have ended the British Raj then and there.

That winter was very cold. Orwell had very little money indeed. I think he must have suffered in that unheated room, after the climate of Burma, though we did, rather belatedly, lend him an oil-stove. He said afterwards that he used to light a candle to try and warm his hands when they were too numbed to write. O yes, he was already writing. *Trying* to write, that is—it didn't come easily. At this time I don't think any of his friends believed he would ever write well. Indeed, I think he was unusually inept. We tried not to be discouraging, but we used to laugh till we cried at some of the bits he showed us. You must remember that we were hard-working women, older than he. To us, at that time, he was a wrong-headed young man who had thrown away a good career, and was vain enough to think he could be an author. But the formidable look was not there for nothing. He had the gift, he had the courage, he had the persistence to go on in spite of failure, sickness, poverty, and opposition, until he became an acknowledged master of English prose.

Orwell's parents had now left London, and were living at Southwold on the Suffolk coast. My friend's parents had a house there too, and our employers had a small business close by. We used to work there for some weeks during the summer—we were all on visiting terms, so that we saw Orwell fairly often, one way and another. He was very good company in the countryside. I remember so well his taking me straight to a nightjar's nest in a featureless sea of vegetation. The nest was just a little hollow in the ground, with one egg and one young bird, a very queer young bird with an enormous mouth, funny whiskers, and a valiant hiss. I expect Orwell had taken bearings on the nest, but he must have watched the old birds patiently to find it in the first place. Seeing the nest was a nice change from squabbling about D. H. Lawrence, which we had been doing briskly as we came along. Orwell thought the world of him, while to me Lawrence was always a gifted writer indeed, but no prophet.[2]

Over the next several years, Pitter and Orwell continued to see each other from time to time, occasionally sharing an evening meal together.

In the meantime Pitter and O'Hara enjoyed the initial profits of the post–World War I boom, earning on average £7 a week each; however, once the boom was over, their wages slipped precipitously to 30 shillings a week each. To economize, O'Hara sublet her flat and moved in with Pitter. As both women believed themselves suited to no other kind of work, they determined to work hard as artisans. O'Hara recalls that Pitter's "economical dinners at this time half killed me; she has a wonderful digestion and can eat anything. . . . Our principal meal on Sunday [was] suet pudding; this was a very good filler, but the after effects for me were not too happy." Pitter herself recalls this period as rather normal, noting that she and O'Hara belonged to a generation of surplus women. So many young men had been killed in World War I, Pitter says, that it seemed quite natural to be unmarried. She and O'Hara soon reconciled themselves to the idea of not marrying, opting instead for independence, a career, and their search for a little home to retire to when their working days were over.

In a letter to her father, Pitter hints at the financial challenges she and O'Hara faced:

Thank you very much indeed for your noble cheque, which will be as you wish, a sheet anchor and a reserve fund. You always used to tell me that a certain sum in reserve enabled one to cheek people when so inclined, and this shall make me, I hope, more independent and self-respecting. I shall put it into savings certificates and try to add to it, and remember that it was your generosity which started the fund. . . . Business is rather slack, but we shall soon have the Ideal Home Exhibition, always a rush. Perhaps you would like to come and look around there. . . . K.[3] thanks you for your inquiry—she is very well and is glad you are better. I have had something—flu or bronchitis—better now. (June 1922?)

The hard work required of Pitter and O'Hara was long and without end. Twelve-hour days, six days a week, was a normal schedule. Indeed, throughout her working life Pitter followed a similar schedule. In doing so Pitter honed her skills as an artisan, perhaps a gift she inherited from her mother's master cabinetmaker father. She was content learning how to make and decorate furniture and household items: "Working with my hands . . . always seemed the only satisfactory way of earning a living; it soothes the mind while 'brainwork' teases it to shreds. I am grateful for having been taught the use of woodworking tools and the ABC's of painting." The other great benefit of this hard schedule was that she learned to discipline herself to use whatever spare time she had to work on her poetry. Often this meant letting ideas play themselves out extensively in her head before getting them down onto paper. This incubation period provided fertile ground for her imagination and poetic maturation.

Pitter's dogged devotion to verse was rewarded in early July 1925 when she received an unexpected letter from Hilaire Belloc, one of the most prolific essayists and writers of the first third of the twentieth century.[4] After offering praise for her verse, he asks: "Can you let me know when I can get your *Collected Verses*? I would like to have them & have never seen them" (July 4). Thus began a twenty-seven-year friendship and patronage that served Pitter even more than did Orage's. In the matter of patronage, Pitter was uncommonly fortunate; while many poets of her day never enjoyed the favor of even one well-connected member of the literati, she came under the care of two. If Orage watered the tender shoot, Belloc cultivated and groomed the blossoming fruit. Orage, though lacking an acute critical eye, did Pitter the favor of publishing her regularly in the *New Age*; Belloc, with a practiced and nuanced critical capacity, did her the greater favor of advocating her work in larger arenas, eventually bearing the lion's share of the cost of publishing her second and third books, *First and Second Poems* (1927) and *Persephone in Hades* (1931); in addition, he wrote the preface to *First and Second Poems* as well as to her fourth book, *A Mad Lady's Garland* (1934).

In his letters Belloc gave her generous advice and pushed her to get her poetry into the hands of book publishers. For instance, in his second letter he urges her to send some of her poems to the *London Mercury* and adds: "As for getting them published, I think that there would be plenty of people who would consent to put them together if I wrote a preface, and that I will do should you be willing. The best way for a book of verse (unless it is about Fox Hunting or the Empire) is to have it done by a small press, and leave them to handle it" (July 15). Her response is gracious but also raises the issue of her work schedule: "I am deeply obliged to you for your advice, and more than grateful for your offer of a preface. It will probably be some months before I shall be able to complete the preparation of the typescript—I have to work till seven nearly every evening. . . . It is unbelievably kind of you to concern yourself with my work. If the thanks of inexperience and obscurity are grateful to you, accept them" (July 20).

It is clear in their correspondence back and forth about what came to be *First and Second Poems* that Pitter had come to see the weakness of her early verse. At one point she writes: "The idea of reprinting [selected poems from *First Poems*] pains me, but I defer to your judgment except in the cases of those marked 'omit' in the script, which pain me so much that in a new book they would affect my health. These verses were produced between the ages of fourteen and twenty, and if I had had my own way they would never have been collected" (Aug. 31). A week later she is equally critical about the remainder of the poems later appearing in *First and Second Poems*, the majority of which were first published in the *New Age* between 1921 and 1923: "Perhaps you will then tell me if [the manuscript] is too small or too large, and I would then adjust it. I have included some things that make me feel like an idiot when I read them, and there are a good many that only a real shortage of material would make me include. So either way I shall be prepared." Pitter also tells Belloc she is using a typewriter to complete the manuscript: "For I have encroached upon my investments to the extent of giving £1 for this interesting Bronze Age machine, and every half-hour that can be spared I devote to working it" (Sept. 8). By January 1926 Belloc had finished writing the preface, and before the year was over the manuscript was nearing publication. As they continued to correspond, Belloc urged Pitter to keep at her writing: "But *go on writing* for heaven's sake! Write every line you can!" (Dec. 31, 1926).

First and Second Poems: 1912–1925 was published in March 1927 by Sheed and Ward. In his preface, Belloc laments the state of English verse:

> The classical spirit has not fallen in disrepute among us: it has been forgotten. It has become alien and strange, so that men coming across it today, in our society, are like rustics coming across some marble of the ancients. It does not repel them, but it hardly attracts them at all—they

can make nothing of it. That reaction against the classical spirit, which began in England with the turn of the eighteenth century and the opening of the nineteenth, the romantic extravagance, the search for violent sensation, the test of poetry by poignancy, the loss of measure, provoked elsewhere a fairly strong resistance and, before long, a reaction.[5]

Belloc is particularly sharp in his attack on how "the romantic extravagance" has damaged English poetry and so praises in Pitter's verse "an exceptional reappearance of the classical spirit amongst us" (7). He admires Pitter's ability "to get [her] rhythmic effect without emphatic lilt; to be subtle in [her] management of results without any apparent complexity; to be an artist without showing [her] art." In addition, he compares her verse to architecturally large and solid buildings while disparaging romantic poetry as "those buildings which are a conglomerate of shining ornament and rubble" (8). Pitter's verse, he adds, captures the essence of an earlier time in English poetry when a fine poem was clear to all: "Really good verse, contrasted with the general run of that in the midst of which it appears, seems to me to have a certain quality of *hardness*; so that, in the long run, it will be discovered, as a gem is discovered in mud" (9). While we are tempted to smile at the quaintness of Belloc's critical evaluation, we admire his devotion to poetry characterized by "beauty and right order, singularly apparent in the midst of such a moral welter as perhaps no society of men ever yet suffered" (10).

Initially both Belloc and Pitter were incredulous that *First and Second Poems* was slow to be reviewed by established London presses. He writes her on May 2, 1927: "Why *on earth* didn't they review it? The state of the English Press gets worse with a gallop, but this sort of neglect is lower than America! I think the decline of culture here in the last 20 years is a portent—but its present level is perilous. It is catastrophic. Whenever I return from Europe I feel *afraid* of the future here." Her reply is more gracious, but nonetheless piqued:

> It is extremely puzzling to me that it should not be noticed at all, as the previous book [*First Poems*], so slight and not more advertised, had numerous reviews, some of them good. This is more important, has been announced, is sponsored by you—what on earth can it be? Perhaps those modern Borgias, never mind who, have arranged for its suppression. This is at least a flattering hypothesis. If I were only consumptive, I might die à la Keats, but I can't even produce a fit of coughing. Never mind. (May 3)

When a review did appear in the *Times Literary Supplement*, neither could have been particularly pleased. The reviewer, while noting Belloc's high praise, offers penetrating insight into the weakness of Pitter's "classical spirit": "The virtue of classicism is to correct romantic extravagance and sensationalism; but it is always liable to stifle instead of to discipline a true impulse, to substitute verbal ceremony for vital image. In much of Miss Pitter's verse we are conscious of such imperfect expression, of emotions too weak wholly to inform the language in which they are dressed, and of words whose 'grave and ordered loveliness' is too self-sufficient."[6] And when he concedes "her verse always has substance and it is finely chiseled," Pitter and Belloc must have felt this was tepid praise indeed.

Gorham Munson is more generous, claiming that Pitter "is not a ragged pilgrim going toward Parnassus, but one who actually dwells on that magic mountain and has climbed from its lower slope to the upper air where true excellence alone can live."[7] He recognizes her debt to Elizabethan sentiment and finds her interest in fairies not a negative, but an attempt to connect to the spiritual and mystical; furthermore, he praises her technical abilities, citing in particular her use of traditional poetic forms (the sonnet, rondeau, ballade, and distinct stanzaic patterns), bold metaphors, assonance, and internal rhyme. Richard Church finds much to admire and agrees that they exhibit the classical spirit. He summarizes the emotional impact of *First and Second Poems* effectively:

> Throughout Ruth Pitter's work this submission of self is the dominant *motif*, lifting up the weariness of her temperament, and making what seems a constitutional despondency blossom into the most beautiful forms of resignation; shapes of reminiscence, and half-gestures of patient wistfulness, conjuring a beauty that creeps into the reader's heart, bringing that almost unendurable pain which one feels on a clear, spring evening, when the sky is shower-green, with a westward-hovering star to remind one of a former scene shared with a beloved person who has since vanished into the grave.[8]

Yet even in Church's high praise there is the tacit admission that the emotion is impersonal and detached. Eda Walton adds that *First and Second Poems* "is almost a literary anachronism," belonging "much more certainly in the seventeenth century."[9] Walton also criticizes Pitter's work as too derivative, although "she should write well, once she clears herself of echoes."

In point of fact, *First and Second Poems* suffers from the same deficiencies as *First Poems*: a voice that is vapid, abstract, detached, impersonal, and unconvincing. Yet Pitter does expand her range of topics to include her love of poesy, the human spirit as a reflection of divine care, existential confusion, inexplicable disillusionment, loss and sorrow, and reflections upon death. Importantly, poems having to do with the fairy world are few. Indeed, the poem "As Silly Child" may be Pitter's recognition that much of her early verse was too naive, too uninformed:

As silly child that wishes all things pleasant
I thought I saw a Land where every peasant
Was gay and wise and far removed from folly,
And statesmen in their secret hearts were holy;

And London in the lap of light was queenly
As cities of dream, and silver Thames serenely
Glided to sea by all her pastured ridges,
Whispering on weirs, and singing through the bridges. (172)

In terms of her impersonal voice, there are promising exceptions among the 133 poems that make up *First and Second Poems,* three-quarters having previously appeared in the *New Age.* For instance, "Young Loves" (161) and "Melancholy" (143)[10] suggest that a more personal voice is emerging in Pitter's verse, while previously unpublished poems such as "The Hermitage" (157) and "My Name Is Peace" (178) continue Pitter's tradition of writing about Hainault Forest.

Although the imagery of "Youth Has Been Storm" is abstract, its mature reflection upon the tempestuous emotions of youth versus the wry insights of age leads aptly to the final realization: "I mourn not bitterly / The vanished green" (174). In "Let Me Not Live" Pitter achieves a subtle poignancy as she notes that her own death, and by implication the death of any human, is not worth remembrance:

Let me not live in a sad monument,
    But let me be
Far from the searching of remembrance sent,
    Sunk in the sea;
The Gods have written death; set not to time
    The trifling bound
Of marble, nor a tablet marred with rhyme,
    No plot of ground;
I was less fair than clouds, and no man makes
    Statues to these;
Forget me; think upon the silent lakes,
    The slender trees. (175)

The inevitability of human death makes grave markers, stones, or crypts pointless. Rather than linger at such empty memorials, Pitter suggests readers should focus upon natural objects. Her clipped "think upon the silent lakes, / The slender trees" is no sentimental sop. Indeed, this honest reflection upon the melancholy reality of the human condition intimates the powerful poetic voice that later emerges.

Stylistically, Pitter writes longer poems and experiments with blank verse and the sonnet. "Pastiche: In Praise" is one of the poems where she pledges her allegiance to poesy, ending in competently written blank verse: "And Heaven shall smile that I forget my soul, / And frown not; for thy silver traffickings / Are thorough Heaven, where I shall light me down / When that thou stayest, and the world is burned" (73–74).[11] These lines also illustrate her more frequent use of the caesura in this volume. Of the six sonnets in *First and Second Poems,* "Sea-Herb" is a clumsy effort. For instance, the diction is forced throughout, as the opening quatrain illustrates: "Fate hath not sown thee by long Lethe stream / That scarce gives back the light of leaden day, / And with her slow wave laps the bitter clay / That which with every wanhope herb doth teem." Oddly varying the rhyme scheme of an Italian sonnet, Pitter's poem about a shore plant clinging to its rocky home never reaches the heroic gesture she intended, as its final couplet illustrates: "And songs of combat from the epic deep / Fling furious brine even athwart thy sleep" (85).[12] The awkwardness of Pitter's handling of this and the other sonnets in this volume suggests that she was still experimenting with the form and belies her later success with the sonnet.

Had Pitter's poetic output stopped with *First Poems* and *First and Second Poems,* she would have deserved the same oblivion as countless other would-be poets. There is little in her first two volumes of verse to suggest the excellence and quality of her later efforts. The reasons for her later success will become apparent, but certainly her good fortune in having Orage and Belloc as early champions gave her the stimulus to continue writing poetry. While Orage's and Belloc's patronage of Pitter's poetry was a boon, her affection for her father was dealt the severest blow by his death on August 18, 1926. In the unpublished poem "The Cottage," written shortly after George's death, Pitter writes poignantly about her memories of her father in Hainault Forest:

My father of that utter loneliness
Was part; he was a man of great desires
Confused, frustrated: the imperfect he
Rejected, and so had nothing in this life.
He talked with spirits of the tenuous air,
And far in the black wood I often saw
His homeward lantern, and would hear him make
Cheerful discourse to one that answered not.
A bodiless music in the frosty dark
One night we heard: one night the snowy owl
Swooped down, and sitting on the gate did cry

As boding woe: he told me one was dead,
A dwarf that lived at hand, and it was so.
He had a friend, a rat, most hoar and old
And blind: he fed and cheered it, caring not
For any ravage that such creatures do;
And fox and squirrel held his store as theirs,
And the sad hound and hard-used lurcher came
To warm them, and when sick they searched for him.
And one that found him not lay down and died
On the deserted threshold in the dark.

And he was harvested last harvest time:
I gathered in his thin, neglected crops
Untended since the sowing, and rooted out
Self-seeded hundreds of forget-me-nots;
And I shall gather in his crops no more;
Saving the lifelong crop of bitter weeds
He sowed in me, that make me hate my kind
But not hate him; such offspring was his fate,
And such a father mine; a majesty
Of darkness orders man's unhappy ways,
And to that empire do I bow, and keep
A steadfast silence. Ours not tragedy,
Nor the perfection of catastrophe,
But the slow victory of the rotten void,
Where nothing triumphs over piety,
Even as in this soil the fungous slime
Rots the proud body of the English oak.

There his old garment hangs upon the door:
There lean his spade and mattock, hedging-hook,
With all their kind: most strange, he does not come,
And I am told he will not come again.
Yet far in the dark wood I hear him make
Cheerful discourse to one that answers not:
And still the hound comes and seeks the fire,
The ghostly place hath but one ghost the more.

This passage evokes Pitter's abiding love both for the cottage and for her father.
As the rich imagery of the cottage and forest suggests, she regularly returns to
them in her mind. More importantly, however, these lines reveal her recognition

of her father's hard life and nostalgia for their shared times of simple companion-ship at the cottage. She acknowledges his effect on her personality—sowing in her "bitter weeds . . . that make me hate my kind"—yet she sees in this a strength since it has toughened her and made her accept that for humankind "darkness orders man's unhappy ways." Her description of his clothes and tools is so apt we almost smell his scent and feel the handles of his tools, worn to smoothness. And the final lines verge on the mystical. That this poem was not published offers commentary on Pitter's reluctance to expose her heart; yet this poem is compel-ling, and it points to future poems in which a personal, intimate voice appears.

Pitter's mother, Louisa, grieved the death of George but sought solace by pur-chasing Oak Cottage, a little country house near Dunmow, Essex. Oak Cottage soon succeeded the rented cottage in Hainault Forest as Pitter's favorite spot when she wanted to escape London, and for many years she cherished the dream of one day retiring to this Essex retreat.[13] In the meantime, weekend visits had to suffice, so she and O'Hara continued working for the Jenningses, with Pitter snatching time here and there to work on her verse. By the end of 1928, however, the Walberswick Peasant Pottery Company was teetering on the edge of closure due primarily to poor management and fallout from the Great Depression.

Facing the loss of a regular income, Pitter and O'Hara gambled on a risky venture. As they were nearing their lowest ebb, one morning Pitter received a letter from the painter Mary McCrossan, who said a friend in Chelsea with a business similar to the Jenningses' was looking to sell out and retire. She wanted a tenant for her studio who would be willing to take over the business, to as-sume the seven years remaining on her lease, and to purchase her few assets for £50. On the face of it, the idea was so fraught with risk that Pitter balked and turned it down outright, arguing to O'Hara that neither of them had experience running a business. Indeed, this might have been the end of it, but O'Hara was convinced they could pull it off. After days of argument, O'Hara finally won the day, and the two young women pooled their joint savings and took the plunge.

What they had done before in the way of economizing was nothing com-pared to what they had to do now. In six months they pulled together stock and capital valued at £500. In addition, Louisa lent them £100 (for which the two women insisted on paying 5 percent interest). Lacking other support, and in fact eager to be independent of outside sources, in early June 1930 they hired a small horse and cart and moved their stock to the Chelsea studio. When they unlocked the studio door, a black cat appeared from nowhere and dashed in, rushed round and round the studio, and then ran out, never to appear again; O'Hara, at least, "felt at the time this was a good omen." Arranging their stock in the two large rooms of the studio, both women were acutely aware of how little they actually had. Nonetheless, on June 18, 1930, Deane and Forester

(Pitter and O'Hara kept the name of the existing business) was officially registered at 55 Old Church Street, Chelsea.

Pitter's relationship with Orwell blossomed briefly during this time. She recalls how he would turn up now and then:

> He liked our large workshop. I remember his changing into very shabby clothes in its shadowy recesses, prior to some excursion into the seamy side of life. He didn't look in the least like a poor man. God knows he *was* poor, but the formidable look didn't go with the rags. He left in the workshop a suitcase full of clothes—to our feminine eyes the most deplorable clothes. He would write from time to time and ask for various choice items to be sent on. Now and then he would ask me to go out with him. I have lively recollections of these occasions, at the same time heartrending and comic. You see, he hardly ever had enough money, and it was terrible to him to let a woman pay. I used to take picnic lunches and help as tactfully as I could, but the heartrending element *would* come in. I used to think, "Well, if it's so awful, why doesn't he get a proper job?" But this, of course; was very bourgeois.[14]

It also became clear that Orwell was looking for more than friendship, and on several occasions he made it clear that "he was after what no nice girl should ever give." In another unpublished poem, "Eros with Chilblains," Pitter gently parodies their relationship at this time:

No longer blind
but of all glory forlorn
appeared the Imp, and blew on his raw hands.
I don't want you
particularly, he said,
but you'd better have me
or you'll get no sexlife,
you must have sexlife.
I cried Good God and eyed the waif again,
meeting the blue suspicious stare.
Mean modern vesture hid not wholly
the shape and port celestial;
the arrogance and the melancholy
veiled him in part but veiled not all,
the arrows of fire, the fiery hair
were chilled and dim, but fire was there.

She then describes comically the tempestuous nature of their conversations—
him wanting sex, her wanting love—while he trolls through the dustbins like a
tomcat looking for a female in heat.

> He spat like a cat,
> he swore like a whore.
> "If you patronize me
> anymore
> if you mention Psyche
> again to me
> I will strike you with lightning"
> caterwauled he.
> "The trollop's trailed me
> three thousand years"
> and he blistered the earth with fiery tears.
>
> If you really want me
> and you are He,
> the door stands open
> and here I be;
> blind no longer
> you should know
> to my bed and bosom
> the way to go.
>
> "I'm damned if I do! it's up to you!
> You must pick me up and carry me too!
> When I was blind the way was plain
> but now I must learn all over again.
> I don't want you but you must have Me.
> Take me in and be damned!" said he.

The comic nature of the poem, with its humorous comparison of Orwell to Eros,
culminates appropriately:

> I flung him out in the yard,
> I hoped he damn well died.
> To count the bites and scratches
> for a long time I tried,
> then gave it up and went to bed,

and listened in case he cried
there in the dark outside.

I could not hear a whimper
save from poor Psyche, whose
sweet holy saving simper
was always bound to lose,
but from the outer dark there rang
an ashbin-lid's defiant clang.

Although Pitter and Orwell continued to meet occasionally, they gradually lost touch as she and O'Hara worked hard to make their business succeed and he followed the path that won him worldwide acclaim as the author of *Animal Farm* and *1984*.

In Pitter and O'Hara's first month of business, they earned only £20, not nearly enough to cover their rent, wages for one assistant, and other expenses. Although they knew the work and were gifted at it, they did not know how to buy, sell, market, or keep accounts. Accordingly, risking even more, they hired a traveling salesman to show their goods to a wider market; unfortunately, he turned out to be dishonest and was quickly released. While O'Hara was able to brave these crises, Pitter suffered torments of anxiety. One fear she inherited from her parents was that of destitution; economic independence and prompt discharge of financial obligations were principles she held to religiously.

Then a near-catastrophic event occurred. In mid-August, only two months after beginning their business, a small can of cellulose paint that Pitter was opening exploded, and the lid flew up, severely injuring her left eye—not only lacerating it but also coating it with amyl acetate and pieces of hard pigment. She was rushed to the nearest hospital, which happened to be run by the Freemasons; for a moment this was problematic because the hospital was only for Freemasons, and Pitter was told they would not treat her. Fortunately, however, the taxi driver who had brought her piped up and said, "I am a Freemason." He signed for Pitter, and she was admitted for treatment. For two months both women feared Pitter would be permanently blind in that eye. This severe injury compounded their financial crisis, as the costs of medicine and the hospital and the loss of revenue since Pitter could not work combined to bring them to the brink of bankruptcy. O'Hara in particular felt the hardship of this period since she had to take Pitter to the hospital each day then bring her back and settle her in the flat and then go to work at the Chelsea studio.

Before either woman gave in to despair, however, they made one more effort with a traveling salesman. When the applicant appeared, he was shabby

and penniless. Yet Pitter and O'Hara liked his look and hired him. This good
fortune probably saved the business, as he turned out to be honest, hard working, and very effective at selling their goods to the larger shops; indeed, he
remained a trusted and important employee until the outbreak of World War II.
Furthermore, Pitter's eye gradually recovered so that by Christmas of 1930 she
was able to work again. Soon orders were coming in so fast their chief trouble
was meeting their deadlines. True to their natures, Pitter and O'Hara redoubled
their efforts, often working from 8:30 A.M. until midnight seven days a week,
catching a meal here and there on the gas ring in the studio. While O'Hara
probably thrived on this, noting that "hard work does not kill. . . . What really
gets one down is worry," Pitter was less sanguine: "Business is nothing but a procession of troubles any way you look at it, and takes every bit of energy bar the
merest dregs—I [had to] write poetry with what [was] left." In another instance
she writes Belloc: "The sanguinary dogfight of commerce in these times has me
heartscalded" (Dec. 3, 1933). Still, within a year, the two women's hard work
and persistence led to solid business connections and financial independence;
they even paid back Louisa's £100 loan. Eventually the business grew to employ
eleven people, and throughout the 1930s their decorated goods, including tea
trays with floral decorations and other household objects from pencil sharpen-
ers to small tables, were shipped to Europe and all parts of the British Empire.

There is no doubt that Pitter's move to London, her friendship with O'Hara,
and the opening of their business had much to do with Pitter's psychological
maturation. In effect she moved from being a rather dreamy, immature girl to a
worldly-wise, anxious young adult. Moreover, the terrible injury to her eye, while
only a short-term physical disability, actually became a catalyst for the maturation
of her imaginative life. Living as an invalid and unable to keep up her frenetic
work schedule, Pitter took advantage of her physical inactivity by exploring in
profoundly deep ways something she had never attempted before: the full exercise
of her poetic imagination. Indeed, one of her most powerful poems, "Stormcock
in Elder," had its genesis during this period.[15] As the poem opens, we see that Pitter has imaginatively retreated to the cottage in Hainault Forest:

> In my dark hermitage, aloof
> From the world's sight and the world's sound,
> By the small door where the old roof
> Hangs but five feet above the ground,
> I groped along the shelf for bread
> But found celestial food instead.
>
> For suddenly close at my ear,
> Loud, loud and wild, with wintry glee,

The old unfamiliar chorister
Burst out in pride of poetry;
And through the broken roof I spied
Him by his singing glorified.

What then follows is a concrete, detailed description of the stormcock, the English missal thrush, made all the more remarkable because this vivid physical description is based exclusively on Pitter's memory from her days in Hainault Forest:

Scarcely an arm's length from the eye,
Myself unseen, I saw him there;
The throbbing throat that made the cry,
The breast dewed from the misty air,
The polished bill that opened wide
And showed the pointed tongue inside:

The large eye, ringed with many a ray
Of minion feathers, finely laid,
The feet that grasped the elder-spray:
How strongly used, how subtly made
The scale, the sinew, and the claw,
Plain through the broken roof I saw;

The flight-feathers in tail and wing,
The shorter coverts, and the white
Merged into russet, marrying
The bright breast to the pinions bright,
Gold sequins, spots of chestnut, shower
Of silver, like a brindled flower.

Soldier of fortune, northwest Jack,
Old hard-times' braggart, there you blow!
But tell me ere your bagpipes crack
How you can make so brave a show,
Full-fed in February, and dressed
Like a rich merchant at a feast.

One-half the world, or so they say,
Knows not how half the world may live;
So sing your song and go your way,

And still in February contrive
As bright as Gabriel to smile
On elder-spray by broken tile.

Pitter's own gloss on the poem's origin connects it to her eye injury: "This poem is very singular to me because it was composed when I had temporarily quite lost my sight as the result of an accident. I'd seen the bird many years before, but it was only then, when I was blind, that its image came back to me in the most minute detail. . . . The small details . . . would not have been seen consciously while the eye was in action. But the image from the unconscious mind came back more complete than anything directly seen."[16]

In effect, then, the eye injury led to the emergence of a genuine poetic voice as she began to write poems crafted less "while the eye was in action" and more by the insights of her unconscious mind. Her enforced blindness caused her to turn within to see. As a result, she attended to her inner poetic voice in new and dramatically transforming ways. Where she once embraced nature visually like the young Wordsworth, her blindness forced her to explore her memories of nature and natural objects in a more deliberate, reflective, and intuitive manner. This pause, this inner exploration, gave her the time to penetrate the mysteries of life whereas before she wrote about the surface of human existence in a flat, unconvincing, ethereal tone. The retreat within, perhaps combined with the fear of never seeing again, drove her to a closer examination of her own poetic vision. Where she once maintained a detached, impersonal relationship with her poetry, now she made intimate connections with the subjects of her verse, often with startling insights about the human condition—its joys, doubts, loves, fears, commitments, uncertainties, convictions, and longings.

Driven into the fertile well of her imagination, Pitter learned how to draw on past memories of the cottage and its surroundings in Hainault Forest as the controlling foci of a vast poetic reservoir. Indeed, over the next twenty-five years, the period of her most memorable and powerful work, she draws frequently and deeply from this pool of memory. In poem after poem the "blind" poet retreats back to her forest of memories, delighting in the sights, sounds, smells, and feel of the paths, trees, flowers, meadows, brooks, birds, and other inhabitants of Hainault Forest. Those early years near the cottage had inadvertently developed into a wellhead of stored memories; the poetic energy that had only trickled out in her poetry up until her thirtieth year began to gush out into a flowing stream through the mid-1950s. Had she not suffered the eye injury and the forced idleness it precipitated, she might never have had the chance to make the imaginative descent into this poetic fountain.

In effect, Pitter's eye injury was a key event that unlocked her voice as a poet. Out of a potential disaster, she reaped a benefit she could never have anticipated, and the promise that Orage and Belloc had sensed in her was released in a way that neither could have imagined. Her repeated retreat into her imagination suggests an unconscious influence of Wordsworth upon Pitter. In *The Prelude* he writes:

> There are in our existence spots of time,
> That with distinct pre-eminence retain
> A renovating Virtue, whence, depressed
> By false opinion and contentious thought,
> Or aught of heavier or more deadly weight,
> In trivial occupations, and the round
> Of ordinary intercourse, our minds
> Are nourished and invisibly repaired;
> A virtue by which pleasure is enhanced,
> That penetrates, enables us to mount,
> When high, more high, and lifts us up when fallen.
> . . . .
> Such moments worthy of all gratitude,
> Are scattered every where, taking their date
> From our first childhood.[17]

Pitter's early days in Hainault Forest provided her countless spots in time that nourished and propelled her imagination and poetry.

While Pitter's eye injury was undoubtedly the key event in unleashing her poetic voice, a secondary one was her evolving decision throughout the 1920s to avoid long-term romantic entanglement. While neither frigid nor a prude, Pitter grew to have a circumspect view of the possibility of passionate love. She writes a friend a few years later: "Have kept out of love as much as possible, as my psychology is such a muck-heap that it takes all my skill to carry on, without jarring impacts, which would ruin all my careful improvements. I lurk, intensely observant, in the undergrowth."[18] Ironically, though a self-confessed romantic, she was unwilling to compromise either her freedom or her poetry for a man. In "The Poet Speaks" she says: "If one had a miserable love affair, and, of course, [I lived] a little bohemian life and one had many, then this was not the stuff . . . I wanted at all. . . . I always had an instinct about mixing love up with things; [it] never seemed right when you'd done it. It wasn't I minded showing my feelings, but the result seemed impure. One hadn't enough control to present the solution one wished." In a later recollection she said:

> Although my private myths [about romantic love] flourished obstinately, over the years, and against odds too, as one after another of the inadequate

opposite numbers faded away, I began to have glimmerings about the dishonesty of the whole thing. I was growing up; terribly slowly, but inexorably. The ideas of Freud and Jung began to pervade human society, and I couldn't help becoming aware of them. But the biggest eye-opener was when somebody fell romantically in love with *me*, for a change. . . . This was a horrible experience, because it was quite obvious that he wasn't in love with me, myself. He didn't know me, didn't want to. All he asked was that I should *pretend* to be the woman of his vision. He was looking past me—looking over my shoulder at a ghost. There is hardly a word in the language rude enough to reply to this attitude, I felt, choking with indignation, and throwing his flowers out of the window. And all the time I had been trying to do this very thing to other people.[19]

Pitter's recognition that this man had been in love with love, not with her, helped her to see her lack of success in romantic love as her own failure. While this angered her for the moment, she admitted: "Most of us don't get the chance to be silly-romantic for more than a very short period of our lives. Romantic love is a flowering. Surely there's a time of life when these bright dreams and alluring myths are all right. You can't live on flowers, of course, but, oh Lord, how sweet they are!" In a later interview she says: "I would look at the boy next door and I would look at young men one met in the course of one's work, and one would say to one's self that they are simply not relevant. One might be very fond of them, but one would realize that, as I always say it would be cruelty to animals to marry them, because there was always this ruling passion [writing poetry], this major preoccupation, in which the poor dears had no share."[20] Still later she adds: "I always said to myself: my true love or none. I will not marry unless I feel I cannot exist without that person. And though it were quite often painful, one realized that this extremely nice person, one would be glad to know better—well to him my work was only marginal. But to me it was absolutely primal, and if the work was only marginal to him, then he was only marginal to me."[21]

Consequently, while Pitter did have friendly relationships with several men throughout her life and was romantically and sexually drawn to several, she also had a powerful sense of self-protection—both against a broken heart and for her fiercely held muse. No poem better expresses this sentiment than "If You Came," first published in 1939:

If you came to my secret glade,
Weary with heat,
I would set you down in the shade,
I would wash your feet.

If you came in the winter sad,
Wanting for bread,
I would give you the last that I had,
I would give you my bed.

But the place is hidden apart
Like a nest by a brook,
And I will not show you my heart
By a word, by a look.

The place is hidden apart
Like a nest of a bird:
And I will not show you my heart
By a look, by a word.[22]

Deftly, Pitter sets this poem imaginatively in a wooded retreat with obvious allusions to Hainault Forest. While the speaker promises the visitor physical comfort, including shelter and nourishment, and while there is sensuous detail in her promise to wash his feet and give him her bed, she will not give her secret self, her heart's true being, because it "is hidden apart." The penetrating core of the poem is the speaker's affirmation that she "will not show you my heart, / By a look, by a word." At the same time, her initial invitation to the visitor is genuine and intimate, suggesting she is open to romantic pursuit, but it has to be initiated by the man. The discovery of her heart is possible, yet the poem ends abruptly, leaving the sense that no pursuit, no discovery, was attempted. In commenting on this poem later, Pitter said: "This poem enshrines . . . the biological fact that a woman expects to be found out about. She expects to be discovered, however secret she makes herself."[23] Of course, this was not the last poem she wrote about love; later poems that also explore her musings on romantic love include "Early Rising," "Weeping Water, Leaping Fire," and "True Love's not Told" from A Trophy of Arms; "The Difference" from The Spirit Watches; "But for Lust," "Lament for One's Self," and "Passion and Peace" from The Bridge; "Hen under Bay-Tree" from The Ermine; and "The Heart's Desire Is Full of Sleep" from Still by Choice. However, "If You Came" offers early insight into Pitter's overall attitude toward romantic love; while beautiful, intense, and desirable, such love was a threat and an ultimately unfulfilling alternative to her devotion to poetry.

Persephone in Hades

Pitter's eye injury and conscious decision to avoid romantic entanglements, combined with her very real need to make Deane and Forester a successful business, concentrated her creative energies, leading to a remarkable outpouring of new verse that broke radically with her first two volumes. Her poetic voice, which had been largely derivative, flat, impersonal, and unconvincing, took on a new, vital tone characterized by humor, multiple points of view, and psychological complexity, eventually resulting in *A Mad Lady's Garland* (1934). However, the first expression of her new voice occurred when she began to experiment with poetic form, leading to the publication of her only narrative poem, *Persephone in Hades* (1931). Once again Belloc championed her cause. Writing her on June 7, 1930, after having read the poem in manuscript, he said:

> The poem excels in vision, that is the first point. . . . Next, on account of this, it excels in metaphor; the metaphors are as strong as they are numerous and that is very rare. The similes also are strong, notably that of the swan and of the jasper. . . . Now as to diction, I should make the criticism that there was not a sufficient presence of the caesura. . . . The passage on the horror, presence and experience of death is, I think, not only the finest in the poem but the finest I know. . . . One last point is the excellence of using the double syllable ending, which you have done with great effect in more than one place, especially in the last lines of the last page of the typescript.

In subsequent letters Belloc is eager to know when the poem is going to be published, "for it is a very fine thing indeed":

> I think it is important that Persephone should appear. Would you like to try the London Mercury? They print acres of bad verse and they have plenty of room for the best verse now going, which yours is. I will ask Squire [the editor] to do it. His own judgement on verse is valueless and anything like advice he therefore resents, but I think I can do it. I hope you will not mind if I try? It is a ridiculous thing that a purely material point should interfere with putting good verse before the public and in no time but ours would such an absurdity be possible. (July 22, 1930)

Apparently Belloc's enthusiasm for the poem was not shared by the editors at the *London Mercury*, nor by book publishers, as Pitter's letter to Belloc of February 27, 1931, makes clear: "It was a great pleasure to hear from you again, and I am very grateful that you should be trying to get poor Persephone a place. I feel rather lukewarm about it myself. No one but you seems to care for the poem. My friends condemn it variously as cold, diffuse, Calvinistic, patchy, morbid, ill-constructed, redundant, monotonous, etc. All say there are good bits, but all select different ones." She goes on in the letter to ask whether Belloc thinks she should contact Doubleday in New York in order to ascertain if an American publisher would be interested in printing the seven-hundred-line poem. The extent to which she and O'Hara are working long hours toward making Deane and Forester a success during the poem's composition is also revealed in this letter: "We have been working extremely hard all the winter, but our business is quickly gaining ground, and although I have written nothing for eight months, I must not regret the time spent endeavouring to lay the foundation of a competence. I hope you are well and happy, and I am most grateful for your untiring interest and help." Belloc's help, once again, was a boon to Pitter's fledging career. After finding no London publisher interested in *Persephone in Hades*, Belloc, who held dual citizenship in England and France, arranged for the French publisher A. Sauriac to print the poem. About Belloc's ceaseless efforts on behalf of the poem, Pitter writes: "Your kindness to me, as well as your zeal for literature, leaves me at a loss for thanks. Through all the demands of business today I have felt the delightful sensation of being *fortunata et felix*, rare enough in neglected minor poets in hard times" (March 3).

Published in August, *Persephone* inevitably attracted no critical attention, primarily because its limited edition of one hundred copies, printed "for private circulation only," meant only a very few people would have access to it. The seven cantos of *Persephone* are Pitter's retelling of the Greek myth of Persephone, daughter to Zeus, chief of the gods, and his wife, Demeter, goddess of the earth and agriculture. Although Zeus had given his consent to Hades, god of the underworld, to marry Persephone, Demeter intervened and prevented the marriage. Desperate to have her, Hades seized her one day while she was gathering flowers and carried her off to his realm of darkness. Demeter, disconsolate over the loss of her daughter, wandered aimlessly, her sorrow spreading infertility over the earth. As all vegetation withered and a severe famine swept the earth, Zeus sent Hermes to the underworld to bring Persephone back to Demeter. However, before Hades would let her go, he tricked Persephone into eating a pomegranate seed, the food of the dead, and so she was forced to return to the underworld for four months each year. Consequently, Persephone has come to be seen as the goddess of both death and fertility, and she is often associated with the earth's revival each spring.

Pitter's *Persephone* is largely faithful to the myth. Canto 1 introduces the narrator as a worshipper of Persephone, and he offers the poem as praise to her, noting the importance of fearing the gods and asking about the reality of everlasting life: "Brightness eternal, the immortal splendour, / Life without end and everlasting power; / Who that is prey to death may celebrate them?"[24] The narrator also suggests that only love can endure death: "What of night, that which is hidden? / What is the end of love, what lies beyond it, / What is love's counterpart? Answer, Love only" (9). While the story celebrates romantic love, the poem is curiously passionless; that is, Pitter works hard to tell us about the love between Persephone and Hades, but she does not show us that love. All their passion is intimated, reported, and chronicled, yet we never see the two lovers as lovers, nor do we hear them speak to each other.

When the scene shifts to Olympus and Zeus granting Hades' request in canto 2, Persephone is pictured as living a happy, contented life on the earth:

> And fair on the far Nysian plain she played.
> The chilly mist that drifted in from sea
> Hung in her hair rich as the hair of Zeus,
> The air above Olympus seemed her eyes;
> Her breast was sacred to her mother Earth,
> And her proud neck and mouth entirely fair
> Mixed august heaven with Demeter kind.
> The pale urns of the autumn crocuses
> Admired her feet, likening them to those
> Strong feet of Hermes, swift upon the hills
> Or in the air: the autumn's clearest star,
> The yellow lily, leaned towards her hand,
> Careless of being gathered, might it see
> The hand that Earth to her sole daughter gave:
> For who beheld it savoured every flower,
> Saw the rich vintage, sheaves and laden wains,
> Honey and milk, abundance of all kinds,
> And all that hands may take from the great Earth.
> And she was white and powerful as the swan,
> The swan in beauty and the swan in flight
> On her great wings that dares the dire abyss. (11–12)

The rich imagery associated with Persephone makes vivid her appearance and recalls allusions to the myth of Zeus and Leda. However, the appearance of autumn foreshadows a change in her happy state. Utilizing the pathetic fallacy clumsily, Pitter describes the clouds weeping in anticipation of Persephone's fate: "Dun fleecy cloud / Formless and ominous, that began to weep / In rain" (13). From under the earth ominous rumblings bellow forth three times, the last one accompanied by a fierce rain that lashes down, stripping and uprooting trees. Throughout these events Persephone shows no fear and stays her ground. Pitter using to great effect an epic simile to capture her courage:

> As the royal stag
> Scents danger, though the ill he cannot see,
> And with dilated eye, but warrior front
> Armed and implacable, still steadfast stands
> While the whole female herd in panic flies,
> So did Persephone outface the unknown. (13)

Suddenly the earth opens up and Hades rises from below: "She fronted Him from whom the fearful priest / Averts his face at the black sacrifice, / Whose name is never spoken, and whose rites / Are secret, and with whispering horror done" (15). Before she can move, Hades strikes her senseless, pulls her onto his chariot, and forces her to go with him into darkness. The earth weeps as the ground closes upon her.

Demeter's fury and hatred for Zeus and the earth's anguish are the focus of canto 3. Driven by despair, Demeter directs her wrath toward heaven; since she has "lost / That dearer life, was lost herself, and strayed / Raving in ragged glens like the fierce wind, / Stalking the mountains like a tempest, torn / With sudden shrieking" (17). To Demeter's passionate imploring that Persephone should have had a "shining mate," one of the bright gods of Olympus, not the dark, dread lord of the underworld, Zeus responds with stony silence: "He / Covered his chastened light with wintry cloud. / The sable curtain fell, and on her heart / Blackness descended" (18). Yet Pitter's verse does not move us to consider Demeter's sufferings. What could be more painful than the loss of a child and the silence of an impassive lover/husband? However, instead of feeling sympathy for her plight, we never sense Demeter's emotional turmoil because these matters are reported to us; we never witness Zeus and Demeter in dialogue, nor are we shown why Zeus made his decision. Zeus's stony silence, on the one hand, is to be expected. He is God and God owes no one, not even another god, an explanation for his acts. On the other hand, if Pitter's intent was to suggest that Zeus's actions had grander cosmic implications worth the short-term pain for himself, Demeter, and Persephone, the impersonal nature of the narrative is inadequate. At the same time, Pitter does show that Zeus is disturbed when he sees the earth ravaged, stripped, and swept by winter, the promise of spring in serious jeopardy:

> Now at the very heart of winter, earth
> Seems dead; now all her lively streams stand still,

The wind's breath ceases, and the ashy snow
Whispering descends, and veils the stiffened clay.
Now the starved beast, coiled in his cave asleep,
Breathes at long intervals and longer, then
Shudders but once, as sleep unites with death.
Flowers are but memory; the ragged stem
Stands lifeless, and all hope lies in the root.
Frost strike no deeper! One inch more, farewell
Promise of resurrection, and farewell
Spring, and new beauty, and the precious seed,
The fruit of all; but roots are quiet in earth,
Feel not the pang of frost, but fast asleep
Await the rising, or unknowing die;
Leave them to heaven, to slay them or to spare. (19)

Illustrating his wisdom and worth as the father of the gods, Zeus sends Hermes to Hades as the canto ends.

In canto 4 Persephone is portrayed as disconsolate before the dark, barren throne of Hades, wishing to be the least creature on earth rather than the queen of the underworld. Pitter does a fine job in evoking the nameless fears associated with the underworld: "Eternal night in the strong-vaulted earth / Covers the throne of Dis, and the lost shades / Surround it with innumerable sighs / And presences unseen yet desolate" (20). Persephone wishes "to be a cloud, a leaf, a grasshopper, / A worm, yea any vile or humble thing, / To have the boon of ceasing: for that dark / Is dreadful, and as chaos come again" (20–21). On earth, at least, she could die; in Hades, she is wracked with pain and can barely remember her day on earth: "Now through her bones was thrust a dolorous pang / Made of all agony . . . hopeless in hell she lay" (21). Grief and horror are her only friends now, and worst of all, she feels unloved and useless. In a moment of existential angst, she doubts the goodness of Zeus:

And in the dreary citadel of grief
The throned negations faced: to be unloved,
Uselessness, and the hell that comprehends
All misery in one mind, the hell of doubt.
She dreamed the gods were not;
. . . .
Fell is despair, and so despairing, she
Craved the return of pain to numb despair,
Offered the flesh to every insult, so

The delicate mind, prone to the greater ill,
Might be redeemed from obscene hopelessness. (24)

Longing earnestly for death, she stares the possibility fully in the face and turns away: "For such is death, no grief nor any pain / Hold equal horror with that Not to Be" (25). By the end of the canto, as she falls asleep, she accepts her fate stoically, rejecting despair but also rejecting any hope as the final two lines poignantly express: "Free at long last from pain, but with no joy, / She sat exiled from time, and place, and life" (26).

Canto 5 serves as the turning point in Pitter's retelling of the Persephone myth. It opens: "But winter will recede: O not for ever / Sleeps the sown grain there in the grave; the earth / Is warmed, and it must upward" (26). After reaching her nadir, Persephone awakens like the earth after winter, oddly affected by three liquid drops representing her own enduring spirit, a throbbing musical note, and spiritual knowledge; we are not prepared for the introduction of the three drops, so their insertion is arbitrarily intrusive. Yet through them Persephone comes to see that by accepting her fate she has become victorious, and her faith in the gods is restored.

The divine heart reclaims its heaven; at last
Of her long travail she is satisfied,
Knows herself victress: ay, and more than all,
Glories in wisdom heaped, in knowledge stored,
The golden granary of grief and pain.
All mystery lies open; now she sees
Clear through the core of being; now she knows
How the immortal gods are justified
And life is crowned for ever. (27–28)

Indeed, by accepting her place in the underworld, she is reborn and her rebirth brings a warm glow to the underworld, revealing the face of Hades as loving, wise, majestic, and powerful: "Perfect in knowledge, beyond knowledge wise, / Proud of her victory, renewed by death, / By death enlightened and initiate, / She saw and loved" (29). When Hades extends a pomegranate to her, she accepts it willingly:

She hungered and she thirsted; forthwith took
With human gratitude, celestial grace,
The orb that made her empress of the shades,
The fruit that slaked her longing, that assuaged
Her dearest need with an eternal wine,

And from the rock of sorrow struck for her
Sweet fountains filled for ever. (29–30)

Her willing acceptance of the pomegranate contrasts with the myth's portrayal
of Hades as having tricked Persephone and heightens the coming together of
two figures representing death and life. Indeed, now Persephone is able to see in
Hades new kinds of beauty: darkness is not terrible but sweet, and night is not
frightening but reassuring. In this integration of opposites—Persephone with
Hades, day with night, light with dark, life with death—her soul can rest, trusting in a unified wholeness of all things.

The upswing of emotion continues into canto 6 as Persephone's newfound
contentment corresponds to the light brought to the underworld by the arrival
of Hermes:

As when the sun into a creviced cave
Darts a white spear, and on the shadowy floor
Makes a bright circlet, so a glorious beam
Plunged into Hades, and illumined there
The ebony throne, and threw a bridal light
Upon Persephone, clothed on with gold
Her divine whiteness, and attired her head
With light, her only needed ornament. (31)

When Hermes reminds Persephone of the earth, her initial desire to return is
powerful: "Now all a daughter's heart within her stirred, / Simple and faithful,
and along the light / She looked, and yearned towards the happy earth, / Remembering she had a mother there" (32). However, the pomegranate rind at her
feet and her genuine love for Hades hold her to the underworld, but in another
variation on the myth, Hades, sure of her love, graciously permits her to go with
Hermes, even blessing and directing her to renew the earth and the flowers:

Go thou, and rediscover the old world!
Go, with renewed majesty salute the flowers,
Once thy dear toys, but now a dearer brood;
Once loved for fairness, but now utterly
Revealed and understood, children of gods.
Let them speak softly of the nether dark,
Thy bed and theirs, and worship in the sun
With silent songs, thy brighter deity.
. . . .
But ancient earth awaits thee; rise and go.
The trees, that seem like heavenly presences,

Long for thee: send up to their mighty hearts
The wine of resurrection, crowning them
Each with proper beauty. (33, 36)

The poem's final canto continues this celebratory theme when Demeter hears
rumor of her daughter's return to earth. Although she initially treats the rumor
with disbelief, not wanting to be hopeful lest her grief be doubly compounded,
she is won over after retreating into a lonely valley where she witnesses the
reawakening of the flowers: "But a breath / Comes from the south, and smiling
in the dark / The violet opens, uttering her heart / In sweetness like a song: the
last of the snow / Melts, and diminishes, and so departs" (38). As Demeter sees
additional evidence that the earth is fertile again and notes how humans are offering sacrifices of thanks to the gods, the earth trembles, opens, and reveals to
her not her daughter of old, but a spectacular, awe-inspiring, majestic goddess:

The Mother bowed herself, and from the earth
Mutely adored the proven deity;
No cherished babe, given back by fate reversed,
But all life crowned, and in full cycle raised
Up to an awful splendour, fate fulfilled.
Her babe had gone down to the dreadful grave
For ever; and the presence that returned,
The same and not the same, seeming to be
Death reconciled with immortality. (42)

The poem concludes with altars being erected to honor Persephone; in addition,
her renewal of the earth and goodwill are shown spreading over the earth.

In *Persephone* Pitter explores the possibilities of narrative poetry, experimenting with the pathetic fallacy, epic similes, sustained blank verse, and the canto.
Unfortunately, her manuscript notebooks of *Persephone* have not survived, so
it is impossible to consider her revision process. Although the narrative quality of the verse is competent enough, the poem's dearth of dialogue makes the
story tedious at times. Still, she handles the pace and rhythm of blank verse
easily, and her enthusiasm for the Persephone myth is one she held from early
childhood; it is not surprising she took it up in her only narrative poem. While
some might be tempted to speculate about possible autobiographical elements
in *Persephone*, they would be very difficult to substantiate. However, Pitter's
interest in the relationship between death and life, as well as the spiritual motifs
of resurrection, suffering, doubt, and renewal, find later expression in her lyrical
poetry. In brief, *Persephone* is an unexpected and workmanlike composition that
helps to mark Pitter's movement away from her ineffective and immature early
poetry and toward her controlled and mature verse.

THREE

Critical Acclaim,

1932–1937

In spite of Belloc's best intentions, *Persephone in Hades* languished outside the purview of critical attention; yet Pitter took no offense. She largely accepted the criticism of her friends about the poem, although she had earnestly tried to write a good poem. No critical reviews of *Persephone* appeared, but Richard Church wrote Pitter a letter praising her effort. In her reply we can see their mutual dislike of "fashionable" modern poetry:

> Many thanks for your letter, and for your very kind remarks on "Persephone." The question you raise with regard to the traditional is indeed a burning one. But it is a very dark matter to me: look at it as I will, there seems wool over my eyes and confusion in my mind. There are hypocrites, posers, and bluffers among the moderns, so much is obvious: and yet there is *something besides*; there is a growing point there which cannot be ignored. Whether this bud is the main stem of our literature, or a side growth, is beyond me. I only know that the language of the Authorised Version, the language of Milton and of Shakespeare, is the language of my heart, and I am content to risk my literary life on it. I have indeed come to see that the deliberate use of obsolete terms is all wrong; but I am not clever in the Eliot-and-Pound manner, and must gamble on my instincts. The pseudo-modern verses I have written lately are a deliberate joke: but some have taken them *au grand serieux*, which shows how ready, and even eager, people are to be deceived, and demonstrates the enormous opportunities now open to the unscrupulous. It may be that English literature is finished, and that the "moderns" are merely the irrelevant chatterers in the foyer after the piece is done. But of traditional English poetry—"when I forget thee, O Jerusalem." (May 27, 1934)

Since she had come to enjoy the narrative poetry of John Masefield and Walter de la Mare, her efforts at *Persephone* may also have been inspired by their work.[1] Regardless, she did not see the failure of the poem as an imaginative setback, and indeed, given the intensity with which she and O'Hara focused upon making Deane and Forester a success, she hardly had time to reflect upon the failure of *Persephone*.

We can see how consuming the work of their business was during the 1930s in a letter Pitter wrote to the Australian writer Nettie Palmer, who befriended Pitter by sending her gifts of seashells and coral and expressing deep admiration for Pitter's verse:[2]

> Why, you must have been reading my stuff for about twenty years. So I send you a fairly recent publication [*Persephone*]. Nobody likes it, so I hope you will. . . . Perhaps you would like to hear how I live. I do hope it will not seem too unpoetical. I am in partnership with another woman, and we do painted things and sell them. We used to work for others, but have been on our own for 2½ years, starting with one assistant—and now we have eight girls and a traveler! We sell to the gift shops, and are rather proud of having come along so fast in these hard times, though heaven knows if our success will last. We do mostly trays and painted glass, and I am going to send you a specimen when I get time to do a nice one. We have four rather nice rooms here, and a big studio and two showrooms in the next street but one. We work terribly hard, and keep very long hours—holidays are almost non-existent.[3]

About O'Hara, Pitter added: "My partner, Kathleen O'Hara, is somewhat older than I, and we are most excellent friends. We have worked together for 15 years, lived together nearly as long, and are now united in financial interests as well. Who says women are incapable of true friendship? We even answer the acid test—not even a man can make us fall out" (Nov. 28, 1932). The grit, savvy, and hard work of the two women was well rewarded, as through this decade their business flourished, and at about this time Pitter and O'Hara's financial stability permitted them to take better lodgings at 2 King's House, 396 King's Road, SW 10.

In spite of, or perhaps because of, her grueling work schedule, Pitter refocused her imaginative life and began a series of poems that marked the passing of her heretofore ineffective poetic voice and heralded instead a newer, more personal one.[4] Orage, back from a quasi-mystical spiritual pilgrimage to America, was now the editor of the *New English Weekly*, so Pitter began sending him poems for that publication.[5] During the years 1932–1934, he published thirty of her poems, the majority offered through the lens of odd, grotesque points of view; the bulk of these were published as *A Mad Lady's Garland* in 1934.[6]

A Mad Lady's Garland

The first of the poems appearing in the *New English Weekly* was "The Kitoun's Eclogue."[7] Pitter, perhaps because the poem was so different from anything she had ever published, and fearing the poem's comic tone might undercut her efforts to be known as a serious poet, used the pseudonym B. Forester. Written from the perspective of a three-month-old kitten, the poem humorously explores the "perfect blessedness" of being a black female cat, especially when it comes to love:

> My sable hue, like Ethiopian queen,
> My raven tincture and my jetty dye,
> Not a defect or blemish can be seen
> By anybody that hath half an eye.
> What sight more welcome than the night above?
> What hue more honoured in the courts of love?[8]

Glorying in her inky coat, she delights that "they kept the sooty whelp for fortune's sake / When all my stripy brethren plumbed the pail." Eating her fill of mice and never fearing the kick of any man "lest he spoil his luck," the little "bogy baby" dreams of the future when she will hear her "lover's voice; / What music shall I have—what dying wails—/ The seldom female in a world of males!" She imagines herself as Venus's servant and "the toms, in gallant cavalcade, / Come flying to the lovesick fair one's aid." Indeed, she counts herself far superior to any mere woman on this account: "What maid could draw her suitors on like me, / Sing such a tune and get away with it?" Nor will she suffer guilt for her promiscuity, another advantage she has over women: "I court no tickle immortality, / And fear no judgment when I go from hence: / No hope, no dread my little grave contains, / Nor anything beside my scant remains!" The poem ends in mock exaltation, as the bogy baby's epitaph will be "O felis semper felix" (Oh, ever happy cat!), while everyone else's will be "mud."

Pitter's droll sense of humor struck a chord with many readers. In a peculiarly ironic twist, one of these was Belloc, who wrote Orage: "How *frightfully* good is the poem by B. Forester in your pages this week, called 'The Kitten's Eclogue'! Send me I pray you 6 copies . . . for I want to send it to several people" (Dec. 26, 1932).[9] Pitter enjoyed the joke, and after Orage sent her Belloc's postcard, she wrote him: "What a lark that you should have been so pleased with 'The Kitten's Eclogue,' because I wrote it. Mr. Orage sent your card. I would not sign it with my own name, as I have an idea that a 'straight' poet can hardly afford to publish comics (you do though: I ought to have remembered that)" (Jan. 1, 1933).[10] The important thing about "The Kitoun's Eclogue," however, is that it marks a critical turning point in Pitter's technique as a poet. Freed from reliance upon the flat, impersonal poetic voice of her early verse, Pitter was able to achieve authorial distance from the subject matter of "The Kitoun's Eclogue." This authorial distancing, given free reign over the next three years as she experimented with other points of view, also liberated Pitter so that she could later explore her own emotional life through her verse; what developed was a mature, highly reflective yet never intrusive poetic voice—a voice that becomes compelling and vulnerable, probing and evocative, introspective yet not maudlin.

Pitter also shared with Belloc how the series of poems comprising A Mad Lady's Garland got its genesis:

> For some months past I have been plagued by all the things I have written turning funny in the middle: so in despair I started to write deliberate comics. I enclose a copy of "The Earwigs Complaynt," which is to appear in the N. E. W. Mr. Orage has insisted on my signing this, and also on printing it in modern spelling, which I think is a pity: and I hope you will relish the version I send. . . . I project another, in which an Hereticall Catterpiller is martyred by his fellow worms for insisting that caterpillars become butterflies. (Jan. 1)

Belloc, still determined to popularize Pitter, immediately began to encourage Pitter to work at collecting her comic verses with an eye toward publishing them; in fact, he offered, as he had with First and Second Poems, to write a preface.[11]

A common theme in the poems is romantic love, although rather than being celebrated, more often than not it is ironically chronicled. For instance, in "Maternall Love Tryumphant, or, Song of the Vertuous Femayle Spyder," we hear a mother spider give her account of being wooed, baited, and mated by "a loving swain, / A spider neat and trim, / Who used no little carful pain / To make me dote on him" (1–4).[12] Even though she had "a tender heart" for her swain, as she neared birthing hundreds of spider babies, her only food consisting of "sorry scrawny flies," she knew the thing to do:

> So I prepared with streaming eyes
> My love to sacrifice.
> I ate him, and could not but feel
> That I had been most wise;
> An hopeful mother needs a meal
> Of better meat than flies.

She justifies her lethal web with a sanctimonious veneer that betrays a distrust of romantic love. About two bluebottle lovers caught in her web who prayed for mercy, she says she cared not a feather: "Food I must have, and plenty too, / That would my darlings rear, / So, thanking Heaven, I killed and slew / The pair that loved so dear." The poem ends with her hopes to be remembered as a virtuous mother—one who gave all for her children, including her husband. And, still sanctimonious, she believes her reward will be a heavenly home, "Where in the mansions of the blest, / By earthly ills unmarred, / I'll meet again my Love, my best / And sole desired reward." Has there ever been a better picture of one who wants to have her cake and eat it too![13] Was the matronly spider's view of romantic love Pitter's own sardonic assessment? Like the mother spider, was Pitter saying that a poet cannot afford to tie up her emotions in loving a man?

In "The Earwig's Complaynt" Pitter pictures a self-possessed vetch as a Homerian warrior, fully armored and eager to recount his latest adventure.[14] We follow him as he describes his journey through a bedroom toward the ear of a beautiful woman, "a goddess of celestial hue and size . . . / From the which spectacle my ravished eyes / Would not return, but on that heavenly she / Fastened instead, and owed no troth to me" (7–11). In his wonder, he claims she represents "continents of beauty," "starry plains," and "an universe of love." He was so moved that he fell to kissing her skin, forgetting that his was a thorny, irritating kiss, which caused his "beloved" to snatch him off and "cast [him] straightway out of bed." Although he is crushed by her rejection, indeed almost insulted that she has turned away from the love of such a brave warrior as he, he finds solace in himself: "Even for Earwig comfort there can be: / Lo! from beneath my mail I spread my wings! / And she—what knows she of such heavenly things?" Pitter pokes gentle fun at how one-sided lovers quickly comfort themselves with their own vanity when rejected by the unattainable.

Perhaps the most grimly humorous poem about romantic love is "The Coffin-Worme Which Consider." Recalling the tone of the old "Twa Corbies" ballad, a pair of worms prepare to enjoy a freshly buried body. While one is reticent to begin, the other urges her on, offering at the same time a utilitarian assessment of the economy of love in death. Indeed, he chides her for holding back: "Why dost thou lag? thou pitiest the man? / Fall to, the while I teach thee what I can. / Men in their lives full solitary be: / We are their last and kindest company" (75).[15] Although we wince at the "kindness" of the narrator, there is a modicum of brutal truth in his claim. Now a philosopher, the worm assures his mate that they actually do the dead man a favor: "Lo, where care's claws have been! those marks are grim; / Go, gentle Love, erase the scar from him." Whether the scars are on the dead man's face or heart, it little matters since the worms will remove them all. Then too, while the dead man may have died of love or for love, ironically his body will now become the place where the two worms and their "generation shall sow love / Throughout that frame he was not master of," hinting perhaps at the way in which romantic love so paralyzes and tortures humans. In a last ironic slap, the narrator tells his mate to offer a final lie about romantic love:

> In his ear
> Whisper he is at last beloved here;
> Sing him (and in no false and siren strain)
> We will not leave him while a shred remain
> On his sweet bones: then shall our labour cease,
> And the imperishable part find peace
> Even from love; meanwhile how blest he lies,
> Love in his heart, his empty hands, his eyes.

In a wonderfully macabre twist, the dead man will finally experience love—the devouring love of worms. Using both classical and biblical allusions in a final ironic flourish—from the deadly love song of the Sirens in *Ulysses* to Paul's arguments for the resurrection of the body in 1 Corinthians 15—the narrator's pragmatic anodyne is a haunting, unforgettable epitaph on the relative hollowness of romantic love; that is, as the two worms settle into devouring the dead man's heart, much, perhaps, as love did when he was alive, the truth is that his heart, hands, and eyes are "empty," the flesh having been quietly consumed by the pragmatic, hard-working worms.[16] In death as in life the man is tricked into believing that romantic love can sustain, nurture, and redeem; instead, it is a trick played upon one like him who is only too willing to be deceived.

"Fowls Celestial and Terrestrial or The Angels of the Mind" considers poetry and the life of the poet. Set as a series of dialogues, the poem presents four different bird personas—a swan, a nightingale, a bird of paradise, and a phoenix. As each speaks, we are offered insight into the life of the poet; furthermore, since each bird often appears in poetry, their comments present incisive inside views. The pattern of the questions and answers is surprising; to simple questions, paradoxical or ironical replies are given, ostensibly undercutting the poetic vision of the bird. For instance, the section on the swan begins: "'Where dost thou feed?' / 'In the river-slime and weed.' / 'Where hatch thy young?' / 'The dank marish-reeds among'" (46–52). When asked about her feet, she says they are "black webs," her fair long neck is only useful to seek food "at the dark bottom," and her beautiful white feathers are just instruments "to sail over stagnant fens." Each of her terse answers reduces a potentially lovely image to mere utility in the face of hard life.

So the questioner poses the obvious question: "Alas, then tell how it may be / Thou shinest so well in poesy?" Here the tone of the poem changes (as does the stanza into a Spenserian one, a more elegant and traditionally honored form—the shift to Spenserian stanzas is repeated throughout each section of the poem) as the swan suddenly becomes the embodiment of all the earlier images she h~~~ ~~~~~~~~~~~:

Al
Sp
Aı
Aı
W
Aı
O:
Tl
Sɪ

The words she speaks link her poetically to elegies, martyrdom, sailing ships, high aspiration, and chastity and culminate in the most famous poetic idea associated with swans: "In the mind's heaven I like an angel go / Down a most silent stream, imagining / Like Narcis [sic] that I see my love below; / And mute I am until that death shall bring / A voice and then that love unspeakable I sing." As suggested by the transfigured bird's "swan song," poets take mundane, everyday words and transform them into beautiful, soaring passages that transcend everyday life.

If the swan song is one powerful poetic idea linked with poetry and the life of a poet, the nightingale "that nests on Earth" offers an equally powerful one. Again the simple questions are followed by clipped, unappealing replies: "'What doest thou all day?' / 'Catch grubs and flies where e'er I may' . . . 'Lov'st thou so sore?' / 'As other birds do and no more.' / 'Why then so sing?' / 'Tis but love madness in the spring.'" As evening falls the nightingale takes wing and cannot be seen; however, much in the tradition of Keats's "Ode on a Nightingale," the bird's "peerless notes of sorrowful delight / Dropped down like pearls," recalling heartbroken lovers such as Dido, "ill-entreated queen." Sobbing "with a muted and serene / Sound," Philomel speaks:

Ill was my fortune, worthy is my fame,
Whence all unhappy poets are my peers:
The luckless lover in my ditty hears
His woes adorned with rarest elegy;
It seems his hurt is healed through his ears;
And so for ever in the company
Of the mind's angels not the least angelic I.

Unlike the swan song of a dying lover, the nightingale's love song soothes the un-requited lover and makes her song no less worthy for the poet than the swan's.

The third bird valuable to poetry and the life of the poet is the bird of paradise. Questioned as to being a legend, it briefly replies: "'In Indian forest do I
breed.' / 'A heavenly place?' / 'Some beauties, much that is most base.'" In addition, it discounts the beauty of its voice, noting instead that "attire is all my
fame"; and, indeed, it is for elaborate and showy plumage that the bird of paradise is best known. In response to the questioner's belief that the bird of paradise
only sings in heaven, she claps her wings and flies to the highest cedar branch,
where the sun gleams off her so dramatically "that now was no more seen / As
earthly fowl, but even as she had been / One of the awful burning cherubim."
When she speaks again, she celebrates her heavenly home, especially the tree
"where of all bliss is endless store: / There sing beside my shining mate for
evermore." That is, while the swan and nightingale evoke the mutability and
hardship of human love, the bird of paradise suggests permanent, certain love.
    Unlike the first three, the phoenix is mythic:

"Where may I find
Thee?" "Only in the aspiring mind."
"Where is thy nest?"
"If thou liv'st truly, in thy breast."
"Nowhere on earth?"
"My death is secret and my birth."
"What is thy food?"
"A fire that burns in solitude,
In the which flame
I mine own child and parent am."

In fact the bird is sitting on "her precious pyre . . . all crowned as with eternal
fire." The questioner stands amazed at how she bears the fire, "the cruel element
that burns her breast." Recalling again 1 Corinthians 15, the bird says: "This
mortal must her immortality / Put on, and this corruptible be made / To that
which shall not perish . . . , / Must with a heavenly body be arrayed." Bolstered
by this truth, the phoenix does not fear death since it knows it will rise from its
own ashes and "bloom in the fire where lately I did fade." The phoenix, therefore, represents never-dying, reviving, resurrected love.[17]
    The four birds comment directly about the life of the poet. That is, if the
poet links the idea of the swan song to the bittersweet song of the dying lover,
the poet's work, her poem, her "final" act of creation, becomes a kind of swan
song. If the nightingale's song suggests the pain of unrequited love, the poet's
work, because it is often misunderstood or misinterpreted, similarly suggests her
disconnect from others. If the bird of paradise in her elaborate, showy, even
artificial plumage can sing of changeless love, the poet's work can speak of that

which is lasting, true, and most real. Finally, if the phoenix sings of the reviving, resurrecting power of love, the poet's work can revive a culture that is in desperate need of renewal. "Fowls Celestial and Terrestrial or The Angels of the Mind" is a serious piece, only thinly disguised in a volume of otherwise comic poems.

Other poems use insects or small animals to reveal human character types, much in the fashion of beast fables. "A Sadd Lament of a Performing Flea" concerns a famous flea who warns his hearers not to envy his fame and fortune.[18] While he is honored by his public, "were I to be new-hatched, ah, then I'd choose / A poor estate, a leaden Louse I'd be" (53–54). He longs for any kind of life other than one under public scrutiny—be it as a "buxom Sheep tick" or under a "flowery thorn." Instead of roaming freely, sucking the blood of princes, "sweet-breathed peasant," lovely ladies, or innocent babies, he must confine his to "the hairy arms" of his keepers. The moral of his lament is: "Example take by me; and O complain / Never too loudly of a low estate / Slandering your boon and longing for your bane."

A similar self-pitying tone occurs in "Ecclesiasticella: Or the Church Mouse," except here the speaker is the proverbial church mouse anxious to justify yet cloak her existence.[19] Yes, she is the epitome of poverty, but for her that is of no consequence: "My name is Poverty, my fame a sneer; / This a light burthen, that a windy breath: / For poor Ecclesiasticella's care / Is nowise for this life which vanisheth" (55–58). The mouse says she would never want rich food, dwellings, or lyings; those kinds of things are for "gross and worldly mice." She is piously content with the crumbs of cake and drops of ginger beer she comes upon in the pews, always, of course, thanking heaven for her good fortune. While she claims she is not troubled by earthly love because her "soul is fixèd fast" on a saint, her saint is the church vicar:

Angelic Mr. Maunder! whose bright face
Mine earthly lamp and heavenly lodestar is,
Thou little reck'st what fount of living grace
Thou art, what ark of holy mysteries;
Could I but pen my feelings as they be,
Then ah what Fan-mail I would write to thee!

She loves, as well, the church bazaars, yet she has been seen by one of the members of the church, who is determined to get rid of her. The mouse ends her poem by resentfully noting that the church should be "free for all to enter in, / Or how should poor mice find the wherewithal / To live in holiness and free from sin?" The parishioner trying to get rid of her will "rot the Church, and be / The heavy cross of pious souls like me." Pitter wryly gives the mouse just the right tone of self-righteousness, having her use the overly pious "thou" and "thee" as well as many verbs ending with "-eth," and she cleverly permits the mouse to misapply a theological term like "grace" so that in the end we see the impoverished mouse is merely self-serving and not deserving of our sympathy.[20]

The speaker in "Cockroach" is an angry, embittered, venomous hardback resentful that modern life has earned a greater reputation for being nasty than he: "Moderns? oh yeah, you call yourselves moderns? / Well, I've been as modern as you / Any time these many million years" (68–72).[21] Beginning as a dialogue between a prehistoric "hepatic plant" who claims she knows all about being nasty, the poem turns when the cockroach takes over and lists the nasty accomplishments of his ancestors over the eons, including living in sewers and dirty ditches. Two items he points out as particularly noteworthy. First, he says "I and no one else invented / Cannibalism." However, the second point is the real topper and finally reveals the primary target of Pitter's satire:

Take stink.
Only think,
A million years I stank alone,
Specialité de la maison
A family monopoly.
If you wanted stink you came to me.
And now look at the competition,
I wouldn't mind if it were two or three
Competent men, but each edition
Of the evening papers
Stinks with such a pleasant voice
Making all the vales rejoice,
Cutting all my cockroach-capers.

Pitter's satire on modernity climaxes when the cockroach says: "Publicity's a dam fine thing / And all that artists have to cheer 'em." The ugliness of the cockroach's personality is mimicked by the ugly mixed meter of the poem.

Perhaps the most sweetly humorous yet metaphysically pointed poem in *A Mad Lady's Garland* is "The Frog in the Well: A True History, and Image of the State."[22] With the tone of a mock epic—beginning: "From the far brink of sacred Helicon / Stoop, kindly Muse, to hymn the tale of one / Poor atomy, whose tragedy was wrought / To comedy by means she never sought" (63–67)—this poem chronicles the tale of a poor tadpole who was captured by cruel boys, placed in a jar, and then thoughtlessly tossed into a well. Poignantly ironic, the poor tadpole, Sabrina, is cut off from the larger world. As time goes by, and although she has little food, she metamorphoses into a frog with huge head and little brain that "wove stratagems the distant top [of the well] to gain." Then

one hot August afternoon a thunderstorm sends a deluge of rain that begins
to fill up the well and lift the imprisoned Sabrina to the brink of freedom. Yet
when only a few inches from the top, the rain ceases "and straight the tide was
stayed, / And slowly downward from the mocking brink / She . . . began to sink.
/ Poor soul! I cannot sing the pains of hell, / And so that last defeat may never
tell." However, a deus ex machina intercedes:

> Now for thy faith! still call on heaven to save,
> And save it shall, though every demon rave.
> The hatch is lifted and a human face
> Looks down into the dim and dismal place:
> The human vision sees the victim there,
> And human reason knows her whole despair.
> A tactful hand (no paw of murderous lout
> But kind Ruth Pitter's) plucks the sufferer out,
> And to a pond where she may soon be fat
> She takes the wizen creature in her hat.

Pitter's comic insertion of herself into the poem leads to one of the few morals
among her beast fables: "Yet, ah believe that if the fates can do / Thus for a frog,
we may be hopeful too / That we shall see this wretched State of ours / Snatched
from the malice of the nether powers!" Pitter muses that while, like the tadpole, we cannot save ourselves, perhaps there is a benign cosmic power that
will save us by snatching us from a "huge despair."[23] This moral hints at Pitter's
theological position at this time in her life; that is, while she cannot affirm with
certainty a dogmatic creed, she can hope that a benevolent Something is in
control of human affairs.[24]

What was the critical reaction to *A Mad Lady's Garland?* Belloc loved it. In
his preface, he lavishes praise for its variety; by that he meant that Pitter had
published poems completely unlike her earlier work.[25] However, his best remark
remains one of the most penetrating critical evaluations of Pitter: "The two peculiar gifts which make Miss Pitter's verse what it is and ensure its permanence
are as clearly present here as in the earlier poems. Those two gifts are a perfect
ear and exact epithet. How those two ever get combined is incomprehensible—
one would think it was never possible—but when the combination does appear
then you have verse of that classic sort which is founded and secure of its own
future." Furthermore, he cites his favorite, "The Kitoun's Eclogue," and offers
somewhat prophetic words: "I could wish to be younger in order to mark the
moment when talent of this very high level reaches its reward in public fame. It
must come." The rest of his remarks demonstrate both his and Pitter's jaundiced
view of the poetry of their day: "But the day in which we live, having no stan-

dards and having apparently forgotten what verse is—and, indeed, what the art of writing is—may keep us waiting for some time. However, I don't feel that that matters much, for stuff which is clearly permanent can wait as long as it likes. The obvious truth that the other kind of stuff washes away like mud, and that automatically the earth is purged of it, is the one consolation we have for living in the chaos we do" (vii, viii). Pitter later writes Nettie Palmer: "I wish I knew what you think of modern verse. I suppose you *can* think about it. I haven't the equipment" (March 4, 1935).

Coinciding with the publication of A Mad Lady's Garland was Pitter's growing acquaintance with George William Russell, the Irish poet who published under the name AE, to whom she had been introduced by Orage sometime in late 1933.[26] About A Mad Lady's Garland AE wrote:

> I would shrink from the grotesque poetry in "A Mad Lady's Garland" with all the shuddering with which we remove ourselves from the vicinity of cockroaches or earwigs, only Miss Pitter makes the creatures of her fantasy . . . speak so classically, with so exquisite an artifice, that I am stayed to listen to them, and admit into my house of soul thoughts I would have closed the door upon if they had not come dressed in so courtly a fashion. . . . I find it astonishing that a poetess who had, before this Garland, written verse of a stellar loveliness, could depart from that serene mood to play these pranks with vermin and insects. But it is all symbolic. We find our humanity in the Church Mouse . . . and the Coffin Worm. . . . The poetess uses the classical metrical forms, yet while following the traditional craft her originality is more apparent; for it is not an originality which depends merely on a novelty in technique and has otherwise nothing original to communicate to us, and is forgotten so soon as the novelty in craft becomes familiar. But I cannot altogether forgive the poetess's irony which led me to see portions of my own nature in the undesirable forms of earwigs, cockroaches and coffin-worms, no matter with what classical perfection of utterance they express the oddities and perversities of our humanity.[27]

A Mad Lady's Garland also received favorable reviews from critics.[28] An unsigned review appearing in the *Times Literary Supplement* offers a wonderful description of Pitter's place in the contemporary poetry scene: "The road up to Parnassus has lately been crowded with notice-boards of warning and stern instruction; the number of shell-holes, indeed, notifies us how desperate the attempt to climb that way has become. Miss Pitter, so to speak, comes up the road on a bicycle, singing cheerfully to the sun and anybody whom it may concern, and—with just an artful glance or two at the notice-boards—she proceeds with this easy speed toward the top."[29] He then links the madness of the volume to "the kind practiced by such seventeenth century poets as Herrick, Lovelace, or Cleveland" and calls the poems "merry fabrications . . . touched with a spirit of parody and imitation."

Richard Church is generous with his praise, lamenting the fact Pitter has been overlooked for years because she has not been writing "fashionable . . . experiments in unintelligibility." He adds: "Nobody wanted to read work that was so quiet, so austere, so honest in its acknowledgment of its sources. It was too 'traditional'; and during the last 10 years, to be traditional in England was to be condemned as dull and imitative."[30] Already familiar with her earlier verse, Church notes this volume "resembles her other work only in its technical excellence," since here she turns to "humor and satire" like Aesop and LaFontaine. He credits her beast fables with "the sanity of her judgment," noting as well that she is "a devoted student of Edmund Spenser. And indeed one might venture to say that her devices of using deliberate archaisms and inversions are copied from him, since he was the first English poet to be so conscious of the historical development of his native tongue as to be able to hark back to words and modes of speech long fallen into disuse." His highest praise comes in the last line of his review, linking his view of Pitter's poetry with that of Belloc's: "[This] is the work of a poet who has labored to know her craft and has practiced it for a long time. That is why I believe that her work will also endure for a long time. It is nonfashionable, like all permanent things, such as bread, and water, or a well-made kitchen table."

Michael Roberts says Pitter critiques human foibles "quietly using a bodkin, not a dagger, [and] does strike home,"[31] while William Benét recommends A Mad Lady's Garland as a book "full of the most original sort of poetic mockery—not without its serious moments."[32] D. G. Bridson refers to the poems as pastiche, but "good pastiche has its proper place in poetry no less than has good satire."[33] While he credits her verse as "exquisite" and her imagination as "ingenious," he comes near to damning her with faint praise when he ends his review: "Miss Pitter may not set out to do a very great deal, but what she sets out to do she does perfectly." Percy Hutchison, however, finds much to enjoy in Pitter's verse: "she has an ear most accurately attuned."[34] He adds that "there is not a person alive who might not be better for reading" her beast fables and ends his review claiming it "is an eminently jocund book with a wealth of human significance."

A Mad Lady's Garland was Pitter's first foray into comic verse, something she returned to later with On Cats and The Rude Potato.[35] It is not a volume reflecting an angry or insane voice; rather, in spite of the obvious bad pun, it is a madcap volume—a comic garland, a poet's laurel wreath given in good fun to herself and others. Nevertheless, we should be careful not to dismiss it for that reason; in fact some of the poems are actually more serious than a first glance suggests. While there is genuine laughter and gentle satire, the volume is also about Pitter's developing poetic voice, especially the authorial distance she realizes by adopting the various animal and insect personas. Such distancing moves her away from her largely ineffective early verse and opens her to examining the human condition with a poetic voice that is honest, incisive, sympathetic, intuitive, and winsome. She moves from being a poet writing thinly veiled poems about herself, and thus, ironically, feeling impersonal and flat to readers, to being a poet writing poems touching on the most important of human experiences— love, longing, loss, beauty, aspiration, religious faith, the desire for a sense of place, nature's appeal, friendship, isolation, and intellectual exploration. In the process she transforms her verse into poetry that disturbs and affirms, that challenges and comforts, that confronts and reconciles. By distancing herself, Pitter paradoxically learns how to enter into relationship with her readers.

Given AE's praise of *A Mad Lady's Garland*, it is not surprising she enjoyed spending time with him, writing Belloc: "I have been meeting AE, and warming my hands at him, with the critical faculty well in leash" (Feb. 2, 1934), and "I have been seeing AE, a blessed spirit" (late April). To Nettie Palmer she confides: "I went to see AE yesterday evening" (May 28). Soon their friendship results in an invitation to visit him in Donegal, as she tells Belloc: "I am going to Ireland on the 1st July to stay for a few days with AE in Donegal: I feel I shall be going as a poet, to a poet, fresh from the approval of a poet" (June 14).[36] Perhaps in order to observe proprieties, Pitter's mother accompanied her on the visit, which lasted a fortnight. Pitter was struck by the physical beauty of the Donegal coast, the poetical speech of the inhabitants, the wild flowers, and "above all that intense feeling of the unseen world only just invisible—as though at any moment gorgeous legendary figures might appear out of that gorge, on to that empty shore, or an ancient ship cast anchor in the bay." Although she claimed she was far from being psychic, she admitted to having felt the supernatural all around her as never before. Staying in AE's small farmhouse, Pitter said, "It was really almost annoying to find how *hypnotic* was the effect of poetry chanted by him in an atmosphere of peat-reek. The walls seemed to melt away."

They enjoyed wonderful weather during the two weeks and took many leisurely walks along the coast. In one instance AE rolled up his trousers, hung his boots around his neck, and waded "majestic among such droves of prawns and shrimps as I have never beheld since." On another occasion they were busy shaping figures out of the sand, "when I looked up, and there was half the village silently roosting on the cliff, completely bewitched by the creative spectacle. AE was rather perturbed, grabbed his boots and dodged round a rock to put them on. It was the only time I had seen him self-conscious." About another outing during which Pitter's trousers accidentally split, she wrote the following unpublished poem:

In Eire land of barbarous wretches,
R. P. climbs rocks while A. E. sketches.
He ends, looks up, and sees a cloud:
Ah come on down! he cries aloud.

But she cannot suppress a dimple.
To come on down is not so simple.
Her treacherous scanties fell flat,
And she has crammed them in her hat.

At the end of their time in Donegal, he gave Pitter five paintings that she treasured for the rest of her life.[37]

AE wrote Pitter after her return to London, and it is clear that he liked her
very much:

> It's damnably lonely here without you. We have to pay for all our delights.
> But I would gulp down a month's dreariness for another week's rambles
> with you. I went for a long walk today and remembered with deep self
> disgust that there were lots of beautiful places I had not shown you, and
> then I reflected that if I had crammed them all into that fortnight your
> young legs would be aching and my old legs would be paralysed. . . . I
> had all kinds of qualms when I wrote you to come whether I could really
> make you comfortable, and then I said Damn it she's a poetess, a genuine
> one, not a made up one and she's bound to be happy once she gets into
> the open air! . . . [I had a dream vision of you and] your eyes were quite
> recognizable only more ultramarinely bluer and more brilliant than their
> physical counterparts. . . . But I must not waste your time now you have
> got back to business and its worries. I only want to say you were an angel
> to come here. You are one of the best of companions. You have the airy
> element in your nature predominant so that you never get entangled in
> things like those with the watery nature. You will rise above London and
> its fogs and its business because of that airy element, which makes you a
> free creature as far as mortals may be free.[38]

Pitter and AE met several other times over the next eighteen months, but events
and perhaps the thirty-year difference in their ages kept them from becoming
romantically involved; she was too busy running Deane and Forester, while he
was too involved in writing and painting; moreover, his health was failing fast
and consumed a good deal of his attention.[39]

The critical success of A Mad Lady's Garland encouraged her.[40] Belloc, ever
her advocate, writes her on October 3: "It looks to me as though your work has

pierced at last. Now that your fame has begun it will grow, & the pace is unimportant. Also the great thing is to continue to work. One can always scrape, but as age approaches one dries up—I know that truth from experience. One must write all one can while one can." Yet the demands of Deane and Forester did sap her time. To Belloc she replies: "I will try to write—what you say about drying up is very true: the cares of the world come upon one, and one's heart no longer flies back to poetry automatically. But it does fly often and often to the few, including yourself, who encouraged it in the past" (Oct. 5). Orage, too, joined in the chorus of praise, writing her on October 15: "I meant to have thanked you for my copy of the Mad Lady but autumnal vicissitudes affect me too! I hope we'll get over them together. The reviews I have seen are as I expected. . . . However, you & I share a common fate—as to public esteem I mean. . . . Hoping to see you soon—with AE or otherwise."

However, on November 6, an unexpected blow came with the sudden death of Orage. She mourns him to Belloc: "My other early champion is gone, alas! I grieved for Orage heartily. In spite of all detraction, justifiable or otherwise, there was something *undeniable* about him" (Dec. 27). In an unpublished poem she celebrates and laments his passing:

Out of the dream he is gone home,
From bright effect into dark cause
Translated suddenly: not come
As most do, against broken laws,
Long pain and slow mortality: O no,
He said a quick good-night, and parted so.

Look up into the enormous dark,
He is flown forth and dispersed there:
Our orphan faces, white and stark,
Peruse the void with piteous stare:
What! No word more, no look, no smile to show
Whether beyond *this* grave our love may go?

Yes; from the empty arch of night,
See where our own griefs, each in kind,
Return like perfumes, seeds of light,
Music half heard and half divined,
Feathers of fire and flowers that breathe and glow,
Small meteors, dens of comfort, plumes of snow.
. . . .
This my warm coat he gave to me—

The fortitude that saves me still:
Our wings that cross death's ocean, he
Fostered: to light on heaven's hill
They beat, they spread, they soar: his bantlings go
Wherever space may spread or time may flow.

The heart that to itself suffices
The word of power that cures the soul,
Heaven's love against all death's devices,
The part united with the whole:
If so much strong felicity I know,
All, save my mere beginnings, here I owe.[41]

In a letter to Nettie Palmer she adds: "Could it be? . . . He is gone! It was not really a good thing to have known such a man so early and so long, because all the rest seemed Poor Fish and Cheap Skates. He once said to me, 'Well, if you don't fall in love with me, you won't with anyone else!' This impertinence amused me at the time—I was twenty—but it has gradually become a Draped Urn in my mind" (March 4, 1935).[42]

Spurred on by the loss of Orage and by a desire to honor his early confidence in her, she writes Belloc about the success of A Mad Lady's Garland: "I suppose my last book has made me a poet by acclamation, as I have had such good notices, and a great many invitations since it has appeared. Profits I do not expect" (Dec. 27, 1934). Yet in spite of her success, Pitter was disdainful of the self-promotion of many writers and artists. She tells Belloc:

I have met a great many well-known writers, and a dreary set they are too, for the most part. They do not converse, they gossip, and that maliciously. It is not difficult to imagine the place of torment reserved for Grub Street below, is it? The tortures would consist in such exercises as speaking the Truth, Verifying your Facts, Meeting one's Obligations, Confessing that one's own stuff might possibly be No Good, etc. The supreme anguish might be a Peep into Futurity to anticipate the Verdict of Posterity. Of course some of them are decent human beings, but these are inclined to inhabit Cloud-Cuckoo-land and to swaddle themselves in clouds of Pale Mauve Fluff. (Dec. 27)

Pitter, while a gifted artist, shunned self-revelation. As a result, she was very deliberate in her attempts to mute her own personality in her verse. In a letter responding to a request to include in a poetry anthology some of her poems from A Mad Lady's Garland she confides:

Very many thanks for your delightful and encouraging letter. A pat on the back does make such a difference. If ever I can get over the effects of being half-educated and worried to death all my life, perhaps I shall do better still. . . . All my life I've played the game of seeing without Being Seen: I cannot bear that it should be possible for any real personal emotion of mine to be detected in my work. Seeing such quantities of degrading emotion *inadvertently* betrayed in many people's stuff—the great want of objectivity which is so general—it has seemed to me that directly one writes out of any direct personal emotion (save enthusiasm for the art itself) sublimation is mined. Or at least that's how I condone my meanness. It's awfully ticklish work to be a poetess: one is so suspected of sentimentality that many a time have I erased a good line, with the remark, "No, that is Girlish and Confiding, with the Hair Down." And then, too, it is a question of being rather malicious, and consequently not wishing to afford any handle oneself. I read the novel of a friend—"Ha ha! What a scream! He's shoved in that awful woman we thought was his mistress: let's go on, we shall be able to find out what really was the state of affairs, if we piece it together. Well, fancy *idealizing* that disgusting old baggage!" The idea that anyone could do this sort of thing to my own work fairly brings me out in a rash: I hope you see what I mean. (July 15, 1935)

Pitter's modest origins, her lack of family or spousal financial support, and her grueling work ethic kept her mind occupied not with herself and her feelings but with earning a living and seeking financial independence.[43] She knew that her poetry, much as it was the focus of her creative and imaginative life, would never support her. Accordingly, she worked hard and carved out time for her poetry as necessity permitted.[44]

Barely eight months after the death of Orage, the news came on July 17 that AE had died. Pitter's letters to friends at the time show she had been aware of his gradual decline; in late May she had gone to visit him, hoping to lift his spirits. After hearing of his death, she writes Nettie Palmer: "It seems you were right about AE. I only thought he had gone to Bournemouth to recuperate, but the day before the operation he wrote to me in unmistakable tones of farewell. I regard his death as an enviable achievement, done with the minimum of pain and the maximum of dignity. He was ready to go, and had decreed it in himself, I think" (July 23). Pitter mourned the passing of AE, but she did not dwell upon it.[45] She was thankful to have known him and to have been his friend, but she had purposely avoided a deep emotional attachment to him.

Throughout this period Pitter continued to visit Oak Cottage whenever she could. After one visit, she writes Palmer:

I am just back from my mother's cottage in the country, where we mus-
tered 8 for Christmas, and where I made beautiful ice-cream with ice out
of the pond, and pruned all the vines. My mother has a gardener who owing to infantile paralysis is stone deaf and speaks a very primitive English
in consequence: it is like talking to a Native. "Wife hospital, pain belly."
"Robin good boy, not kill." "Gentleman love lady, not kick lady backside"
(this last apropos of some local wife beater). This gentle creature over-
crowds all plants, and seeing six hoary old vine-trunks, all cowhorn snags,
lying chopped down after my exertions, moaned pitifully, "Too much cut!
All good!" On being told to copy the names of seeds from packets to labels, proudly exhibited forest of labels with the noble inscription, one and
all, "seeds that can be relied on." (Dec. 30, 1935)

After the grit and grime of London, the treasured visits to Oak Cottage were
like an oasis and recalled the pleasures of the cottage in Hainault Forest. There
she could enjoy the beauty of nature during all the seasons, and the local environs, while never able to take the place of Hainault Forest in her imagination,
could offer refreshment and respite.

A Trophy of Arms

Pitter and Belloc continued to correspond, and he urged her to keep writing.[46]
In fact, when he took over as editor of G. K.'s Weekly he solicited material from
her: "Can you send me anything for G. K.'s Weekly. . . . Do! I hardly ever take
verse but I would take yours. We have to go voluntary: no one gets paid. It's like
the old New Age in that. But you would be read by good judges, a worthy audience" (Sept. 14, 1936).[47] Actually Pitter's A Trophy of Arms appeared the same
day. Belloc was delighted and wrote:

This reminds me that a friend has given me your book which I had not
seen. I am even now doing a signed review of it which will appear in my
first number on Oct 1st. It cannot be sufficiently praised. It is quite admirable work. I heard a story about it last night at dinner, when my friend
gave me the book which I hope will amuse and please you. One of the
younger generation, between 30 and 40, who apparently had not come
across your work (which is understandable considering the stuff they read
and alone have the chance to see), came rushing in to a big restaurant,
shouting that he had found a new poet who was worth all the others put
together, and waving your new book in his hand! (Sept. 17, 1936)

Pitter replied: "I shall look forward eagerly to the signed review, and think it typical of your generosity that you should do it—in your first number, too! The restaurant incident was most gratifying and amusing. Many thanks for relating it" (Sept. 23).

Like many of the poems in A Mad Lady's Garland, most in A Trophy of Arms were first published in the New English Weekly, several appearing in manuscript notebooks as early as 1926. Unlike A Mad Lady's Garland, which is unified by its use of animal and insect personas, its beast fables, and its pervading comic tone, A Trophy of Arms is a collection of poems that explore the melancholic reality of the human condition; yet it is neither depressing nor despairing. Instead, it is a clarion call to embrace sorrow, loss, and loneliness through either the lens of nature or a veiled, transcendent power. Technically, A Trophy of Arms continues Pitter's reliance on rhyming couplets (most often tetrameter but in one case heroics), alternate rhyme, tercets, terza rima, sonnets, modified sapphics, and blank verse. Throughout we see Pitter expanding the range of her poetic voice; she does this primarily by creating a persona that offers her the opportunity to write about deeply felt personal experiences while at the same time providing her a useful distancing device. The poems can be grouped according to four dominant themes. The first concerns the cottage and Hainault Forest. While "Stormcock in Elder," discussed earlier, harkens back to the forest cottage, her beloved "dark hermitage," her deep affection for this place is more vividly portrayed in "The Lost Hermitage" as, during a return trip to the hut, she insists that

My heart dwells here
In rotten hut on weeping clay;
Tends here her useful herbs, her bloom;
Will not away,
May not be startled to one tear,
Is tenant of her little room
For ever.[48]

Even though she cannot live at the hut, imaginatively she will always inhabit it. She lists the many birds there (stock dove, storm cock, finch, blackbird, jay, starling, titmouse, nightingale, and "song-thrush hatched in a cup of mud") as well as particular images, such as "frost on the grass, / The lonely morning, the still kine, / Grief for the quick, love for the dead." Akin to a Wordsworthian "spot in time," Pitter claims: "All these are laid / Safe up in me, and I will keep / My dwelling thus though it be gone." Her memory will lovingly stay upon the ramshackle cottage even if she is back in Chelsea and the cottage itself tumbles in upon itself: "My store is not in gold, but made / Of toil and sleep / And wonder walking all alone." Her affirmation of the permanence of the cottage in her imaginative life and its power to renew her link "The Lost Hermitage" to Yeats's "The Lake Isle of Innisfree."[49]

Pitter's nostalgic affection for the cottage is also apparent in "O Where Is the Dwelling":

> O where is the dwelling I love the most,
> And what but the one poor place can please,
> Where the penny I lost and the faith I lost
> Lie buried beneath enchanted trees?
>
> O there is the dwelling I love the most,
> And thither for ever my feet are bound,
> Where the youth I lost and the love I lost
> Lie buried, lie buried in holy ground! (46)

Of note here is how she connects her longing for this place with a series of profound losses, including her faith in the fairy world, youth, and love; that is, while there is pain associated with the forest cottage, it is more than assuaged by the "enchanted" and "holy" ground this place is in her imagination. Pitter's ability to communicate this tension simply in her verse is one mark of her growing poetic maturation. She continues this theme in "The Return," although in this case she longs to escape imaginatively from the toil and trouble of everyday life in London: "So, since the battle goes so ill, / Let me lie down and dream of home: / To-night I'll lie upon the hill . . . / Between the leaves and the loam: / Lie there where quiet was / Between the bough and the grass" (85–86). She sees in her mind the tree where the nightingale sings, the mists drifting over the brooks, and the heavily scented lilies, woodbines, and hyacinths. Yet in this instance her memories are not enough to sustain her:

> To no end but to be old and poor,
> To lose the good, and to get the bane:
> To find no door like the rotting door
> Which I find not again:
> To weep in my bed at night
> And forget the tear of delight.

Drawing strength from these images momentarily refreshes her; however, the imaginative return to the cottage cannot trump the hard reality of her everyday circumstances.

Other poems are almost certainly inspired by experiences in Hainault Forest. "The Viper" is a lovely piece reminiscent of Emily Dickinson's "A Narrow Fellow in the Grass."[50] Yet while Dickinson objectively focuses upon the visual as the snake "wrinkled and was gone," leaving the viewer with "a tighter feeling / And Zero at the Bone," Pitter instead links "the lovely serpent" with the spiritual: "Fair was the brave embroidered dress, / Fairer the gold eyes shone: / Loving her not, yet did I bless / The fallen angel's comeliness; / And gazed when she had gone" (26). In "The Strawberry Plant" Pitter writes perhaps her best descriptive poem:

Above the water, in her rocky niche,
She sat enthroned and perfect; for her crown
One bud like pearl, and then two fairy roses
Blanched and yet ardent in their glowing hearts:
One greenish berry spangling into yellow
Where the light touched the seed: one fruit achieved
And ripe, an odorous vermilion ball
Tight with completion, lovingly enclasped
By the close cup whose green chimed with the red
And showered with drops of gold like Danaë:
Three lovely sister leaves as like as peas,
Young but full-fledged, dark, with a little down:
Two leaves that to a matron hue inclined;
And one the matriarch, that dressed in gold
And flushed with wine, thought her last days her best.
And here and there a diamond of dew
Beamed coolly from the white, smiled from the gold,
Silvered the down, struck lightning from the red.
The overhanging rock forbade the sun,
Yet she was all alight with water-gleams
Reflected, like the footlights at a play:
Perfection's self, and (rightly) out of reach. (65)

That this humble yet beautiful plant cannot be plucked thoughtlessly by a passerby gives the poem a wonderfully lasting impression; we can imagine this delicate natural beauty sitting forever undisturbed in her rocky throne.

The second group of poems in A Trophy of Arms coalesce around the idea of romantic love. "Early Rising" could very well be set in the cottage in Hainault Forest, but its focus is less upon the natural environment than upon the sense of lost or unspoken love. Pitter begins: "I arose early, O my true love!" and then

describes the quiet pre-dawn beauty of the forest: "It was an hour of Eden."
Happy musings follow, but they are negated by the poem's ending:

> And I was sad, O my true love,
> For the love left unsaid:
> I will sing it to the turtle-dove
> That hugs her high-built bed:
> I will say it to the solemn grove
> And to the innocent dead. (31–32)

In "Weeping Water, Leaping Fire"[51] the speaker angrily rejects the idea of love,
given the hardships of life that she faces:

> Weeping water, leaping fire,
> God and my grave are my desire.
> With swarming strife and scanty joy,
> Little ease and long annoy,
> I am damned and drowned in rue—
> With love then what have I to do? (48)

In spite of the second stanza's less violent tone, she still ends by asking, "Then
what have I to do with love?" The final two lines appear to address Cupid (or
perhaps the boy in question): "Lovely boy, I know you lie: / Frown as you will,
but pass me by." If "Weeping Water, Leaping Fire" insists love should be avoided,
"True Love's not Told" argues that it is impossible to communicate about love:
"What said I even now? True love's not told; / I'll tell my love when we shall
meet in heaven, / My Love: till then my love I shall not know" (55). Despite a
kind of leap of faith here, the fact remains there is no possibility of connecting
to her beloved on earth.

Contrasting to these jaundiced views of romantic love, "Fair Is the Water" is
more hopeful. Again the setting may be in or around Hainault Forest as Pitter
describes the life-giving effect of water on the land, "on the braided tresses of
the barley," and on the rose. However, the emotional peak of the poem comes
in its conclusion: "Fairest is water when the heart at evening / leads the fond
feet to the familiar places: / fairest is water when it falls in silent / dew where
thou liest" (58). The ending is admittedly ambiguous since we wonder about
where the person is. Is he asleep in a nearby bed? Is he beneath the earth? Or
is he only in her memory? "As When the Faithful Return" is a poignant statement about unrequited yet patient, hopeful, faithful love: "As when the faithful
return to valleys beloved, / little lamenting the winter, alone with the pensive /
genius, the soul of the place, and when the profane ones / fly with the summer,

and lewdness and folly are vanished: / so I with thine image at last shall abide in silence" (45). The persona insists that when others deride, forget, or reject the beloved, "mine shalt thou be in dateless eternal affection." More than that, the persona senses the beloved will eventually return to her: "Quiet and clean is the house, and here I await thee: / thou by familiar groves, by the river of water, / under the snow-laden yew, the sun-gilded rose, / reverend with years, with youth immortality blooming, / silent advancest, and sittest down in my dwelling." The simplicity of the diction and the crisp, evocative phrases ("quiet and clean," "snow-laden," and "sun-gilded") contribute to the beauty of the lyric's suppressed passion. As these five poems suggest, and notwithstanding various statements by Pitter about avoiding romantic entanglements, her heart's affection could not simply be silenced.

The poems constituting the third group are connected by way of contrast, as they concern joy and pain. "Sudden Heaven," discussed later in chapter 10, explores the unanticipated joy that can suddenly visit when least expected. "Gentle Joy" is an insistent praise for joy in spite of man's sorrow, sin, and darkness; while "tears are no majesty," sighing "a blight unholy," and melancholy not admirable, joy burns like the daystar in the heart where it lives. Although man rises and passes, "thou canst not die, and never mayest / From Paradise thyself dissever: / Thou risest; all is cured, forgiven: / Joy is on earth, and earth is heaven" (14). On the other hand, "Storm" is as ominous as its opening line: "I have seen daylight turn cadaverous" (18–20). The remainder of this stanza offers a powerful description of how a summer's day can go from being peaceful to violent, beautiful to threatening, charming to frightening. Then in the second stanza, in an often-used poetic device, Pitter links the idea of the outer storm to an even more turbulent inner storm: "Have I not seen the sudden storm in the mind, / Conceived of anguish brooding wastefully, / Heaping the sullen forces baulked by life, / Harvesting blackness, gathering up rage." The third stanza celebrates the way an external storm clears the air, cools the atmosphere, and provides life-giving rain. However, the fourth stanza rejects this possibility for one experiencing a terrible inner storm: "Truly there is a tempest-following calm; / But if there be one of the mind I know not, / For I have never seen it. Her day is dim; / Her fairest day is one without alarms; / Cold was her dawn, colder shall be her night." Pitter's incisive ability to cut to the bone, her refusal to pretend that it will be all right, and her rejection of the pathetic fallacy make a poem like this read true to human experience.

One poem, "Joy and Grief," attempts to bridge the gap between joy and pain. It begins with Pitter admitting her joy has faded "while Grief, great growing boy, / Devours, invades" (82–83). Grief "my whole having eats," but joy, finding no food, "by my chimney sits / In dying attitude." She then resigns herself to dwelling only with grief once joy is completely gone. In fact, she posits that grief "may gentler grow, and be / In my cold age / A comforter to me, / The wounds he gave, assuage." In the meantime, however, before joy deserts her, she affirms she will "nourish both, / The devourer and the dying." The poem ends with a stoical resolve:

> I am strong, I cast away sloth
> And do but little sighing;
> See the sad purity
> Of the white sky and the stream!
> On these, and the winter tree,
> I will gaze, I will dream.

Turning to nature for comfort, perhaps with her memories of Hainault Forest providing the impetus, Pitter rejects despair and embraces both joy and grief.

However, by far the largest number of poems in *A Trophy of Arms* center around spiritual themes, including God, the soul, the meaning of human existence, and death. "An Impatience," with its angry rejection of God in favor of nature, is unusual for Pitter.[52] In the poem she creates a contrast between the teachings of the Bible—"In anger have I closed the book / That lusts to make all men believe"—and the humble beauty of an impatience—"A soul that lived in solitude . . . The lone wildling creature's look / Homage demands and shall receive" (4). While the ideas in the Bible are "vast, yet shapeless things," the flower "brings completeness." Most striking by way of contrast, the message of the Bible is fearful while that of the flower is peaceful: "Your way, your ends are dread to me, / When in your hell I share your dream: / But when this dies, I seem to see / Five petals on the sliding stream." Pitter is not the first poet to find in nature a friendlier benevolence than in heaven, but her poems focusing on spiritual themes are more often conciliatory. For instance, "To the Soul" makes this clear from the beginning with its subtitle, "That she would cease from troubling."[53]

> Feared and adored, the guest unsatisfied,
> Chaos-derived and destined to the abyss,
> The keystone of all mysteries,
> Scourge of the flesh and urgent guide,
> Why troublest thou me? (22–24)

Pitter blames her soul for causing her to yearn for fame, to fear the future, and to be discontent with her present: "Is life so light it should be burdened so, / Labour so sweet, death fair, / That thou with thorny doubts the way dost strow, / With portents fillest the air?" All this makes her long to be a soulless nymph, a gentle beast, a tree, or a flower: "After no heaven I hear them sigh, / Not for the soul's sake have they need / To watch and weep, to groan and bleed." In the poem's conclusion, she entreats her soul to permit her "some moments with a kind of peace," and relief from the fear of death. "Still, still to hear the lonely Muse / Let fall her voice amid the dews, / And be possessed / But for a moment, by her rest!" Pitter longs for the muse to bring solace to her soul.

"A Solemn Meditation" continues this conciliatory tone but begins by noting the ominous signs of the time: "These discords and these warring tongues are gales / Of the great autumn: how shall the winter be?" (75–77). The discords and warring tongues may refer to more than the harsh autumn weather; indeed, Pitter may be referring to the sinister events brewing in Europe and the growing threat of fascism. Yet the tone of the poem shifts to one of hope: "Think not that I complain, that I must go / Under the ground, unblossomed, unfulfilled; / Though our stem freeze, in the earth's bosom I / And you sleep: under snow / We shall be saved." Her affirmation is more than a reference to the natural cycle of birth, life, death, and rebirth; instead, she urges the full embracing of death: "The swift fall wings the ascent: close eyes / And hurl head down and sheer / Into the black of life unfathomable."[54] In her descent into death, she catches a vision of God, praises Him that she was born, rejects her earthly aspirations, and emerges renewed:

Then Alleluia all my gashes cry;
My woe springs up and flourishes from the tomb
In her lord's likeness terrible and fair;
Knowing her root, her blossom in the sky
She rears: now flocking to her branches come
The paradisal birds of upper air,
Which Alleluia cry, and cry again,
And death from out the grave replies Amen.

In finding sustenance from her descent into death, in finding nourishment in pain, and, indeed, in finding praise in her wounds, Pitter makes a theological affirmation that testifies to the important place religious belief played throughout her life. While not a committed or even a practicing Anglican at this time, clearly she is imbued with the central ideas of Christian orthodoxy, and these ideas underlie all her theological ruminations and musings. "A Solemn Meditation," therefore, is her most theologically informed poem prior to her later conversion to Christian belief.

Another poem expressing a conciliatory attitude toward spiritual themes is "Thanksgiving for a Fair Summer."[55] Here Pitter considers how mistaken beliefs about the end of summer may be compared to mistaken beliefs about the meaning of human existence. She says, "We had thought the summer dead: / . . . But now hot camomile in headlands grows"; moreover, bees are busily working the woodbine and "scarlet bean" (28–30). This late season fecundity—its ample grain, sweet berries, and heavy apples—becomes a token of grace leading to a larger realization:

> That life is yet benign,
> That this our race
> Still doth possess a pleasant place:
> For many a doubt
> Assails us, and might overthrow,
> Were not the bow
> Of blessing high in heaven hung out;
> Our time is dark,
> And save such miracle as this
> Where is the mark
> To steer by, in our bitter mysteries?

Pitter's deft use of biblical terms and motifs (grace, doubt, rainbow, miracle) melds with but does not subsume the fact that human life is dark and bitter. She finds in the joys of late summer a reminder that existence is not simply a matter of hard times and eternal questionings. Pitter, while certainly not one to look at life through rose-colored glass, consistently finds ways to see past the darkness of life and to affirm a greater, larger, and, as she says in this poem, more benign reality.

Perhaps her most explicitly religious poem is "Help, Good Shepherd." Pitter invokes Christ, the Good Shepherd, and asks him not to spend his time considering the beauty of the constellations, the forests, water, the sunrise, the pipe and tabor, or even "thy crown-destined thorn" (27). Rather, Pitter urges the Good Shepherd to

> Sound with thy crook the darkling flood,
> Still range the sides of shelvy hill,
> And call about in underwood:
> For on the hill are many strayed,
> Some held in thickets plunge and cry,
> And the deep waters make us afraid.
> Come then and help us, or we die.

The frightening tone of this poem, particularly its picture of humankind trapped and entangled in the underbrush like helpless sheep, recalls by way of antithesis both Psalm 23 and Luke 15:4–6. The "good shepherd" (the Lord) of Psalm 23 makes for green pastures and still water, and even though the valley of the shadow of death must be walked, there is no fear of evil, "for Thou art with me." And the Luke passage compares God to a shepherd who is not content to lose even one of his hundred sheep: "What man of you, having an hundred sheep, if he lose one of them, doth not leave the ninety and nine in the wilderness, and go after that which is lost, until he find it? And when he hath found it, he layeth it on his shoulders, rejoicing. And when he cometh home, he calleth together his friends and neighbours, saying unto them, Rejoice with me; for I have found my sheep which was lost." Similarly, Pitter appeals to the Good Shepherd to use his crook and to help her and others who are ensnared by their own fears, be they philosophical, intellectual, moral, or political.[56]

"Of Silence and the Air" also affirms life's larger purpose, but in this poem Pitter is spiritually ambiguous.[57] Written in modified sapphics, this poem captures Pitter's sense of quiet wonder as she stands outside on a cold, clear, crisp night. She glances up at "Hesper [Venus] and a comet," and "void of desire, but full of contemplation," she considers the message of "the frosty air" (33). What is the message? "Nothing / save but that silence is the truth: the silent / stars affirm nothing, and the lovely comet / silent impending." While the final lines use biblical terms and motifs (worship, eternal), there is not a leap of faith toward a benign transcendence: "Shall not I also stand and worship silence / till the cold enter, and the heart, the housewife, / spin no more, but sit down silent in the presence / of the eternal?" Pitter captures in this piece the human tendency to set one's self before the vastness of the universe and to find that a humbling, awe-inspiring experience, one that leaves the soul in silent worship at the infinity of the universe.

Three poems focus specifically upon death. "A Trophy of Arms" is given from the perspective of a stone statue in a graveyard: "The primrose awakens, but / I lean here alone / Where the proud helmet is cut / In the hard stone" (1). The statue guards a "nameless tomb," even though he does not know why; yet he is faithful to his task and hears the voice of honor call out: "The mighty are not fallen, / Nor the weapons of war perished." The statue's detached, impersonal avowal that death is somehow not final, that it has a larger purpose, is furthered in "The Paradox," where Pitter explores the well-known argument between the body and the soul regarding the permanence of death.[58] On one hand, the body insists that "our death [is] implicit in our birth, / We cease, or cannot be; / And know when we are laid in earth / We perish utterly" (53). Yet, on the other hand, the soul argues otherwise because it "knows / The indomitable sense / Of immortality, which goes / Against all evidence." What can bridge this impasse? "See faith alone, whose hand unlocks / All mystery at a touch, / Embrace the awful Paradox / Nor wonder overmuch." While Pitter is not clear about the object of such faith, her affirmation that faith mediates this age-old argument marks this as another poem exploring spiritual matters.

"Call Not to Me" is Pitter's sharpest confrontation with death. In effect the speaker advises death not to expect to take her in the summertime.[59] "Call not to me when summer shines, / Death, for in summer I will not go" (21). In some of her most charmingly lyrical alliterative lines, she says:

> While under the willow the waters flow,
> While willow waxes and waters wane,
> When wind is slumberous and water slow,
> And woodbine waves in the wandering lane,
> Call me not, for you call in vain,
> Vain in the time when flowers blow.

Instead, she is willing to go with death in winter, "when all is bare." After the beauty of summer and the rich harvest of autumn, then, she acquiesces to go with death: "When hail is the seed the heavens sow, / When all is deadly and naught is dear—/ Call and welcome, for I shall hear, / I shall be ready to rise and go." While she displays here false bravado, nonetheless, her desire to control the uninvited guest who comes to all resonates with many readers.[60]

Critical responses to A Trophy of Arms were overwhelmingly positive. James Stephens, whom Pitter had met through AE, sets the tone in his preface to the volume.[61] He praises Pitter as "a pure poet, . . . perhaps the purest poet of our day. . . . When one has read this book one says—This poet is, naturally and beautifully, a poet, and is such in the security, and innocency, of that Uranian term" (xiv). He saves his highest compliment for the last lines of the preface: "Were I asked—Who is the poet now best using the English language? I should answer, W. B. Yeats—considered as from ten years ago: and were it furthered enquired—Who is the next, the companion poet to that fine artist? I should answer, Ruth Pitter" (xvi). John Gawsworth contends that Pitter "attains an almost perfect fusion of feeling and thought. Her verbal music is the outcome of a clean technique of absolute simplicity. Although as classically precise as ever before, her verse here is not so constricted. There is a new freedom apparent."[62] He also echoes Stephens when he adds "she is a natural poet." Belloc adds to the chorus of praise, noting: "Pitter feels immortality in the night . . . [and her philosophy] holds its place steadfastly in such as continue the intellectual affirmation, the process of the reason, whereby the natures of man and his Creator are discovered."[63] Eda Walton agrees with Belloc but says the poems express less a philosophy than "a seeing with the eyes of the spirit. All the simple things of nature are transfigured in her verse by the light in which she sees them."[64]

Dilys Powell is more measured in her review, finding Pitter's introspective poems more effective than those dealing with everyday reality: "To the unmystical reader she communicates . . . a distant sense of her own immobility in joy;

beyond that, however, he feels her remote. . . . But its relation with her inward life is clearly a matter of immense importance to her; and it is this vital connection which gives her poetry something of its integrity and its strength."[65] Michael Roberts is uncertain about the effectiveness of Pitter's introspective poems, claiming that when her "poems are interpreted in terms of the outer world, they are liable to appear sentimental."[66] Siegfried Sassoon takes direct issue with this view and says Roberts is actually unhappy because "Ruth Pitter has not consulted any neo-pedantic recipes for writing flat verse with a lofty political purpose. Could she hope to satisfy those clever critics who know everything about poetry except how to recognize the real thing when it is put under their 'adult-minded' and propaganda-loving probosces?" Sassoon goes on to say that "poets do not fight for their existence. They are not made, but born. They either write poetry or fail to do so. Ruth Pitter writes poetry."[67] He cites her ability to write about her inner world "with perfect control of visual imagery, writing with serene honesty and a craftsmanship which is always in harmony with its material." Also worthy of note, Sassoon says, is Pitter's variety of form as well as how her poems capture a new awareness of the world: "Reticent strength and sensuous alertness, epithets temperate, transparent and surprising; an utterance urgent, flexible and direct."

Finally, Dallas Kenmare finds Pitter's ability to write poems reflecting the soul's sense of displacement particularly effective: "The poet, like the saint, is inevitably ill-at-ease in his strange temporary abode, a homeless alien looking everywhere for the lost, dimly-remembered refuge, and finding reassurances only in flashes, suffering in love and beauty the nostalgia of the outcast for his native land. In Miss Pitter's poetry the nostalgia is scarcely to be borne; the simplest lines ache."[68] He also celebrates her writing "exquisitely of Nature," her simple diction, and particularly her "innocence of maturity" (something, he says, that links her verse to William Blake's):

At some moment of his experience every poet is crucified by the sins of the world; there is the descent into hell, and at last the golden resurrection and the new, strong life. So we find in the poetry of Ruth Pitter, as in Blake, the limpid imagery, the child-like simplicity, allied to imagery that is sordid and ugly; the passionate love of beauty warring with a mystic hatred of ugliness. . . . Always the chaste, the virginal, the clear vision triumphs; evil is the dark shadow intermittently blurring the mirror, a somber phantom to be wrestled with and overcome in order to reach the lovely lake that is ever waiting. And Ruth Pitter never fails to reach the lake.

Kenmare finds in Pitter's poetry the "non-subjective quality of all great art: the ego, while living deeply withdrawn in solitude and silence, yet flows out continually to life, giving and gaining, relating every experience to the whole, always trying to piece together the fragments of the pattern, never content with the sensations of the 'I' in themselves, but always questioning, searching for the meaning." Among Pitter's early reviewers, no one offered more penetrating and nuanced insight than Kenmare.

In addition, Pitter received many letters of thanks and praise for her work. Perhaps the greatest praise came from Lord David Cecil,[69] winner of the Hawthornden Prize in 1929 for *The Stricken Deer* and later a great friend and supporter:

> Dear Miss Pitter, I hope you will forgive a total stranger writing to you. But I feel I must tell you how very beautiful I think your poems [A *Trophy of Arms*]. I read them last week in a fit of drab depression brought on by the condition of the world: and I cannot tell you what a ray of light spread out on my horizon to discover that some one cared still to write such firm spontaneous glowing poetry—could feel the essential normal beauties of soul & body, so freshly, so strongly, so unsentimentally. I read your [M]ad Lady's Garland too & had liked that very much especially the Fowls Terrestrial & Celestial: but in your new book you have soared still higher. Thank you very, very much. (Sept. ? 1936)

Other letters brought requests for permission to put her poems to music or to include them in poetry anthologies, as well as invitations to parties and other events, or led to new friendships, the most notable being with Lady Ottoline Morrell,[70] who befriended Pitter and took her on as a protégée. Another new friend was Herbert Palmer, through whom she later met and began a friendship with C. S. Lewis.[71]

Accordingly, it was not entirely surprising that A *Trophy of Arms* won the Hawthornden Prize in 1937. The Hawthornden Prize, the oldest of the major British literary prizes, was established in 1919 by Alice Warrender to recognize annually the best work of imaginative literature by a writer under forty-one years old.[72] Warrender herself gave Pitter the good news: "I don't know if you heard of the Hawthornden Prize. It is awarded annually for what the committee of it consider to be the best imaginative work of the year & I have the pleasure of telling you that you are the winner with 'A Trophy of Arms.' Please don't tell anybody [for the time being]. . . . The presentation will be in June, I hope and I will let you know in good time when the date is fixed for you to be there" (Feb. 17, 1937). Lady Morrell, upon hearing the news, congratulated Pitter, who replied: "How kind and good of you to write, with your little strength, to congratulate me. David Cecil told me that he had proposed my book to the committee, and a little bird told me that you had brought it to his notice: so I know where thanks is due. You are a true friend to all poets" (June 12).

Telegrams and letters of congratulations poured in. John Masefield wired: "Hearty congratulations on well deserved success" (July 11). Laurence Whistler wrote, "I am such a bad letter writer that that is the one and only reason why I have not written to you long ago to congratulate you most warmly on winning the Hawthornden. . . . It is an honour that any poet must be delighted to earn, and there is no one who deserves it more than you" (Sept. ? 1937). Christopher Hassall was effusive in his congratulations, claiming A Trophy of Arms was "an event in the lives of all those who for the last two decades . . . had thought all such delicate thinking, passion, and classical reserve had been cleared out of the twentieth-century mind" (Sept. ? 1937).[73] W. H. Davies later complimented her: "Although you asked me not to send anything in return, I feel that I must let you know how much your two little books have been enjoyed. It is not often that prizes go into the right hands, but in your case I feel certain it has. May you continue to do such good work for a long time to come" (Aug. 25, 1938). Even T. S. Eliot recognized her achievement. Pitter and Eliot used to attend Chelsea Old Church in London, often taking communion at the same time. Pitter gave Eliot the news about her winning the Hawthornden while they were standing together in a bus queue; he graciously replied, "And you much deserve it."[74]

By the end of 1937 Pitter was finally recognized as a gifted young poet. Both A Mad Lady's Garland and A Trophy of Arms were critically successful and opened to her new opportunities. At the same time, she continued her hard work at Deane and Forester; it was one thing to have critical success as a poet, but quite another to have financial success. Nonetheless, her labors at Deane and Forester paid the bills and provided enough snatches of time for her to continue to write. In the six years since the publication of Persephone in Hades Pitter had achieved profound personal and poetic development. Although she lost the support of Orage and AE, Belloc continued to be a strong advocate, and she gained the considerable attention of Lord David Cecil, who would remain a loyal friend until the end of his life. No longer encumbered with an impersonal, flat voice, she had learned how to reach her readers, drawing them into her comic verse via unusual narrators, and her serious verse via simple, direct diction and compelling themes that spoke to the underlying realities of the human condition. She was ready to move forward with her poetry as the darkening shadows of war slowly spread across Europe.

FOUR

War Watches,

1938–1941

Although now a successful poet, Pitter had little time to bask in her fame, as the demands of Deane and Forester were unrelenting. In addition, the political rumblings across Europe left both Pitter and O'Hara worried about the future of their small but prospering business. This may explain in part why Pitter contacted BBC radio on July 4, 1938; submitted a story, "The Clean Woman"; and offered to read it on air. Fees paid by the BBC were modest (typically about ten guineas), but every little bit of income was worth the effort. Although it would be two years before her first BBC broadcast, this contact set the stage for a working relationship with the BBC that lasted until the mid-1970s. Moreover, while she continued to publish a few poems in the *New English Weekly*, the *London Mercury*, and by special invitation in the *Virginia Quarterly Review*, her production of new verse was modest. She confided to Nettie Palmer: "I haven't written anything to speak of lately: have been in low spirits" (Aug. 7, 1938).

This may explain why Pitter decided to go on holiday to Norway in August 1938. During her fortnight journey she enjoyed the beauty of the seas, the fjords, and the coastal scenery. Day trips were highlighted by frightening drives on high, narrow mountain roads; exhausting but exhilarating hikes; and delicious, expertly prepared meals. Because she was touring with a larger group, she sometimes joined in their activities. After one event, she writes: "Sunday morning went to church. English chaplain. Liked sermon, which seemed to me both scholarly and thoughtful. Remarked as much to Miss C. G. and evoked flood of evangelism, which offended and disgusted me. Culminated in invitation to pray. Damn the impertinence. Shaking with annoyance, must keep out of the way" (Aug. 14, 1938).[1] Despite such irritations, she found the natural beauty breathtaking, and she was particularly impressed by the glaciers, the friendly Norwegians, and the wide, expansive sky. She even made a half-dozen sketches of favorite scenes and places, and her poem "The Mountainous Country," which appears in *The Spirit Watches*, was inspired by this trip.

Upon her return to London she was pleasantly surprised to find a letter from Walter de la Mare asking her permission to include several of her poems in an anthology he was editing.[2] She replied, "Of course I shall be honoured for any work of mine to appear in an anthology of yours.[3] . . . It was a great pleasure to me to meet you. I had long hoped for this, and was sorry afterwards that I had not thanked you for the kind praise you gave a former collection of mine [A Mad Lady's Garland] when my publishers caused me, rather against my will, to send you an advance copy. I thank you now, and heartily" (Aug. 24, 1938). An additional honor followed when she was invited to join the Royal Society of Literature in November; furthermore she was now in demand to give readings of her poetry in places as far away as Scotland. Yet the pressures of Deane and Forester were never far from her mind. To an inquiry from a well-wisher, she writes: "My position is rather a queer one for a writer. I earn about £30 [per year] by poetry, and spend about £50 [net] on activities connected with it, not reckoning clothes. The rest of my income is earned in business, at which I work long hours, and which (if I continue to be honest to my associates) prevents my having any spare time to speak of" (Jan. 18, 1939).

Her relationship with Herbert Palmer was becoming exasperating because of his anger over what he perceived to be a conspiracy by the critics to ignore his verse. In one letter she tells him: "As for selling [your verse], why do you attach such weight to it? Almost no one, surely, can sell enough verse to make a living now: and of course it is no index of merit. Are you not content to abide the judgment of posterity? I hate to think of you, or anyone, wearing out his mind with resentment and anger. Don't do it!" (Nov. 20, 1936). In addition, it maddened Pitter that he would often send her the poetry of others and ask her to offer critiques. After one especially unreasonable request, she writes:

Why is it so often assumed that poets must take an interest in other poets' work? I wish you would not push the work of these dreary females on to me. Think how inevitable it is that I should dislike this one: we are both women, and therefore enemies: she boasts of her misfortunes, I devour mine in silence: she is a romantic, I a classic (as far as I may): I accept the pains of life, she rebels, etc., etc., etc. Further, she hails from a British Dependency, which is automatically fatal to any possibility of literary merit. Don't do it any more, Herbert! . . . Do recollect that I have to work at least 54 hours a week before I can get one single hour to write or read in. (Jan. 26, 1939)

Pitter, ever the independent woman, did not suffer fools lightly, although rarely was she as blunt about her feelings as she was with Herbert Palmer. Her reluctance to read and assist other writers, while in part connected to the demands of her labor at Deane and Forester, lessened to some degree over time. However, throughout most of her life she avoided reading the poetry of others, reserving free time for her own verse and gardening.

While Pitter had to bite her tongue at times in her dealings with Herbert Palmer, her life was soon to be greatly enriched by her growing friendship with David Cecil and his wife, Rachel. While he had already written Pitter regarding A *Trophy of Arms*, their developing friendship dates from a letter Pitter wrote Rachel on March 7, in which Pitter congratulates her on the birth of her son, Jonathan.

> I hope with all my heart that you will be blessed in your child, and he in his parents. Whenever I look at a newborn infant, I feel at once and very strongly its individuality. No one is like anyone else except in parts, but everyone is intensely himself from the very hour of birth. It must be exceedingly strange to behold another *person* who till a short time ago was part of oneself: but mothers, I believe, do continue to feel that their children are parts of themselves. All the same, a new personality, a fresh factor, has arrived on the scene, complete with mind, temperament, physical idiosyncrasies and everything. One is "teased out of thought" by the miracles, just as when we start to think about space and time.

What eventually resulted was a warm friendship and correspondence between Pitter and the Cecils that lasted until the end of their lives.

Pitter's wider recognition as a gifted poet was rewarded by an invitation to publish three poems, "The Chimney Piece," "The Spirit Watches," and "O Come Out of the Lily," in the *Virginia Quarterly Review*.[4] Moreover, she was delighted to be asked to send other new poems to the journal as she saw fit. At the same time, she continued to try to befriend and encourage Herbert Palmer. Perhaps because of her exasperation with him in earlier letters, she tries to encourage him in another letter written from Oak Cottage, probably in the summer of 1939:

> You seem always to be plagued by petty piracies and injustices, which seem to be your lot in this world. I entreat you to apply that greatness of soul, which you undoubtedly possess, to rise superior to them. It is not easy for a man who is unwell and tired to death, but if you could do so, it would greatly alleviate these very conditions. . . . I know well enough that pugnacity is a normal, if secondary, male characteristic; but there is a way of refusing to be pugnacious which makes one more, not less, than man, and converts the energy which would otherwise be squandered in resentment (even just resentment) into solid working capital for mind

and spirit. I speak as a pugnacious individual, not as one who has never felt the enormous rush of a just indignation.

She also reveals in the letter how much she enjoys being out of London: "I am staying here for a week with my mother. It is a treat to us both, as I love the simplest country life, and she, poor soul, has such bad eyesight now that it is a great joy to be able to talk, to be read to, and to have an early cup of tea brought up." Unfortunately for Pitter and the rest of Europe, such summer countryside bliss could not last, as World War II effectively began with the Nazi blitzkrieg of Poland on Sept. 1. In the first week of the war her letters do not reflect a personal preoccupation with the conflict, but as the conflict gets closer to English soil, her letters offer fascinating and disturbing details. In a letter to de la Mare she makes a veiled reference to the war while revealing that she does have another volume of verse about to appear: "We are embarked upon a phase of existence which must change life for us all, but we can go forward in the light of such visions as this, trusting in life and in ourselves. I have a new little book in the press [*The Spirit Watches*], but it seems weary stuff to me.[5] Never mind. The fair day of humanity and of art must come—it is *promised*" (Sept. 14, 1939). To David Cecil she writes about her growing fears that the war will affect Deane and Forester:

We are trying to stick to the remnant of our business, believing that the taxes we pay are of more value to the country than our unskilled labour at "national" work would be. So far it has not been too bad—about half our staff are still here, the rest at war work; many of our trade customers, corporally in the "safe" areas, are finding business better than it was. Supplies are difficult, of course, and many things unobtainable. But we shall continue as long as we can. I find I can keep up my spirits in the face of this real disaster better than against our usual worries. At least the horrible tension is lessened and instead of selfish preoccupation, one simplifies the mind to the pattern of tragic necessity. (Sept. 29, 1939)

She also tells him about the impending publication of her next book, *The Spirit Watches:* "My new little book of poems is, I believe, in process of printing, but they are not so good as the best in the 'Trophy.'" The blossoming nature of their friendship is revealed as she ends the letter by inviting him to stop by Chelsea on an impending visit and offering kind regards to Rachel and Jonathan.

By late October she sends more poems to the *Virginia Quarterly Review* and admits that the war is beginning to take its toll:

We are settling down to the war now, and I believe we are happier than a year ago, when we felt that we had yielded to the thrusts of tyranny, and betrayed the causes of weaker nations not less in love with freedom than ourselves. It will make us poorer in substance for our own generation at least, but that does not seem to matter. And the more cautious strategy we are now employing will, I hope and pray, prevent some of the awful waste of life we experienced in the last war. I expect to be a good deal poorer both on account of taxation and reduction of business, but I shall take a lot of this sort of thing before I am beaten, having a natural gift of economy and contrivance. And really, the feeling that we are making a firm stand at last is worth any sacrifice of the kind. (Oct. 19, 1939)

Pitter's obvious support for the war and its larger aims was common in Britain. In addition, her willingness to sacrifice in order to ensure that the Nazis did not triumph was shared by many. Of course no one could have known how severely such resolve would be tested, but her convictions are testimony to the moral outrage felt by most people in Britain as they saw the terrible threats posed by Nazism.

The Spirit Watches

It is telling that the title of Pitter's new book, The Spirit Watches, offers assurance that human events are part of a larger story. As in A Trophy of Arms, a number of the poems in The Spirit Watches were first published in the New English Weekly; however, Pitter's fame as the winner of the Hawthornden Prize gave her greater access to other periodicals so that some first appeared in the London Mercury and, as has been noted, the Virginia Quarterly Review. Pitter's publisher, Cresset Press, also wanted to capitalize on her literary fame and urged her to work on a follow-up volume. She willingly complied, and her manuscript notebooks show that all the poems appearing in The Spirit Watches were written between 1936 and 1939. This relatively quick turnaround after publishing A Trophy of Arms explains both the smaller number of poems appearing in The Spirit Watches (thirty-three versus fifty-seven) and the thematic similarities between the two volumes.

For instance, the cottage and Hainault Forest once again serve as a focus for one group of poems. "Time's Fool" is a careful visual reconstruction of Pitter's memories of the cottage. The poem begins ironically as Pitter admits she is time's fool, although not heaven's, because in spite of her longing to rekindle her memories of the cottage, she "hope[s] not for any return."[6] Her tender affection for the cottage comes through as she recalls its contents: "The rabbit-eaten dry branch and the halfpenny candle / Are lost with the other treasure: the sooty kettle / Thrown away, become redbreast's home in the hedge, where the nettle / Shoots up, and bad bindweed wreathes rust-fretted-handle. / Under that broken thing no more shall the dry branch burn." To refer to these worn-out, tattered objects as "treasure" heightens the poignancy of her memories and serves to reinforce her almost childlike determination to hold on to this spot in time. She goes on to claim that all these objects, while insignificant and of little value, were to her at one time "all comfort" because there "the heart was at home." Again, her memories are powerfully evocative: "The hard cankered apple holed by the wasp and the bird, / The damp bed, with the beetle's tap in the headboard heard, / The dim bit of mirror, three inches of comb." No amount of logic or knowledge of the apparent meanness of the cottage can negate its powerful hold upon her imagination:

I knew that the roots were creeping under the floor,
That the toad was safe in his hole, the poor cat by the fire,
The starling snug in the roof, each slept in his place:
The lily in splendour, the vine in her grace,
The fox in the forest, all had their desire,
As then I had mine, in the place that was happy and poor.

Pitter's strong sense of nature's pull, her desire to merge with and be a part of this place, and her longing for a return to her adolescent happiness rarely come through more effectively than in this poem.

"The Hut" continues this theme, picturing the cottage as willingly and gradually being overcome by nature. "Stuck, like a snail upon a wall, / On what we called a hill," the hut leans against an apple tree "whose laden branches lay / On the hot roof voluptuously, / And murmured all the day" (28–29). Imagining that a dryad is warming the hut for her own mysterious purposes, Pitter notes how "the sapling ash had mined the floor, / The chimney flew the bine," and "the doorway was without a door, / But flaunted eglantine." Not only have trees, vines, and flowers invaded the hut, but animals have as well: "The swallow built upon the beam, / The rat was much at home." This woodsy home is the imaginative center of Pitter's world, since "there one foolish child would dream, / Where sorrow could not come." The cottage is also the focus of "Bloweth Where It Listeth," which takes its title from John 3:8.[7] In the poem Pitter suggests that while her body is bound to an earthly spot, her spirit "like any wandering moth . . . flits abroad in air; / Seeking the unsought, and loving what is lone." Not surprisingly, her spirit ranges over the earth until it comes "to a cottage in a solitary lane, / Where the sparrow, nested in the neighbouring tree, / Brooded the shabby eggs which no one loved but she" (58–60). Seeing a "poor soul" within, her spirit peers "in anxiously, to mark the look of care, / But for once in this sorry life sorrow was not there." Indeed, while sorrow has once been there, it has now fled, leaving her spirit joyful and content: "For it took her tenderness with it as it went: / For it goes about blessing, and will not be gainsaid, / The wild weed in the waste land, the ruined wall, and the dead; / And the hearts of poor women in the cold country-side / It goes about blessing, and will not be denied." In effect, her spirit's retreat to the cottage nourishes Pitter as it returns to her conscious mind.

The fourth poem of this group, "Lament for the Landless," considers the nurturing power of nature and the harm caused to those who have no direct access to the countryside: "Love of the earth leaps up, and falls in a sigh for my fellows / . . . Alas, for the man who has never smelled the thick-flowering / [Grape]vine in its bursting glory / . . . Alas for the disinherited, the earthless, the uprooted— / No crocus, no primrose, no blessing of natural increment!" (48–51).[8] Other natural objects whose absences are lamented include the flower of the plum, the hedge sparrow's brood "with buttercup-yellow gullets," strawberry and violet plants, and "the azure crescent / Of the [robin's] half-eggshell." The lament peaks when Pitter says, "Who is forlorn of these is the godforsaken." Accordingly, she opts for immediate sensuous experience: "I eat of the fruit of the tree where the good dog lies / Meshed in the quiet root, and my hand busy / On wrinkled stems that were planted by the forgotten." Additionally, she wants to meld with nature: "And I must be numbered with them and neglect the seasons, / Though somehow I know that a flower is remembered for ever, / And eyes, and the shape of a bird for ever remembered." These four poems harkening back to the cottage and the forest not only communicate Pitter's visceral love for nature but also indicate her secret desire to withdraw from the coming conflict, the distant but advancing chaos of war.

The second group of thematically linked poems in *The Spirit Watches*, like those in *A Trophy of Arms*, concerns nature's pattern of life and death. For instance, in "The Vine in Bloom," a poem inspired by the lush grapevines kept by her mother at Oak Cottage, Pitter explores the beauty of the cycle of life by contrasting her personal aging with nature's pattern of rebirth:

It matters not to grow old, when the vine is breaking:
The years have no weight when the holy vine is in bloom:
Soon I must be sleeping, but this shall still be waking,
The promise of birth is breathed in the word of doom;
She gives me the flower now, then the cluster that comes in its room,
But soon I must be giving and the vine taking. (9)

That is, as she sees the vine so heavy with blossoms that it sags to the point of breaking, rather than feeling sorry for herself as she considers her own "fullness" of years, Pitter does not fear death. There is "no grudge, . . . no quarrel," between her and the vine; instead, the comforting eternal verity of nature's ongoing activity brightens her day and is heightened by the last image in the poem: "And the speckled bird, / Murmuring her care and her busy kindness, is heard / Nourishing next year's songs in the bonny laurel." In the end, Pitter emphasizes her sense of joy rather than pain in this musing upon death and rebirth.

"Burning the Bee-Tree" similarly reflects upon nature's ongoing, revitalizing power.[9] She describes the final fiery destruction of a tree that once housed an active beehive: "We threw their tower down on the mould, / And split it open wide, / But they had taken away their gold, / And there was none inside" (12–13). As others gaze on what's left—"the embalming stain," "a few shards of comb," and "a breath as of the clover-plain"—Pitter watches the "spiced funeral vapours" curl upwards and wonders: "What do you see above, what fair / Visions salute your eyes, / What reverend memories repair / The breach of centuries?" This final destruction of the hive's empire, however, does not evoke sadness; rather, as in "The Vine in Bloom," Pitter finds solace in the unending cycle of nature this event suggests. The burning bee-tree becomes an archetype for all that nature renews and recombines: "The labour, and the bitter sting, / The cells' meticulous range, / Honey, which makes a perishing thing / Immortal, do not change." Far from leading to her bitterness, the burning bee-tree encourages Pitter to recommit herself not only to life, but, more importantly, to writing poetry: "Life, make one couplet that I sing / As deathless, and as strange!" While death is certain, Pitter finds in nature's cycles and rhythms continuity rather than finality; we die but our lives are only a part of a larger ongoing reality.

While "Struggling Wheat" (19–20) also finds in nature an exemplar for the human condition—that is, how the desperate struggles of a field of wheat to survive too much rain and then too much heat may be likened to "ill-fated" man's existential dilemma—"The Stockdove" is a poignant lament connecting the death of a bird with human death.[10] Catching sight of the stock dove, Pitter is at first arrested by its immobility. She wonders if it is caught by a snare, but seeing that the bird is not frightened or panicked, Pitter senses the truth that "death shakes her like a winter storm" (21–22). It is only later in the poem that we learn the bird has been poisoned by tainted grain set there to put down foraging birds like the stock dove. With a certain dignified resignation, the bird "half lifts the wing, half turns the bill, / Then leans more lowly on the clay, / Sighs, and at last is quiet and still, / Sits there, and yet is fled away." Pitter finds in the gentle, quiet, peaceful passing of the bird an event worthy of great sorrow—"the epoch will not suffer me / To weep above such humble dead, / Or I could mourn a century / For all such woe unmerited"—yet rather than give in to angry recriminations, Pitter takes a different direction:

My questioned spirit's sidelong look
From her old fortress answers me,

From where she reads her secret book
On the tall rock Infinity:
From where the innocent dead to that
High place is fled away from grief,
And whence as from an Ararat
She brings the silver olive-leaf.

That Pitter connects the death of the stock dove to the dove in Genesis 8:11 is interesting. There the dove calls to mind the sign of God's peaceful intentions toward man when it returned to the ark resting on Mt. Ararat and brought Noah the olive leaf. Perhaps the point is that while Pitter may have been holding away at arm's length religious faith, she clearly is aware of an internal spirit that offers her counsel, although the question of whether this spirit is transcendent or merely personal is not clear. What we can take out of this poem, however, is Pitter's acceptance of death as inevitable, not something to rail against. As in the previous poems in this group, she finds in death not something to fear or dread, but something to embrace and welcome.

"The Spring" also has theological undertones and can be linked to "Sudden Heaven" in *A Trophy of Arms*. Where "Sudden Heaven" finds an unexpected epiphany in ordinary events, "The Spring" begins by noting a lack of joy and life's bleakness: "Where is the spring of my delight / Now every spring is dry? / There is no blossom in my sight, / No sun in the sky" (45). The puns on "spring" are effective; on one hand, Pitter wonders where to find the sources of delight, and on the other hand, she senses that both the sources and the season itself are arid. This melancholy continues as Pitter says, "The birds are still and love is past, / . . . And life itself now looks aghast / And birth becomes an ill." Yet in the midst of this sterility, perhaps because of nature's rhythms and cycle, she is surprised by delight: "The spring of my delight / Leaps up beyond belief, / As if it sprang in very spite— / In very spite of grief." Pitter suggests that happiness is often counterintuitive; when we least expect happiness, it "leaps up beyond belief" and gives the lie to grief. The poem's conclusion hints at a theological source for the spring of all happiness: "And yet the secret stream of grace / Flows on, and swells the same, / As if from out another place / Where sorrow has no name." While Pitter does not refer directly to heaven, the idea of grace or unmerited favor finds its source there, the "spring" of all happiness.

Pitter's poems ruminating on the human condition are measured. For instance "1938," a prewar warning, complains about man's inhumanity to man, and the human tendency to destroy, to ravage the earth, and to belittle goodness: "The gentle are ground into earth / And the tender despised: / Honour's an ass-head, a bauble, / The mark of a profitless fool" (34–36). All that remains is the deserved grave, since we have "despaired of wisdom." Yet in the poem's conclusion there is not despair; rather, man's foolishness is contrasted with nature's ongoing life: "The earth is as fruitful as ever, / The sea still teeming with fishes, / The sun still lusty; but we / Have failed to love, and must perish." Even in a poem where she embraces despair, like "A Natural Sorrow," which on the surface contradicts the theme of "The Spring," Pitter does not simply abandon herself to anguish. If "The Spring" celebrates the unexpected arrival of joy, "A Natural Sorrow" explores its opposite: "Silent as a falling leaf / To my heart there came a grief: / With a cold and pure despair, / Angerless, it settled there" (30). She resigns herself to this grief, content that it will stay until "it waste from mere decay" or "spring's uprush-ing tide / Thrust the skeleton aside." Moreover, she will employ the dead leaf as a reminder of the inevitability of sorrow: "I will not grudge to feel it so, / This dead leaf, this natural woe, / Neither will rage nor yet repine, / But let it lie there as a sign." She finishes the poem by noting three other signs of sorrow—a pyramid, a gravestone, and an empty bird's nest. While it is impossible to know the particular grief that served as the impetus for this poem, the final image of the empty nest suggests it may have been unrequited love, since she uses the same image in "If You Came," the only poem in *The Spirit Watches* explicitly dealing with romantic love: "The place is hidden apart / Like the nest of a bird: / And I will not show you my heart / By a look, by a word."

The third group of poems centers around spiritual themes, including God, the soul, and the meaning of human existence. The title poem of the volume, "The Spirit Watches," is a confession of sorts, at least in the sense that Pitter hints that she believes in some kind of transcendent being in control of the world; however, she is never explicit about who or what this God is.[11] The spirit addressed in the poem is largely cut off from human activity, although it is com-pletely cognizant of what is going on:

> She hangs the garland in her hair,
> Smiling above unending pain:
> She knows the worst, and does not care:
> Her beauty says, to foul and fair,
> Tears are wrong, and all repining vain.
> What fearful thing is she, that sees
> Joy failing, and the gaping grave,
> That knows our bitter mysteries,
> Our death, our life of little ease,
> The coward's hell, the anguish of the brave. (1–2)

In answer to this question, Pitter says this spirit is "love's apotheosis." Although the specific identity of this spirit is still veiled at this point, Pitter turns the focus upon humankind's blindness to the activity of this spirit: "We are not worthy of the soul! / Through light and dark, through love and pain, / We see our sphere of being roll, / And will not face the living whole / That sent us forth, and calls us home again." Our shortsighted preoccupation with this world and our activities, Pitter notes, keeps us from understanding the reality at the center of the universe: "Into the centre from the verge / Turning again because we must, / She draws us, until we remerge / Into the One: her fearful urge / Is his inviolate law, and he is just."

If the "he" of these lines refers to a transcendent God, then this still-unknown spirit is the agent God uses to pull humankind back into a cosmic universal pool of "one-ness." In fact, the poem's ending resolves, at least in part, this mysterious spiritual agent: "She is our part in God, to shine / Where all abiding glories are; / Even through my tears, I see her twine / Among her deathless locks divine / The star of evening, and the morning star." Venus, the poem suggests, is God's active agent in universal redemption; in effect, Venus is the evidence of God's love in the universe.[12] We take away from "The Spirit Watches" the sense that humankind is not alone in the universe; in spite of our blindness to spiritual reality and our obsession with human activity, including war, pain, and grief, Pitter posits a benign if impersonal God who will make all things well. Although this poem verges on being naive, given that Pitter, along with the rest of Europe, was facing a war, it is not surprising she affirms the ultimate meaning and purpose of all things as directed by a benevolent though distant God.

Another poem in *The Spirit Watches* centering on this distant God is "O Come Out of the Lily."[13] Here Pitter finds in natural beauty signs of that mysterious "something" at the back of the universe, and she longs to get closer to it: "O come out of the lily to me, / Come out of the morning-glory's bell, / Out of the rose and the peony, / You that made them, made so well" (42). The other natural beauties where she finds the hint of God are the ermine's eyes and the butterfly's wings, leading her to call forth to God: "Sleep no longer, nor lurk behind / Hate and anger and woeful pain: / As once in the garden, walk again, / Centre and spirit of human kind." Employing again an allusion to Genesis, Pitter longs for the pre-fallen world of Adam and Eve and their easy and immediate access to God. Pitter's mystical longing for God also appears in "The Bird in the Tree," although here the concern is with how difficult it is to see that "something" at the back of the universe. In what is written almost as another confession, Pitter expresses her frustration at finding archetypes in their earthly types:

That tree, and its haunting bird,
Are the loves of my heart;
But where is the word, the word,
O where is the art,

To say, or even to see,
For a moment of time,
What the Tree and the Bird must be
In the true sublime? (57)

The Platonic contrast between the earthly copy and the "real" form of the tree and the bird is brought further into relief when Pitter writes: "They shine, they sing to the soul, / And the soul replies; / But the inner love is not whole / And the moment dies." Yet her deep longing to experience the "real" bird and tree lead her to pray, "O give me before I die / The grace to see / With eternal, ultimate eye, / The Bird and the Tree." Pitter's desire to experience firsthand these eternal objects is akin to her mystical affection for God; in both cases the physical world is not enough, and so she wants more. This longing for union with the "something" behind the universe is still several years away from being satisfied, yet its appearance in these poems marks an important milestone in Pitter's spiritual journey.

"The Difference" shifts away from God and toward the human spirit, offering a contrast between how nature and humans handle hardship. For example, she evokes the sound of a happy lark that "leaps up loud with his love into the clear grey"; however, if the lark loses his mate or his nest, "he must cease from the song" (24). Yet humans cannot simply cease when they experience pain: "But you must sing ever in spite of all wrong, / Whatever is lost, strayed, or stolen away." Similarly, while a beautiful flower, when exposed to a cold wind, will "sink, . . . fall down there, . . . [and] die in her grace," a human must persevere: "But you must bloom still in the desolate place, / Whatever is frozen or withered away." The resiliency of the human spirit in the face of hardship is perhaps a gift from God, but it is not necessarily a comfort. Instead it is a tool to survive the inevitable flux of human existence.

Other poems illustrate Pitter's continuing maturation as a poet. Two poems consider animals, but unlike A Mad Lady's Garland, they are not comic. "The Tigress" shows Pitter's debt to William Blake's "The Tyger," but while Blake muses upon the character of the creator of such a fierce animal—"Tyger! Tyger! burning bright / In the forests of the night / What immortal hand or eye / Dare frame thy fearful symmetry?"[14]—Pitter considers the terror and the tenderness, the horror and the beauty, and the power and the gentleness of a mother tiger before drawing a connection to human existence. The poem begins by em-phasizing the savage power of the tigress: "The raging and the ravenous, / The nocturnal terror in gold, / Red-fire coated, green-fire-eyed, / The fanged, the clawed, the frightful leaper" (31). Yet the irony is that this "great-sinewed, si-lent walker," this "implacable devil of slaughter," this "she-demon matchless in fury," is also a tender mother "matchless" in her love for her cubs. Pitter then gives us the incongruous picture of the tigress "cleaning the stains of slaughter" from her jaws, and then cleaning and licking her young "delicately as a doe: / She blood-glutted is the angel / To their blindness, she is minister / Between life and these feeble young / In barren places."

However, the poem shifts its focus from a wild tigress to one imprisoned in a zoo. The caged animal, almost as if to spite its human keepers, disdains to rear the cubs she has been "cheated into bearing" and "abandons all at birth, and bids them die." The tigress does not equivocate: "Utter love and utter hatred / Cannot compromise; she gives / Her whole being to their being / Or rejects them into death." In addition, the tigress is not burdened by the human capacity to reason or reflect: "No thought intervenes; her justice / Is not mind-perverted." Yet, Pitter wonders, if the tigress could have but one thought and by "compunction burn," would it be "for all these millions / Mind-infected, mother-betrayed: / No beast so hapless as a man"? Pitter is struck by the tigress's complete commitment to either love or hate, perhaps suggesting something about her own view of the world in the late 1930s. The uncompromising energy of the tigress is an attractive anodyne to human vacillation, compromise, and indecision. While Pitter is not rejecting her own humanity or that of others, clearly she finds in the unreflective, instinctive life of a tigress an appealing alternative.

"The Bush-Baby" is a wistful desire for connection to the animal world. Standing outside a lemur enclosure, Pitter intuitively longs for a closer relationship with the furtive, delicate creatures: "I would rather hold this creature in my hand / Than be kissed by a great king. / The love for what I do not understand / Goes from me to this slight thing" (46). In the velvet coat and round, nocturnal eyes of the lemurs, she sees "an image out of Paradise," and she blesses the bush baby. As in "The Tigress," however, Pitter ends by focusing upon humankind: "To see a glory in another kind, / To love, and not to know. / O if I could forsake this weary mind / And love my fellows so!" The attributes of the natural world—its forests, gardens, and animals—to offer beauty, rest, and peace is almost always preferred by Pitter over interaction with other human beings. And the deeply impressed memories of the cottage and Hainault Forest are at the heart of such longings for retreat to the natural world.

"The Military Harpist" is a study of incongruities, as the opening line suggests: "Strangely assorted, the shape of song and the bloody man" (25–27). The poem considers an old, hard-bitten soldier in full regimental dress who plays with fervent passion a beautiful, seemingly fragile harp with "rainlike strings." Pitter's striking visual presentation of the soldier is memorable: "Prawn-eyed, with prawnlike bristle, well-waxed moustache, / With long tight cavalry legs, and the spurred boot / Ready upon the swell, the Old Sweat waits." That such a fierce, blunt, hardened man—given "to ruminate interracial fornications"—

could at the same time stroke the delicate strings of the harp and produce ethereal music seems impossible. Yet when he plays, he is transformed and "his wicked
old mug is David's, / Pastoral, rapt, the king and the poet in innocence, / Singing
Saul in himself asleep, and the ancient Devil / Clean out of countenance, as with
an army of angels." Indeed, his music may do more to him than to his listeners,
since when he plays "he is now where his bunion has no existence. / Breathing
an atmosphere free of pipeclay and swearing, / He wears the starched nightshirt
of the hereafter, his halo / Is plain manly brass with a permanent polish, / Requiring no oily rag and no Soldier's Friend." However, Pitter likens him not only
to David, "the beloved poet of Israel" who played the harp in order to calm the
evil spirit that haunted Saul, but also to the wandering minstrels of Provence;
to Blondel, the troubadour who rescued Richard the Lionheart from prison; to
"the morning discourse of saints in the island of Eire"; and, perhaps most closely,
to priests harping "at the Druid sacrifice, where the golden string / Sings to the
golden knife and the victim's shriek." The exquisite inappropriateness of the
battle-scarred soldier and his heavenly instrument makes this poem both compelling and memorable.

"Old, Childless, Husbandless" is a tender study of one who knew no love
yet extended it sacrificially to one in her keeping: "Old, childless, husbandless,
bereaved, alone, / She knew more love than any I have known" (47). Well
acquainted with illness, Mary comforted the older woman she nursed, even
sharing her bed so that she could respond quickly to "the threadbare whisper
in the night of fear." When the older woman died, Mary quietly tidied up the
room and took pains not to bother anyone else, "unwilling, kind heart, to call
anyone, / It was so late: all finished, down she lay / Beside the dead, and calmly
slept till day." In Mary, Pitter sees grace, kindness, and generosity of spirit she
admires yet, perhaps, cannot emulate: "What could child or husband be / More
than she had, to such a one as she?"

The Spirit Watches is a natural extension of A Trophy of Arms, as the thematic
similarities between the two volumes illustrate. The one notable difference between the two is the preponderance of references to heavenly bodies—stars,
moon, sun, planets—in The Spirit Watches. In addition to the poems discussed
above, "The Downward-Pointing Muse" celebrates Venus, "An Old Woman
Speaks of the Moon" finds comfort in the beautiful night orb, and "The Primordial Cell" invites readers to remember the life-sustaining power of the earth.
Urania, the muse of astronomy, appears in several poems, and the sun is often
invoked as well. Collectively these heavenly references in The Spirit Watches
convey a sense of humankind's place under the stars; our story is not greater
than the universal one, but we are intimately connected to and perhaps even
guided by the cosmic confluence of stars, moon, sun, and planets. Whether or
not a benign but distant God is above these heavenly bodies, directing them

and humankind, is never explicitly stated in *The Spirit Watches*, but Pitter hints that this is so.

The critical reception of *The Spirit Watches* was mixed. Stephen Spender dismisses it out of hand: "Miss Pitter's poems are admired by [many] . . . , but . . . I consider them a fake. Her music, her imagery, her observation, have a mistiness as of the gauze let down in front of the stage. . . . One has an uplifting sense of someone thinking beautiful things, but nothing is focused either in the Here or the Hereafter."[15] Desmond Hawkins criticizes what he terms her "unholy love of inversions—'deathless looks divine,' 'hedgerows wet,' 'effort grim,'" and her "funny noises like 'rosy daisy.'"[16] He also complains about "an artificially 'poetic' atmosphere," "a solemn hush while the moth-balls are shaken out of the priestly robes," and material that is "trite and faded." Placing her in the lyric tradition of W. H. Davies and Walter de la Mare, he grudgingly admits she has talent. Yet he undercuts even his brief praise by concluding: "*The Spirit Watches* reveals a genuine talent working capably in an inherited vein which is always in sight of exhaustion."

However, the reviewer for the *Times Literary Supplement* finds much to admire, particularly her "sensitive blending of the timeless with the things of time and their transmutation from natural objects into meaningful symbols."[17] Also noteworthy is that "in many of her lyrics the image of perfection which she grasps heightens her sense of the intruding gulf between the actual and the real, the realm of innocence and of marred experience." The overall message of the volume, the reviewer notes, is "that the spirit is eternally victorious" in spite of very real human grief. Eric Forbes-Boyd does not think *The Spirit Watches* is as effective as *A Trophy of Arms*, but not because of a falloff in technical excellence. Instead, the subject matter itself is problematic for him since Pitter, having "retreated" within herself, is too "aloof": "We are conscious, indeed, that this is poetry, that there is subtlety and intensity in it, but it awakens no perception; she retreats only to become more 'advanced' to the point of obscurity."[18] Still, he finds much to commend, especially Pitter's "essential ability to impart a strangeness to her verse, and to arrest or startle us with a sudden peculiarly expressive phrase."

Louise Bogan also offers tempered praise, admitting that while *The Spirit Watches* lacks ardor, it reveals Pitter's "eye for detail, her delicate imagination, and her compassion."[19] Another critic is more certain of Pitter's work in *The Spirit Watches*: "There are very few dead lines and no imitative ones. . . . Though she writes seriously, even when she writes of little things, her tone has not the assurance of one confident of having found the Truth but the questioning note of one still seeking. But though her convictions may be tentative, her poetic touch is sure."[20] Louis Untermeyer is also generous in his compliments: "The surface of this poetry is smooth and graceful; beneath the gently changing con-

tours the shaping mind is firm and surprisingly edged. The idiom is simple, quietly conventional; the statements are seemingly casual; but the craftsmanship
is extraordinarily disciplined and the tone is unmistakably the tone of poetry of
high order."[21] He notes the influence of Blake and the later Yeats, but he adds
even so, "One hears Miss Pitter's own accent—exact but not finicking, patri-
cian but not pedantic." His review ends by claiming Pitter "assumes full stature
as one of the indubitable poets of a dubious time. She is that rare thing: a mystic
with a sense of humor, an initiate whose revelations are immediate, eager, seldom arcane. Tender yet never mawkish, exquisite but stern, Miss Pitter is a joy
to discover and a happiness to recall."

Another critic noting the connections between Pitter and Yeats was the poet
May Sarton. In her review of Yeats's *Last Poems* (1940) and Pitter's *The Spirit
Watches* she says: "It is something to have been born in an age, however terrible, which can produce two such poets, two books as pure, violent, and noble
as these."[22] In particular, Sarton praises the two poets because they write poems
that "contain completed actions of the spirit, perfectly expressed, so that it
seems as if they had never been written. They exist like stones and trees. They
can be taken out of their environment in space and time and set down beside
any living poem from the past. They are not modern. They *are*." About Pitter,
Sarton emphasizes her gender: "We have had many women poets—those who
have taken up the tradition of the woman-poet as lover only, those who have
reacted violently against this and are trying to be masculine poets, movers and
shakers of the world." Sarton argues this is not what Pitter has done. Instead,
"she stands where women stand, rooted between the rational and the mystic,
extremely observant of the natural world (the poems are full of magical detail),
skeptical of the supernatural, convinced of the power of the spirit, bound to
love. Among her contemporaries she stands almost alone, but the muse is beside her."[23]

While the critics may have been split in their evaluation of *The Spirit Watches*,
David Cecil was enthusiastic in his praise:

> I need must tell you how honoured & delighted I was to receive your
> present. I have read it with very great pleasure. Perhaps you are right; I
> do not know if I admired anything in it as much as I admired some things
> in The Trophy of Arms. But—& I say . . . this in all sincerity—I enjoyed
> The Spirit Watches more than the work of any other poet now writing
> in English. It is partly the exquisite accomplishment of your craftsman-
> ship; it is still more a sort of deep aloof severity of sentiment, which heals
> & strengthens the heart. And God knows one is grateful for that today.
> I think the poem I liked the best is "The Spirit Watches" itself. But I
> also thought very beautiful "The Solitary," "The Primordial Cell," "The

Downward Pointing Muse," "The Vine in Bloom," and "The Military Harpist." But I like all the others too. I cannot tell you how gratified I feel to have been given them by the author. (Nov. 1939)

On November 27, 1939, Pitter replies to Cecil:

Many and heartfelt thanks for your delightful letter, which affords me more pleasure and sustenance than I can express. I shall place it among my few treasures—few, because I am no letter-keeper in general. What you say about the severity of sentiment in my work fortifies me exceedingly, since I well know that to deserve this I must have traveled a long way from the beginnings of poetry in me, which were certainly characterized by all the usual sappiness of young work, though never, I thank Heaven by the shameless self-revelations indulged in by some. They say that in poetry the myth should be implicit: so too the voice of the self must not be the leader of the orchestra.

Lacking a university education, Pitter found the enthusiastic support of a scholar like Cecil a great encouragement both aesthetically and intellectually; his praise of her poetry validated, nourished, and affirmed her as nothing else could have. We can only imagine the genuine pleasure she felt when reading his complimentary letters. In addition, Cecil's recognition gave her simple delight—the delight anyone laboring in relative obscurity deeply cherishes.

To Cecil she also frequently admitted to the struggles she faced living in World War II London during the blitz, commenting at various times on how her ornamental painting business was nearing collapse, as well as the constant threat of bombing: "I am really very well, and less tired than is usual at this time of year, as owing to the lighting restrictions we cannot work such long hours as heretofore. I am cook to the establishment, and this is very congenial to me—most poets like cooking, you know. We have at present more business than our reduced staff can handle, but of course the usual spring slackness will be worse than ever: but if we can keep going it is all we ask" (Nov. 27, 1939). The new year brought continued hard work and pessimistic news about the war. In an unpublished poem written in January 1940, "Seagulls in London," she confesses to the difficulty of these days yet affirms her faith in the benign, distant God:

They stormed upon me like catastrophe.
All fear of man was gone: scenting the food
The harpy-crowd gathered and broke on me:
These, bred in solitude
Among the sea-pink in the salt sea-marsh,

Moated about by creeks of quaking slime
Lonelier than mountain deserts, now with harsh
Throats besought alms at this most bitter time.

My hands, cold-palsied, felt their crooked bills;
Their pirate sails struck on my stiffened cheek:
Their cold wet feet touched me with fleeting chills,
Frail and inadvertent, that seemed to speak
For all the fury, of existence weak:
And one was lame,
Lagged on the turn, got nothing when he came.

Heart-withering hunger! How the terror whips
The shrinking mind! Knowing ourselves curtailed,
More steel, less grain lading the threatened ships,
We, for whom plenty never yet has failed,
Feel the frore shadow of what famine now
Clothes the bowels of both foe and friend,
And while all Europe shudders in the snow,
Dare not foresee, nor think upon the end.

And I am moved to ask you to forgive
If I have hope: if like a stubborn seed
The heart turns tough, determined still to live,
Made a mere dormant centre of the need
For bare existence, of the will to be:
If this is hardness, O forgive it me!

Pardon the faith that will not be denied,
One with my life, and needing not a name,
That like these wings over the freezing tide
Beats upward, and not knowing whence it came
Battles with hunger, anguish, and the sea:
If this be impious, forgive it me!

When Finland fell later on March 11 and 12, Pitter is less resilient, writing in a journal: "Meat rationing starts. Bought none. 1d allowed per coupon if you carry away your own meat. Bus cond[uctor] said solemnly they see more strange things in 1 day than we in a lifetime. . . . Finland surrenders. Felt all day as if stuffed with arid smoking rags. Made [cake] for K's birthday tomorrow with 2 hearts on it—but my own heart is very heavy."[24] Deane and Forester also suffered due to a lack of supplies and workers as one after another was called away to war work. Given the dangerous conditions in London due to the steadily increasing German bombing, Pitter took every occasion to retreat to Essex and Oak Cottage. She writes Herbert Palmer: "I am always fairly happy here with my mother. There is any amount of work to do in the garden, but in the country I become a peasant, working and dreaming, not thinking or writing, so I do rather run to waste. . . . The Gerries are buzzing around and the bombs dropping as I write this. We had a very special one a mile away last week. What a wallop! Shook some odds and ends off this old house" (Sept. 26, 1940).

However, her letters to Cecil are very explicit about the bombings. On January 13, 1941, she tells him:

We have been dividing our time between Chelsea and Essex. The business, though much diminished, is still going—there are plenty of orders, but we are limited by law to a small fraction of our usual turnover, and this is further contracted every six months. It would be a serious matter if we had to close, as we should be quite at a loss as to what to do with our furniture and stock—we could not afford to stay here if the business had to close. However, I have been moderately happy and useful in the country, trying to make my mother's garden more productive. At both places we have had bombs very near. I was alone here one night when a big one fell on the warehouse next door. It wrecked the glass roof of the workshop here, but we were very lucky that it was no worse. The warehouse has been condemned as unsafe, and we have no neighbours on either side. In the country, every house in the village has been damaged, one wrecked, yet not a soul was hurt. On Sunday we went for a drive to see some of the city damage. It is heartrending—the frightful mess alone gives one a horrible feeling. To see St. Clement Danes a shell, All Hallows (by the Tower) a heap of rubble, and whole acres of ruin where familiar buildings stood, makes one conscious that for better or worse this is the end of an epoch. And yet there is the sense of opportunity with it. There is nothing lost which cannot be bettered in the future. Of the loss of life I do not speak: the only response, I think, is not to fear or grudge the loss of one's own life should it be required. Nothing can be withheld when there is tyranny to be resisted.

Again, reflecting the general tenor of the British public, Pitter doggedly refused to be done in by the constant bombings and unsettling conditions. At the same time, there is no question her poetic output was compromised by such tension. Unable to find time alone free of war concerns, she was writing fewer serious poems, although she found some relief in writing comic pieces partially inspired by her visits to Essex. In the same letter to Cecil, she confides: "I do not write much, and don't much like the little I do. My calm is intact, but there is no felicity—there has to be some felicity to enable one to write poetry."[25]

Pitter, ever fortunate in literary mentors, had Cecil to thank for introducing her to the books of a writer who would come to play a unique role in her life as admirer, friend, and supporter: C. S. Lewis. On February 1 Cecil writes Pitter: "I shared [your poetry] with C. S. Lewis the teacher of literature at Magdalen here & a very remarkable man—he wrote a book on medieval romance called The Allegory of Love, which is a superb piece of vital, vivid criticism—& he was deeply struck & went off to buy your poems." In a lengthy letter Pitter replies: "I am much interested and honoured by what you tell me of C. S. Lewis. I shall indeed like to have his [*The Allegory of Love*]" (April 16, 1941). She also takes the opportunity to express to Cecil her regret at not having a university education: "Now that I am no longer young, I see the misfortune of having had no University life. Except for the good offices of friends like yourself, one is cut off from and unconnected with the general body of thought and feeling on one's subject, and indeed on all academic subjects—one is a mere cell of literature floating in a sea of dissimilar organisms."

Yet another matter taking time away from poetry was the failing health of her mother. Pitter shares in the same letter that she and O'Hara "are both worried and perplexed about our mothers—old, sick people do find life tragic now, their habits broken up, and the old life shattered, and no power of readjustment." She also reveals how the demands placed upon her by the war have revealed qualities in her she had not previously appreciated:

> I don't know how long we can carry on here—it depends on the Govt. policy with regard to home trade—we can but be stoical and take our quietus if and when it comes. My "bit" consists of furious work in my mother's garden whenever I can get at it. I don't know what I'm made of (except that I'm quite sure it's not sugar and spice, as some have told me) but I do marvel at being able to do heavy work, such as digging, for twelve or fourteen hours a day, and for days at a time. Of course I have always been accustomed to a certain amount of hard labour, but I do think it is nice to be so terrific. This week I have had a harder job even than digging—tearing out the suckers that fruit-trees will throw up. You have to rend them out bodily—cutting makes them more vigorous.

Yet again, as in her early days in Hainault Forest, Pitter confesses that she draws strength from living in close contact with the natural world: "But I am always entirely at peace on the soil. It is one of the beauties of a late spring to see everything bound forward when the weather improves, as it has this week. One day—nothing much except the low-growing spring flowers—then suddenly the trees blossom, and the butterflies (I saw peacock, brimstone, tortoiseshell, and fritillary) come out of their beds, many [get] in the house, and have to be rescued and let out." When she tells Cecil about how her gardening in Essex has led to another volume of comic verse, *The Rude Potato*, she is somewhat apologetic: "I have a little book of simple verses about gardening almost ready, but I am not happy about it, as there are coarse bits, and when you are not sure that the coarse bits are funny enough, it is rather harrowing."[26] She continues: "I have already a major schism in my public, which is too small to be split. There is a sacred public for my serious verses, and a profane one for the satirical, and they seem unconnected, except in America. If I print this lot I may have a silly public. I had a very small one of this kind a long time ago, when I used to write about fairies and what not, and they were indeed sloppy."

Still in this same letter, Pitter reflects on how the war intensifies interpersonal conflicts:

> Recently I have been thinking a good deal about the peculiar isolation and antagonism one finds in so many people. They can't get on with others. Perhaps this has not actually increased of late, only become more evident owing to the war. Of course the evacuation troubles are the best-known example, but it is so common in family relationships too. It chills and sickens one so. No doubt when people are desperately worried (and perhaps afraid) it makes them misanthropic, but it could not do so if they had a shred of religion to hang on to. It does seem that the more wretched people become, the less they rely on this support. And then, too, knowing that their troubles are very real, and that oneself is perhaps so much more fortunate than they, one cannot preach to them: they would say, no doubt justly, "wait until you have as much to put up with as I have—you'd soon feel the same." It would be very like exhorting the extremely poor to resignation—a mean thing unless one is very poor oneself. No, cheerfulness and resignation under misery are lovely to see, but one cannot demand them. So often it is really health that is wanting—for most of us, strength of mind largely depends on that. But how to help them?

Almost certainly this is a veiled allusion to her mother, but it also offers insight into the general ill humor infecting many with whom Pitter had to live, work, and interact during this time.

By the summer of 1941, Deane and Forester existed only in name. While Pitter and O'Hara continued the business on their own, they had no employees, and supplies were difficult to secure. Still with the same tenacity with which they began the business a dozen years before, they held on, determined to produce enough to make ends meet and survive the war. Furthermore, because of the bombings, Pitter was spending more and more time in Essex. She writes David Cecil on July 17: "I do feel that we (the country, I mean) have got along better so far than might have been hoped, and we must lift up hearts and face the rest of the road with a determination equal to what we have shown hitherto. At least there is not the formless horror we felt before we had been under fire." Having heard of Rachel Cecil's pregnancy with her second child, Pitter offers delighted congratulations. In addition, she responds to David Cecil's musing in his recent letter regarding whether one is really doing enough to help the war effort:

It is natural, I suppose, to be exercised in one's mind as to whether one is doing what one ought. There must be many who, like ourselves, have wondered, and explored possibilities, only to conclude that if we are needed elsewhere we shall no doubt get the necessary orders. When France fell I [marched] to the nearest Labour Exchange and offered myself in any capacity, only to be told that it would be better to keep off the books unless I needed a job, as many of similar age, etc., were unemployed. They would not put me on the National Register at all—no special qualifications. I can't afford to do voluntary full time work, and if I stick to my present occupations at all there's no time for part time voluntary work. So I work at growing food as often and as hard as possible, put out any fire bombs I can get at, and try to be a Stable Element.

While this letter reveals Pitter's resolve and resilience, it is even more telling in its lengthy description of a recent series of bombings in London:

The last three raids in London were not nice to be in. That of April 16 (I believe I wrote to you during its early stages) was not so bad, because we had a lot of action in the immediate neighbourhood and had to get busy.[27] But the one three days afterwards was horrid. I had a bad reaction by then, and there was nothing quite close, so I sat in the cellar and had the horrors. The May one, when the House of Commons was hit, seemed very bad here: though there was nothing close by, they must have been using very heavy stuff, for the earth seemed convulsed. I don't like to think my nerve is going, after living through so much. . . . The poor old Church! There is only a fragment left, but that fragment does contain the finest tomb of all. Sir H. Sloane's monument at the SE corner of the site is also perfectly intact. I think this was a man so fortunate that his good luck even extends thus far, when nearly all else on the spot is blasted to powder. We picked up sundry old bones, fallen out of the walls, no doubt. How little the possessors could have imagined this disaster to their relics! One poor gentleman, tolerably complete, was put into a dustbin. . . . My niece, who is doing orthopedics, said he must have waddled in his gait, and gave the reasons. Most strange, to see a blooming girl of 18 standing among the shattered tombs with an old thighbone in her hand, calmly discoursing upon it: and yet with reverence and regret too.

Pitter's detailed description of how the recent bombing had devastated her local church and her somewhat wry comment about her niece provide an intimate look at wartime London.

Pitter did enjoy the occasional invitation to read her verse. Although her view of some of the poetry groups was jaundiced, the opportunity to read was irresistible.[28] Moreover, her poems were appearing more and more frequently in collections and anthologies. Any delight she received from such recognition was tempered by the news that her mother died on October 7. While Pitter was a devoted daughter, Louisa's last years had been full of pain and suffering, so her death was a release and blessing. Pitter wrote Herbert Palmer: "My mother died in October, but we could not grieve much, her life had been a burden for so long."[29] Then she adds: "The business, I am afraid, is quietly expiring for want of stock and labour, though orders are very plentiful. Maybe I'll be called up. I don't know." Palmer, still angry with the world, had written Pitter complaining about his most recent imagined slights. As she had done before, Pitter chided him:

> Haven't defenseless old maids, with their living to get, enough to bear in these times, but you must rise in their path shrieking woe and execration and damning yourself like a fiend, you selfish old incubus? The worst of it is I know your pains are genuine: if it were a pose I wouldn't answer. But how hellish to get stuck for life in these adolescent quagmires! To have learned no cunning to circumvent them! To go about emptying your psychological dustbin on our various heads without a pang of compunction! I feel for you right through my (thank God) thick hide: but do pray try to feel for the rest of us. Not one of the things you complain of (save the ill-health which may be the cause of all) ought to disturb a poet. If you do your best, and I think you do, let others do their worst, be still, and leave it all to Heaven. . . . Don't take my cursing in a bad spirit, but do take it to heart. The key of Giant Despair's castle is in thine own bosom: why liest thou in that stinking dungeon? (Dec. 9)

In the same letter she tells him that her *The Rude Potato* had been published by Cresset in October: "It is a mere potboiler, but on the rumour of its being a bit risqué it subscribed 2,000 before publication." Nine days later she adds: "The new book sells because it has some coarseness and because it is about *gardening*. Think what a vast public this appeals to."

The Rude Potato

The Rude Potato is an anomaly in more ways than one. First, unlike the poems that comprise her other volumes, few of the poems appear in her manuscript notebooks, suggesting that she worked on these poems separately and relatively quickly. Second, and following from the first, none appeared in print prior to the volume itself, which appeared in October 1941. Third, it is her only volume that is illustrated, and the ink drawings by Roger Furse add to the comic tone since the majority of them are cartoon-like portrayals of characters in the poems. Finally, unlike *A Mad Lady's Garland*, which relies primarily on satire, *The Rude Potato* is broadly comic; rather than making fun of human behavior as she does in *A Mad Lady's Garland*, in *The Rude Potato* Pitter indulges her love of gardening—soil, compost, tools, plants (both good and bad), pests, weather— and the simple satisfactions of working the earth and growing nice things. Yet several of the poems move beyond the merely comic and offer brief reflections on the human condition.

"Cider in the Potting Shed" concerns a gardener who, during a rainstorm, relaxes inside and enjoys a tankard of cider and a bit of bread and cheese with another gardener. He is content sitting on a "heap of mould," and the other on a "pile of sand." As a wise gardener, he delights in the rain and takes advantage of the respite to "look at the bloomy Apple-trees" and "the rainbow . . . above the wood," and to hear "near and far, in solitude, / The Maytime cuckoos call."[30] Although Pitter's father, George, had been dead fifteen years, it is not hard to imagine that he served as the inspiration for this contented gardener. This peaceful reverie is then followed by the title piece, "The Rude Potato," a brisk jingle in rhyming tetrameters of a gigantic, crudely shaped primitive potato that, according to Jimmy Burr, one of the characters in the poem, "was the rudest he had met." Yet the deformed spud works its own magic: "Its shamelessness was quite complete, / Warming the honest gardener's heart / By asking no least touch of art, / Which nearly all such gems require / To make them apt to our desire" (3–5). The magic continues, for when others see the huge tuber, they burst into laughter, and when Jimmy takes it to the local pub, the Rose and the Crown, the landlord buys the potato, hangs it high on the wall as an attraction, and sells more ale as a result. Perhaps with tongue in cheek, Pitter ends the poem:

O Science! can you make us mirth
Like this dull apple of the earth?
And what in art can do us good
Like this, so nourishing, so lewd?
Only by life such joy is lent,
Wild, bracing, and inconsequent.

The felicitous tone of these two poems demonstrates the influence of Pitter's lifelong love of gardening as well as the weekend retreats to Oak Cottage; if the horrors of war were the workaday reality of Chelsea, the withdrawals were the longed-for earthy reality of Essex.

"Gardeners All," "The Diehards," and "Other People's Glasshouses" picture different kinds of gardeners as well as the different ways greenhouses are stocked; given Pitter's penchant for her mother's grapevines, it is not surprising that she lingers longest at the vines in the greenhouse: "Ah sacred sight, the grand symbolic Plant, / Assuaging many a deep-felt human want / Filling the eye with beauty, and the mind / With old associations deep and kind" (29–35). But it is not just the mind that is nourished by the vine: "Which for the body's use / Distils that peerless and poetic juice, / So evident a blessing from above, / Whoso rejects it, him I cannot love." Her tastes are so refined that she passes by the Black Hamburg, the Colmar, the Canon Hall, and the Tokay, for her eye and palate have only one desire: "Take the whole garden, friend, but leave me this, / The Alexandrian Muscat, plant of bliss, / With long and taper bunches hanging down / . . . Whose savour reconciles the glee of youth / With the grave mellowness of heavenly truth." Indeed, when she tastes this grape "perception seems to be / Translated into purest poetry, / My griefs transfigured to supernal gold, / At once by nature and by art consoled."

The two funniest poems achieve at least part of their affect from Pitter's use of Cockney. Even though she was born in the East End, Pitter eschews a facile employment of Cockney in her earliest verse. However, it is perfect for "The Weed," the saga of a mother weed who struggled to survive and raise her children. Written from the perspective of a daughter weed that is about to be pulled up, the poem's humor is rich: "Don't pull me up! I got to live, / The same as what you got to do, / And uman people never give / A thought to what a weed goes through—/ Unted and acked and oed to death" (17–23). She protests further, saying she's not a "thievin scum," but only following the example of her mother, who told her to grow deep roots: "She ad er roots all right, ad Ma, / As Tom the gardener's boy could tell; / E said they reached Australia, / And sometimes that they went to—well, / E'd lug the tops off poor old Mum, / But in a fortnight up she'd come." The daughter chronicles what a good "mum" she had—how her mum trained her to grow next to "some borjwar" (bourgeois) plant so she would not be easily detected; how she urged the ants, wireworms, capsid bugs, and slugs to attack the plants the "silly people love to grow"; and how she stretched her roots to steal all the manure. But the day of reckoning finally comes when Tom "fetched a fork with orrid prongs" and "said e'd ave our mother's blood":

Jab went the fork—it turned me bad,
E stuck it in so far below

Poor mum—a gruntin from the lad
I eard—I eard er taproot go!
Er roots laid naked in the sun!
E'd got the lot—poor Ma was done.

In her dying words, however, she urges her child to carry on: "You'll be alive when I am dead, / So don't you go and grieve for me! / Take all the umus you can get! / Suckers and seeds, we'll beat em yet!" Yet as the daughter weed gets caught up in her mother's propaganda, believing that "the weeds will win! / We'll get the ole world for our own!" the poem returns to its opening: "Ave you the eart to kill me now, / After my touchin story? . . . OW!!!"

The second Cockney poem is "Rhubarb Pie (or the Rival Pastrycooks)," a delightfully comic commentary on the fickleness of children and the vanity of cooks. When a mother has to run into London one day, she arranges for her neighbor to give lunch to her five children: "She's always very kind to me. / So she agreed like, quite content" (43–44). Returning home later that evening, the mother asks for a report: "And when I got back, pretty late, / I said to my twin girls, what's eight / 'Now Dawn and Eve,' I said, 'come on, / And tell me all you been and done. / I hope that you were very good, / And nicely-mannered with your food.'" Of course the mother assumes her neighbor was not able to cook anything to please her children: "I'm certain sure that Mrs. Price / Took pains to cook you something nice; / Not like your own mum, but she'd try." But the mother is shocked to learn her kids had "chop toad and roobub pie," since they had always hated rhubarb in the past. However, she is even more surprised when her girls tell her: "But Mum . . . we ate a lot! / It was so nice, and fresh, and hot! / We said to Mrs. Price, O my / This is a lovely Roobub Pie!" Believing her children's tastes have changed, the mother decides to make a few rhubarb pies herself for the next week, but when she serves the pie, she is sadly disappointed: "D'you think they'd touch it? Oh dear no! / They sat the whole five in a row; / They sat and looked me in the eye. / They said, 'We don't like Roobub Pie!!!' / And goodness knows the reason why!" The Cockney slang adds to the humor as we realize that the children probably do not like their mother's rhubarb pie because her pastry is not as tasty as Mrs. Price's. The mother fails to see this, believing instead their refusal of her pie is simply childish fickleness.

"The Morals of Pruning" is not comic; in fact, it is a sober metaphorical look at pruning as a commentary on human life: "When I, who stand as fate to this strong Vine, / Take up the steel, and the devoted shoot, / Not for its own felicity, but mine, / Eye sternly, and determined that the fruit is to be here and thus, so much, no more—/ I think of miseries that men deplore" (51). As humankind has its hopes curtailed like the cluster of grapes she clips off, as human life is interrupted like the stem she nips, and as human certainty withers like the branches she throws on the fire, she considers: "Such surgery / Life does upon my fellows, and on me." However, the poem's moral is stated less as a certainty and more as a hope, recalling something of the tone of *The Spirit Watches:*

> If we could think our pain but part designed
> By some such purpose as evokes this great
> Delicious cluster, where we else should find
> All wasteful and all trivial, then our fate
> Might be absolved, and we more calmly grow;
> At least they cannot prove it is not so.

Pitter's view here is clearly more hopeful than Thomas Hardy's in his poem "Hap."[31] Indeed, it may echo faintly John 15:1–2: "I am the true vine, and my Father is the husbandman. Every branch in me that beareth not fruit he taketh away: and every branch that beareth fruit, he purgeth it, that it may bring forth more fruit." The longing for purpose and meaning in the midst of wartime England, while not perhaps expected among the otherwise-comic poems of *The Rude Potato*, illustrates the pervading seriousness of life that Pitter and others were experiencing during the early days of the war.

The final poem, "For Us All," continues in the same serious vein. Here the comparison is between spring and human renewal. Unlike what we might anticipate, however, this is not a poem about the warmth of spring: "It is the spring of the year and a cold morning. / It is a late spring too, and nothing wakes / Save the first primrose, hugging the moss she was born in, / And the pink-studded branch that the wind shakes, / Wafting the delicate colour down in flakes" (55). Instead, this poem employs the idea of the hardy primrose thrusting its petals into the cold spring as an exemplar for human hope: "It is the spring of our time, the time for dying, / If hope is too heavy to lift and you cannot find / Strength to endure the east, see the petal flying, / To weather the last weeks and the most unkind / Of the whole winter, living upon the mind." If the primrose can survive the final cold blast of the late spring, so can the human spirit if it will insist on looking for hope and turn its back on despair. The poem concludes with a stoicism most British: "Side by side with the old joy and the old sorrow / We bear the unheard-of hope and the new pain. / Like winter wheat under the iron harrow / We grasp the soil and await the April rain; / Toil and endurance shall earn the harvest again." Stiffen oneself, buck up against the odds, and endure, for that is all one can do, and the primrose is nature's signal to man that this is the surest way to survive.

The sober ending to *The Rude Potato* is significant because it demonstrates that Pitter's primary voice is not comic but serious. While Pitter enjoyed writing comic pieces, they should be seen as diversions, not as her central concern.

They also reveal that Pitter did not take herself too seriously, particularly as she aged. Angst, melancholy, worry, and fear would always be a part of her personality, heightened, no doubt, by the war. Yet Pitter was not one given to despair in spite of the very real challenges she would face in the next four years. In fact, she does reach her lowest emotional, spiritual, and psychological point as the war reaches it crisis point, matters we explore in the next chapter.

FIVE

Crossing Over,

1942–1946

The new year brought with it more hard work, little leisure, continued ration-ing, nightly bombings, and general malaise. Pitter and O'Hara found their busi-ness reduced to what the two of them could produce and market, and given the short supply of materials, they were uncertain how long they could continue. While neither was particularly fitted for war work, both knew it was only a mat-ter of time before they would be required to engage in labor that would help in the defense of Britain. Pitter was physically stronger, but O'Hara was mentally stronger, so as their business neared collapse, Pitter grew increasingly depressed. She had poured so much time, energy, and labor into Deane and Forester that she could hardly bear giving it up and losing her independence; indeed, the fact that she and O'Hara had been able to make a go of the business, in spite of the toll upon Pitter's creative output, had been an invigorating and satisfying validation. In addition, the unsettling war news, the real question of whether or not the Allies would prevail, and the uncertainty over the future further contributed to Pitter's sinking feelings.

Yet she did find solace in her friends and continued to write Herbert Palmer, revealing her increasing distress with the state of English poetry. Writing about their mutual friend John Gawsworth, she says:

You know although [he] vituperates the [T. S.] Eliot school, both in title and matter he now tends strongly to imitate them; not by any means to the detriment of his work, but it does reduce a man's importance, as well as reflecting on his sincerity, when he follows a mob while cursing it. Has he got poetry in him, or is he a vain little opportunist pretending to po-etry? It is odd that so lean and bitter a trade should attract hypocrites, but it does; and when J. overdoes the trappings—I mean booze, love-affairs, insolvency, duns, enemies, etc.—I ask myself whether he is a poet or just another Grub St. grub. It is certain that his later work is less bad, however, and while there is development we must not entirely condemn. Probably also I should be the last person to see his merits, tending as I do in such different directions. (Jan. 4, 1942)

Given Pitter's love of traditional English verse, it is not surprising she disliked the modernist movement represented by Eliot and its influence on writers such as Gawsworth. While she misjudged the genuine literary and poetic merit of Eliot, she did believe he was a gifted poet; nonetheless, Pitter became increasingly willing to voice her discomfort with what she believed was the wrong path of modern English poetry.

She also continued her correspondence with David Cecil, to whom she revealed both her fears and hopes. About the inevitable failure of Deane and Forester, she writes on July 13: "We are still here, but perhaps not for much longer; a forthcoming Order may finally quench what trade there still is, and I must register [for war work] in the autumn. It is hard, when we have struggled on through the blitz and all the difficulties. . . . I am striving for two things—resignation to events, and some idea of what it would be best to attempt." In commenting on *The Rude Potato*, she is apologetic, claiming that she only wanted to see if she could write a book of popular verse; that it was modestly successful was a real concern to her American publisher: "Macmillans of N.Y. were simply horrified at it, refused to print it themselves, and earnestly begged that as I valued my reputation I would not try to get it published at all over there. They called it a great many names, ending with *island British*, an insult which is easy to bear. Of course they don't like my cutting such capers when they have striven to represent me as a dedicated spirit."[1]

Her great love of gardening, the impetus that led to the poems in *The Rude Potato*, is also clearly expressed in the same letter:

You ask if I have ever been a full-time gardener—no, but I could and would be nothing else if free to do so; I am sure I have the strength and skill enough; only I think I should subside into a vegetable peace almost without individuality; I should be happy, but it might not be right. My present habit of spending about 3 days out of 14 wholly in cultivating food suits the mind very well. Sometimes that may mean 40 hours digging! I will not deny that this capacity has produced tempting offers, notably from Lockley, the bird man in Pembrokeshire; he wanted me to go and do the vegetables for a co-operative farm there, and I was sorely tempted; but I really can't desert K. O'Hara after all these years. A farm life would be impossible to her. . . . Never mind, I have learned and am learning no end about the subject, and shall hope for more opportunities of using it.

It would be another eleven years before Pitter retired to the country so that she could fully indulge her gardening passion.

In the letter Pitter goes on to reveal her struggles with writing poetry as well as her continuing interest in C. S. Lewis: "Although there is little [time] to get, I find time absolutely crammed with jobs of a bothering nature, and don't write much. This isn't a real excuse; the actual reason for not writing is that I am a miserable sinner devoured by *acedia*. However harassed the life, the creative gift can be exercised if we are in a decent state of mind, and this ought not to be perpetually subject to the state of the world." Then she adds: "The few things I have done [probably poems later appearing in *The Bridge*] are not unsatisfactory, leaving out of account some pretty awful doggerel about cats. Do you know, cats are as hard to write about well as to draw well?" Yet she continued to work on the cat poems, culminating in the publication of *On Cats* in 1946. Regarding C. S. Lewis, she tells Cecil she has read *The Screwtape Letters:* "I found the book which has excited me more than anything has done for a long time—'The Screwtape Letters.' . . . I do hope you have read it. He must be a phoenix; it says in the book that he is a Fellow, I forget of which college, but am nearly sure it is an Oxford one, so very likely you know him. I have actually bought the book."[2] Cecil, eager to foster a relationship between Pitter and Lewis, responds: "Did I tell you C. S. Lewis of Magdalen College is far the most brilliant English Literature man in Oxford, admired your work so earnestly when I showed him. His own poetry is fine I think. . . . I would like to know what you thought of it" (Aug. ? 1942).

In the autumn Pitter ran into George Orwell, and she was shocked to find him in very poor health. She shared a meal with him and his wife, Eileen O'Shaughnessy; this was the last time she saw him, as he would die in 1950. Her memory of this evening is worth quoting in full:

> I had met [O'Shaughnessy] at the BBC, where he also was working, and she'd asked me to supper. They were living in a damp basement flat. She was worried about the rent—£100 a year—which she said they couldn't afford. He was known as a writer now, but not to the extent of getting much out of it. Eileen was a small slender woman with nice clear Irish features and rather curly dark hair. She told me about his recent illness—she had not realized what a sick man he was, and a sudden severe hemorrhage had terrified her. The last straw was that when he had been got off to hospital she looked for the cat to hold in her arms for a little consolation, but it had disappeared, and she never saw it again. Eileen had been through a bad time, and was soon to die herself; she didn't have much of a share in Orwell's brief time of success and prosperity. When he was wounded so badly in the Spanish war, she actually managed to get out there to nurse him. She took a job in Madrid and, I suppose, earned some sort of living, for both of them.

While we were talking, and working away at cooking supper (I remember part of it was apple-pie, and she was nervously anxious not to leave a scrap of core in the apples, as she said he disliked it so)—we were working and talking, Orwell came in. Like a ghost. No doubt he was showing the effects of his recent illness, and of course he did live another 7 or 8 years, but I thought then that he must be dying. The emaciation, the waxen pallor, the slow, careful movements, all shocked and distressed me. But he seemed cheerful, fetched some beer, and sent out again to see if his mother would come in—she was living close by. I had brought with me two things impossible to buy in London at that time—a good bunch of grapes from my mother's home in Essex, and a red rose—two rare treasures. I can see him now, holding up the grapes with a smile of admiration and delight on his ravaged face, and then, cupping the rose in his wasted hands, breathing in the scent with a kind of reverent joy.

That is the last vivid image I have of him. After that evening I never saw him again—I never knew him as the immensely successful author he became. How he did adore life! His nature was divided. There was something like a high wall right across the middle of it. A high wall with flowers and fruit and running water on one side, and the desert on the other. I think he was much more fastidious and conventional than one might think from his work—more than he knew himself. Not liking any core left in the apple-pie, for instance; and do you remember in "Down and Out in Paris and London" how he threw away the milk which was the only food he had, simply because a bed-bug had fallen into it? Too fastidious for a starving man. And his anger at the idea of letting a woman pay—that was very conventional.[3]

Pitter's relationship with Orwell was very much hit or miss, but it was something she treasured all her life, reflecting many times later on how fortunate she was to have known and been friends with him.

However, she had little time to worry about Orwell since Deane and Forester was no more, and she was forced to turn to war work. One of her first efforts was a foray into troop education, as she was asked to read her poetry and offer lectures to soldiers stationed nearby. She writes to Herbert Palmer: "Our business is virtually at an end—a new B[oard] of Trade order makes most fancy goods illegal. I am supposed to be starting a little Army Education job next month. . . . I have prepared a reading-talk on the Ballads, and one on 'The Ancient Mariner,' and am now stuck for ideas, which must of course be of primitive simplicity" (Nov. 11). Eventually she gave five lectures and had several more prepared, but the troops were called up before she could deliver them. She tells Palmer: "I think I've been put on the Army Education panel of lecturers, but I

imagine no one will want me, as this Poetry for Troops stunt was a wild experiment on the part of a very go-ahead officer. I'm to go for interview, too, in a
few days (National Service) so perhaps everything will have to go now" (Dec.
5). One bright note during this period was Pitter's blossoming relationship with
the BBC. Winifred Holmes, BBC talks producer, wrote Pitter on November 19.
The two eventually met on December 7, and Pitter agreed to try writing a radio
script. On December 22 she writes Holmes: "Here is the effort. I have tried, but
have been bothered so much lately that I'm not very sanguine. But it has done
me good to have a shot, and cheered me no end to have been asked." This was
the start of an important professional relationship between Pitter and the BBC
that would lead to many later appearances on both BBC radio and television. In
fact, she began receiving small royalty checks from the BBC, as her poems were
now being occasionally read over the air.

Despite this bit of unexpected good fortune, the beginning of 1943 marked a
very dark time for Pitter. In mid-January both Pitter and O'Hara went to work
in Morgen's Crucible Factory, a wartime munitions plant located across the
Battersea Bridge and within walking distance of their flat. Physically removed
from Chelsea every day, and brought to work in a situation antithetical to her
artistic temperament, Pitter suffered new emotional lows. She writes David Cecil: "You time your letters with a blest if unconscious precision. They always
arrive to rescue me when I am at the lowest ebb. We have had a rather bad time
since January; indeed we have both been working in a factory since the middle
of that month. The people are very good to us, and as jobs go the work (in the
office) is not too bad, yet one's own life is quite gone, and then having to leave
one's home to go to rack & ruin is terribly depressing to females" (March 17,
1943). Compounding this had been the death in action of a favorite nephew
of O'Hara's who had served in the RAF and had often visited the two women
in Chelsea. This bad news was another severe blow to Pitter's already-flagging
spirits: "There is always a chapter of smaller misfortunes too at a time like this,
to make one feel completely forlorn—and all the time I know I'm a humbug
and my troubles are nearly all due to original sin and that doesn't help one to
a better frame of mind. Ah well, God help us all, but I was glad to get your letter." While she thanks Cecil for his comments on one of her recent poems and
relates that she manages to travel to Oak Cottage for a few hours each weekend,
it is clear she is deeply depressed. To another friend she writes: "Now we are
both working in the offices of the big factory just over the river. It is practically
impossible to write; one is never alone and there is no spare time. I cannot say
we are very happy, but we are trying to do what we can" (June 1).

Working in the munitions factory meant long, hard days. She tells Cecil: "I
should love to see you if you are to be in town soon, but I don't know how it
can be managed unless you would be so kind as to call after dinner. The fac-

tory hours are so long. We are in by about 6.15, should you wish to telephone, but away on Saturdays. Life is one continual effort—an effort that is never sufficient, but I know well enough that I've no real cause for complaint. I get dozens of ideas, but not a chance to work them out" (Aug. 23). She tells Herbert Palmer, "I write a bit, about the average for me, and go to my country home for a few hours each weekend. Have struck up an acquaintance with D[orothy] Wellesley[4] who is very interesting about Yeats in particular & life & poetry in general. She demands a degree of genuineness in life & letters that scares me, hypocrite as I am" (Dec. 29). She is also candid about her sagging spirits: "We got this job before the M[inistry] of L[abour] thought out any worse one. We work in the offices—very dirty place and long hours & work not exactly inspiring: people very decent, as they mostly are. It is pretty hard for my partner, who isn't exactly young. Of course she isn't forced to work except by economic necessity. Our income is under ¼ what we are used to, and the feeling of compulsion is (to me) sickening and enraging. Also I am becoming rheumatic, and the pain makes me savage." Her unpublished poem "Autumn 1944" reflects the general tenor of war malaise that gripped Pitter during this time:

Now the earth is assuaged and the lawn lies dewy all day,
And work is lightened, as it has need to be;
For the sixth winter finds us fewer and feebler,
Older and sadder; all of us now old soldiers
Familiar with death and privation; strangers to liberty
For a large part of our lives; and we are weary.

Autumn in England, after an unkind summer;
And I with these last few flowers, these small carnations
Held in my hand; more real than the vast victories
Whose pulse we can hear across the narrow waters
As we heard it before, long ago, when we were young.
Weary of thought, I hold them for consolation;
The colours like flame without heat, like innocent blood.

I lament the innocent blood; weary and guilty
Lament the innocent blood that is shed for me;
Mourn the young dead I knew, and the young living
Think of with anguish as though they were my children:
Though childless I know this not, the heart of anguish,
For thus to the solitary the woe is tempered;
Lacking the joy, theirs not the sword in the bowels.

But the childless were children, and we can say to the mothers
That we know the kindness; because we can remember
That first breast faithful, we to their present anguish
Bring the sweet barren flower, and lay it by them.

The poignancy of this poem—with its admission of war weariness, its linking of
the current war with World War I, its focus on the concrete reality of the few
carnations she holds in her hands, and its offering of flowers to the mothers who
have lost their children in the defense of England—is compellingly tender and
reveals how deeply Pitter feels the sacrifices of others; she knows that her own
war privations are little compared with those of families who have given all.

Yet as she neared complete despair, unsolicited hope came from an unlikely
source: depressed after a hard day's work in the factory, she heard the BBC radio
broadcasts of C. S. Lewis, later published as *Mere Christianity*.[5] She recalls:

There were air raids at night. The factory was dark and dirty. And I remember thinking—well—I must find somebody or something because
like this I cannot go on. I stopped in the middle of Battersea Bridge one
dreadful March[6] night when it was cold, and the wind was howling over
the bridge, and it was as dark as the pit, and I stood and leaned against
the parapet and thought—like this I *cannot* go on. And it didn't come to
me at once but some time afterwards I heard the broadcast talks of C. S.
Lewis, and I at once grappled them to my soul, as Shakespeare says. And
I used to assemble the family to hear because I thought that they were so
good that even from the point of view of enjoyment people shouldn't miss
them, and I got every word of his that I could, and I could see by hard
argument there was only the one way for it. I had to be intellectually satisfied as well as emotionally because at that time of life one doesn't just fall
into it in adolescent emotion, and I was satisfied at every point that it was
the one way and the hard way to do things.[7]

The site of this spiritual crisis later becomes the focus of the title poem of *The
Bridge*, and while Pitter's conversion to Christianity was several years away, hearing Lewis on the radio was a critical step down the path to Christian faith.

Although Lewis's broadcasts help to cheer her "dark night" of the soul, it is
hard to calculate the extent of emotional damage Pitter experienced working
in the factory. On April 3, 1945, she writes Cecil: "I'm still working in the Dark
Satanic Mill, and getting very tired now, like everybody else; it's an awful thing
to hate figures & yet be fairly good at them—and the manpower situation gets
steadily worse, which means that the pressure steadily increases: but we're all in

the same boat." Yet the best possible news came on May 8 when VE day (Victory in Europe) was declared and six years of war in Europe came to an end. For Pitter this meant she could look forward to ceasing her factory work. To Herbert Palmer she confides: "I am still at the ghastly factory, but hope to be free (free to starve) by the end of August; but as the time approaches, I feel very depressed at the idea of leaving the people, whom I love dearly, and think they like me. However, it would be silly to stick there, as I don't earn enough to keep me, and the work is beastly; can you imagine a poet balancing the filthy insurance stamps with deductions from the stinking payroll? That's what I have to do, about £500 worth a week" (June 19).

Later in life she remembered these as very dark days indeed, yet as she intimated to Palmer, she also came to love the people in the factory. She tells Hilary Smith: "It was very distressing to lose one's business. One had sweated blood to build up and it was a very successful little business too, but I wouldn't have missed that factory for the world because it was a new world to me. [The isolation and loneliness of the factory was very real] but it was very fertile you know."[8] She tells John Wain: "I remember very well the great factory I worked during the war, some five thousand people, and the wonder it was to me to see the beauty and indeed the moral beauty of many of the people, working in this old industrial population, all their lives, and in dirty surroundings. And there was one most beautiful young woman whom I saw but never, I think, spoke to, who was afterwards killed in the blitz. . . . But humanly speaking I wouldn't have missed that factory for the world."[9] With Hallam Tennyson she recalls:

[During the blitz I worked in] Morgen's Crucible factory at Battersea, which was, of course, a very dirty factory. They made carbon brushes for electric motors and that sort of thing, and I worked in the personnel office. . . . I did one spell a week in a very dirty machine shop just to show [I was] willing. And this was really more tragic because I didn't know the ways of the work people or realize how hard their life was. And it was an old industrial population—very easy to rough them up, and I did rough them up once or twice. And I shed some bitter tears in that shop, but I learned a lot there, all the same. And in any case it was heartening to find how fundamentally good and nice these people were who had such a hard life, because I don't think any factory's a fit environment for a human being, let alone a dirty and old-fashioned one. . . . I wasn't so very far from the plebes myself. I had never been to university, [and] I had lost a little, frail business we had struggled so hard to build up. In these respects I was on a level with them, and in the dirt, and, one wouldn't say the degradation, but [given] the dearth and the strictures which we were all enduring, we were all troops together.[10]

Pitter writes Nettie Palmer on August 23, also giving a snapshot of her mixed feelings at the time:

> Can't keep on any longer—weary to the very bone, and eyesight suffering from endless figures: nothing serious, only fatigue. But the canteen meals will be sorely missed. . . . Our clothes are nobody's business, and our hous-es are beginning to be infested with various creatures, from old bomb-debris & enforced neglect. We've been driven out of 2 of our rooms by fleas: luckily they don't bite, only tickle, but it is horrid, and the authori-ties are too bankrupt of manpower to be able to help at all. People now tend to become very tough, so that one feels that no one cares whether one sinks or swims, and on the whole they'd rather one sank. It's natural, when people's whole lives are one long worry, deprivation, & debility. . . . But we won! And we are thankful to have all our legs & arms and even furniture still. We've lost our good business (no prospect of reopening yet, no labour or material) but, my word! When I think of Dunkirk and the Battle of Britain and the blitz! To have got rid of the blackout is alone a great blessing. . . . I shall hate leaving them—the general verdict on that factory is "Lousy dump! Lovely people!"

Indeed, leaving Morgen's Crucible Factory for the last time on September 15 improved Pitter's emotional state and gave her a hopeful outlook for the future. Soon she began working again on decorative furniture, this time out of the flat at 55 Old Church Street, Chelsea; however, due to the lack of materials, her earnings were meager and the likelihood of reopening Deane and Forester was remote. She tells Nettie Palmer on November 9: "Thank God, I left the factory 8 weeks ago: and do you know, much as I love them all, it cost me a real effort to go and see them: I've a kind of phobia of the place. I feel 20 years younger already." Weekends would often find Pitter and O'Hara at Oak Cot-tage or the home of Dorothy Wellesley, the Penns in the Rocks, Withyham, Sussex. Wellesley, who had been great friends with W. B. Yeats, enjoyed Pitter's company, and Pitter, for her part, felt sympathy for Wellesley and admired the natural beauty of the Penns.

The Bridge

Despite her depressed emotional state and the difficulty she encountered as she tried to write throughout the war, Pitter published *The Bridge: Poems 1939–1944* early in 1945, an introspective volume of poetry clearly influenced by her wartime experiences.[11] A review of her manuscript notebook of this period confirms that all the poems were written during the dark days of the war. Like *A Trophy of Arms* and *The Spirit Watches*, where small clusters of poems have clear thematic connections, *The Bridge* continues this pattern; in addition, this volume is characterized by recurring images and symbols, particularly water, birds, and flowers. Also Pitter does not entirely lose sight of the benign, distant God she writes about in *The Spirit Watches;* although his presence in *The Bridge* is not as pervasive as in *The Spirit Watches*, her conception of God is clearly moving in the direction of orthodox Christianity. In the few poems in which she writes about God, it is clear she is on the verge of a spiritual conversion. Also of note is that the overall melancholic tone of the poems marks it as a volume profoundly influenced by Pitter's wartime experiences; yet, characteristically, she never gives in to despair.

The title poem, "The Bridge," functions at multiple levels. On the literal level, it is a poem about her forced move from working in Chelsea to working in Battersea across the Thames; on another level it is about her forced move from the life of an artist to that of a factory worker; and on still another level it is about the conflict between the ideal and the real. The bridge in this case is Battersea Bridge, the span she had to cover twice a day, a three- or four-block walk from her flat, and the site of her spiritual crisis. The opening lines of the poem illustrate Pitter's conflicting emotions between giving in to and resisting the pull toward despair: "Where is the truth that will inform my sorrow? / I am sure myself that sorrow is not the truth. / These lovely shapes of sorrow are empty vessels / Waiting for wine: they wait to be informed."[12] Next Pitter contrasts the very different kinds of things made on either side of the river: "Men make the vessels on either side of the river; / On this the hither side the artists make them, / And there over the water the workmen make them." That is, while artists make beautiful, delicate vessels, workmen make shell canisters: "These frail, with a peacock glaze, and the others heavy, / Simple as doom, made to endure the furnace. / War shatters the peacock-jars."

Yet in spite of this ominous reality, Pitter does not look to run away; instead she says, "Let us go over. / Indeed, we have no choice but to go over." Although Pitter's letters quoted above testify to her loathing for the factory, the poem takes on metaphorical dimensions in her declaration that "we have no choice but to go over." Life demands that she go over, that she endure, that she face her worst fears; there is no shirking, no shrinking back from the inevitable: "There is always a way for those who must go over; / Always a bridge from the known to the unknown. / When from the known the mind revolts and despairs / There lies the way, and there we must go over." It matters not that she does not want to leave the artist's life—the known, the comfortable, the given. She "must go over" to bridge her fears to the unknown, the discomforting, the unpredictable. Still, this is not easy, for there are no guarantees: "O truth, is it death there over the river, / Or is it life, new life in a land of summer?" She cannot know as she moves across the bridge whether or not she will live and thrive physically, emotionally, spiritually, or poetically. Make no mistake, she affirms: going across the river is risky business.

The poem's conclusion returns to the image of the vessel, moving away from those made by artists and workmen and focusing instead upon the vessel of the mind: "The mind is an empty vessel, a shape of sorrow, / Fill it with life or death, for it is hollow, / Dark wine or bright, fill it, let us go over. / Let me go find my truth, over the river." The only way to answer the poem's opening question—"Where is the truth that will inform my sorrow?"—is to embrace the unknowable. The only way to find truth is by confronting life head on; hanging back, avoiding reality, hiding out cannot "inform [her] sorrow." Would she rather stay on her side of the bridge in Chelsea with the other artists? Probably. Would she rather not go to the factory and participate in producing its vessels, "simple as doom"? Probably so. Would she rather live in the ideal rather than the real world? Probably so. But Pitter knows retreat is no answer. The mind must be filled with something, "life or death . . . dark wine or bright," or it will despair. Finding truth, for Pitter, involves action, and so she crosses over the river, into the world of the factory, and into the frightening reality of war.

Poems about the war comprise the largest thematic grouping in *The Bridge*. The first of two poems about swans, "The Cygnet," may be Pitter's most comprehensive statement about the war (11–16). Here a young solitary swan "rocking on turbid water," yet to outgrow his gray feathers, serves as an emblem of the human spirit; just as the polluted Thames—"Water that has been fouled by wicked creatures: / Water whose loveliness dies of pollution"—defiles the body of the cygnet, so the war pollutes the human spirit. Always deeply drawn to swans, Pitter lavishes great detail on her description of the cygnet: "For male pride, in the spring, he lifts his feathers, / Grey though they be; and thus with overarching / Pinions he goes, and lays his long neck backward, / Down-pointing the fierce narrow head and livid / Bill, that now is leaden, but shall be scarlet." As he sails alone past already-mated pairs of swans, he is looking for his own mate "among the secret marshes / And from their joy regenerate his passion: / Himself a mode of these, he passes hissing, / Dark in the face of love, mourning division." The angry, immature, yet passionate and unconnected gray bird becomes a mirror of the human spirit in war-torn London.

Although the city has "gap-toothed black scribbled skylines such as madness / Might scrawl in dungeons," the cygnet reminds her that within the city there are "dark places" where "beauty is imprisoned" and where people dream "at times of happy love and childhood." As the poem telescopes down, Pitter takes us into one of these places, a bomb shelter, and we read one of her few sustained passages of what it must have felt like to live in London during the blitz:

The fiery tears are falling; red and silver,
They change and drift and wane, stars of disaster;
Gold clusters, like the sparks in burning paper,
Silently glimmer, then from haunted darkness
Leaps their long shuddering voice of formal horror:
White sheets of light flicker and flap and vanish;
The steel-blue fingers, stark, intent and rigid,
Deliberately seek their prey in heaven.

In the midst of such death and destruction, Pitter ironically finds great beauty as she highlights the brilliant red, silver, and gold colors of the bombings in the night sky. Yet "the fiery rain is falling, and the vision / Of love is lost in the funereal blackness":

I heard a music once, but it is silent,
The bellowing night derides it and devours it
With loud destruction, varying but unceasing;
Where are the harp and the pipe now, my darling,
The loved voice murmuring in the leafy shadow?
All fallen silent, and all buried with thee.

The fiery doom is falling; fear and horror
Engulf me as the wave of steel roars over:
Shuddering with terror and the cold of winter,
Empty of life and yet impaled by duty,
I tremble as the dry stalks in a meadow
Tremble in barren wind, in stark December,
Sere, sere and barren as those bones of summer;
Where is my hope, O where lies any promise?

Pitter's simile describing her emotional state in terms of dry stalks of wheat in December, "sere and barren as those bones of summer," is powerful and leads to the existential query that is similar to the opening line of "The Bridge": "Where is the truth that will inform my sorrow?"

In fact, however, the question here is only rhetorical: "And loud within life undefeated answers. / Even while the icy wind of terror rattles / In the dry brain, the thought comes quick upon me / Of seed blown from the skull-shaped pod and scattered, / Preparing a new beauty, an awakening." The key for Pitter, much in the manner she explores in "The Bridge," is the certainty that she must not give in to despair, that she must keep going, that there is a "germ of hope undying," and that it will "flower in that immortal, promised summer, / When

the sky weeps no fire, but only water." This fierce determination to continue
on is symbolized by the redemptive power of water, which assumes an almost-
sacramental dimension: "Water shall bless them, water out of heaven / Washing
from earth the stains of wicked creatures." By invoking the cleansing power of
water, Pitter pictures a baptism:

> Water in rain, water in dew at evening
> Falling through clear air, stealing through clean grasses,
> Dwelling in darkness in our mother's body,
> In secret springs welling and murmuring through her,
> Gathering in brooks and lapsing into rivers,
> Rolling magnificent down glorious tideways
> Deep for the mighty hulls, clean for the salmon,
> Pouring predestined to unfathomed ocean.

In addition to the language of baptism, Pitter's use of the theologically loaded
"predestined" underscores her belief that life's meaning is anchored on more
than just a personal commitment to going on; in fact, "The Cygnet" affirms
Pitter's faith in a benevolent, distant God, but the God she writes about now,
unlike in *The Spirit Watches*, is sounding more and more like the God of Christianity: "Restore our innocence, return with water / Bliss for the blood-guilt
of the wicked creatures, / Whose life . . . sickens / At the denial of its inmost
nature, / Loathing its vileness, longing for its pardon."

Baptism is a metaphorical and theological picture of death and resurrection;
those who go under the water have their old nature buried and are reborn as
new creatures.[13] Thus, when the inhabitants of the bomb shelters emerge, they,
too, experience a kind of rebirth, even if only short lived:

> The blear smoke crawls, the dawn glimmers, the children,
> With their wan mothers, creep from dens that hide them
> A little from their terror; they turn homeward
> To the poor dole of food allotted strictly,
> To each his portion, just and insufficient;
> To the grey day; labouring on till evening,
> Then turning blindly to the earth for harbour
> As beasts do, bolting into holes for terror.

Pitter's frank portrayal of war's crushing daily weight—the fear of incessant
bombing, the nightly scurrying into the shelters, the limited access to inadequate and unsatisfying food, and the sense that it will never end—reflects the
everyday experience of London's weary inhabitants. Yet the baptismal theme—

the notion that resurrection follows death—is highlighted in the poem's conclusion and its return to the cygnet, who is now a year older: "It is broad day; / on the polluted river, / Thick with impurity yet crowned with honour, / There sails a creature raised above pollution, / Proud and immaculate as winter ermine, / He who was last year's Cygnet; now from greyness / Wholly redeemed." With physical maturity, there is also spiritual maturity: "Anger is past with him; the hissing madness / Of unrequited passion is forgotten." For he is no longer alone, and together he and his mate find "in love the only cure of sorrow, / Abandoning themselves each to the other, / Losing the separate self, the seed of anguish." In Pitter's farewell to the mated pair, she blesses them and urges them to be "fulfilled for ever." The transformation of the gray, dingy cygnet—lonely and angry—into the white, royal swan—mated and noble—becomes a symbolic promise for Pitter and her fellows: "While we, still bound in anger and pollution, / Battle through dreary days and nights of terror / Until our spirit flowers, and we follow." "The Cygnet" tells us that Pitter's wartime experiences were frightening, debilitating, and depressing; yet the transformation of the bird holds out a hope that the human spirit will be similarly transformed if it maintains itself against despair, keeps an implicit if not overt faith in a benevolent deity, and affirms the redemptive power of love.

Another war poem, "The Sparrow's Skull," offers a similar conclusion. Subtitled "Memento Mori, Written at the Fall of France," it is a sober reflection on the "moment of death" of a sparrow that had become so familiar to the speaker that it was almost tame; moreover, the death of the sparrow is likened to the fall of France.[14] The poem's opening lines are poignant and sober: "The kingdoms fall in sequence, like the waves on the shore. / All save divine and desperate hopes go down, they are no more. / Solitary is our place, the castle in the sea, / And I muse on those I have loved, and on those who have loved me" (19). In confronting an awful reality—both her own and England's isolation—Pitter's instinctive pull is toward finding love: "I gather up my loves, and keep them all warm, / While above our heads blows the bitter storm: / The blessed natural loves, of life-supporting flame, / And those whose name is Wonder, which have no other name." One of her loves had been a fragile little sparrow, and quietly invoking the graveyard scene from Hamlet, Pitter holds up her Yorick: "The skull is in my hand, the minute cup of bone, / And I remember her, the tame, the loving one, / Who came in at the window, and seemed to have a mind / More towards sorrowful man than to those of her own kind."

Pitter's sense that this bird was more at home with humans than other birds may be more imagined than real, yet it offers her solace since it suggests that fear can be overcome: "And I will keep the skull, for in the hollow here / Lodged the minute brain that had outgrown fear: / Transcended an old terror, and found a new love, / And entered a strange life, a world it was not of." Pitter uses the skull to reflect on her own fears about the wearying effects of the war and the rushing tide of Nazism: "Even so, dread God! Even so, my Lord! / The fire is at my feet, and at my breast the sword, / And I must gather up my soul, and clap my wings, and flee / Into the heart of terror, to find myself in thee." Like the sparrow who flew toward the terror of the humans who befriended her, so Pitter resolves to fly into the terror of the Lord. While it would be wrong to call this a "fox-hole religion" poem, it must be admitted that Pitter's use of "my Lord" shows she is moving ever closer to Christianity. Urania may be a comforting notion in the face of personal doubts and inarticulate longings; Yahweh, the God of the Bible, however, is what she wants when human understanding and scheming are exposed as incomplete, ineffective, and impotent. In the midst of terror, Pitter does not want a distant albeit benevolent God; instead, she wants a real, powerful, personal deity whose intervention in human history has satisfied many human hearts.

While birds and water function as important images in "The Cygnet" and "The Sparrow's Skull," the next two war poems employ flower imagery. "Flowers in the Factory" reflects upon the incongruous appearance of beautiful, fragile, delicate flowers inside a dirty wartime factory. Perhaps with Morgen's Crucible Factory as a background, these flowers are silhouetted against the light of the smelting furnaces: "The firedew, the glow-worm light / Phosphor-radiance, molten heart, / Make a clearness in the night; / Lend these poor a little part / Of the beauty of the sun!" (57). Although some might disparage the appearance of these flowers in a place like this, Pitter knows they are a balm to those who love beauty:

> None can tell who does not know
> How such stars in beauty run
> With cold sweetness like the snow
> Through the silent, suffering mind,
> Through the grime and through the gloom,
> Like the fair, the fleeing hind
> Through the forest to her doom,
> Followed till she vanishes
> By beauty-tranced, by yearning eyes.

The intuitive power of beauty to comfort those open to its influence is sufficient argument to keep flowers in the factory. What is more, the flowers can even change human attitudes: "Give them blossoms, what you can. / What is nature in your hand / Changes in this mood of man." Although Pitter's artistic instincts are thwarted by factory work, flowers such as these nurture her aesthetic longing.

"Funeral Wreaths" goes outside the factory to consider the many flower wreaths brought there as memorials to those killed in the nightly bombings: "In the black bitter drizzle, in rain and dirt, / The wreaths are stacked in the factory entrance-yard. / People gather about them. Nobody's hurt / At the rank allusion to death" (58–59). Visitants read the cards sent with the wreaths and find "delight, and a sense of ease." Pitter wonders at this:

Is it only that flowers smell sweet, and are pretty and bright,
Or because of the senseless waste of so many pounds
Or because in that dreadful place the unwonted sight
Of a heap of blossom is balm to unconscious wounds—
The mortal wounds that benumb, not the sharp raw pains
Of the daily misery, but the fatal bleeding inside?

Whereas the flowers in "Flowers in the Factory" bring solace, here they almost mock the seriousness of wartime death, trivializing the terrible loss of life: "Here is the supernatural to be bought with the gains / Of the spectral torment. The soul can go for a ride / On the high-heaped car that has nothing to do with bread, / Nothing, nothing at all to do with the war; / The soul can go for a ride with the rich young dead." Then Pitter lists the tawdry wreaths: one is in the form of the gates to heaven ajar; another is a broken column; another is a pillow that says, "Rest in peace"; and yet another is a "sham Harp with its tinsel string allusively" burst. The mawkish artificiality of all this peaks when one of the most important symbols of Christianity is contrived into a "three-quid Cross made of flaring anemones." There are also "gibbeted carnations," "skewered roses," tulips "turned inside-out for a bolder show," and "arum lilies stuck upright in tortured poses / Like little lavatory basins." Ironically, though these wreaths are intended to honor the dead, Pitter sees them as empty, futile, and vacuous: "Mindless and pagan offering, wicked waste, / This is the efflorescence of godless toil, / Something that has no meaning, that has no taste." If the flowers in "Flowers in the Factory" serve as poignant reminders of beauty and pointers to a reality beyond the temporal, those in "Funeral Wreaths" are insincere attempts at mourning wartime deaths.

While *The Bridge* reflects Pitter's wartime experiences, not all the poems in it are concerned with the war. As in *A Trophy of Arms* and *The Spirit Watches,* several poems coalesce around nature and her memories of the cottage in Hainault Forest. Given the harshness of her days in Chelsea during this time, it is not surprising Pitter writes poems that are dreamy returns to the cottage. In "Retrospect" she envisions her spirit returning to the cottage, "a sylvan place, a distant time, / An owlish and an elvish air" (38–39).[15] Her spirit "looks upon the ragged tree, / It broods along the darkening glade; / It sees what I no longer see." Yet she cannot make the kind of connection she desires with her spirit: "It hears what is to me unheard: / If it could only speak to me, / Shaping the wonder to a word, /

If it could speak the ancient spell." In "Rainy Summer" she tries to "remember, though we cannot write it, the delicate dream" (45). Notwithstanding this claim, she does a wonderful job remembering: "We repose in our secret place, in the rainy air, / By the small fire, the dim window, in the ancient house; / Kind to the past, and thoughtful of our hosts, / Shadows of those now beyond thought and care, / Phantoms that the silence engenders, the flames arouse." Her precise memories recall "Stormcock in Elder": "The secret bird is there, . . . betrayed / By the leaf that moved when she slipped from her twig by the door, / As the mouse unseen is perceived by her gliding shade, / As the silent owl is known by the wind of her flight." The sustaining power of the cottage is again underscored in the poem's final lines: "We remember the delicate dream, the voice of the clay; / Recalling the body before the life was begun, / Stealing through blood and bone with bodiless grace / In the elfish night and the green cool gloom of the day."

Still another poem that dreams of the cottage is "The Hill of the Kindred," which opens: "Would you remember if I asked you / The ruin in the hanging wood?" (51). She recalls the close grove, the hillside, the broken stones, and the "cold black gaping chimney-place, / . . . Like a skull's face." Perhaps by contrast with the ruins Pitter sees all about her in London because of the nightly bombings, the memory of the ruined cottage is sustaining: "A ruin is to me / A place of peace, where restless care, / Parting, and toil, and usury, / And all our sorrows buried are." But beyond remembering the literal ruin, she harkens back to the people who once were there: "I think how she who baked the bread / On this poor hearth when it was warm / Sleeps like a queen among the dead." This almost certainly alludes to her mother, as Pitter recalls the delightful days that her family spent in the Hainault Forest before World War I. The solace she imaginatively experiences as she lays her "head / Down on the green neglected stone, / Loving the cold hearth of the dead," gives her the strength to carry on in the midst of hardship: "Not timid, like an untried child, / Nor bitter, like an angry lover; / For life and I are reconciled, / The grief is done, the care is over."

Several poems relate specific experiences in nature. "The Tall Fruit-Trees" is an exuberant celebration of autumn harvest as Pitter glories in the joys of climbing heavily loaded plum, pear, and apple trees: "But while I am able O let me ascend the plum-tree / And poke my head out at the top, where the lovely view / Has a foreground of scarlet plums with a wash of blue, / And I am away from earth in the starlings' country" (30–31). The pleasure she receives from this high vantage point suggests a deep desire to ascend life's everyday toil and pain and become lost instead in the swaying fecundity of the great trees. While Pitter's poem lacks the existential subtleties of Robert Frost's "After Apple Picking" ("For I have had too much / Of apple-picking: I am overtired / Of the great harvest I myself desired"), it nonetheless reflects Pitter's strong affection for the natural environment: "But the great old trees are the real loves of my heart, /

Mountains of blossom and fruit on the stalwart timber." "The Bat" recounts Pitter's unexpected pleasure in handling an injured bat brought into the house by her marauding cat. Initially she is horrified to see the bat, since she thinks it "unholy" and has always thought its "murky and erratic wing" was "made of stuff / Like tattered, sooty waterproof, / Looking dirty, clammy, cold, / Wicked, poisonous, and old" (32–33). Yet because "even fear must yield to love / And pity makes the depths to move," she picks up the creature in order to save it from the cat. As she lifts the night flier, she is curiously moved: "Strange revelation! Warm as milk, / Clean as a flower, smooth as silk!" In contrast to what she had believed, she finds the bat's body to be delicately charming: "O what a piteous face appears, / What great fine thin translucent ears! / What chestnut down and crapy wings, / Finer than any lady's things." As the tiny, fragile creature clings to her, Pitter is not repelled; instead she intuitively sympathizes with it and blesses it as she releases it: "Warm, clean, and lovely, though not fair, / And burdened with a mother's care; / Go hunt the hurtful fly, and bear / My blessing to your kind in air." This sense of connectedness among all living creatures is one that finds expression in many of Pitter's nature poems, and the unexpected pleasure this heretofore frightening creature brings is reminiscent of her reaction to the snake in "The Viper" from *A Trophy of Arms*.

"Wild Honey" is a measured harangue at the stupidity of a man who is consumed with the surface and the trivial: "You, the man going along the road alone, / Careless or wretched, rarely thoughtful, never serene, / Possessing nothing worth having; man of the sickly pleasures, / Man of the mawkish, wrongheaded sorrows, typical man" (52). This superficiality causes such a man to pass by and miss a rich, sweet, and sustaining vein of goodness:

There in the riddled tree, hanging in darkness,
There in the roof of the house and the wall-hollow,
The new like pearl, the old like magical amber,
Hidden with cunning, guarded by fiery thousands
(See where they stream like smoke from the hole in the gable),
There in the bank of the brook the immortal secret,
In the ground under your feet the treasure of nations,
Under the weary foot of the fool, the wild honey.

This parable on humankind's tendency to live on the surface and its inability to see the nurturing truth beneath the crust of everyday activity is neatly done, and Pitter's descriptions of where the wild honey may be found are masterful. She suggests that we waste our time with the facile, the obvious, the mundane, while missing richer sources of meaning and purpose, a notion she also explores in "Burning the Bee-Tree" from *The Spirit Watches*.

The last group of nature poems concerns birds. Unlike "The Cygnet" and "The Sparrow's Skull," which offered commentary on the war, "Freemasons of the Air" is a careful observation of sand martins flitting and darting about a sandy bluff as they scrape out their nests: "With turning wing and forky tail, / And highest in the diamond light / The swifts like boomerangs in flight, / The spirits who can sleep on high / And hold their marriage in the sky" (17). Pitter finds simple delight in watching these birds joining together to build their homes: "They sport, they sing in unison, / Their noble perils make them one." If the implication here is that humankind should learn something about unity from the sand martins, Pitter offers a patent moral in "The Crow," a poem about how an injured crow is cared for by a group of children. In spite of their kindness to him, the crow never warms to his captors; instead, "friendship [he] damned with all he knew" (21–22). Pitter uses this bitter crow as a jumping-off point for comparison to someone from her past: "I knew a man, I knew a man / As thin as any grudging crow. / He also had his bitter *damn* / For all his jailers here below. / And also for the one above. / His hatred was a kind of faith." She wishes this man could be born again so that he would "think less of getting, more of giving; / In short, to learn the art of living." Although there is no way to establish who she has in mind, it is not hard to speculate this is a poem about her father, George; his socialist principles were sickened by the poverty and misery he saw in the lives of the elementary school children he taught, and Pitter's memories of him in the unpublished poem "The Cottage," discussed earlier, also suggest this possibility.

"The Swan Bathing" is the second poem in *The Bridge* about her favorite bird; however, the overtly sexual context of this poem is unique in her corpus.[16] Even the title of the poem connotes a sensuous, if not sensual, experience, and this is made explicit in the opening lines: "Now to be clean he must abandon himself / To that fair yielding element whose lord he is" (18). Throughout, the swan is the image of masculine activity and the river of feminine passivity. Accordingly, the picture Pitter paints as the swan washes himself is clearly one of sexual encounter and climax:

There in the mid-current, where she is strongest,
Facing the stream, he half sinks, who knows how?
His armed head, his prow wave-worthy, he dips under:
The meeting streams glide rearward, fill the hollow
Of the proud wings: then as if fainting he falls sidelong,
Prone, without shame, reveals the shiplike belly
Tumbling reversed, with limp black paddles waving,
And down, gliding abandoned, helplessly wallows,
The head and neck, wrecked mast and pennon, trailing.

His passion spent, as the metaphor ("wrecked mast and pennon, trailing" and its obvious verbal echo of "penis") makes explicit, he continues his dominance: "It is enough: satisfied he rears himself, / Sorts with swift movement his disordered tackle, / Rises, again the master; and so seated / Riding, with spreading wings he flogs the water / Lest she should triumph."

The violence of his mastery is further reflected by the river: "In a storm of weeping / And a great rainbow of her tears transfigured, / With spreading circles of his force he smites her / Till remote tremblings heave her rushy verges / And all her lesser lives are rocked with rumour." Once his dominance is ensured, the swan and the river "are reconciled." Having expended himself, he moves on: "With half-raised pinion / And backward-leaning head pensively sailing, / With silver furrow the reflected evening / Parting, he softly goes." While the primary attention of the poem up until this point has been the swan, the end focuses tenderly upon the river. As the swan sails away, "one cold feather / Drifts, and is taken gently by the rushes; / By him forgotten, and by her remembered." The all-too-common pattern of sexual consummation—the male's conquest, satisfaction, and then moving on versus the female's submission, partial satisfaction, and longing for intimacy more lasting than mere copulation—is beautifully and poignantly portrayed in this ending. Although Pitter often insisted she avoided romantic entanglements and was extremely guarded about affairs of the heart, only someone who had experienced a physically intense if ultimately short-lived sexual relationship could write a poem as passionate as "The Swan Bathing."

Other poems about romantic love lament how it is thwarted by lust. This is nowhere clearer than in "But for Lust": "But for lust we could be friends, / On each other's neck could weep: / In each other's arms could sleep, / In the calm the cradle lends" (50). But even the possibility of genuine friendship is trumped by unbridled eros: "But for passion we could rest, / But for passion we could feast / On compassion everywhere." Despite lust's destructive certainty, Pitter insists tender, compassionate love is possible: "Even in this night I know / By the awful living dead, / By this craving tear I shed, / Somewhere, somewhere it is so." "Lament for One's Self" also deals with how lust bedevils love. Presented as a dialogue between an impartial narrator and an unhappy respondent, in this poem Pitter writes of the difficulty of finding love that sustains and fulfills: "Did you find the true heart / For whom you were born? / Never, for cold lust did part / Us in this place forlorn" (54–55). Moreover, even friendship is hard to find: "It is either that we all are mad, / Or my heart was born blind, / For every kind of love went bad / Between me and my kind." However, like the hopeful ending of "But for Lust," "Lament for One's Self" resists despair:

No matter what the body felt,
No matter what it saw,

My inmost spirit ever knelt
In a blind love and awe:

And dead or living knows full well,
Sick or whole it knows,
The secret it may never tell
Of joy and of repose.

Even though human experience and past encounters argue the contrary, Pitter
never gives up on the hope that selfless love will win out.

This is true in a slightly different way even in "Vision of the Cuckoo," a poem
portraying a speaker bitterly outraged over thwarted love. As she watches and
listens to a cuckoo in the roses outside her window, Pitter reflects upon its "sweet
voice, sour reputation" (20). Even more significant, "I with the eye possess you
and your meaning." The cuckoo's reputation as one who lays her eggs in another
bird's nest, leaving her chicks to be raised by the foster mother, gives Pitter the
means of laying aside her own fierce anger: "I by the world and by myself offended,
/ Bleeding with outraged love, burning with hate, / Embattled against time my
conqueror / In mindbegotten, misbegotten space, / Drink with fierce thirst your
drop of absolution." In the cuckoo Pitter sees "no love, no hate, no self; only a
life, / Blooming in timelessness, in unconceived / Space walking innocent and
beautiful." That the cuckoo can move on and resign the past to the past stimu-
lates Pitter to make a similar resolution: "Guiltless, though myriad-life-devouring;
/ Guiltless, though tyrant to your fellow-fowls, / You live; and so in me one wound
is healed, / Filled with a bright scar, coloured like the roses." As in "But for Lust"
and "Lament for One's Self," in "Vision of the Cuckoo" Pitter veers away from
despair and finds a way to cope with her disappointments in love.

While Pitter finds ways to handle her own frustrated romantic relationships,
she is still an acute observer of human unhappiness. In "Man Accuses Man" she
contrasts how pleasant the natural world is—"I made for it, and it for me"—
with human antipathy. Indeed, the poem's Edenic ethos is marred by "the curse
/ . . . on my head from human kind" (42–43). This curse marks every good thing,
threatening to destroy the possibility of human happiness. In "The Lost Tribe"
Pitter is certain she has been somehow cut off from "the blood-relations of the
mind" (44). She does not know "why I am alone, / Nor where my wandering
tribe is gone," yet she longs to find them and whole, nurturing relationships.
This disconnect is extended in "The Serious Child" as Pitter considers a child,
perhaps one growing up in wartime London, who has had to grow up too fast:
"O which is more, the pleasure or the pain, / To see a child who knows / At
nine years old, the tale of loss and gain, / The weight of the world's woes" (46).

As she considers the child shouldering this weight "mournfully," she includes herself and makes an intuitive leap of faith: "Child, are we lost? and shall we ever find / The far abode of joy? / Only within, in kingdoms of the mind, / My little careworn boy."

If human discord is certain, Pitter's determined resistance to despair, her naive faith in joy, and her self-reliance militate against a completely melancholic view of the world. Moreover, as has already been noted, many poems in *The Bridge* suggest she is moving toward belief in the God of Christianity. "Polymorph Pervers" recalls "Sudden Heaven" from *A Trophy of Arms*. Set "at the blind end of the house / Where the weeping stains of rain come creeping down," where "no one goes," this poem headed seemingly for unhappiness abruptly changes its course: "Sudden joy, the shooting star, / Rootless joy burst out like the wild rose, / Shattering sorrow, breaking winter's bar; / Furious joy leaped up in me, / Where little joy or none might be" (53). This epiphany results from Pitter's witness of nature's promise of rebirth in "the clean, the fruitful tree," the "buds of young desire," and "the next wave of the tides that never tire." Overt religious language is used: "In the presence of the blessing, the pure woe, / [Broke] like a winter wave." "Wherefore Lament" (subtitled "Written during an Attack on London 7 October 1940") also evokes the idea of blessing: "Wherefore lament, thou fond ephemeral? / Thy salve is very sure; / Thy wound shall cease, thy wrongs be cancelled all, / Thine hurt hath certain cure" (41). Although the initial blessing is that the grass will cover our graves, the larger blessing is of God's controlling hand:

> Let the great tempests of the spirit blow,
> Fanning that seed of fire,
> Until the flaming tree of life shall grow,
> And flourish, and aspire,
>
> And fill the universe, and bear the stars
> Like birds on every bough;
> In whose pure eyes these wild and bitter wars
> Profane the heavens now.

Pitter's deft use of religious imagery, particularly "the flaming tree of life," and her insistence that the immediate conflagration of World War II will not forever "profane" the heavens, shows this to be another poem revealing her gradual move toward Christianity.

Two final poems take us even closer to Pitter's conversion. "Better than Love" is a prayer calling upon God to intervene in human affairs:

Are you there? Can you hear?
Listen, try to understand.
O be still, become an ear,
For there is darkness on this land.
Stand and hearken, still as stone,
For I call to you alone. (34)[17]

Noting God's powers to create beauty, to sustain life, and to effect justice, she says: "Hear me, you solitary one, / Better than beauty or than love, / Seen in the weed, the shell, the grass, / But never in my kind, alas!" The failure of humanity to appreciate truth, to honor life, or to practice justice leads Pitter to read God's message in natural objects, so that "the ragged weed is truth to me, / The poor grass honour, and the shell / Eternal justice." She is content with these spiritual emblems for now, but her prayer is for when "I see / The spirit rive the roof of hell / With light enough to let me read / More than the grass, the shell, the weed."

If "Better than Love" hints at the sacramental, the sonnet "Lilies and Wine" is sacramental: "The white and gold flowers and the wine, / Symbols of all that is not mine, / Stand sacramental, and so bless / The wounded mind with loveliness" (49). While the lilies, symbolic of Christ's death and resurrection, and the wine, symbolic of Christ's sacrificial death, together speak powerfully about the possibility of new life, of spiritual rebirth, at least in this poem they are just "symbols of all that is not mine." That is, even though Pitter is drawn to the literal and symbolic beauty of the lilies and wine, she is still on the outside, looking in. Yet in the immediacy of the poem, she hints that something is about to change: "I knew and loved them long ago; / But now the white, the gold, the blood / Dawn doomlike, not to be withstood." In fact, as the poem concludes, she stands on the threshold of conversion: "At the white, gold, and crimson gate / I and my heart stand still and wait." As we shall see in the next chapter, Pitter's conversion is still several years away, and it is not until *The Ermine* (1953) that she writes poetry clearly marking her move to Christianity.

Critical reaction to *The Bridge* was favorable. Of course, David Cecil was delighted with the poems: "This is only to say how beautiful I find your new volume. I had of course seen several before—notably 'The Swan Bathing' . . . but I read this again with enhanced pleasure; & what beautiful reviews there are! 'The Estuary' seems to me a perfect piece of writing & there are several others as good—'The Coloured Glass' & 'Hoverfly on Poppy.' And 'The Cygnet' is very fine. . . . You know how deeply I admire your art: & how it speaks to my heart as well as my taste" (April 2, 1945). Pitter, ever grateful for Cecil's attention, replies: "Your very kind letter does me good. I don't care if nobody reviews the thing now. And indeed it looks as though nobody means to: but having had the Hawthornden, and your approbation, has satisfied me—I mean this quite seriously: I can't express what your praise has meant to me. These last pieces have not been so closely meditated as the former ones, but that is due to circumstances" (April 3). Two months later Cecil is even more enthusiastic:

> I hardly dare to write to you—nine weeks ago you sent me your poems & I have not written a word. . . . [My busy schedule has prevented me.] I hope you did not think me very rude. I feel this way about it because I admire the poems so very much. Your poems have always been able to move me in a way no other poems of our day do: & these are no exception. Indeed, you seem, if I may say so, to here combine the two strongest [elements of your writing] in a way they have not been combined before—I mean your beautifully exact descriptive style, with your rare abstract & symbolic manner. In the *Trophy of Arms* they appeared, as a rule, separately. Here they come together, as in "Retrospect," "Vision of the Cuckoo," "Rainy Summer," and "Tree to the North," "The Swan Bathing," & "The Death of a Beauty." . . . I do so admire your beautifully apt yet slightly . . . unexpected words . . . the "elegiac programming" of the lily etc. They give a more exquisite sharpness to language. And as usual the quality of your emotion, so severe & yet so sensitive, noble, . . . shows its peculiar power to heal, soothe my spirit. Thank you very, very much for letting me have the privilege of seeing them. (June ? 1945)

The good favor of Cecil was reinforced by brisk sales and favorable reviews. She confides to Nettie Palmer on August 23: "I feel I've got very dull as regards poetry, but 'The Bridge' has been well reviewed and sold out (paper shortage rather than merit, I fear)." Later she tells Palmer: "I go to the country when I can, and am trying to be a bit literary too: but here I feel discouraged and outmoded. For me poetry was always an expression of happiness, and now, what with the atom bomb & all, it seems to be pointless: especially as the unhappy gulf between tradition & Eliotism seems to be widening. It's like two different languages" (Nov. 9).

Pitter's modesty notwithstanding, the critics found much to admire in *The Bridge*. For instance, one of the earliest reviewers cites Pitter's power to evoke mystical insights: "In her vision of the cuckoo, her picture of the estuary, or her invocation of the one yew-tree protecting the old house to the north, the timeless world in which the guilt of time is redeemed is part of the natural image, flows through it and invests it with more than temporal reality."[18] Wilfrid Gibson says Pitter "is most successful when she writes simple nature poems—nature poems that, nevertheless, have a telling human relevance."[19] Another reviewer praises Pitter's technique: "The variety of her rhythms, within a firm metrical framework, show how it is possible to unite conversational freedom with classic form."[20] Still another compliments Pitter for responding "to the terrible stress of the times with a subtle and pleasing sense of affirmation. . . . Without being in any sense 'modernistic' she seems abreast of and attuned to her times."[21]

One dissenting voice was that of G. W. Stonier: "Miss Pitter rejoices some; those, I suspect, who need a chapel to go to, where they can examine the stained glass; no light, however, comes through the windows."[22] Stonier, like the reviewer for the *New Yorker*, who writes, "Now that a good deal of artificiality has disappeared from Miss Pitter's work . . . [she is] more modern and capable of larger effects," reveals more about his own tastes in verse than about the excellencies or deficiencies of *The Bridge*.[23] A more important dissenting voice is that of American poet and critic Randall Jarrell. He dismisses the poems in *The Bridge* as "in approximate silhouette, Robert Bridges versions of Walter de la Mare," although he does not provide examples of what he means.[24] He also faults Pitter for being "'traditional' in the bad sense of the word" while granting that "her own sensibility and formal intelligence interrupt and occasionally transfigure her delicate, orthodox, and reasonably interesting exercises in what one might call Attic modes." Jarrell's belief that Pitter essentially writes derivative verse makes him see real limitations in *The Bridge*.

Christopher Morley, an equally important critic, counters Jarrell by extolling Pitter's "little book [as] a testament against despair."[25] He urges readers who "have a craving for the tingling-tart, for the inside-outs of feeling, for the taste of snow or the smell of moss, [or] a dull ache for the kind of thoughts you would like to think but never have, . . . [and] a gust for words used with incomparable freshness" to spend time with *The Bridge*. Fredrick Brantley is helpful when he points out that Pitter persistently shows "hope still exists . . . [as] a private kind of courage to place against the sorrow of an age of 'anger and pollution,'" but he misses out on the depth of the volume when he claims that "for the most part the poems are unambitious, gentle descriptions."[26] Babette Deutsch is of two minds in her review. On one hand, she argues that Pitter "has the gift of compassion, bred of pity and indignation, and she has also a fine discernment of the requirements of the lonely mind, a delicate discrimination of those essences on which the solitary soul must feed."[27] On the other hand, however, "taken in its entirety, the book fails to satisfy. Miss Pitter has not always escaped the effect of staleness that is produced by a too facile use of traditional forms. Her delight in the lovely trivia of existence, especially the winged and petaled inhabitants of gardens and orchards, is the occasion for a grace that is rather pretty than sturdy." Theodore Maynard praises *The Bridge* for the very same reasons that Deutsch criticizes it: "Once again Ruth Pitter has given us a remarkable book of poems—remarkable in every one of its separate items and remarkable in the totality of it effect. . . . [It] marks also an advance both in its wider range and in a technique that always finds new devices while remaining essentially the same."[28] Where Deutsch faults *The Bridge* for being "traditional," Maynard praises it:

> Miss Pitter is unmistakably of our time, but she has the advantage . . . of also being timeless. She is fresh and original without effort and without eccentricity. Serenely, securely, perfectly she accomplishes, each time, what she aims at. It is all so quietly done that in those quarters where a premium is set upon the queer or unintelligible she may not receive adequate attention. . . . All that one wishes is that work of such unfailing distinction were more widely recognized for what it is. A few more such poets in place of the mountebanks on the one hand and the twitterers on the other, and poetry would be rescued from its present disrepute.

What is most clear is that reviewers of *The Bridge* attack or defend it in terms of their own critical biases. Accordingly, modernist critics such as Jarrell and Deutsch find it ultimately unsatisfying, while traditional critics such as Morley and Maynard cannot praise it enough.

What all these critics fail to consider completely are both the context and the profundity of *The Bridge*. The context of these poems—written during the terrible early days of the war when the very survival of Britain was in the balance and throughout the wearying years of nightly bombings, mounting civilian deaths, strict rationing, the systemized destruction of London's infrastructure, personal isolation, short tempers, and the pervasive fear that things might never get better—lends to *The Bridge* a power not seen elsewhere in Pitter's verse. A poem like "The Cygnet" is far superior to the earlier "The Swan," and a poem like "The Sparrow's Skull" is so different from "The Birds Mourning" that one might think they were not from the same hand.[29] In other words, Pitter's awful experiences in Chelsea during World War II infuse the poems in *The Bridge* with a vision of wartime reality that is at once more immediate and personal than Pitter's early impersonal musings, and at the same time her vision of the war does not lead to despair.

Indeed, it is the war context of these poems that lends them their profundity. "The Bridge" dramatizes an existential crisis as Pitter faces squarely the issues of meaning and purpose. Who am I? Where am I going? What is there after death?—these are all implicit questions posed by the poems. "But for Lust" is almost a mirror image of "If You Came" from *The Spirit Watches*, but with the added idea that lust is the natural enemy of love. And "Lilies and Wine" poignantly leaves us with the sense Pitter is standing at a church door, desperately desiring to go in and receive the sacrament of the Eucharist, but not quite ready to enter: "At the white, gold, and crimson gate / I and my heart stand still and wait." While Pitter's poetic technique in *The Bridge* is essentially the same as in A *Trophy of Arms*, this does not matter to readers who want poetry to take them to the deep, secret places of the human experience—readers who want someone to write about our shared fears and hopes, our yearnings for genuine human love, our sense of a longing for a transcendence beyond the temporal, and our growing belief in the mystery of life. With Pitter, we want to "find our truth, over the river."

The success of *The Bridge* coincided with renewed interest from the BBC, and her work with BBC radio finally took off early in 1946 when she did a broadcast on Alexander Pope.[30] In the broadcast she notes his well-known irritable temperament, but in excusing him she may be offering an insight into her own psyche: "Now to be a poet is a painful thing. It means showing one's tenderest feelings in public, with the certainty of having them badly hurt." In her extended discussion of Pope, Pitter illustrates that her lack of university education was no critical handicap. She moves easily in and out of Pope's poetry and is clearly cognizant of the important political, literary, social, and religious ideas of eighteenth-century England. For example, she points out that Pope did not produce any great works of creative imagination, in part because of the age itself: "It was a political age, with a system of patronage which tended to make writers subservient to parties and factions. . . . The leaders of taste were all politicians or men of fashion. The universities didn't count for much. . . . And the church, amid the antagonisms and upheaval [sic] of the time, had saved its connection with the State by a compromise—a compromise which had seriously weakened its moral authority." She also notes that English literature was neglected, as the most attention was paid to the classical writers of antiquity; literary criticism was based primarily on personal bias and blind dogmatism. Moreover, the people best suited to rule the country and offer positive role models were consumed with self-interest and artificiality: "The Court, the Parliament, the clubs, theatres, and coffee-houses, provided places where the intrigue, malice, envy, and treachery could work, to the accompaniment of endless gossip, rivalry, and abuse. It was an age of hatred." Accordingly Pitter assesses Pope in light of these realities: "He had a high conception of human dignity, and humanity was parading before him like a procession of apes, dressed up in the motley rags of every kind of vice, corruption, and folly. Nature had indeed made Pope a poet; his age made him a satirist." Pitter shares her delight in her BBC work with Nettie Palmer on January 22, 1946:

I've been rather stimulated by getting a little work from the BBC—the first time they've given me a chance. I've done a talk on D. Wordsworth's journals, and a programme on Pope: and shall be doing one on Collins. These are all for the Far Eastern English service. They also let me take part in a Poet's Quiz, which some people thought infra dig, but it was fun, and the poets won. I can't tell you how much I hope they will let me go on. I feel there's nothing like the spoken word, and there's room for so much improvement in radio. Also one can do the necessary reading & writing anywhere, and as I move about so much, this is a great attraction. As you say, one only needs a little margin of restoration & well being to have the extra energy needed for composition.

As was true throughout England, Pitter had tired of wartime rationing, yet now that the war was over little relief was on the horizon. So she was both slightly embarrassed and greatly excited to receive parcels of hard-to-get food-stuffs sent by friends and well-wishers from Australia, Canada, and the United States. After receiving a package from Nettie Palmer, she writes:

A lovely parcel arrived today, quite intact—I think it must be the New Year one, with the tinned meat, sweets, cheese, jelly crystals and—*what* a kind thought—envelopes. It had been such a gloomy day, too: whether it was the sunspots, or one's glands, I don't know, but I felt as if in an oubliette, and an unsanitary one at that. The moment your parcel came we ate several sweets without pausing for breath, and felt quite different. Blood-sugar gets low, I expect. But it's the kindness too that is so restorative. Thank you with all my heart, Nettie. We—the whole nation—have been so depressed by the further ration-cuts. People are getting peeved with the Govt., though I don't see how they can help it, when the causes are world-wide. Of course we shall grow every scrap we can this year. You can't think how precious are the few things we store for the winter, now quite unobtainable in the market: for example, onions, apples, and pears, and tomato pulp and bottled fruit. Last season we had good crops. Some very hard pears which we call "clock-weights," which never get soft, we have discovered are first rate baked. You'd laugh to see the scrupulous fairness with which they are doled out, as if we were Arctic explorers. At first sign of frost, we rush to stow the onions between the mattresses! God help those—and they are many—who have to subsist on the bare rations. But we know that we are far from being badly off in comparison with our neighbours. (Feb. 7)

Such packages were a welcome supplement to her scarce rations and meager diet. To another friend she writes: "We are all pretty sickly & depressed, as our food, clothes, houses, & prospects exhibit a uniform squalor. I don't much care: we have got used to life at this low level: the itch for profit has left me, and I refuse to be afraid of anything one is likely to meet now, having seen such a variety of lethal effects! But I should like to be a bit cleaner. The dirt of everything, which there has been no noticeable efforts to tackle so far, is horrible. I have a country home, thank God, so I get out of it at weekends" (March 27).

To still another correspondent, Eugene Walter,[31] she adds: "Well, I don't deny that we are feeling the pinch pretty well everywhere, but I don't forget the millions worse off. What I should really like is a bit of soap that doesn't skin my face, and a little jam or dried fruit. We live mostly on bread, fish, & potatoes, and the trouble is that they taste so dull, especially when we haven't any milk or fat to cook the fish nicely" (April 26). She was especially grateful to receive a package from Walter: "I got back from a weekend in the country today, and found your delightful parcel. I was as pleased as a child. I think the thing that touched me the most was the saved-up sugar. I only hope you haven't been doing without it and drinking unpalatable coffee. But everything was so exciting. The figs, so much better than any we ever got even in good times: the dried orange juice which I'd never seen before, & which is most delicious: the luxurious soap, a real boon, because not only is there no good toilet-soap here, but even the ration of common soap is being cut" (June 24). Over the next five years Pitter would receive numerous packages from Nettie Palmer, Eugene Walter, and others, and as the letter above illustrates, she was always deeply grateful.

As Pitter's radio work with the BBC increased, she was also now being increasingly sought as a literary arbiter. For instance, she served as a judge for a competition focusing upon spoken verse. Her fellow judges were Alida Monroe, L. A. G. Strong, C. Day Lewis, Richard Church, Clinton Baddeley, and Dylan Thomas. At another event, she recalls the latter's behavior: "Dylan Thomas, quite intelligent & nice when sober—oh dear! He came to our nice respectable Poets' Club dinner and threw rolls at the President—a dreadful affair" (Aug. 5). She also spent time with Virginia Sackville-West, visited Dorothy Wellesley at the Penns, and enjoyed the hospitality of Rachel and David Cecil. After returning from a weekend with them, she writes: "I am in a state like Catherine Morland's [from Austen's *Northanger Abbey*] when she returned from her gaieties and had no appetite to go on making her brothers' shirts. I must look out some sermons for myself, as I've no mother to do it for me. But I am most grateful for the weekend, which was full of delight, and interest, and kindness, and comfort. And really, I do think the children are remarkable—intelligent, *sympathiques*, and so unspoiled" (Aug. 26). Other friends of this time included the poet Laurence Whistler and, especially, C. S. Lewis. In fact, Pitter's friendship with Lewis is so important, it is explored more fully in the next chapter.

SIX

Friendship with C. S. Lewis,

1947–1949

Before we explore the details of how Pitter and Lewis became friends, it is important to note here that Lewis's earlier influence on Pitter through the wartime BBC radio broadcasts contributed to her eventual conversion. Given that her poem "Lilies and Wine" from *The Bridge* shows her standing on the threshold of confirmation, it is not surprising that she formally joins the church in September 1946. This is Pitter's comic account of the event:

> I wanted to be confirmed in the country, because I belong there, and because I thought it would please our Vicar [Rev. Dr. J. C. Morrice], an old, learned, and very zealous priest, whose cure in the notoriously godless regions of East Anglia gives him very hard work and little joy. The day was arranged and everything ready; but some impulse urged him to check the time and place, when it was found that the venue had been changed to a more distant village, and no one had notified him. However, he won that trick.
>
> The service was rather late in the evening, and he was to have called for me in his car. But though it had been going like a bird up to a few hours before, it simply would not start. After sweating over it for ten minutes, the poor Doctor flew to the telephone, but could not get my number. Any other number, oh dear yes, but the operator said there was no getting mine. The Doctor, by this time frantic, rang up a neighbor, who sent me a message. I rang up a garage (finding nothing wrong with my end of the phone) and the man came immediately. We picked up the Doctor, and drove 32 miles in 50 odd minutes. The country got wilder, the evening darker, the roads became little deep lanes, patches of marsh and forest appeared, sullen fires ringed the horizon (that was only straw from the combined harvesters burning in the fields, but it looked awful), the man no longer knew the way, but we were never misdirected and never had to cast back. A lighted church appeared—we pulled up and tumbled out,

but it was the wrong place. At last we arrived, a quarter of an hour late, but the Bishop was giving a little preliminary homily for the young, so it didn't matter.

One might have expected, in a little ancient church in a remote place, to see only a few peasants, but one quarter of the nave was a solid mass of khaki—young soldiers from a neighbouring camp; the corresponding quarter was filled with girls in white veils, and the place was as full as it would hold. The lads made the responses very loudly and precisely, as one man, and it had a heartening effect; so had the appearance of the local vicar, whose breast displayed a spread of medal-ribbons like an angry sunset, and whose face was like a Churchill tank.

A very large and leisurely bat, with much less fear of humanity than it should have had, cruised in a deliberate manner up and down the nave, then perched on a cornice, eyeing us all with a black leer; presently, with a gesture of whose meaning I was not sure, it suddenly shook itself, flung its obscene wings about its body, and crawled into a crevice out of sight.

We drove home exulting, the Doctor relating school and college pranks, and also some strange dreams which he has had from time to time.[1]

It is unlikely that Lewis knew about Pitter's confirmation, but in later letters she directly connects her conversion to his writings. For instance, she writes Nettie Palmer: "Did I tell you I'd taken to Christianity? Yes, I went & got confirmed a year ago or more. I was driven to it by the pull of C. S. Lewis and the push of misery. Straight prayer book Anglican, nothing fancy. . . . I realize what a tremendous thing it is to take on, but I can't imagine turning back. It cancels a great many of one's miseries at once, of course: but it brings great liabilities, too" (Jan. 16, 1948).

Pitter's desire to meet Lewis had been fortuitously advanced when Herbert Palmer began corresponding with Lewis in the autumn of 1945; Palmer soon agreed to help Pitter meet Lewis. In a letter of November 15 in which she comments briefly on several of Lewis's books, including *The Pilgrim's Regress*, she writes Palmer: "Are you really going to see Lewis? One of the few people it's worth getting excited over, I think. I know he is a good poet. I daresay he never heard of me, but I wish you would tell him that his work is the joy of my life. One's homesickness for Heaven finds at least an inn there; and it's an inn on the right road. You're absolutely right about his importance—*portentous*." Palmer replies and says Lewis was surprised to learn of her interest in him; Palmer quotes from Lewis's letter to him of December 15: "I am astonished at what Miss Pitter says and am most deeply rejoiced to find that my work is *not* (as her rash kindness betrayed her into saying) the 'joy of her life,' but the occasion which sometimes awakes that joy into activity. The little I have seen of her work I admired very greatly" (Wednesday [late Dec.?], 1945).[2] To this high compliment, Pitter says: "I am quite [exalted] at receiving the message from C. S. Lewis, for whom my enthusiasm is of a kind I thought dead in my bosom—haven't felt anything like it for 30 years." Then she adds:

> No, I haven't got "The Great Divorce" yet: I'm on the trail. I'm half way through "The Allegory of Love." Pretty hard going, too, for the likes of me: but Herbert! could one ever have expected to see the neatly mummified & discarded Gower so brought to life & given a new importance & significance? True creative, constructive criticism: what has been without exception the scarcest article for half a century: and for why? Because authoritative criticism must be founded on moral law. Isn't there a great change here? It seems to me that in our lifetime we have passed from the wreck of liberal humanism to the beginning of a new recognition of dogma: isn't it rather tremendous? Now it's years since I looked into Swendenborg (doesn't Lewis tick him off rather neatly in "The Pilgrim's Regress"?). I retain an impression of something fantastic & not first-rate. As for Spiritism, I am entirely with Lewis. The whole thing seems to me suspect and (when all's said & done) in bad taste. AE (peace to his ashes) can't escape the imputation either. (Feb. 15, 1946)[3]

Palmer further piques Pitter's interest in Lewis when he writes:

> I spent last Friday evening [May 17, 1946][4] with C. S. Lewis. He is a convivial Irishman, and looks like a cross between a jolly priest and a publican—with a dash of the fox-hunting squire thrown in. We had a great time and read our poems to one another until midnight. Actually I discovered him first, for if you turn to my "Post-Victorian Poetry" you will find a note on a long allegorical poem called "Dymer" by one Clive Hamilton. I did not know till a few days ago that "Clive Hamilton" was C. S. Lewis. . . . He does not like women, but says he would like to meet *you*. He says all the women he knows are saints or devils, chiefly devils, and that he knows no betwixts and betweens. I imagine that he would include you among the saints, for he couldn't possibly put you with the devil class and you are not average or mediocre. . . . Do you know his "That Hideous Strength"? Mine might better have been entitled "That Innocent Strength" but never thought of it. (Tuesday [May 21?], 1946)

Pitter expresses her gratitude in her reply: "I would do any honest thing under the sun to know C. S. Lewis, and so am very grateful to you" (June 19). She adds in the same letter: "I should say I *did* know 'That Hideous Strength.' Haven't been so excited since I was about 14. I've just got 'Out of the Silent Planet' and 'Perelandra' . . . and have read both 3 times, and watched too the utter absorption of several very various people I've lent them to. Have been wondering just how learned one would have to be to realize *all* their implications: and yet merely as stories they are so rich. It's no use—there's a parcel of girls chattering—superlatives are feeble."

Palmer's next reply further heightens Pitter's anticipation when he quotes from Lewis's letter to him of July 5: "C. S. Lewis sends you his Duty, and says you may see him when you like (Sunday [July 7?]).[5] On July 8, Pitter writes Palmer: "Many thanks for the kind messages from C. S. Lewis. I will write to him, and ask if I may go to see him: and in this prospect I feel more excitement, and more diffidence, than I have felt since the age of 18 or so." Pitter then writes Lewis and asks to meet him. In his response to her letter, he expresses surprise that she was hesitant in asking for the meeting: "But what you should be 'trepidant' about in calling on a middle aged don I can't imagine" (July 13).[6] Pitter's July 17 letter to Lewis recalls the visit:

> I have hunted these out wishing you to see something more recent than the "Trophy," and particularly that you should see "A Mad Lady's Garland," which though only grotesque & satirical (with the exception of "Fowls Celestial and Terrestrial", included as a deliberate archaism) I think is my best & most original.[7] Please keep the other two if you have a mind to them, but perhaps I may have the "Garland" back some time, as it is the only copy I have bar the American. My visit to you has discountenanced all the gypsy's warnings of people who say "never meet your favorite authors. They are so disappointing."
> With heartfelt thanks.[8]

Lewis quickly reads *A Trophy of Arms* and writes Pitter on July 19: "[*Trophy of Arms*] is enough for one letter for it has most deeply delighted me. I was prepared for the more definitely mystical poems, but not for this cool, classical quality. You do it time after time—create a silence and vacancy and awe all round the poem. If the Lady in *Comus* had written poetry one imagines it wd. have been rather like this." He comments on his favorites, noting in particular that "Cadaverous in Storm" is wonderful and that "'alleluia all my gashes cry' [from "A Solemn Meditation"] just takes one up into regions poetry hasn't visited for nearly a hundred years. . . . Why wasn't I told you were as good as this?" (720–21). It is not hard to imagine the thrill Pitter received upon reading Lewis's high praise, particularly since she admired him as writer, scholar, and sage, ever mindful of how his radio broadcasts and books had nurtured her faith.

Hardly before she could catch her breath, a few days later Lewis adds that while he is not fond of A Mad Lady's Garland, he finds good things in The Spirit Watches, including "Old Fashioned Song," "Love & the Child," and "End of Fear"; about The Bridge he is even more emphatic, praising specifically "The Bridge," "What of These?," "The Bat," "Aged Cupid," "Retrospect," "The Sparrow's Skull," and "But for Lust." He ends the letter by sending her several of his poems and inviting her critique of them, assuring her that he is unlike Herbert Palmer and will not be offended by any negative criticism; what he most wants to know is if they are "real poems" or only good ideas forced together by metrical ingenuity (722–24; July 24).[9] Pitter was delighted by Lewis's effusive praise. In her journal recollection, she writes: "This of course is the sort of letter a poet can live on for a very long time; not least because it shows that the work has been closely read" (July 19 and 29).[10] She does not disguise her excitement about having met Lewis when she writes Nettie Palmer on August 5:

> My most exciting adventure of late has been making the acquaintance of C. S. Lewis. I think more of his work than anybody else's now, and shd. never have dreamed of bothering him: but Herbert, who is of tougher fibre, wrote that he had been seeing him, and egged me on until I actually took a day off & popped down to Oxford: invaded sacred precincts of Magdalen, and found Lewis in his study (what a perfect place to live in). I took him the "Trophy," and he afterwards wrote to me about it—the most generous praise. But he doesn't like the "Garland," and I can only hope he will never discover the "Rude Potato." Well, I can't hope that so saintly a man would sympathize with my bawdy side—I'm not sure that I sympathize with it myself. But Nettie, what a privilege to know anyone so learned and so humane. He is a poet too—has sent me some pieces in MSS. Almost appallingly clever in form, and fits the profoundest thoughts into it entirely without distortion. . . . I think this skill is Celtic—he is a black Ulsterman. Is only 48, has been Fellow & Tutor for 21 years, and is said by learned people to be the dominant figure in Oxford—yet he received kindly the likes of me and poor Herbert. He is very dubious about his own verse—knows its strong thought & formal skill, but doubts if it's poetry. Nettie, I do glory in knowing this man, and to think that he admires my work.[11]

Within the fortnight Pitter replies to Lewis, and although her letter has not survived, we can surmise her critique of Lewis's poems based on Lewis's letter of August 10. After thanking her for taking the time to respond, he says he is relieved that she found the poems effective and confesses "that in most of

these poems I am enamoured of metrical subtleties—not as a game: the truth
is I often lust after a metre as a man might lust after a woman." In the same
letter Lewis discusses at length how epithets function in poetry and refers her
to Owen Barfield's *Poetic Diction* (735). On August 28 Lewis writes Pitter that
he looks forward to her next visit to Oxford, and on September 24 he thanks
her for sending him reviews of his books done by Americans: "I like American
reviewers: they do read the book" (738, 741).

As the pace of their correspondence accelerates, Lewis clearly desires to get
to know her better. For instance, Lewis invites her to a luncheon on October 9
in his rooms at college; he sweetens the invitation by telling her that his friend
Hugo Dyson, who holds Pitter's poetry "with something like awe," will be there
and very much wants to meet her (742; Sept. 27). On October 2 Pitter writes
Theodore Maynard about this invitation: "The thing that looms largest on my
present horizon is the prospect of a luncheon at Magdalen College on the 9th.
C. S. Lewis has very friendly & unexpectedly invited me. I hear the David
Cecils will be there, whom I know & like very much."[12] Pitter, in recalling this
luncheon, wrote: "I remember at this lunch Mr. Dyson's saying 'Can't we devise
something that will get her here to Oxford'? and feeling my chronic Jude-the-
Obscure syndrome somewhat alleviated."[13] Pitter writes Lewis late in December
of 1946 and asks whether David Lyndsay's *Voyage to Arcturus* (1920), which had
recently been broadcast on BBC radio, was a parody of *Perelandra*.[14] On January 4, 1947, Lewis explains in a lengthy reply that *Perelandra* actually owes its
inception to Lyndsay's thriller. In addition, he sympathizes with a writing block
Pitter is experiencing and then adds: "I've just had a poem . . . refused by the
Spectator for the first time—I mean, the first time since I was a youngster. Very
tonic: I'd forgotten the *taste* of that little printed slip" (754). About this letter,
Pitter writes Herbert Palmer on January 7: "I've had a delightful letter from
Lewis, which goes far to console me for my present poetic barrenness and the
crushing difficulty of life. I am so grateful to you for the introduction. Won't it
be lovely when we all meet in Heaven, if we can only get there—to be together
in perfect innocence & felicity & death & sorrow gone & past for ever? Perhaps
we shall speak of it then."

Lewis began to write Pitter regularly about his own verse, admiring her native ability and appreciating her critical insights. In effect, Pitter became Lewis's
mentor as a poet. For instance, on February 2, Lewis asks her to judge between
two versions of his poem "Two Kinds of Memory": "I have written two different
versions of a poem and all my friends disagree, some violently championing A
and some B, and some neither. Will you give a vote? Firstly, is either any good?
Secondly, if so, which is the good one? Don't be in the least afraid of answering
No to the first question: kindness wd. only be encouragement to waste more
time" (758). In recalling the poems, Pitter writes that "both versions are very

fine, of course: the skill in form alone is enough to drive a small poet to despair: and then the melody, so strong and so unforced, and the solemn images and the contrasting moods" (Feb. 2)[15] She also believes Lewis was going out of his way to be generous to her, although there is nothing in the letter to suggest this: "And see how he deprecates giving trouble, when one was of course only too eager: I have sometimes thought he would devise little jobs because he knew very well what pleasure it would give."

Clearly Pitter relished Lewis's attention, particularly his desire to have her views on his poetry; however, she misjudged him if she thought he was patronizing her when asking her to comment upon his poems. Instead, he genuinely respected her opinion; after all, she was the established poet—the winner of a prestigious literary award for poetry—and he was the would-be poet. While she may have been Lewis's mentor as a poet from his perspective, it is unlikely she would have seen it that way. She was too keenly aware of Lewis as a "great man" to consider herself superior to him in any way, even as a poet. When she writes back and gives her judgment in favor of version B, he writes: "I also was pretty sure of B: the slower rhythm suits the meditative theme. A is too like a jig" (762; Feb. 8). Lewis soon returns the favor; after reading *Persephone in Hades*, he tells her that "I think it is remarkable work" (762; Feb. 12). In her journal recollection of this letter, Pitter says: "On re-reading this letter after more than 20 years, I am impressed anew by Lewis's generosity & the thoroughgoing way he tackles the thankless job of reading & genuinely evaluating another person's poetry (an anguish to most of us [poets]). Both his encomiums and his strictures find a home in the heart" (Feb. 12).[16]

Pitter's enchantment with Lewis at this time comes through clearly in letters to her friends. For instance, on April 24 she writes Herbert Palmer: "I've been trying to fix a date to take Sir Ronald Storrs to see Lewis—it's very difficult, as Sir R. seems to think everybody's engagements shd. give way to his, and I feel the same with regard to Lewis: am shocked, in fact, that anyone should not regard him as a Being of Another Sphere (the hero-worshipping old maid *will* come out)."[17] In addition, Pitter's deep admiration for *Perelandra* led her to ask Lewis if she might transcribe the ending of the novel into Spenserian stanzas. At first he is amused—"I'm rather shocked at your wasting your *verse* on my *prose*" (771; April 27)—but this soon gives way to curiosity: "When am I to see the Spenserians?" (776; May 8).[18] Two months later he responds to Pitter's Spenserian transcriptions: "I like them—and you manage to be closer to the original in verse than some of my continental translators seem to get in prose" (789; July 6). Concerning the difficulty of arranging the meeting with Storrs, Lewis tells her to set a date for a luncheon for the three of them sometime during his summer vacation, noting that if Storrs can't make it, the two of them will do just fine since they will have plenty to discuss on their own (776–77;

May 8). On June 6 Lewis confirmed the luncheon for July 16 (780).[19] While a detailed account of the luncheon has not survived, Pitter does summarize it for Laurence Whistler, who had been in correspondence with Lewis about the possibility of beginning a new literary journal that "would have a Christian or at any rate a 'spiritual' point of view."[20] Pitter writes Whistler on the day of the luncheon: "I hasten to report on the meeting with C. S. L. today. Of course it was delightful. I took Sir R. Storrs, who whatever else he may be, is a good classic. The conversation of the 2 men was so good that I was content to listen: a high tribute from the Sex. First rate lunch, too."[21]

Pitter's delight in getting to know Lewis better through meetings like this was keen, perhaps leading her to harbor hopes for an even closer relationship. While Lewis, at least in his letters, never encourages a relationship beyond friendship, he clearly was comfortable with Pitter and enjoyed spending time with her. On her part, she did all she could to promote their friendship, continuing to critique the poems Lewis sent her. For instance, he sends her the poems "Donkey's Delight," "Young King Cole," and "Vitraea Circe" and invites her criticisms (790; July 6).[22] She recalls being flattered Lewis would think her view on his poems important: "[They] are magnificent poems to my mind, the technique staggering, vocabulary so wide, learned, & choice, discrimination (moral or spiritual) so lofty. As well might a lion request a mouse to criticise his roaring: and yet I can imagine a lion doing so."[23] The ease of their friendship is sometimes spiced by Lewis's characteristic humor. For instance, concerning Pitter's *The Rude Potato*, Lewis writes: "Thanks for the [book]. I look forward to finding out how rude a potato can be. All the ones I meet are civil enough" (796; July 21).[24]

More than a year goes by before their correspondence picks up again, a conscious decision on Pitter's part, as she tells Herbert Palmer: "Seen anything of C. S. L.? I met him at dinner at the David Cecils last month. . . . C. S. L. seemed pretty chirpy. I should like to write to him often, but have determined not to plague my betters unless they plague me" (Feb. 22, 1948). On August 31, Lewis, impatient to hear from Pitter about the three poems, writes and chides her for waiting so long to send her remarks: "On a railway platform this morning . . . I made a resolution. I said 'I will no longer be deterred by the fear of seeming to press for an opinion about my poems from writing to find out whether R. P. is dead, ill, in prison, emigrated, or simply never got my letter.' So it was with great pleasure that I found your [letter about them] awaiting me" (874). Pitter confides to David Cecil the essence of her critique of these three poems, to which Lewis uncharacteristically had not promptly replied: "I have had some correspondence with C. S. Lewis lately about his poems. I had to tell him that I think he has a tinge of the Flaubertian *haine et mépris de la vie* [a hatred and disdain for life]. Since then a dense and bodeful silence. Well, one has to get down to brass tacks about poetry—one can't criticize *round* it. Technique is all very well, but it's a man's profound feelings about life that make or mar poetry" (Sept. 22).[25] Within the week, however, Lewis, still musing on her criticism, writes and thanks her for the penetrating critique. He tells her he has waited to respond because he is still trying to take in her criticisms, and, more to the point, he has hesitated to respond because he fears her criticisms about his poems are actually muted because of her great regard for his prose (881; Sept. 29).

Pitter's journal recollection of this incident provides the most detailed account of her personal evaluation of Lewis as a poet:

> Now, I wonder. *Is* his poetry after all not? About how many poets or poems would readers agree 100% or even 50%? "The peaks of poetry are shiftingly veiled, and different readers catch different glimpses of the transcendental." I should like to know more about the actual process of conception in his case. Did his great learning, & really staggering skill in verse inhibit the poetry? Did he ever (like most of us) catch some floating bit of emotional thistledown & go on from that, or did he plan on a subject like an architect? (Producing perhaps short epics?) He had a great stock of the makings of a poet: strong visual memory, strong recollections of childhood: desperately strong yearnings for lost Paradise & hoped Heaven ("sweet desire"): not least a strong primitive intuition of the diabolical (not merely the horrific). In fact his whole life was oriented & motivated by an almost uniquely-persisting *child's* sense of glory and of nightmare. The adult events were received into a medium still as pliable as wax, wide open to the glory, and equally vulnerable, with a man's strength to feel it all, and a great scholar's & writer's skills to express and to interpret. It is almost as though the adult disciplines, notably the technique of his verse, had largely inhibited his poetry, which is perhaps, after all, most evident in his prose. I think he wanted to be poet more than anything. Time will show. But if it was *magic* he was after, he achieved this sufficiently elsewhere. (Sept. 29)[26]

While clearly sympathetic to Lewis's poetry, Pitter comes to believe it is in prose such as the passages at the close of *Perelandra* that he made "magic."

Still Lewis continued to send Pitter his poems. In late November he sent her "The Saboteuse," and asked for her opinion.[27] Her reply must have been positive, because on December 6 he thanks her: "I feel a little guilty at bombarding you with these things but my men friends (none of whom is a good a poet as you) give such contradictory opinions that I must have a Court of Appeals." In the same letter he discusses Matthew Arnold's *Sohrab and Rustum* and concludes: "I sometimes wonder whether we know anything about poetry" (893).[28] Pitter's reply must have suggested that lyric poetry is most often the province of the young, since less than a week later Lewis wonders why narrative poems tend to be written in a poet's mature years, citing *The Winter's Tale, Samson Agonistes*, and *Philoctetes* as examples. Then he adds: "A flash of love-liking, a bird's song, a momentary depression, can hardly appear to age with that apparent isolation & self-sufficiency wh. they have in youth. One knows now where they come from and where they go to and it is *that* one wants to talk about—the summer not the swallows?" In a final postscript, he says: "Goethe, I'm told, kept on pouring out first class lyric to the end. But that is because he kept on having love affairs—a recipe I wd. deprecate" (894–95; Dec. 11).[29]

In addition to their lively correspondence, they continued reading each other's poetry and meeting regularly over the next two years.[30] Moreover, on July 16, 1949, Pitter received an unexpected letter from one of Lewis's oldest friends, Owen Barfield: "By showing me your very kind appreciation of my poem *The Unicorn* Marjorie Milne has emboldened me to imagine that, if I asked you to lunch with me, you might consent not *merely* out of charity, but with a dash of inclination to lighten the burden. Would you feel so disposed one of these days? It would be a great kindness." As Lewis had often referred Pitter to Barfield's *Poetic Diction*, it is not surprising that soon the two were arranging to meet for luncheons. In fact, Pitter has numerous meetings with Owen Barfield and Lewis.[31] On August 1, Barfield writes and offers high praise for her poetry, particularly "Fowls Celestial and Terrestrial" from *A Mad Lady's Garland*: "It is, in its own right, a very noble poem with a life to it that occasionally makes one catch one's breath. And if a poem doesn't make me catch my breath, I may feel very politely towards [it] & be quite glad to read it, but—well! You know the difference." Barfield shared with Pitter and Lewis a love for traditional English poetry and distaste for modernist verse. His compliments continue: "I can well understand that you enjoyed writing the Garland most. You *are* the Trophy, but you only wear the Garland, and therefore can keep on taking it off and looking at it. . . . I wish I could get hold of the *Trophy* somehow. And have you a lending copy of *Persephone in Hades*, which the [local] library does not possess? I have a special weakness for Persephone and hope it is really about her and not about a giant grain elevator of that name in Wisconsin or a pylon in Beverly Hills." Pitter must certainly have felt pleased by the way he ends this letter: "May I keep the M. L. G. a little longer, please? Why don't we all live in your 'Heroic Couplets' [from *A Trophy of Arms*] mansion and spend our time reading our own poetry to each other, and the great poems of antiquity together, except of course when we were dancing . . . on the sunken lawns and playing the viol de gamboys?"

After receiving a copy of *Persephone in Hades*, Barfield writes on August 13:

Thank you very much for both your letters and I ask your forgiveness for not having acknowledged the precious *Persephone* at once, but I did want to read it at least once first, and had no chance all last week. Even now it has only been a hurried and furtive reading, but enough to convince me of its unusual strength and beauty. The first section with its preponderance of doubling endings, somehow faintly recalling the Sapphic line, made me doubtful at first, but finally got me. I am venturing to keep it a little longer in the hope of a more leisurely reading. Is that permitted? . . . I have been struggling with 4 Petrarchan sonnets—most irresponsibly as I shall hardly clear up my affairs before getting away even with them!

Pitter's widening acquaintance with Lewis's friends like Barfield was something she treasured, especially since she always felt her lack of a university education. Moving in the circle of Lewis's bright, literate, and intelligent friends offered Pitter both solace and intellectual stimulation.

A fortnight later Lewis tries to arrange a luncheon meeting, noting that it is maddening she should be in Oxford and they not meet; he wants to lunch with her so they can read their works to each other (966; Aug. 13). Two other letters from Lewis follow posthaste and when he learns of Pitter's new friendship with Barfield, a luncheon is set for the three of them on September 20 at Pitter's flat in Chelsea. Before the luncheon Lewis and Pitter correspond about *The Tell-Tale Article*, a book by Sir George Rostrevor Hamilton, which Pitter wanted Lewis to review.[32] Lewis defers to Pitter and says she should write a review since he has already written to Hamilton about the book. His continuing enthusiasm for her poetry is also evident when he adds: "I re-read most of *The Bridge* last night. A lot of it is stunning good, you know" (972–73; Aug. 24). The September 20 luncheon was a great success.[33] In recalling it two days later, Lewis lavishes praise on the painted tea tray she has sent him: "The Tray arrived . . . to create general delight and put up my domestic stock. No one had been the least impressed when I said I was going 'to lunch with a poet in Chelsea,' which sounded good enough to me; but now that you have risen to be 'someone who paints lovely trays' it is a different matter. . . . The only snag is that I detect already a tendency to call it the Good Tray and prevent its ever being used." Then he goes on to compliment her unpublished poem "The World Is Hollow," which she had read aloud to him and Barfield during the luncheon.[34] As for the luncheon itself, he adds: "You gave us a lovely day. A fine hazy air of cornucopia ('beyond all rule or arte, enormous bliss'[35]) hangs over it. . . . My only regret is that my acquaintance with the Blitzekatze [didn't] prosper as I shd. have wished" (981–82; Sept. 22).[36] Barfield is equally appreciative: "So many thanks for both your letters and—'the Pitter tray,' as it will inevitably be christened. My wife and I are both delighted with it, and she is talking about redecorating an entire room to go with it." He also thanks Pitter for sending him a copy of *The Bridge*, noting, "That is 3 volumes you now favoured me with—2 of them your only copies. I do indeed appreciate the honour and my strivings to deserve will only be excelled by my amazement at being thought worthy of it."

His only uncertainty has to do with how he conducted himself during the luncheon: "In general I had a sense of having behaved rather badly—in the quite odious schoolboy sense of not passing things at table!" He also comments on the great fun they all had: "I hope you and Jack kept it up well into the small hours, capping carryout with carryout, besting ballade with ballade, vying in virelays and triumphing with triolets. Isn't he terrific company?" His letter ends with the promise of another meeting and a conspiratorial suggestion:

> I gather we are to meet anyway at the end of December at Oxford under the broad umbrella of Marjorie Milne; but I hope we may meet again before then also. Couldn't we form a new literary club—G[eorge] R. H[amilton]; Laurence Whistler; and you would have lots of impressive names. "*Rule 1*. The names [T. S.] Eliot & [Ezra] Pound will not be mentioned without the consent of the Chairman first asked and obtained. Fines for breaking of this rule will be strictly enforced." But I am babbling on green field like Falstaff. We could get CSL up occasionally no doubt. (Sept. 25)

Pitter's warm friendship with both men flourished during the remainder of the year. For example, after Pitter and Barfield lunch together on October 2, he writes: "I am impressed by all I have read of *The Bridge*; you do seem to have a perfect sense of the *weight* of words. And Oh, what a difficult thing it is, when they are one's own words! How the last pennyweight keeps coming on and off every time one reads them afresh deliberately" (Oct. 9).

A week later he asks if he may now address her as Ruth ("Dear Miss Pitter—or, if you think I might now dispense with this tiresome pitter-patter—Dear Ruth"), and then he comments on how much better her later poetry is compared to her earlier work: "What has struck me about all these volumes [*A Trophy of Arms, The Spirit Watches*, and *The Bridge*] is how different they seem from [*First and Second Poems*] (the one with the Preface by Belloc), which I got from the library a year or two ago, and which, for the most part, I found too difficult for enjoyment." Then, perhaps much to Pitter's liking, he links her poetry with Lewis's:

> The truth is that both your poetry and, in a different way CSL's, have a delivery about them which makes me despair and feel like a bulldozer in a field of asphodel—not as a critic, but when I look at my own stuff. In your case, at all events, the delicacy is not of sentiment only—which is not much use—but, well, syllabic. And you keep making those long shots of imagination, as in the last 3 lines of "Rainy Summer," and elsewhere. On the whole,

I think "One Tree to the North," "The Tall Fruit Trees," and "The Sparrow's Skull" fetched me most completely, but it is hard choosing.[37]

On October 22 he comments more upon their using first names: "I really believe this is the first time I have taken the name step, certainly so with anyone of your sex." But it is poetry that they most share: "All else apart, your poems were so obviously standing in tears amid alien corn. As to 'betters,' I am too proud of my humility to compete, but it is at your service with any other crumbs of virtue I possess."

With Lewis Pitter asks if she may publish her Spenserian transcriptions of the end of *Perelandra,* to which Lewis readily agrees. About the unpublished poem "Hen under Bay-Tree" she sent him, he says: "The Hen (in your poem) is lovely: unfortunately the hens I meet aren't very like her" (997–98; Nov. 17).[38] On December 10 he writes and asks if she will lunch in his rooms at college with him, Barfield, and Miss Milne after the conference "Women in the Priesthood" (1008).[39] Clearly Pitter is excited by this opportunity: "I'm going to Oxford on Friday, to assist at a 2-day debate on whether women ought to be parsons. I think not, though it's not easy to say why. It's going to be held in C. S. Lewis's rooms at Magdalen [College], & some of us are going to lunch with him afterwards. This interests me a good deal more than the debate" (Dec. 28).[40] While being with Lewis and the others had been a great treat, the conference itself was tiresome: "We did 3 hours on Friday and 3 this morning on Could Women be Parsons, & if not why not? Oh dear, how exhausting! Although it is a pleasure to hear intelligent people debating, 3 hours at a time is a bit much" (Dec. 31).[41]

On Cats

Pitter's evolving relationship with Lewis, of course, was not the only thing holding her attention during these years. Although she was writing serious poems and sharing them with Lewis and Barfield, she was also working on another comic volume. If *The Bridge* was Pitter's sober wartime collection reflecting her metaphysical wrestling with the darkness threatening to engulf her, *On Cats* was a welcome postwar lighter touch, whimsical yet shaded with melancholy.[42] She was a lifelong lover of cats, as the unpublished sonnet "For the Little Cat Murphy" written in the mid-1930s reveals:

Friend, now so long under the laurel sleeping,
Or in eternal meads with many a bound
Hunting in glee along the enameled ground,
Or at celestially-painted insects leaping,

How we remember thee! For in our keeping
Perfect in kind and courtesy thou wert found,
Lovely in look and action, sweet in sound,
Patient in pain, even when we were weeping;
Mirror of manners! Though above thee grow
Grass of three seasons, still among the flowers
Thou liest, where are lodged all buds that blow;
Safe in my love, thy love from winds and showers
I keep, as one to whom it is given to know
Choice spirits, though in other forms than ours.

So it is not surprising that she devotes her third and final volume of comic poetry to felines.

Pitter's affection for cats was shared by many, including several contemporary writers who waxed poetically and philosophically on cats. For instance, in a letter to a friend Lewis says: "We were talking about cats and dogs the other day and decided that both have consciences but the dog, being an honest, humble person, always has a bad one, but the cat is a Pharisee and always has a good one.[43] When he sits and stares you out of countenance he is thanking God that he is not as these dogs, or these humans, or even as these other cats!" (March 21, 1955).[44] In *On Cats* Pitter, sometimes with her tongue in cheek, surveys the melancholy life of cats. Her cat poems often explore the hard daily challenges cats face; accordingly, in the midst of the comic touch there is a dark undercurrent throughout *On Cats* that reflects in part Pitter's own daily challenges of earning a living.

The first poem, "Quorum Porum," opens ominously: "In a dark garden, by a dreadful tree, / The Druid Toms were met. They numbered three, / Tab Tiger, Demon Black, and Ginger Hate. / Their forms were tense, their eyes were full of fate."[45] In a scene reminiscent of the opening of *Macbeth* and the three witches chanting, "Fair is foul, and foul is fair. / Hover through the fog and filthy air," Pitter has her three druids engage in a caterwaul challenge:

An hour of ritual silence passed: then low
And marrow-freezing, Ginger moaned "OROW",
Two horrid syllables of hellish lore,
Followed by deeper silence than before.
Another hour, the tabby's turn is come;
Rigid, he rapidly howls "MUM MUM MUM";
Then reassumes his silence like a pall,
Clothed in negation, a dumb oracle.
At the third hour, the black gasps out "AH BLURK!"
Like a lost soul that founders in the murk;

And the grim, ghastly, damned and direful crew
Resumes its voiceless vigilance anew.

The poem ends when the three "stiffly rise, and melt into the shade, / Their Sabbath over, and their demons laid." Although there is something of the mock epic about this poem in the tradition of Chaucer's "The Nun's Priest's Tale," at the same time Pitter deftly captures the ominous ethos of an evening showdown between her brooding druids.[46]

In a letter of May 25, 1947, Lewis had made playful compliments about *On Cats*, particularly wondering about "Quorum Porum" and the Latin declension of *porum*: "Thank you for the *De Porum Moribus* (How does the whole declension go? Puss, Puss, Purrem, Purris, Purri, Purre, Purres, Purres, Porum, Pibus, Pibus?). A very cheerful and companionable work. I think the first piece is the best: so finely observed that I wd. treat it as serious—but that is a foolish distinction" (776).[47] Pitter comments: "He is referring to the first (and yes, much the best piece in it), 'Quorum Porum,' i.e. a meeting of cats: 'quorum' a competent number, 'porum,' genitive plural of 'puss.' Now, if declined as a boy would, in the commonest way for nouns in '-us,' this has decidedly (childishly) rude results. Those concerned for the elegance of their Latinity will be grateful to Lewis for his ingenious & graceful declension, so skillfully avoiding the pitfalls (which of course were the object of the exercise)."[48]

That a cat's life is always tenuous and dangerous is the focus of "Mister the Blitzkit (for K.)," a poem inspired by one of Pitter's cats that Lewis had met.[49] Its opening also invokes *Macbeth*, although in a comedic fashion: "Double, double, toil and trouble, / Crumps and bumps and lumps of rubble." In its portrayal of an orphaned kitten looking for a home, the poem captures the youthful but worldly-wise savvy of Blitzkit: "Little Mister, six weeks old, / Hungry, frightened, dirty, cold, / Has no mother, home, nor dinner, / But he's sharp for a beginner" (9). Street-smart, Blitzkit, in hiding, surveys the human passersby on the street since "from their faces he can tell / Who would treat a kitten well." He rejects a policeman ("good but gruff . . . [who'd] pop him in a certain Van"); a nice-looking matron (whose "four fat kids" would eat all the stew and "give him hell"); and then, in order, a warden, a soldier, and a sailor. At this point poor Blitzkit is at his nadir: "Cripes, he could down a bit of food. / And O hell, here comes the rain." However, before he gives in to despair, he sees his mark, a kindly-looking young woman:

In her countenance he reads
That she will satisfy his needs.
Food, fire, bed—he ticks them off—
Worm-dose, mixture for his cough,

Velvet mouse for when he plays,
Brush and comb, and holidays
In the countryside afar,
Or boarded out with loving char.

Certain she will "pick him up correctly / And always touch him circumspectly," he darts out in front of her and looks up "with piteous grace." His streetwise ways serve him well:

Six weeks old—but what a grip
On the art of salesmanship!
Youth, dirt, fear, all play their part
In the lady's feeling heart.
A word of love, a mutual kiss,
And he is hers, and she is his.

Blitzkit's melancholic present is redeemed for a bucolic future, as "he finds he did not err / In his estimate of her"; she takes him home and gives him warm milk and "a nice old woolen vest." As he drifts off in peaceful sleep, he knows she will brush his fur: "And in the evening she will seal / Their love with a substantial meal, / And let him lay his clever head / Close to her own warm heart, in bed."

If Pitter's druidic cats represent dark melancholy and Blitzkit streetwise savvy, Plainey of "The Neuter-Cat's Apotheosis" illustrates that there is still life left in old bones. Certainly he has seen better days:

Aged, thin-legged, tabby-and-white, and wise,
Poor Plainey held his tongue, and used his eyes.
Full seventeen years a hunter's life he led,
With seldom better food than broth and bread,
The heartless mess that rural England pours
On dirty plates for faithful carnivores.
And what with this, and his declining years,
He showed thin fur, stiff joints, and cankered ears. (15)[50]

Much of his reputation rests upon the day early in his life when he "KILLED THE STOAT," yet now "as a mere yard-cat, he had his share / Of want, and cold, and wretchedness to bear." A special torment to him is the Demotic Venus, the female of the yard: "She, / Never had any sort of use for he: / Insultingly aware he was no suitor, / She cuffed his chops because he was a neuter." In addition, food, really his only comfort now, is not very good. Although he sometimes finds some "eave-scooped nestlings" in the spring, such pickings are meager and "not a bellyful." Furthermore, he disdained "to eat rats and such" since "rodentophagy's a feline vice." And sleep, which ought to have been another comfort, is thwarted by summer cold, and "winter meant the cart-shed and its drip."

However, Plainey's life is invigorated after a mean-spirited neighbor sells out:

> And Kick-cat Hall, where Plainey dared not show
> His clay-hued nose for fear of sudden blow,
> And where conditions gave his nerves the jitters,
> Became (O happy day) a nest of Pitters.
> These kindly people served a charming god
> Whose creed associated Cats with Cod;
> Who put into their heads, when fowls they had,
> That Giblets make the feline bosom glad.

Plainey finds himself welcomed into this new kitchen and condescends to permit the new owners to pet and groom him from time to time. More blessings follow one Christmas when his newfound hostess, who is wrestling to remove from a turkey dry meat "that she does not deem a treat, / But half despises," hears his plaintive purring: "Hard times . . . have taught me discipline; / I ask no more than some odd piece of skin." So moved is his hostess that she rips off an entire leg and holds it down to Plainey. He knows what to do:

> For sudden Plainey leapt,
> And seized the trophy like a true adept;
> And who shall say whether his clutching claws
> First touched it, or his well-instructed jaws?
> One moment, with the hunter's cunning old,
> He stayed to jerk it to a better hold:
> The next, like skimming Monoplane was seen
> (With turkey-leg for wings) to scour the green.

Retreating into his lair under the woodpile, he realizes "a neuter lifetime's frustrate love: / To have enough." Even though Plainey experienced many hard knocks in life, his encounter with grace via the Christmas turkey leg is his apotheosis; he transcends his heretofore melancholic existence by feasting on this gift of the incarnation.

While Plainey finds grace, the mother cat in "The Matron-Cat's Song" personifies one who knows how to bear trouble with a loving yet detached resignation.[51] The poem opens immediately after she has given birth to her latest litter:

So once again the trouble's o'er,
    And here I sit and sing;
Forgetful of my paramour
    And the pickle I was in:
Lord, lord, it is a trying time
    We bear when we're expecting,
When folk reproach us for the crime
    And frown with glance correcting. (34)

Admitting that she feared someone would kill her kittens soon after they were born, she has found an ironic sanctuary: "The surly cook, who hates all cats, / Hath here a little closet, / And here we nest among her hats—/ Lord save me when she knows it!" Reflecting on her litter, she smiles to herself as she thinks about the future of her "girls": "Lord, lord, to think upon the sport / Which doth await the hussies; / They'll be no better than they ought, / Nor worse than other pussies." However, her real pride is her boys, with one minor hesitation: "How harsh their manly pelts will be, / How stern and fixed each feature—/ If they escape that cruelty / Which man doth work on nature!"[52] Considering her immediate future, she resigns herself to caring for her kits. Though their voices are small, they will still demand her whole attention; more problematic, however, is that their noisy crying will attract "dishonourable mention," possibly leading to their discovery and unhappy end. She ends her melancholic musings by noting: "But then, alas, I shall not care / How flighty they may be, / For ere they're grown I'll have to bear / Another four, or three." The matron cat's practical wisdom and seasoned experience speak to all who find a loving but detached resignation the best way to plow through life's stony fields; that is, she resolves to do what she can for her kittens because she loves them, but she will not get bogged down trying to manage things beyond her control.

On Cats was a minor sensation among feline lovers. Pitter received numerous letters about the poems. Lewis writes Pitter: "I think just as you do about the Anglo-Cats. Their prevailing quality is the very non-catholic one of disobedience. They will obey neither our own book nor Rome" (762; Feb. 8, 1947). Dorothy L. Sayers sent Pitter a copy of her cat poem, Aeneas at the Court of Dido,[53] with a note reading: "Dear Miss Pitter, I hope the enclosed may give you a few moments of entertainment in exchange for the vast pleasure I have had from your book of verses On Cats" (June 9).[54] Later Sayers sent Pitter a copy of her A Cat's Christmas Carol as a private 1947 Christmas card and enclosed the following note: "I meant to send this in time for your cats to sing at Christmas, but had momentarily mislaid your address. But it may be suitably sung till Twelfth Day! With all good wishes for 1948."[55] David Cecil writes Pitter on June 23: "I have never thanked you for your book of cat poems. It was very bad of me, because I simply loved them. Your cats are much more genial and full-blooded and comfortable than [T. S.] Eliot's which always seem to me to suffer from a touch of New England primness. Yours have a nice Dickensian vitality. I am so pleased to be acquainted with them."

In addition to her growing friendship with Lewis and the publication of *On Cats*, Pitter's postwar years were characterized by her friendships with poets May Sarton, Dorothy Wellesley, and Herbert Palmer; her growing BBC radio career; her grateful reception of care packages from American well-wishers; and her renewed business success. Sarton, who had written a favorable review of *The Spirit Watches*, visited Pitter in the summers of 1947 and 1948.[56] Their mutual interests in poetry and gardening led to a number of meetings over the intervening years. Anxious for Wellesley and Palmer to meet, Pitter worked tirelessly to arrange for Palmer to visit the Penns. After a number of false starts, Palmer finally visited Wellesley on June 7, 1947, and the two remained polite if not intimate friends. Due to Wellesley's increasingly poor health, Pitter made frequent trips to the Penns to lighten her spirits and offer companionship.[57] After Wellesley moved into a convalescent home at a convent in Kent, Pitter continued to visit and offer her friendship.

Since Pitter's BBC broadcasts on Pope, Dorothy Wordsworth, and William Collins had been well received, she was invited to do additional broadcasts. On November 26, 1946, Pitter appeared on the new BBC radio program, *Woman's Hour*, and on November 30 she was featured along with Virginia Sackville-West on another BBC program, *Poetry Readings: The Book of Verse*. Six months later, on May 31, 1947, Pitter was the featured reader and commentator on another *Book of Verse* program, this time on Shakespeare's *As You Like It*. Pitter returned to *Woman's Hour* on July 10 with "The Most Important Thing I Have Learned in Life."

Due to the continuing postwar rationing, basic food staples in England, including sugar, lard (shortening), tea, eggs, milk, and butter, were in short supply. Pitter, who already enjoyed the generosity of Australian Nettie Palmer and American Eugene Walter, soon had an even more beneficent American well-wisher, Mary E. Cooley.[58] After Cooley's first letter arrived, Pitter writes on March 25, 1947: "Indeed I should be very glad to have a parcel. I live on my rations—eating out takes time and money, and I don't like it anyway . . . . The only thing there is enough of (apart from imported fruit at prices only the pro-letariat can afford) is the commoner kinds of white fish. Lady, you try to make a dinner out of plain cod, with no fat or milk. Oh, we're not starving—only the deprivation of so much for so long, is really making us rather neurotic—person-al relations are getting terribly difficult, that's the worst of it." Upon receiving Cooley's first package, Pitter thankfully replies:

Your most kind gift was received by me today, which seems wonderfully soon after first hearing from you. It really is a most splendid parcel, reinforcing our diet just at the weakest points, and reinforcing too one's faith in humanity, because there is nothing at all to compare with the direct, personal helping hand. It's like the old times when good people gave away servings from their own dinner in basins to poorer neighbours—it really does warm the heart. As a point of interest, you may like to know that the 2lb. or so of butter included is equal to four months' ration for one person; you may imagine therefore how greatly this is appreciated. The cheese is equal to about 8 weeks. The tinned meat is unobtainable here—each tin will be the foundation of a gala meal and a great treat. It was wonderful too to get an extra pound of sugar! After 8 ozs. per week for years on end, it has become very precious. (May 1)[59]

When Cooley later asked if Pitter knew of others to whom she might send packages, Pitter suggested David and Rachel Cecil, indicating that even titled families suffered postwar food deprivations.

Although O'Hara effectively retired from ornamental furniture painting in January 1949, Pitter continued her hard work, which was only briefly thwarted by another self-inflicted injury to her eye, as she writes Cooley on January 12, 1949: "[On January 6] I had a horrid accident—I'm almost ashamed to tell you, it was so criminally careless of me. I filled the eye-bath with ammonia, and calmly applied it to my right eye! Oh, I did all the first aid in grand style, and got a doctor in a very short time: but why didn't I *smell* it? It was a complete lapse of mind for a second or two. There's no permanent damage, and I shall be able to go on as usual in a day or two from now, when the atropine has cleared off, but I've lost at least a week's work."[60] Fortunately, the injury did heal quickly and Pitter was hard pressed to keep up with the large number of orders for her painted tea trays. Out of gratitude to Cooley, Pitter sends her two tea trays and provides one of the few descriptions of her work:

There are 2 rectangular ones coming as well—large enough to be really useful. I forgot to sign them—how silly. I'm afraid the trays themselves are rough & clumsy, but they are very strong and rigid, & great in use. They will stand a good wash with soap & water, and a polish with cellulose polish such as is used for cars: or the old-fashioned liquid metal polish (as used for brass) is very good. If any slight white marks appear on the black ones after use with hot pots, a good gentle abrasive cleaner (as used for the bath) well moistened, will generally remove it. This all goes for the decoration too, which is cellulose like the surface finish. Mind, they are for you to give away or keep just as you feel inclined—no strings attached at all as I've been doing this work all my life and it's like plumbing or hair-dressing to me. (June 3)

On November 24, Pitter underscores the difficulty of her work: "I've been frightfully busy with painting; everybody seems to want my work, and I've been working all hours," and on December 8 she adds: "I have been working like mad, but customers are never satisfied."

By the end of 1949 Pitter was a much happier person than she had been in 1946. The horrors of World War II, while not forgotten, particularly as the postwar rationing continued, were at least solidly in the past. Her growing friendships with Lewis, Barfield, Wellesley, and Cooley were heartening, and the promise of additional BBC work was a certainty. Her conversion to Christianity and confirmation in the Anglican Church gave her a spiritual home and put to rest most of her theological uncertainties. Furthermore, the renewed flourishing of Deane and Forester as a one-woman painted tea-tray business provided sufficient income so that she did not worry about financial ruin. Indeed, while O'Hara had already retired, Pitter could now begin thinking about her own retirement. Although Chelsea had been a good home for the two women throughout their working years, both were thinking and talking about finding a place outside London for their retirement years. And for Pitter the poetic muse was not dead; as we shall see in the next chapter, she makes both a physical and poetic transition leading to a new life near Oxford and ultimately culminating in her finest volume of verse, *The Ermine*.

SEVEN

Lurking in the Undergrowth,

1950–1953

As the 1950s opened, Pitter was comfortably settled in Chelsea, earning a good living, yet ever ready to head out to Oak Cottage whenever circumstances allowed. Indeed, she increasingly desired to leave London permanently, so she and O'Hara began to discuss the possibility of moving to the Essex cottage. O'Hara was reluctant to do this, given her more refined tastes—life at the cottage was very simple, if not in some ways spartan. Tired of the crowds, the traffic, and the general bustle of city life, Pitter longed to live in the country, where she could fully indulge her love of nature, gardening, and animals. In addition, Pitter's friendships with Lewis and the Cecils were flourishing, and the fact that they lived in or near Oxford came to influence her thoughts of retirement. Although thwarted for the time being, it would not be long before Pitter's dream of a country life would be realized.

She continued to receive care packages from her friends, most notably Cooley. As strict rationing in England began to ease and many basic foodstuffs became more readily available, Cooley started sending more specialized items. On January 17, 1950, Pitter thanks Cooley for a delightful and hard-to-get treat: "No doubt you will be delighted to know that having received your last magnificent box of chocolate, I am in a state of having-had-enough unequalled since 1939. Altogether you must have sent about 9 lbs in the 3 packages, and, as you can understand, this is almost stupefying to those [living] on a basis of 1 lb a month. . . . The stuff is so beautifully fresh, coming straight from the factory like that." Later in the month she writes Cooley about the death of Orwell: "Today I went to the funeral service for 'George Orwell' (Eric A. Blair). I have known him & his family for almost 30 years. He was a very interesting but I think ill-fated man. . . . I really feel quite oppressed with grief about it: I didn't know I could still feel so much. . . . For years past I've always said 'I don't mind people dying, if it amuses them. It's the ones who won't die that get my goat.' But I minded this death" (Jan. 27). Orwell's death certainly reminded Pitter of her own early days of struggle when she and O'Hara were starting Deane and Forester, so to lose him as an acquaintance from her young adulthood was a blow. In fact, as the inevitable march of time toward death begins to take its toll on Pitter's friends and acquaintances, death becomes an increasingly prominent theme in her poetry. Many of the poems she writes during this time that later appear in *The Ermine* deal with death.

The 1950s were also the period during which Pitter increasingly received regular letters from admirers, for the most part ordinary people who were profoundly moved by her poetry. One of these admirers, Richard E. Blackshaw, a native of Liverpool but at this time living in Illinois, first writes Pitter on February 10. Dating his love of her verse to his purchase of *First and Second Poems,* he offers praise of his favorite poems from *The Bridge;* he also admits to his disaffection for modern poetry, singling out T. S. Eliot for particular criticism, completely unaware of how much Pitter agreed with him:

I dislike the bulk of T. S. Eliot. . . . I find the "moderns" worse than difficult. Of course they justify their obscurity by opposite illustrations from the past. Only theirs is obscurity obscured. Thus in their eyes I become an enemy of newness and innovation. But, after all, their claim is but a claim, and should be examined with care, candor, and skill. Their subjects presumably come home to the bosoms and business of man today, but I feel that it is the job of Poetry to deal with the great and lovely things that have always disturbed the minds and hearts of men.

Blackshaw adds that his favorite moderns are Walter de la Mare, Robert Frost, Robert Graves, W. B. Yeats, and, of course, Pitter. In addition, he heaps praise on seventeenth-century poets Henry Vaughan, Andrew Marvell, John Donne, Richard Crashaw, and George Herbert. Pitter replies on February 19: "I was so glad to have your very kind letter. Fancy you knowing my work so far back! It *is* nice to hear from such a faithful reader. And I do agree with your feelings about modern poetry in general. For half a lifetime I have patiently striven to understand (making little headway) but now I have made up my mind that the qualities that confuse us are BAD."[1] She goes on to tell Blackshaw to get a copy of Hamilton's *The Tell-tale Article* since his critique of modern poetry is one she shares. A lively and literate correspondence developed between Pitter and Blackshaw that both deeply enjoyed.

In addition to letters from admirers, during this same period Pitter continued to receive letters from other writers and poets who enjoyed her work. Roy Campbell writes Pitter on February 25 and tells her, "Ever since I saw that superb poem about the Earwig I have been a fervent admirer of your work."[2] He adds that he had hoped to meet her the previous weekend at the home of mutual friends and had been "extremely disappointed" when she had cancelled. He also tells her he had just stayed the night at Magdalen College, where he found "you had a great admirer in C. S. Lewis." Pitter's steady if incremental success as a poet led Cresset Press to decide to do a collected edition, so after attending a class in choral verse speaking at her diocesan conference in Oxford in early July, she was busy correcting galley proofs. While working on the collected edition excited her, she tells Cooley that "I have become so dull lately that I don't know what will happen to me. My one aim in life seems to be not to get mixed up in anything whatever. This is not quite the thing for a poet, I am well aware; at least, not until one is, say, 70 or so. I have been re-reading Milton, and am delighted to perceive that I can now focus him critically, which I was unable to do at all while young. This sort of thing consoles me very much—as long as one can see some kind of development, all is not lost" (Nov. 7).

Several weeks later her collected edition, *Urania*, containing selections from *A Trophy of Arms*, *The Spirit Watches*, and *The Bridge*, and with a title-page illustration by Joan Hassall, appeared.[3] In a later letter to Nettie Palmer she explains why *Urania* does not contain selections of her early verse: "A good many people have deplored the omissions in 'Urania,' & indeed some were actually overlooked, but as regards the early ones—well, I looked at them, & consulted various people, & decided against: if I had put them in I should have patched them, and this wouldn't have been right. I couldn't let them go as they were. There is a definite 'watershed' in the work about 1932–33, and all on the far side is really immature. They can go back & look at it if they want to" (Dec. 28, 1951). Pitter's critical insight about the poor quality of her early poetry is perceptive, and it illustrates as well her lifelong distaste for self-promotion. Had she wanted to pad *Urania* with her early verse, perhaps as a way of trying to redeem it, Cresset Press probably would have acquiesced. By including the early verse in *Urania*, Pitter could have tried to make the point that she had always been a poet capable of winning the Hawthornden Prize. Pitter's personal and poetic integrity, however, militated against such a "sellout." She knew that it was only after *Persephone in Hades* that she found her poetic voice, so she was content to "lurk in the undergrowth," working hard every day as an artisan in order to earn a living and quietly crafting her poetry in the precious spare moments she could find.

In general critics reviewed *Urania* favorably. David Cecil, writing for the *Observer*, is predictably positive: "The critic's first impulse is one of gratitude. For in this selection, one of the most distinguished of living writers has gathered the best of her achievement. The result is a book of extraordinary beauty."[4] Cecil admires Pitter's unique gifts as a poet, particularly her use of language, and her "careful, fastidious aptness of phrase which time and again, escapes preciousness triumphantly to achieve felicity." However, most satisfying to Cecil is how Pitter has joy at the center of her verse: "Not a carefree joy: Miss Pitter is acutely sensitive to the tragedy of life, especially of modern life. The still and moonlit exaltation, to which at moments she attains, is that of a spirit who has surmounted suffering but not forgotten it. It is this which makes her work, for all its classic restraint, so poignant; and so consoling." The reviewer for the *Times Literary Supplement* notes that *Urania* shows Pitter's "growing mastery of her material."[5] He also is perceptive enough to see in the poems Pitter's own spiritual pilgrimage: "The fine perception of the life of flowers, birds, and animals and of country people is the recurring note: it is the pastoral world of eighteenth-century lyric, delicately formal: it is also a visible expression of God." He praises her work as "idyllic, gentle, most beautifully musical verse." In particular, he cites one poem: "'The Cygnet: A Song of the Thames' raises the poet's achievement to a new level. It is a poem in the light of which we re-read all her previous work, and in which her favourite images fuse into a manifold symbol of tragic splendour."

The appearance of *Urania* was deeply satisfying to Pitter since it validated her place as an important if undervalued poet. In addition, its appearance gave her an opportunity to write Lewis with the news, while at the same time complimenting him for his *The Lion, the Witch and the Wardrobe*, the first of the Chronicles of Narnia, which also appeared in 1950. Lewis was delighted to hear from Pitter: "What a delightful surprise! You cheer me up to no end, and provide a makeweight to letters from a headmistress which tells me the book will cause confusion and terror, and many people are much 'distressed' at my having written it. But I get nice letters from actual children and parents. . . . But next time you write, don't write all about *me*: what are *you* doing, and how are *you?*" (Nov. 28, 1950).[6] Encouraged anew by Lewis's attention, she tells him about her latest gardening efforts, and a month later he confesses that he cannot keep up with the scientific names of vegetables and finishes by noting he has enjoyed reading the poetry of Dorothy Wellesley (79–80; Dec. 30).[7]

Lewis's friendship with Pitter leads him to share with her his thoughts, feelings, and ideas. For instance, a week later Lewis writes and frankly reveals his frustration with modern literature, wondering why he should bother reading contemporary authors if he does not care for the work they produce (83; Jan. 6, 1951). Two months later he writes Pitter with praise for *Urania*, noting that the book is beautiful and his favorite poems look even better in a new book. One "reason why they look better is that they are better than I remembered. I find that my very favourite 'The Sparrow's Skull' had in memory preserved only its poignancy and lost a great deal of its delicacy and poetic breeding. . . . I say, 'Sinking,' which I hadn't properly noticed before, is a corker. So indeed are dozens." He also recalls the wonderful grapes she had shared at an earlier luncheon, and he uses this letter as an opportunity to cajole Pitter into a visit: "When next term cd. you come down and lunch? There's an extra reason: you have property to reclaim. Groping in the inn'ards of an old arm chair lately (a place which rivals the sea bed for lost treasure) I fished out a spectacle case which, being opened, revealed your golden name wrapped in your silver address" (95; March 17).[8] Pitter is surprised both at having lost her spectacle case in Lewis's armchair and at his only recent discovery of it. In response Lewis says, "May I book [our luncheon] for May 10th: 1:15? . . . I didn't know arm chairs were ever cleaned: should they be?" (101; March 26).[9] To Cooley on May 9 Pitter writes and expresses her excitement about her luncheon the next day with Lewis: "Old Bertrand Russell is doing a series of radio pep-talks, trying to sell us the hoary fallacy of being radiantly happy on an ethical basis! I wonder who let the darned old fool loose. I am going to Oxford tomorrow to see C. S. Lewis, who puts the blame where it belongs, on our fallen nature!" After the subsequent get together on May 10 Lewis writes her: "It is I who have to thank you for making my little party a success. You supplied the air and fire." He also thanks her for being willing to read and critique more of his poems: "My own MS will go to you as soon as it is typed. Don't let it be a bother: what I want is only a *Yes* or a *No* or *Doubtful*. It is very kind of you to undertake the job, for a job of course it is" (117–18; May 18).

The summer of 1951 also brought a visit from Sarton; another trip to Oxford, where Pitter taught a verse-speaking class each day at the diocesan conference of the Worship and the Arts Association; service as a judge for a poetry contest (she tells Cooley, "Terribly hard work, and not very rewarding, for most of the competitors are just plain dull"); and an embarrassing yet humorous escapade involving T. S. Eliot. She was out walking with her acquaintance Dorothy Tyler:

It was one of those muddles that one can get into in one instant—nothing that really mattered, but a perverse little twist of fate. As we were passing the big block of flats facing the river, I just remarked that T. S. Eliot lived there with his friend John Hayward. Miss Tyler popped in to see if she could see his name on the board, but there weren't any names shown at all, so she asked the porter which flat it was, as I didn't know. The demon porter at once said brightly, "No. 19, madam!' and flinging open the elevator, invited us to ascend. Now this is where I should have held back, but I was indecisive, & Miss Tyler, after looking doubtful for a minute, got in and I followed, for I couldn't desert a guest at that point. We got to No. 19 and Miss Tyler rang the bell—a nice housekeeper came and I said here was an American lady who would so much like to see where Mr. E. worked—and to my horror she said Mr. Hayward was at home and she'd go and see. I sent in my name because I do know him slightly. The housekeeper presently took us to him. He is dreadfully crippled (I think it is extensive disseminated sclerosis) and couldn't get up, and there we stood while he said it was quite impossible, people weren't supposed to know, etc. He wasn't rude or unkind, only extremely stiff, and it was so silly really, because I can remember old Tommy Rot since he was smaller than Ezra Pound. We got out in a hurry. (June 16)

Three weeks later Pitter ran into Eliot in church, and Pitter recalls the meeting in a letter to Cooley: "He was sitting at the back when I came in. I went & spoke to him—said, 'Good morning, it's only Ruth Pitter.' He said 'Ah yes, it's so many years since I saw you.' I said 'I'm so glad to see you here.' I don't think anyone else recognized him. He looked miserable, I thought. I prayed for charity among poets (!) meaning mostly myself" (July 16).

On July 7 Lewis thanks Pitter for her remarks about the poems he had sent her earlier: "Very many thanks for reading the MS. The idea that you should also thank [me] is to me fantastic: I was 'making use of you.' You were a thermometer" (130). No matter how overwhelmed Lewis became with the massive correspondence he was now receiving, he always enjoyed receiving Pitter's letters. Back from a trip, he says finding her letter among the many waiting for him "is a bright spot in a hailstorm of correspondence" and promises to visit her during an upcoming trip to London (Sept. 12).[10] He is particularly gracious in his New Year's remarks for 1952: "Congratulations on [*Urania*] being a Book of the Year for '51. Whenever I re-read your poems, I blame myself for not re-reading them oftener. . . . All blessings. I will drink to your health (not 'only with my eyes') at lunch time" (Dec. 29).[11]

Blackshaw writes at year's end to tell Pitter that she had been favorably praised in R. A. Scott-James's *Fifty Years of English Literature, 1900–1950*.[12] In addition, he apologizes for being "gushy" in an earlier letter but finds solace that "Scott-James comes close to my sudden remarks in his appraisal of your work" (Dec. 10). In her reply Pitter says, "No, I didn't think your letter 'gushy.' I thought it the letter of a man with lively feelings, a warm heart, & the courage of his convictions—all excellent things. People nowadays are much too shy of expressing their feelings—it is a very immature attitude" (Dec. 19). Then she reflects upon how beneficial it is for a poet to hear from readers: "Poets have to expose their emotions a good deal, and it's wonderful to think that we can sometimes touch the hearts of others & they write & tell us so—the radar signal comes back from the cold void of space & tells us there's another living, feeling being out there who wishes us well." Regarding Blackshaw's closing comment, where he says he hopes she is weathering the "commotion and distress of the times," almost certainly an allusion to the Korean War, Pitter writes, "Yes, I get along well enough: I have what most poets have not, great bodily strength, and I have a quiet pleasant trade which gives me a living without having a boss, and a little country place I can fly to at times: what more could one want? I share the general anxiety, of course, but as a Christian I do not ask for security—my security is elsewhere—though I pine & grieve to think of all the misery of the countless victims." Pitter's reference to her Christian faith as a sustaining force in her life is measured and indicates how closely held her spiritual commitment is.

Writing to Cooley, Pitter offers an insight into the kind of paintings that appeared on her tea trays as well as a humorous Christmas anecdote:

> I'm glad you gave your mother the little tray. I do sometimes think that, humble as this work is, the love I feel for the flowers etc. does come through. Certainly the demand supports this theory. But of course I can't do more than a certain amount, so I'll never get rich on it, though I daresay it will yield bread & butter as long as my eyes keep good enough. Those gazelles I copied at first from Persian paintings, but soon gave them my own feeling. When I was younger I portrayed them leaping & running: now I am older I paint them having a nice set down, as we Cockneys say. What a lot of lovely associations they leave in literature. Tell your mother that the creature really is a gazelle, quite close in type to the reedbuck of the Sudan—a pretty sand-coloured thing about 3 feet high.
>
> We spent Xmas here, not liking crowded travel at that time. We had a bachelor friend with us, who had given up his quarters so that his sub-tenants could have their family round them. We went to the midnight service. I cooked Xmas dinner—goose & trimmings. The goose cost an awful lot, but lasted well. I made all the sauce, gravy, etc. the day before, & put them in preserve jars & heated them *en bain marie*. A good time was had by all. The bachelor friend washed up & did the fires, and when all was restored to order I read Milton's "Nativity Ode" with great feeling to be greeted by terrible snores half way through. The midnight service and the dinner had got the better of my friends. (Jan. 17, 1952)

After Christmas a final important letter of the year comes from longtime friend Nettie Palmer, who tells Pitter how much her poetry has influenced her own life. Pitter, of course, is delighted: "Your encouragement is so generous & so discriminating—a rare thing, to find a kind woman & an experienced professional writer in one person" (Dec. 28, 1951). When Palmer laments the fact that Pitter, in spite of modest fame, is not more widely known, Pitter muses: "I still feel obscure, because although fairly widely known now, I am distinctly not fashionable, and still have to work hard at painting to make a living. But at the same time I know that I have been, and am, a great deal noticed considering everything, and I have some steadfast friends whose judgment, like yours, I respect, who consistently approve of my work." She adds that her production of verse has been limited as of late: "I haven't written much since the war; one lives in much too close quarters & there are too many chores, but better writers than I are in the same boat. I have plenty of ideas, but they drop off without opening. Perhaps times will improve."

During the first three months of 1952 Pitter did have a burst of poetic output, as her manuscript notebooks show. Furthermore, Pitter was not only active in writing poetry. Because of her growing reputation, she was invited to address the Royal Institution of Great Britain. On February 22 she delivered what was, in effect, her poetic manifesto, "A Return to Poetic Law."[13] Here Pitter argues for her deeply held belief that the future of English poetry is directly linked to a return to what she calls the "traditional laws and rules of art." In general, what she means by this is the kind of poetry she loved and grew up memorizing—that of Chaucer, Shakespeare, Spenser, Milton, Pope, Wordsworth, Shelley, Keats, Blake, Hardy, and Housman. Such poetry relies on tried and true forms, diction, imagery, figurative language, meter, and rhythm. What is more, traditional poetry concerns itself not with the bizarre, the transient, the immediate, but instead it deals with issues intimately connected to the human condition—love, death, existence, beauty, meaning, God, fear, doubt, joy, hope, grief, and so on. Early in the address she says: "During the last century or so there has been unprecedented impatience and disgust with the traditional laws and rules of art, and a corresponding profusion of experiment and of ephemeral fashions, which we in England hold in great awe. . . . Poetry has thus been brought into disrepute: it has tended to become despised, and of late increasingly neglected."[14] Along the way she cites Barfield, Lewis, and George Rostrevor Hamilton (especially his *The Tell-Tale Article*) for support and, predictably, lays much of the fault for the state of modern British poetry at the feet of T. S. Eliot. The fundamental error she sees in modern poetry is that it "consists in separation, division, abstraction of elements of life and of thought one from another, resulting in false exaltations, false degradations, and impious, unreal enmities."

Because of this, Pitter argues, "contemporary poetry is now cut off from the generality of English-speaking people. It has become a minor specialist's subject like stamp collecting. The public has not deserted poetry; it is poetry which has deserted the great public, the people who are too honest to pretend an interest they do not feel." While a few educated men and women labor on with contemporary poetry, Pitter says the majority avoid it because "it bewilders and somehow humiliates them. . . . They have been given stones for bread, and are delighted when one suggests that they should cease the pretence of eating them." Then she parodies claims she has heard: "I have read the assertion that poems comprehensible in one reading must be bad poems. I have been given to understand that pleasure in poetry is a bad symptom. I have heard a poet of some reputation announce in public that he was about to read a poem of his own which we should not understand, and should not like if we did understand it." It was the attempt by modern poets to isolate their work as a subspecies of abstract thought that most infuriated Pitter.

When she explains what she means by a return to poetic law, therefore, it is not surprising that she affirms the idea of universal law: "The first two laws of poetry, as of all human affairs, are love of God and love of one's neighbour." Pitter's attempt to apply these biblical injunctions is worth noting, since it illustrates her poetic credo. About this first law, Pitter says: "Every poem should start from a waiting upon the spirit; from poetic experience, from inspiration. There is no mistaking the thing when it happens, for it carries an impression of reality far beyond the reality of everyday life." To support her contention, she cites a passage by the French poet Paul Valéry: "A poem is above all a rhythm. That is to say, it is an explosion at the centre of one's being, the force of which expends itself in successive waves reaching to the very limits of the surface. Without this explosion there is no poetry. By this we know the true poet."

Then Pitter offers her most sustained explanation of how she believes poetry works:

> I believe that the structure of a poem is inherent in that poem from the moment of conception, as the structure of the living organism is inherent in the fertilized ovum. The rhythm is set up by the successive waves from the first "explosion." The whole can be projected from the fragment; if a phrase suddenly embodies itself, the shape of the rest can be inferred; in fact the whole poem will gradually form and organize itself about this small bud. The rules are used as tools to help the parts to their places, once we can see what form the poem wants. Such a poem, lawfully begotten and faithfully reared, will carry its own spiritual credentials, and strike home to the heart of the receptive reader at once. It may be felt as a physical shock. . . . [Great poetry] most comes home [not to the familiar], but to something deeper and more unknown: like music, it is the language of spirit to spirit, instantly recognized, and received in the same act.

Pitter's first poetic law is at odds both with modernism and postmodernism: with the former because of its focus upon the personality and personal experience of the poet, and with the latter because of its assumption that readers no longer share a common worldview shaped by shared religious, spiritual, and cultural traditions.

She says, "The second great law, of poetry as well as of life, is the love of one's neighbour," thus revealing her debt to traditional views of the role of poetry held by writers such as Aristotle, Longinus, and Sir Philip Sydney. That is, the function of poetry "is to give delight; various kinds of delight, of course, some of them very severe; but always to delight. This must mean, I think, that the poet is to make his work as lucid as possible, to communicate with his neighbour as perfectly and as widely as he can." Certainly Pitter intends this as a contrast to the kind of poetry she believed Eliot and his followers were writing. She admits that poets adhering to this second law may not always be successful, yet she believes something good can still result because of a connection back to her first poetic law: "He will not always succeed in being perfectly lucid, but there is a mystery here. If he strives faithfully for clarity . . . , his involuntary obscurities, and even his ignorance, may be used by the spirit to give an uncovenanted richness." In another sustained passage, she summarizes her argument:

> In embodying a poem, and in clothing it, the poet should be mindful that the body is nobler than the dress, and the spirit than the body. He must therefore have regard to inspiration, reason, and poetic form, in that order. Poetic form, however rich, must never knowingly be allowed to obscure reason, nor must either of them conceal, or distort, or debase the spirit. Thus the poet will not go too far from colloquial speech and its natural rhythms. He will discard poeticisms, such as inversions, in so far as they merely serve the form. He will be as lucid as his matter permits, for love's sake, without whom he is sounding brass and tinkling cymbal. He will not deliberately exhibit psychopathic symptoms. He will not be able to exclude them altogether, whatever his vigilance. No one can do that. There will be unresolved psychopathic residues in every work of art, but this does not mean that raw clinical material can be presented as art. Poets are miserable, to be sure, but poetic misery is not poetry, unless and until it can be so resolved by power and skill that a proper catharsis is induced in the reader.

For Pitter, the poet's psychology should never be the exclusive focus of a poem.[15]

In the conclusion of "A Return to Poetic Law" Pitter's traditionalist and anti-modernist bias is brought into succinct relief: "True poetry is a spiritual thing; its joy is supernal joy, its corruption is more dreadful than natural corruption. True poetry, like peace, is whole and indivisible. Delight is as native to it as grief, and as indispensable; and our part in fulfilling the law of its nature and genesis, both as poets and as readers, consists in love and gratitude, in courage and rejoicing, in faithful work, and in all possible humility." All this leads her to have renewed hope for English poetry: "Let us move on into the opening era, with its hopes of a new poetic magnificence worthy of the glory of the mighty English-speaking nations." In this, her most complete attempt to articulate her thinking about poetry, we find much to inform our understanding of her work, both the early immature verse and the later mature work. Through her poetry, Pitter longs to make connections to the intuitive, the spiritual, the mysterious. Life for her is not simply a matter of that which is observable, measurable, or quantifiable; physics, chemistry, and biology can describe the physical world, but they cannot portray the human condition. Accordingly, when Pitter writes verse she is striving to connect to the world beyond nature while finding in nature clues that offer insight into the world of the spirit.

Having completed and presented "A Return to Poetic Law," Pitter turned to thoughts of the future, and she and O'Hara begin talking in earnest about moving out of Chelsea, the biggest hindrance being that the lease for their flat was in effect until 1954. While this was an impediment, Pitter's desire to be nearer Lewis and the Cecils led her to look for opportunities to settle around Oxford. Her continued contact with both men also probably contributed to her desire to move near them. For instance, Lewis's playfully writes Pitter about how unrhymed alexandrines are better than blank verse, offering an example with Pitter as the subject: "I know far less of spiders than that poetess / Who (like the lady in *Comus* in the perilous wood) / Can study nature's infamies with secure heart." He also humorously invites her to one of his lectures: "It always seems a bit of cheek to send anyone (especially the likes of you) a ticket for one's lectures, unless one could do it in the Chinese style 'In the inconceivably unlikely event of honourable poetess wishing to attend this person's illiterate and erroneous lecture'" (182–83; April 16, 1952). Pitter recalls the lecture:

That lecture! It was in London, I forget where: a biggish hall with a gallery. This lecture was a keypoint in my mental life, but I must warn the reader that my mind goes on elaborating anything that strikes it forcibly, and allowance must be made for the accretions. . . . On arriving & taking my seat about halfway down the body of the hall, I was struck at once by the arresting character of the assistance. Right in front there were what seemed to be several retired lady dons, checking deaf-aids and simply beaming with anticipation. The rest of the two front rows seemed to be filled by individuals mostly well-known enough to be recognized, nearly all with people they shouldn't have been with, and glorying in it. Behind these were several rows of earnest Christians, also beaming, though looking (as I am afraid we usually do) rather mere and moth-eaten. Back under the gallery were more well-known persons, variously accompanied, and this lot not courting the limelight. Over the edge of the gallery appeared from time to time the heads of sundry well-known authors, having a swift peep and popping back. "Now what," thought I in my ignorance, "what can possibly have drawn this heterogeneous assembly together?" I was soon to know. In strides Lewis, full of bonhomie, competence, and matter—on to the platform—vast applause—bows, & begins, "This is a very warm poem ['Hero and Leander']!" Of course! The Christians were out to hear dear Lewis, the dons for this and the learned exposition, and the scandalous—well, for the warmth. I learned a lot that afternoon. Wonder-ingly, I realized what times could be had in the academic shades. . . . What a pleasure to hear Lewis lecturing or broadcasting! Splendid voice, never a check, hardly a note, not a dull phrase.[16]

Furthermore, Pitter enjoyed a visit to the home of the Cecils in Oxford because of its contrast to the busy streets of London. She writes Rachel on May 5: "I got home safely & uneventfully, complete with flowers and wine, and well pleased with the lovely week-end, surrounded as I had been with comfort, kindness, & entertainment. . . . I was so glad, too, to see the children again. They are most interesting and individual, and friendly too. London seemed horrible after such a lovely time, even if the sun had begun to shine." Thus, as Pitter and O'Hara continued to talk about leaving Chelsea, the idea of finding a home near Ox-ford became more and more attractive. O'Hara was more interested in finding a good house than in a particular regional location, while Pitter, also desiring a good structure, believed her friendships with the Cecils and Lewis would be greatly enhanced by a move that would bring her closer to Oxford. Eventually the two women agreed to focus their search in the greater Oxford area.

In midsummer Pitter was visited at the Essex cottage by one of her American care-package benefactors, Eugene Walter. Having long admired Pitter's poetry and wanting to promote her to a wider reading audience, Walter asked if he might reprint portions of *Persephone in Hades* in the periodical he edited, *Bot-teghe Oscure*. Pitter writes him after his visit:

Here is "Persephone" in redemption of my promise. I know you'll be care-ful to let me have it back, as it's my only copy. It was nice to see you at the cottage. I've always had a kind of myth at the back of my mind, the essence of which is "that some day, some very nice man will care about my work enough to come and search me out in the country where I belong." At the old cottage we had when we were young in the forest . . . I was always on the watch, and though lots of nice people came, it wasn't for that. It wasn't vanity, but faith: if the work is valid, it will be answered. Now in my "jubilee" year (it's 50 years since I first tried to write a poem) it has happened. I could go on about it forever, but mustn't. I shall hope to see you in Paris later. (July 23)

After another relaxing weekend with the Cecils in early August, Pitter hears from Walter again, who thanks her for sending him *Persephone in Hades* and offers to make a protective book jacket for it. Pitter thanks him for this and for the copy of his periodical: "I did get the copy of *Botteghe Oscure* safely, and apologise for not having acknowledged it at once. Do you know, I have hardly had time to do more than glance at it yet, and have only just discovered that it contains three delightful poems of your own. They are all endearing, but the first is my favourite: I like the form, and the theme is as noble as (alas) it is rare" (Aug. 28). She finishes the letter by wishing Walter could be with her again at Oak Cottage: "I wish you were . . . going with me to North End this evening. It will really be dusk when I get there, for the Dogstar is waning. We have been glutted with greengages, the grapes are about ripe and the pears & apples coming along—the late apples, that is—the early ones have been in use since a few days after your visit. I feel you will be there again." Unfortunately, Pitter's trip to Paris in September fell through, so she never visited Walter there.

By October Pitter had reluctantly decided to sell Oak Cottage, writing Cooley: "I have had to make a sad decision—to sell off our productive little country place. . . . I can't keep up the cottage except by living there, and it's too rough & unsocial for K. We mean to look for a country home elsewhere, & leave London" (Oct. 2). On November 18 Pitter writes to offer Cooley condolence for a friend who has suffered a painful operation, and she shares her own sadness: "I am in grief too. Yesterday I left the cottage for the last time. It has come sooner than I expected, and is a real trouble; I did so hope I could finish my days where my mother lived and died." She also writes Walter about this: "Yes, it was sad to leave North End, when I had hoped to end my days there, but there is a credit side. I shall have a little more time & a very little more money now I haven't 2 lives to run, and the journey, especially in winter, was very trying, though the distance was small" (Dec. 16). And for the first time she mentions that her next volume of poetry is in process: "No, *The Ermine* won't be out till spring; it always happens like that to my books. It's my own fault for not raging round to parties & reminding people of my existence."

Lewis writes on January 2, 1953, and gives her New Year's greetings, consoles her on the loss of Oak Cottage, and compliments her on "A Return to Poetic Law," which she had earlier sent him; he notes that unfortunately, those who most need to read it will probably never see it (273–74). Lewis's wry comments about what he believed was a ruling literary clique and their predilection for modernist verse certainly found a sympathetic ear in Pitter. Pitter writes Rachel Cecil explaining the sale of the Essex cottage and sharing her desire to move closer to Oxford: "As soon as the disposal of this house is arranged we shall set about finding something not too far from Oxford—say 10 or 12 miles, or even a little more—I know that places at all close in must be very scarce & expensive" (Jan. 8). Good to her word, Pitter begins writing the London County Council in order to ascertain whether or not the tenant occupying the lower floor of 55A Old Church Street would be permitted to sublet the top two floors from Pitter and O'Hara for his electrical supply business.

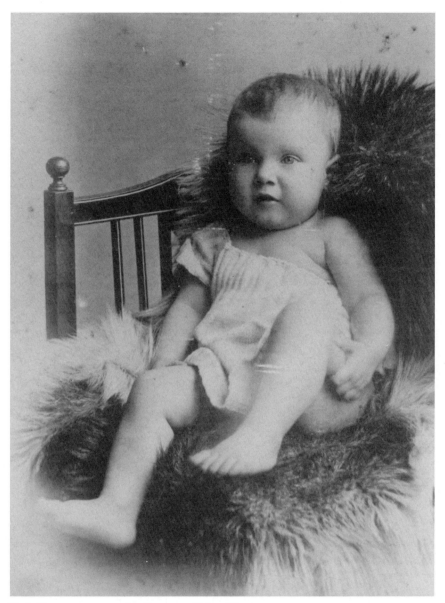

Ruth Pitter at one year old. Courtesy of Mary Thomas.

Front row (left to right): Ruth Pitter, Olive Pitter, and Geoffrey Pitter. Back row (left to right): George Pitter, Kitty Murrell, and Louisa Pitter. Ca. 1903. Courtesy of Mary Thomas.

Pitter in mid-1920s. Courtesy of Win Murrell.

Pitter outside Oak Cottage, early 1930s. Courtesy of Ann Soutter.

Mervyn Peakes's line drawing of Ruth Pitter that first appeared in *London Mercury* 36 (July 1937): 236a. Used by permission of David Higham Associates Limited.

Pitter and her mother outside Oak Cottage, early 1940s. Courtesy of Ann Soutter.

Pitter gardening at the Hawthorns, mid-1960s. Courtesy of Mark Pitter.

The Queen's Gold Medal for Poetry, awarded personally to Pitter by Queen Elizabeth II, October 19, 1955. Courtesy of Thomas McKean.

Mark Pitter. Photo by Don King.

In February Pitter replies to Theodore Maynard, who had written and asked Pitter to update him on her life and writing. She remarks humorously: "No, this house was not destroyed, though it well might have been. I believe one of the U.S. works of reference said it had been—I think they were pepping-up my biography a bit, as they also knocked 10 years or so off my age" (Feb. 19). Pitter must have been both flattered and cheered by such an error. Then she adds: "I am slower than ever at writing—I think there is some little excuse besides the middle-aged loss of lyrical impulse, as I simply cannot get peace even to think consecutively. There is nothing between one and the noise & confusion of life. I think I am getting a little schizophrenic, as I notice myself hating & fearing people for being about to speak to me! However, I did a sort of Collected Poems a year or two ago, and have a new book (very small) on the way ('The Ermine')." Pitter's confession about her difficulty writing foreshadows the fact that The Ermine is her last volume of verse containing mostly new poetry.

The Ermine

The Ermine: Poems 1942–1952 appeared in the spring, and it marks a deliberate turn in Pitter's poetic and spiritual life.[17] Of special note is the fact that no poems focus upon Hainault Forest or the old cottage; in addition, there are no poems dealing with romantic love, either yearning for it or lamenting its loss. Instead, it is a volume filled with poems inspired by stories or memories from her childhood and poems exploring death and the spiritual life. By the end of the book, Pitter's faith in a benign but distant God such as we see in A Trophy of Arms is replaced by a powerful affirmation of her faith in the God of the Bible and in Jesus Christ in particular. Yet this movement is not presented as an evangelical tract; instead, Pitter uses all her skills as a poet to communicate her religious commitment obliquely through suggestion, indirection, and intimation. When she does finally reveal her faith at the end of The Ermine, she has done a masterful job preparing the reader for her theological "coming home." This way of organizing the text makes The Ermine unique: it is the only one of her volumes of lyric poems that, at least in some ways, tells a story. Fittingly, the story is of the culmination of Pitter's spiritual pilgrimage.

"The Stolen Babe," the first poem based on childhood memories, is a dramatic monologue from the perspective of a gypsy woman who has stolen an ailing baby out of the garden of a well-to-do family. Pitter heard several variations of this story during her childhood, and her version, while not approving of the gypsy woman's actions, does humanize her, capturing her loneliness and desperate desire for love. Knowing the child is ill, yet fearful of being exposed if she takes the baby to a hospital, the gypsy pauses for awhile in a churchyard: "See the green grass and the flowers on the graves! / There's a baby's head on that old stone there—/ Smiling, smiling, between the little wings, / Smiling in the darkness under the yew."[18] This gravestone foreshadows the impending death of the stolen child, and this is made certain when the woman, seeing a little bee go "home to her little burrow under the stone," says: "Ah, she's the lucky one, she's got a deep shelter, / Out of the cold wind, out of the rain, / Out of the bad luck, under the ground: / A good safe place, baby, under the ground." This poignant yet tragic retelling of a child abduction leaves us wondering about the pain and suffering not of the gypsy, but of the family of the child; perhaps Pitter creates greater sympathy for this family by keeping them at a distance, focusing instead on the desperately lonely but ultimately unsympathetic gypsy woman, whose own selfish needs drive her to do the unforgivable.

"Herding Lambs," dedicated to Pitter's sister, Olive, recalls an instance from their childhood when they were drawn by "the high bleat [of the lambs], / And the low voice of the ewes" to the gentle passing of a sheep herd one beautiful spring morning (16–17). On this "daffodil day" they heard "the rainlike / Rustle of feet" and ran out to see "three / Old grey men, and five children" herd a small group of sheep "to the fresh lea." She remembers "when a silly lamb / Turned back in fright / A withered or an infant hand / Guided him right."[19] Throughout the poem there is a calm assurance that all is well: "The early mist muffled their sound / Muted that double chime / Trembling along the grassy ground / From the morning of time." The delightful metaphor of "the rainlike / Rustle of feet" cleverly helps us hear the busy but gentle movement of the sheep. While "Herding Lambs" is ostensibly about the memory of this event, it serves the larger purpose of illustrating Pitter's sense that humanity is protected by a loving, personal God.

"The Father Questioned" may be another of Pitter's recollections of her father's anger at the injustices of man toward man. Set in the graveyard where he was buried—"Dead father, your bones lie under the cedar"—Pitter remembers a series of disturbing scenes from her childhood:

O father, who was the noseless man, and the child
With angel eyes and face all covered with sores?
What was the woman screaming? why did they take her
Away, and where? had someone hurt her, father?
The unemployed are marching, singing of hunger.
Why are they hungry? the shops are full of food;
Why can't they have it? now they've turned into soldiers,
And must fight and die. Why must they die, dead father?
Who says they cannot have food, and then says, "Die"? (23–26)

In a sudden shift, the poem turns to the "hyacinth, crocus, daphne," lovely flowers that "speak so plainly, do not ask an answer." Such as these, Pitter says, "are
what we seek." Yet the question remains: "Why is the rest not so?" That is, what
is it "behind" the beauty of nature that can counterbalance man's inhumanity
to man? Still addressing her dead father, Pitter offers an answer: "Father, there
is something I cannot tell you. / There are no words. It lives behind the sky. / It
is there in the tree, and in some people's faces, / Like music, like the lily of the
valley, / Like a green grave and like a happy morning: / O, even in the grass,
even in dew." In earlier volumes of verse, Pitter might have referenced this "it"
to the distant but benevolent God she believed was behind all things; now,
however, she says that it "is love that lives behind the sky," a love so powerful
that it can help her bridge man's inhumanity and nature's beauty. Indeed, this
love, this "living father," tells her as much in the poem's conclusion: "It is you
who make them one. That is your treasure. / Can you seize earth and heaven by
the two horns / And bend and string them? Can you be that Eros? / The child
must understand the sun's affliction; / Green grave, and weeping night, and
happy morning." Recalling Blake's "Without Contraries is no progression" from
The Marriage of Heaven and Hell (1790–1793) but going beyond that, Pitter intimates that only a loving, personally involved God can help her and others to
live in proper balance between human injustices and nature's beauty.

Poems reflecting natural scenes or settings include "The Cedar," written to
memorialize a favorite cedar of Lebanon that Pitter loved looking at when she
stayed with Dorothy Wellesley at the Penns. Peering out the upper-floor windows and into the garden below, Pitter sees more in the cedar than just trunk,
branches, and needles. Instead, it becomes a conceit for the landscape of the
world—its microcosm becomes a macrocosm:

> Plant or world? Are those lights and shadows
> Branches, or great air-suspended meadows?
> Boles and branches, haunted by the flitting linnet,
> Or great hillsides rolling up to cliffs of granite?
> Those domed shapes, thick-clustered on the ledges,
> Upright fruit, or dwellings thatched with sedges? (21)

Her imagination sees much more than the majestic tree; in fact, it "is a country hanging in the morning. / Scented alps, where nothing but the daylight
changes, / Climbing to black walls of mountain ranges." In this vivid description, Pitter offers a vision of pleasure and comfort, a "dwelling of the blessed in
the green savannahs."

"Hill and Valley," a poem dedicated to David Cecil, is almost certainly set
in the countryside near Oxford. In this poem Pitter tries to capture the peace

of an idyllic scene, moving imaginatively from a lush hillside down "by deep drinking-places where the cattle go" (22). She hears mowing "falling with whispers" and the shrill cry of a lark, and she watches in silence as "grape-coloured shadows" lengthen down the hill. For a moment she wants to stay there, where she "could mind the sheep on the hill for ever," but then she believes she was "made to live by a great river, / Watching the cattle drinking in dimpled gleams, / Winding the wands of willow that spring by the streams." Although she would soon move to the Oxford countryside, when she writes this poem she is still living in Chelsea near the Thames, the "great river." Longing on one hand to live closer to the natural environment, on the other hand she senses that her present calling keeps her in the city. Consequently, she delights in the quiet, natural setting of this hill and valley, using them as "spots of time" that she can later draw on for refreshment.

"Dew" is a word picture describing the action of falling dew. Pitter uses metaphor extensively in order to capture the omnipresence of the dew: "Freshness of violet, richness of rose, / Bloom on the blade of the green grain, / Misty and waxen veil of the beautiful heath, / Incense-tear from the cedar, weeping its balm, / Pearl on the cheek of the peach, film of the breath / Of the cold night coming with gradual calm" (28). As it touches the objects of nature, dew acts almost like the water of baptism—cleansing, blessing, and enlivening: "Dew, the water of life, the pardon, the peace." "The Tuft of Violets" has a similar effect and can be glossed to "Sudden Heaven" from A Trophy of Arms and "Polymorph Pervers" from The Bridge; like the two earlier poems, "The Tuft of Violets" finds unexpected joy, this time when a small patch of early violets "breathes" upon Pitter during a late March walk. The powerful scent awakens her as well to the joyous song of a missel thrush and a foraging bee "kissing each modest face." All this leads to a Henry Vaughan–like mystical vision:

Time ceased, as if the spring
Had been eternity; I had no age;
The purple and the wing
That visited and hymned it, were a page
Royally dyed, written in gold;
Royal with truth, for ever springing;
For ever, as of old,
The sunlight and the darkness and the singing. (36–37)

To find in everyday experience these sudden epiphany-like occasions brought joy to Pitter, sustaining and nourishing her when she perhaps least looked for such.

"The Tree at Dawn" takes us on an early morning mowing expedition where Pitter contrasts the overwhelming beauty of the scene—probably set near Oak

Cottage—and the felicity of the animals nearby with human discontent and un-happiness. Up before the rising of the sun, "in the cold grey, and all alone," she takes up her scythe ("the hook"), "and while the dew would serve my turn / I cut the nettles strong, / The mowing grass and parsley-fern / The garden hedge along" (3–6). Reflecting on the quiet isolation of this experience, she muses: "How lone-ly seem the creatures then; / How lonely, even trees; / But the conceiving minds of men / Are lonelier than these." Echoing ideas she explored earlier in "Lament for the Landless" in *The Spirit Watches*, Pitter says nature's great advantage over man is that its objects are not aware of their loneliness: "They do not know them-selves alone, / And knowing would not care; / But holiness invests each one / In the grey morning air." Struck by this thought, Pitter drops her scythe—ceasing her "sacrilege"—and peers intently as light begins to infuse the scene: "Still as a plant I stand, and look, / And now no longer break / The breathing silence with my hook, / But watch the colours wake." Her attention focuses upon a gigantic tree, with its great bole of "glittering green ore," its boughs "dark green as the deepest sea," its sap that contains "the spirit of the dreadful night," and its fruits that "burn in the light / Of their last dawn, and bleed."

Then she turns this vision of the tree upon herself, noting that while the fruit of the tree "bleeds," the tree is not in pain; she contrasts this with her own experience: "For all the pain / Is in me who behold, / And mine, not his, the crimson stain." Pitter's "bleeding" is her awareness of her disconnect from other humans; this is a pain that nature can never know. As the light continues to grow, it mystically illumines the tree and other objects beyond it:

> But his that life mysterious,
>   And sacred, as I well see,
> And well companioned; glorious
>   Beyond the great old tree
> The pale-blue velvet cabbages
>   Stand lovely as a dream,
> And violet and pink sweet-peas
>   Clearer begin to gleam,
> With white that glimmered long ago,
>   When from my bed I came.

The intensity of this mystical experience—in the tradition of Thomas Tra-herne—is fleeting, as it is ironically washed out by the rising sun: "The clouds begin to glow, / The east begins to flame; / The god leaps up, the day is here, / The heat pours from the sky: / The tree is commonplace and dear, / And I am only I." In this poem we move along with Pitter as she rises before dawn, intent on getting some practical work done—to fulfill the agenda she set that day for herself—and experience instead her unexpected sense of isolation and loneliness in the face of nature's mysteries. For a moment we behold her "dappled-dawn" epiphany and find supernal value in the familiar objects of nature that she also explores in "The Bird in the Tree" in *The Spirit Watches*, but then the common light of day turns all into the ordinary, the mundane. Perhaps in no other poem does Pitter capture as effectively her intuitive understanding of the mystical power of nature as in "The Tree at Dawn."

In "The Captive Bird of Paradise" Pitter reflects upon a beautiful bird of paradise she loves to watch in a nearby zoo.[20] Although the bird is confined by the bars of the cage, Pitter has a mystical connection with the bird. Indeed, for Pitter this bird is a type of a miraculous creature in captivity. She longs to understand, to connect, to know intuitively all the bird stands for: "Give me the bird of Paradise, though dying, / Exiled and doomed, ravished from the Elysian / Forest where I shall never see it flying" (18). Her descriptions of the bird's colors, including "the rose-death purple mantled on with fire" and "the dying-dolphin green," are memorable. The poem ends with Pitter, although regretting that she will never see an even more mysterious bird, the phoenix—"Though I shall never see the sudden turning / Into a sphery monstrance, globe of splendour, / The ecstasy that is beyond our learning, / The action and the attitude that render / Love back to whence it came, the phoenix burning"—reflecting that she will be more than compensated by experiencing a mystical communion with the bird of paradise: "Give me the bird of paradise, the wonder." The bird as an object of natural beauty fascinated Pitter, and through it she makes a mystical connection to transcendent beauty.

The last poem of this group is "Hen under Bay-Tree," less about the natural setting and more an allegorical comment upon Pitter's life. Self-effacingly, she pictures herself as "a squalid, empty-headed Hen, / Resolved to rear a private brood" (43). As a result, she flies up from "the social pen" and perches in "noblest solitude" on the branches of a bay tree. We should not miss the irony here, since Pitter, who never married or had children, portrays herself as a brooding hen; her "offspring" are her poems, and her flight to the bay tree connotes the laurel wreath, the classical mark of honor given to poets. Hinting at the sense of being cut off from those who could understand her, also explored in "The Lost Tribe" from *The Bridge* ("I never found my people yet; / I go about, but cannot find / The blood relations of the mind"),[21] Pitter says the hen waits: "Alert she sits, and all alone; / She breathes a time-defying air." While above her songbirds shake the tree with their carols, the hen is content to occupy the lower branches: "Unworthy and unwitting, yet / She keeps love's vigil glorious; / Immovably her faith is set, / The plant of honour is her house." While some might object to ending the poem with such an obvious moral, Pitter affirms through the hen several things. First, as a poet, she is a loner, and given her penchant for following traditional forms and rejecting the modernism of T. S. Eliot and his imitators, this is no surprise. Second, she will be true to her muse, never involved in self-promotion. Third, she will affirm the redemptive power of love in all its manifestations, but particularly God's love. Finally, the only validation she needs is having written poetry she believes in—that which speaks directly to the heart, the soul, and the spirit of others.

Three poems focus primarily upon death. "A Worn Theme" considers the age-old question of what happens when we die: "Fairest is soonest gone— / But O gone where? / . . . Where has the spirit fled, / Whence did it come?" (29–30). For Pitter these are rhetorical questions that she answers this way: "Ah, when a beauty is dead / Its soul goes home." In fact, the ending of the poem has something of a death wish:

Then let us go there too;
Dearly I long to be
Where lives the vanished blue,
The moment's light at sea,

The smiles and the tender graces,
All gone by,
The flowers and the faces
That were born but to die.

Let us go, let us go
To their immortal day,
For all we have to do
Is to be fair as they,
And die, and flee away.

The ease, simplicity, and peace of death are attractive to Pitter. There is no fear of the grave, no fear of the worm, no fear of the rotting body, reflecting her conviction that physical death is a release and the entryway to union with God.

"Old Clockwork Time" and "The Lammastide Flower" are very much companion poems. "Old Clockwork Time" uses a stereotypical scene from a country churchyard: a large-faced clock perched at the top of a church tower gazes down upon a graveyard. Pitter contrasts the pitiless movement of time and its consumption of all physical things with the simplicity of natural beauty: "Old clockwork Time beats in his tower, / I hear his wintry, wheezing breath; / His faded face looks down; a flower / Answers *Eternity* beneath" (33). While "the seconds creak, the quarters chime, / The light dust fall, the heavy doom," the clock inexorably "beats his anvil, and his blood / Moves to its measured pulses still." Yet in the face of this, a "humble angel carved in wood / Looks up to its immortal hill." It seems untouched by the passage of time: "With moveless, dedicated eyes, / It gazes on, while all the waste / Seconds and minutes, hours and days / Plunge to that echoing gulf, the past." It is the contrast between the inevitable ticking away of time and the wonder of eternity represented by the flower and the carved angel that leads to the poem's deft conclusion: "What does each Adoration care / For sorrow measured off by sound?" Death may be certain, but it is not the last word.

In "The Lammastide Flower" Pitter also explores immortality. The poem considers the death of a man who was well known to Pitter, as well as the ac-cidental drowning of a child. Both deaths were untimely, and the second had followed the first closely. In the poem two late autumn flowers, the toadflax, with its orange and lemon colors, and the sky-blue harebell, function as symbols for the two dead individuals. Placed on the graves of the dead man and child, they are peering happily up at the sky "while like a weary prodigal / Man counts the harvest of his pain" (34–35). Both flowers cause Pitter to ponder what they may be saying to her:

> You yellow spires of Lammastide
> That look not at me but beyond;
> You silent bells that mirror sky
> Yet hang so meekly to the ground;
> What, either far or deep descried,
> Holds you so rapt, in such a bond,
> One looking low, one looking high:
> What is that silence you have found?

Each flower offers an answer. The toadflax tells her to be still: "I see the Pow-ers, they see me, / I see those Two, and both are gold: / Two golds in one, and both are true." The harebell adds: "In the blue." And together: "'Two golds,' they said, and 'In the blue.'" The essence of what they tell her is that the two dead people live on in the gold of the sun and in the blue of the sky. They are only dead to the earth; that which is eternal, immortal, and everlasting about them—call it their souls, their spirits, their metaphysical essences—lives on and transcends physical death.

The last group of poems explores Pitter's gradual movement toward Christian orthodoxy; by the end of the volume Pitter makes a definitive statement about her newly realized faith. The title poem, "The Ermine," takes as its starting point three ideas traditionally associated with the ermine: it will die if its beautiful white coat is soiled ("he dies of soil"), it is an emblem of chastity ("he is the snow"), and its pelts have been used to make extravagant, lavishly expensive robes for royalty (1). However, Pitter's concern goes far beyond these notions; her real concern is to suggest that the ermine, a creature that is immaculate except for the characteristic black spot on its pelt, is a type of the saint on earth who has his own "dark" spot of sin: "Royal he is. What makes him so? / Why, that too is a thing I know: / It is his blame, his black, his blot; / The badge of kings, the sable spot." This vivid black-on-white contrast gives the pelt its rich value and reminds the saint that even the holiest is tainted by sin: "O subtle, royal Ermine, tell / Me how to wear my black as well." As Pitter moved toward orthodox Christianity, she realized that settled faith can lead to spiritual pride and self-righteousness. The ermine's spot reminds her that even the whitest, even the purest, even the most set apart is still marred by the black spot of sin and so must learn "how to wear my black as well."

"The Neophyte" records an incipient, struggling, imperfect movement toward faith: "Something I see and feel, / But I must not speak. / It lives, O it is real, / But cold and weak / As a far light in a cave" (2). The religiously loaded title prepares us for this theme since a neophyte is a new convert, a novice, a beginner in the faith. Appropriately, therefore, Pitter uses a series of additional metaphors to describe her fragile hold on faith: "as the faint glow / That green glow-worms have," "as stars of snow," and "as tenuous jellies" seen "on a wall / Where the tide has been." The image of the withdrawing tide is particularly effective, especially because of the promise of its return: "Where the tide has been; / Whence the great swinging deep, / With its bell-mouthed roar, / . . . Has gone, falling away / Far to the main: / But with the day, with the new day, / Shall come again." Although she intimates her imperfect hold on faith in this poem, nonetheless she insists on its daily rebirth.

Similarly, "Penitence" is a religious poem referring to the redeeming effects of repentance upon the soul. Using the metaphor of rain falling upon young corn that has been parched because of a fierce drought ("sent down by divine law / To save the blade and the seed"), Pitter notes the need for repentance in the human heart: "Love leaps to send and draw / Sweet water got by fire / Out of a cloudy grief." Just as the blessed rain saves the corn, so tears of repentance save the soul: "Sweet dew of strong desire / To save the flower and the leaf" (27). "The World Is Hollow" is another religious poem about childlike hope, adult despair, and God's jealous insistence on holding man's attention. Although a child has been told the world is hollow, empty of transcendent or supernatural truth, the child instinctively rejects such a claim: "Father, they told me that the world is hollow, / A thing no child believes, / . . . Hope is its kingdom, and the mortal future / Holds love, the captain-jewel of the creature" (19–20). Yet the child's hope is countered by the adult's despair: "But man's despair is like the Arabian sun, / When the last morning cloud / Melts in the fire; then the lost wretch alone, / . . . Falls in the sand, and cries his need aloud, / Full-grown at last to love, when he can find / No cloud, no rock, no shelter in the mind." In fact, the world *is* hollow if man hopes to find meaning and purpose solely in the world. The truth is that the world can never "be filled / Save by the One supreme." In the end despair is used to drive men away from earthly contentment, and, by implication, toward God: "Despair, that burning angel, by the child / Unperceived even in dream, / Stands sentinel by Eden, and the beam / Unmitigated, doom pronounced by light, / Glares from his arms, and blinds the earthly sight."

The culmination of Pitter's spiritual pilgrimage occurs in the final sequence of poems, "Five Dreams and a Vision" (52–62).[22] These poems unfold the fascinating drama of a soul's movement toward faith in Christ. They are Pitter's most sustained attempt at writing religious verse, and the fact that she recounts her conversion experience via dreams and visions suggests that it was less a decision of the will and more an unconscious, intuitive, and mystical process. In the preamble to the sequence, Pitter writes: "All life is strange: / Waking no less than sleeping; all / Mantled in mystery of perpetual change, / Like the ephemeral / Blushing and whitenings of a wasting fire" (52–53). Yet man, she says, works feverishly to avoid facing the mystery, futilely committed instead to finding meaning and purpose in the activities of temporal experience: "[We] build us palaces without a name, / We write our timeless, spaceless histories there, / And read ourselves, before we are quite spent, / In that more swiftly wasting element." However, in contrast to human activity, Pitter says that the fine details of nature and the inarticulate breathings of simple creatures speak volumes if only we open ourselves to them:

> [The] shifting sands and brooks that wander
> And the way twigs lie;
> They may say things silently:
> And the toothless babe may speak
> To resolve the mother's doubt;
> The cat and dog and ass call out,
> The strong be guided by the weak;
> The powers can use a little leaf
> As a simple to heal grief;
> Simple or symbol; and a dream
> Be more than what such things may seem.

That dreams may speak to us about deeper truth, about the mystery of life, is Pitter's premise.

The first dream, "A Stranger and a Sojourner," has numerous biblical echoes, most notably concerning Abraham: "By faith Abraham, when he was called to go out into a place which he should after receive for an inheritance, obeyed;

and he went out, not knowing whither he went. By faith he sojourned in the land of promise, as in a strange country, dwelling in tabernacles with Isaac and Jacob, the heirs with him of the same promise. For he looked for a city which hath foundations, whose builder and maker is God" (Heb. 11:8–10). After the Israelites escaped from Egypt, they wandered in the desert as strangers and so-journers, looking to find the Promised Land. Indeed, Abraham and the Israelites become types of the Christian pilgrim, who is never satisfied with this world because he is always looking for a permanent home not of this world. Pitter has in mind this biblical passage:

> These all died in faith, not having received the promises, but having seen them afar off, and were persuaded of them, and embraced them, and con-fessed that they were strangers and pilgrims on the earth. For they that say such things declare plainly that they seek a country. And truly, if they had been mindful of that country from whence they came out, they might have had opportunity to have returned. But now they desire a better country, that is, an heavenly: wherefore God is not ashamed to be called their God: for he hath prepared for them a city. (Heb. 11:13–16)

Recalling as well "The Lost Tribe" from *The Bridge*, "A Stranger and a Sojourn-er" opens with a profound sense of displacement: "Always the unknown place, / The place where I have not been. / Always an unknown face / In a strange scene; / Always the people whom I do not know, / In a mysterious land" (53–54). In the surreal landscape of this unknown place, the speaker is not afraid, noting, "There is no shelter here. I will go on." As the houses crumble and the roads fail, the speaker senses that "there is life where never yet / Air blew or water ran, / Where time is not a tragic theme, / Where the misery of man / Has not cast his bitter dream." In this life "unfallen spirits rest / Like the swan upon her nest, / Moated round with innocence." With the swan Pitter returns to her favorite bird, this time as an image of the pilgrim who has found her real home.

The second dream, "Forms with Infinite Meaning," explores the significance of a landscape hinting at something wonderful. At dawn "in a grey land that was not sorrowful," in the hollow of "low smooth hills," there were shells: "Whether small shells, and near, / Or mighty shells reared up before the hills, / I do not know; but dear, / Dear with a worth beyond all earthly price, / And clothed with such significance / That their melodious stillness was a dance" (54–55). Pitter may be making a connection here to the biblical idea of the pearl of great price, the notion that all should be given up in order to find God.[23] The stillness of this scene is broken: "And then there came a voice, / And up the clean sky rushed a whiter sun, / And there was done / Some great solemnity, which yet was play." What this all means is just beyond her understanding, yet she is not frustrated or upset: "In that strange dream my heart kept holiday; / Forms more than forms are shadowed in my mind, / My loves for ever, though of alien kind." Is this a land untouched by sin, a land filled with the voice of God, yet a land just beyond her comprehension? Pitter does not know, but it is a land she loves.

The third dream, "The Tree," is about another surreal scene. Pitter describes how once in a dream she looked down into a hollow, where she saw a tree with curious flowers: "What were those flowers of flame, / Hanging so still, unblown, / Pendent upon a great and great-leaved tree / In the deep-shadowed glade before the door / Of the veiled cavern?" (55–56). Descending into the hollow, as she nears the tree she sees "pendent from stalks, those flowers that were men, / Asleep, and beautiful." As she watches them gently breathe, she "wept with gladness" because she "had feared to find that they were dead." The poem ends by suggesting this dream was about the preexistence of the soul: "This was a blessed people not yet come to be." The next poem, "A Vision of Extreme Delight," is almost a companion piece to "The Tree" since it is also about "another people" who are living in a world "under a sky / Dark as our midnight but intensely blue" (56–57). This world is dominated by "palmlike forests of the very hue / That shines unearthly in our glaciers / . . . Melting into the green the glow-worm bears." At the same time, this world is "pulsing with a life untold," populated with people who "showed like monoliths of living ice, / Streaming with rays of visible delight. / O there is no device / Of language for them." However, her vision of the world and its people has made an indelible mark upon her mind: "If I were blind, / I should still see palms waving without wind, / And living jewels, cataracts of bliss, / Against the dark of other skies than this." This, too, is a world without sin, filled instead with the blessed—the kind of world Pitter longs to experience.

The fourth dream, "The Transparent Earth," marks a distinct break with the earlier poems in this sequence; initially in this dream of the earth, gone are the images of pleasure, delight, peace, and blessedness. Instead, there is heaviness and burden: "Earth is bowed with a weight / Hard and heavy to bear; / Bowed and curved round the great / Core of despair" (57–58). Images of the grave and the earth as man's inevitable resting place follow: "Earth is weary and old, / So men have always said; / Earth is heavy and cold, / On the cold breasts of the dead." However, the poem shifts radically via a dream in which she sees the earth "clear / As a drop of dew":

> Like a crystal was her sphere,
> And the sun shone through:
> Standing at midnight in the street
> I saw the sun between my feet,
> Shining up into my face
> Through earth colourless as space;

Through an earth as clear as wine,
Colourless and crystalline.

The power of this dream to transform her dreary impression of the earth into a brilliant, transparent world hints at the spiritual transformation going on inside Pitter. Because of her growing faith, she can see the world not just as a place of hardship and misery but instead as a place redeemed and renewed by the hand of God.

The fifth dream, "But My Neighbour Is My Treasure," recalls the second most important law of the New Testament—Love your neighbor as yourself—and serves as a fitting preface to the last poem in the sequence.[24] In essence "But My Neighbour Is My Treasure" says that while "solemn and lovely visions and holy dreams, / Mysterious portents," are very important, they pale in comparison to the significance of people: "For I am listening for that mortal tune, / The broken anthem of my fallen kind, / And seeking for the vision of those I see / Daily and here, in this poor house with me" (59). It is her friends, especially Kathleen O'Hara, her acquaintances, her customers, her neighbors in Chelsea, and so on, who hold Pitter's attention: "Their name is Wonderful, a holy name; / These in the light of heaven I shall behold, / If I can come there, standing in the flame / Of glory, with the blessed in their gold." Moreover, the call to love people is of utmost importance: "There is no dream more wonderful, for they / Are worth the whole creation, each alone. / Grant me to see their beauty on that Day! / There is no vision to prefer, but One." Several important things stand out in these lines. First, at this point in her life Pitter values people even more than the natural world; while much of her early poetry celebrates the natural world, perhaps because of her disappointment with people, here she affirms people over the natural world. Second, this poem is actually a prayer for God to permit her to see all those people on the day they are glorified in heaven. Third, this vision of the eternal importance of people is most to be desired, save "One."

This most-to-be-preferred vision is the subject of the final poem in this sequence. "The Great and Terrible Dream" hardly seems to be the most preferred vision since it begins as an apocalyptic nightmare:

Dark valley, or dark street: arches or trees
Or rocks? Shadow of evening, or of cloud?
Fear in the air, and a profound unease;
The panic-driven feet, and from a shroud
Of dust or darkness, ravings as of men
Running in horror from some sight so dire
That the flesh cannot stay, or turn again,
But mindless flees, as hand is snatched from fire.

Fixed in pure terror, horribly afraid,
I listened to that frenzied multitude. (60–62)

Yet in the midst of this nightmare, Pitter hears a "calm, solemn voice" say:
"*They fear the blood.*" To Pitter these words mean "love was alone / And in
extremity," so she hurls herself against the frightened crowd: "And wounded,
naked, trampled, torn, and bruised / I fought against them for a weary time /
Willing to die before my heart should break; / I thought them murderers fleeing
from their crime, / And what they feared so madly, I must seek."

But then, just as suddenly as the tumult began, it is over, and Pitter again
hears the calm, solemn voice say: "*He is there. Look on Him. That is He.*" Initially this causes "the fear of death" to come upon her as she remembers from childhood an incident in which a coffin opened when the men carrying it slipped.
However, she cannot resist the imperative: "Torn with love and awe, / I saw the
Face, the plaited thorns, the stain / Of blood descending to the beard I saw; /
And felt the power of life conquering death, / More dread than death, for death
is vincible." The poem is a vision of Christ's crucifixion, and Pitter's desperate
struggle against the crowd in order to assist "love in extremity" illustrates the
profound degree to which she tries to identify with Him. The culmination of
Pitter's spiritual pilgrimage is revealed in the final four lines of this poem and
of *The Ermine* as a whole: "[Christ's face] struck me down. It stopped the very
breath / Itself had given. But the dream was well: / O well is me, and happy shall
I be! / Look! He is there. Look on Him. That is He." Pitter's search is over when
she looks into the loving face of the sacrificed Christ. His sacrifice becomes
hers, and the benign, distant God of her earlier poems is revealed to be the one
she had always known but resisted. Moreover, she now points others to this
face: "*Look! He is there. Look on Him. That is He.*" While not an evangelistic
pronouncement, it is a bold statement that Pitter believes spiritual fulfillment
can best be experienced through the sacrificial love of Christ on the cross.

The Ermine not only chronicles the culmination of Pitter's spiritual search. It
also contains her most mature poems—well crafted, thought provoking, emotionally powerful, and aesthetically pleasing. The poems in this volume are far
from her early verse published in the *New Age*. *The Ermine* illustrates how Pitter
grew as a poet over the years—often working in snatches of time, worn weary
by the demands of trade, but ever true to her muse, ever seeking ways to share
through poetry the longings of her heart, the fears of her mind, and the convictions of her soul. Critics found *The Ermine* to be her most mature work; this con-
sensus is best typified by the review appearing in the *Times Literary Supplement*:

The Ermine is perhaps Miss Pitter's most beautiful book of poems, and
this, of a poet so constant in her inspiration and accomplishment, is to

say much. Maturity deepens the true poetry in her always skillful work, without changing it in kind. The same deft, plangent music, fresh eye and human warmth, the same religious faith and poetic inspiration quietly at one with each other, distinguish these new poems. . . . All are marked by a confidence characteristic of this writer but unusual among contemporary poets. It derives from a rare personal harmony with life, a vigorous, unsentimental, loving acceptance of our mortal and our modern lot.[25]

The reviewer also notes how difficult it is to write compelling poetry of happiness—"by which is meant that state of contained, lively serenity that lies between bliss and animal contentment"—and he argues that Pitter excels in such poetry. At the same time, he notes that Pitter also confronts dark themes: "God, for her, is certainly in his heaven, but earth is squalid as well as lovely, and man a fallen creature." His greatest praise comes when he says: "At times she succeeds so well that, through sheer plainness, not beauty only but magic alights on a line—that spell nothing can ever explain, . . . [and that] is perhaps the secret all poets most hungrily desire to win."

Lewis was awed by *The Ermine*.[26] The day after he receives a copy from Pitter, he writes:

Dear Miss Pitter, or (to speak more accurately) Bright Angel! I'm in a sea of glory! Of course I haven't had time to read it properly, and there'll be another, more sober, letter presently. This is just a line to be going on with, and to assure you at once that the new volume is an absolute CORK-ER. I had feared that you might be one of those who, like Wordsworth, leave their talent behind at conversion: and now—oh glory—you come up shining out of the frost far better than you were before. "Man's despair is like the Arabian sun" [from "The World Is Hollow"]—I seriously doubt if there's any religious lyric between that one and [George] Herbert on the same level. And then my eye strays to the opposite page and get the "dying-dolphin green." And "what we merit—A silence like a sword" [from "The Other"]. I wonder have you yourself any notion how good some of these are? But, as you see, I'm drunk on them at this present. Glory be! Blessings on you! As sweet as sin and as innocent as milk. Thanks forever, Yours in great excitement, C. S. Lewis. (327–28; May 12, 1953)

Several days later he is still effusive about *The Ermine:*

The brightness does not fade: appealing from Lewis drunk to Lewis sober, I still find this an exquisite collection. When I start picking out my favourites, I find I am picking out nearly all. "Tree at Dawn" is full of delight for eye and ear. "Great Winter" is extremely new and delightful in rhythm: and "storm of suns" is wonderful. . . . The *noises* all through "Herding Lambs"— not only "rainlike rustle of feet," tho' that is the most striking single aural image—are wonderfully conveyed. "Captive Bird" is pure gold all through: so lovely fair my sense "aches with it": and I still think as I did about "The World is Hollow.". . . "Penitence" is taut and accurate as a Yeats poem. . . . The "The Five Dreams" do, I don't know how, build up to a whole greater than the parts. . . . I do congratulate you again and again. I hope you are as happy about the poems as you ought to be. (328–29; May 15)

Pitter was delighted by his praise.[27] Of special note is how carefully Lewis has read and reread the poems and how enthusiastic he is in pointing out his favorites and commenting on the parts of others he finds noteworthy. In other words, Lewis's close reading of *The Ermine* reveals a would-be poet being swept off his feet by a genuine poet. Lewis deeply admired *The Ermine* because he longed to write such good poetry himself.

David Cecil was similarly impressed by *The Ermine:*

I did not write before because I wanted to read the poems properly. Now I have read them. All I can say to you is the same kind of thing I have said before—only more so, if possible. They seem to me in the highest degree possible noble and beautiful. As I have told you before, your work does something to me that no other modern writer's does: consoles, illuminates—and it is a little difficult for me to criticize it or relate it to other people's work. But striving to preserve my detached critical judgment, I would say that your art was both developing and consolidating in this last book. In particular, I liked "The Tree at Dawn," "The Father Questioned," "A Worn Theme," "Reflection after Victory," and "The Tuft of Violets." Your blend of strong classical form, vivid actual observation of nature now and again transfigured by a gleam of unearthly light is, surely, unique. Thank you very, very much. These poems have made a great difference to me in these last few weeks. (May 22)

Before ending this letter, Cecil adds: "I have not thanked you for the very beautiful poem dedicated to myself ["Hill and Valley" (To D. C.)], which should also be in my list of favourites."

With the praise of Lewis and Cecil in her heart, Pitter was determined to move near Oxford. As she and O'Hara looked for a house, they found the prices to be formidable, especially the ones closest to Oxford. For several months it was hit and miss as one possibility after another fell through. She writes Rachel Cecil after another weekend visit to her home that included some house hunting led by David: "We have firmly made up our minds to be within a reasonable distance of Oxford, though, & will persevere. I am filled with glory as regards the social side of the week-end. The intimate kindness & sharing of family life, the spirit-renewing meeting with Lewis, the music & flowers, . . . Coronation talk—all like one lovely dream—and then the visit to John Betjeman in that sweet place—how rich you make me" (June 16).[28] On July 26 Pitter tells Cooley: "We haven't got a house yet, but there are lots in the market and the prices are on the down grade. . . . We can pay cash, thank God, so we feel time is on our side. We have seen some nice places, but not just the right one yet. I think the one I regretted leaving most was a square stone Rectory, with 20-foot rooms, fine windows, and good old shutters. It had an ancient burial-mound right in the garden, and the old churchyard, with crazy old stones leaning over, just beyond. Just the job for a good poet. But K. was downright scared of it, even in the daytime."

Pitter and O'Hara, taking it on faith that they would be able to sublet their flat in Chelsea, continued their dogged search throughout August and were rewarded during a visit to Long Crendon, a village fifteen miles northeast of Oxford. While looking at a large, expensive, rambling house, Pitter noticed at the back of the property a small cottage that just suited their needs. Negotiations moved quickly, so that on September 12 Pitter writes the estate agent: "We have inspected the above [the Hawthorns, Chilton Road, Long Crendon], and subject to surveyor's report and contract, we wish to purchase this property at the price named in your particulars, £4,000, which includes the whole of the land offered, about 2½ acres. We are not offering a lower price, as is usually done, as we think the house and land are worth the price asked if the surveyor's report proves satisfactory."

The next several weeks were taken up with frenzied negotiations, agreements regarding minor renovations, and the arrangement of legal documents. By the first of October, Pitter and O'Hara had signed an agreement to purchase their long-awaited retirement cottage in Long Crendon. Pitter writes Lewis with the news; in her journal recollection she writes:

[Kathleen and I] had now found this house at Long Crendon, and moved in just before Xmas of this same year. The village is too consciously pretty for me (though our end is like any outer suburb): I come from half-pagan Essex, (and I mean half-pagan, not just lapsed Xtian), and Long Crendon has long been "full of old maids and widders, abuying bits of places and a-doing of 'em up." But we thought the 1910 villa, very solid, with a good bit of ground, the best value we had seen for what we could afford: and we had earned every sixpence of the price ourselves, starting in business without

training, during the worst of the recession, on a capital of some £600,
our joint savings; and we are rather proud of the achievement. (Oct. 3,
1953)[29]

Pitter also wonders if after seven years she and Lewis might begin addressing
their letters to each other with their Christian names. Lewis replies on October
3: "'Rachel' has been ready for a long time: you know I am of the generation
who was brought up to hold that the initiative must come from you. Long Crendon—long since endeared to me because Owen Barfield used to live there—will
now have a second good association. . . . Warnie [Lewis's brother] joins me in
our duties and warm welcome to these parts. It is, as you have seen, a lovely
village" (367–68). And, in fact, for the first time he addresses the letter "Dear
Ruth," and he signs "Jack Lewis." In her journal recollection, Pitter says: "I had
now known Lewis for seven years (I had asked 'if I might now have Rachel,' alluding to Jacob's seven-year service), and thought perhaps he would not mind
if we now used Xtian names. It was all very well for him to say that the request
should have come from [me, because] he would never have made it."[30] Later
Pitter writes Cecil about this: "I have managed to get on Xtian name terms
with CSL after seven years' acquaintance; quite soon enough for decency, if
one thinks as I do that undue or premature familiarity tends to make real intimacy meaningless" (March 13, 1954). The formality of their salutations and
signatures in their correspondence up until this point may strike us today as
odd; however, both Lewis and Pitter were of an age given to such formalities.
Indeed, such formality marked both proper upbringing and good taste. At the
same time, this formality also suggests that both Lewis and Pitter were reticent
to move their relationship beyond that of friendship. On the part of Pitter,
while she may have wanted to have more than just a friendship with Lewis, she
did not want to be the one to push it; this reticence recalls the lines from her
poem "If You Came" from *The Spirit Watches:* "The place is hidden apart / Like
a nest of a bird: / And I will not show you my heart / By a look, by a word." On
the part of Lewis, in spite of his genuine affection for Pitter, he was careful to
avoid affairs of the heart. Ironically, whatever possibility existed for some future
romantic relationship between Lewis and Pitter was about to be complicated by
the arrival of American Joy Davidman Gresham into the life of Lewis.

Regardless, Lewis was happy Pitter was moving to Long Crendon. Pitter
wanted to share the news with her other friends as well, so she is quick to
write Cooley: "We have found our house, at Long Crendon on the borders of
Buckinghamshire and Oxfordshire. It is a solidly-built 'villa' . . . with about 2½
acres of neglected nursery-garden and orchard. It has been 'done up' to sell, like
new, and has plenty of light and 2 quite large rooms. We should have liked an
antique, but we feel that this will be a warm clean healthy house, and that it

is the best value we have seen yet. It's not exactly ugly, only very plain, with a tiny classical feeling" (Oct. 7).[31] David Cecil, hearing the news, writes Pitter: "How very exciting that you should have got a house at Long Crendon! And how delightful it should be so near Oxford. I shall look forward to seeing much more of you. That is a very pleasant thing to look forward to" (Oct. 8). Pitter and O'Hara were determined to move before Christmas, so for the next two months they were in a whirlwind of preparations—signing legal documents, subletting 55A Old Church Street, packing up their things for shipping to the Hawthorns, and notifying friends and business associates of their change of address. On December 11 Pitter and O'Hara left their Chelsea flat for the last time and spent their first night in Long Crendon—what would be Pitter's home for the next thirty-nine years.

Lewis is quick to offer a warm welcome: "Welcome to what Tolkien calls the Little Kingdom, at least to the marches of it. . . . I hope much happiness awaits you there. It will be interesting to see how soon you rusticate—grow slow-witted like us and believe that the streets of Thame (now your metropolis) are paved with gold and shiver delightfully at the thought of its mingled wickedness and splendour" (389–90; Dec. 21). He also adds something that may have dampened Pitter's hopes of seeing him more often:

> We have had an American lady staying in the house with her two sons aged 9½ and 8. I never knew what we celibates are shielded from. I will never laugh at parents again. Not that the boys weren't a delight; but a delight like surf-bathing which leaves one breathless and aching. The energy, the *tempo*, is what kills. I have now perceived (what I always suspected from memories of my own childhood) that the way to a child's heart is quite simple: treat them with seriousness and ordinary civility— they ask no more. What they can't stand (quite rightly) is the common adult assumption that everything they say shd. be twisted into a kind of jocularity. The mother (Mrs. Gresham) had rather a boom in USA . . . as the poetess Joy Davidman: do you know her work? The Vac. is pretty chock a block so far (oh if we could have Christmas without Xmas!) so that I rather hope than expect to knock on your door. Meanwhile, all good tidings to you both.[32]

In spite of the news about Joy Gresham, Pitter was buoyed by her move to the country. She anticipated indulging her passion for gardening without restraint. Freed from Chelsea, she planned to lavish attention on cultivating the bit of brown earth she and O'Hara now owned.[33] In addition, she hoped that being nearer Oxford would bring about more time with the Cecils and Lewis. In many ways, therefore, the end of 1953 marked the beginning of a new life for

Pitter. With the success of *The Ermine,* her critical acclaim was at its height; with the move from Chelsea to Long Crendon—and its inevitable associations with Hainault Forest and the old cottage—her personal happiness seemed ensured; and with the resolution of her theological uncertainties, her spiritual search found a home in the Anglican Church. What might have been a quiet retirement, however, was not to be, as future fame, a new career, and new relationships were waiting on the horizon. If Pitter's personal life as an artisan was beginning to slow down, her public life as a BBC radio and television commentator was about to take off.

⌁ EIGHT ⌁

Unexpected Turns,

1954–1955

One can hardly blame Pitter and O'Hara for considering the Hawthorns an idyllic retirement spot as they quickly settled into life there. Looking around the grounds of the Hawthorns, both women had what they most wanted. The two large common rooms downstairs were light and airy, perfect to serve as studios for each woman. O'Hara, the better painter, especially enjoyed her studio. Pitter, while continuing to paint tea trays, looked outside to the two-and-a-half acres of orchards and fields for her pleasure. With rich memories from Hainault Forest to draw upon, Pitter could now anticipate many hours outdoors—clearing, digging, planting, cultivating, pruning, and harvesting. But not quite yet; while O'Hara was completely retired, Pitter still soldiered on with her work as an artisan. Pitter writes Cooley about her conflicting emotions: "At the moment it is brilliantly sunny, but with a strong cold wind. The only outdoor work possible is gathering wood & cutting branches out of shrubs, but perhaps this is as well, as I must really set to and earn money again. I had three weeks off during the move, and I honestly believe it was the longest spell I had since leaving school 38 years ago. Well, my work is not much of a strain, though it means long hours—it is hardly work at all in the sense of having to cope with difficult people & situations, so it is no hardship really" (Jan. 31, 1954).

Now settled near Oxford, Pitter could more easily visit and be visited by her friends. Pitter writes Cooley about the Cecils' first visit: "The David Cecils turned up last Sunday, to our great delight. I was in the garden, and suddenly heard his rather comically decided voice 'This is it! I can see her—through the hedge!' We were so glad to see them—now we know we are near Oxford" (Jan. 31). Lewis, happy to have Pitter living nearer to Oxford, writes her that he would have come for a visit but is suffering from gout. He presses her to come to Oxford soon so they can lunch together (Jan. 4).[1] It did not take Pitter long to make the somewhat involved trip to Oxford; she writes Cooley: "I am going [to

195

Oxford] for the first time since the move, to lunch with C. S. Lewis to-morrow. It's only about 13 miles away, but when you have to take 2 buses it seems a great undertaking" (Jan. 31).

Ruth Pitter, C. S. Lewis, and Joy Davidman Gresham

Although Pitter entertained hopes of more frequent visits with Lewis, the difficulties of transportation were little compared to a second and more complicating factor: Lewis's blossoming relationship with Joy Gresham. In fact, when the luncheon with Lewis mentioned above did take place on February 1 at the Eastgate Hotel, there was a third party present: Gresham. It is time to explore the dynamics of Lewis's relationship with Pitter and Gresham. Despite widespread interest in the life and work of Lewis, other than Lyle Dorsett's 1983 biography of Gresham, And God Came In, very little scholarship exploring the nature of Lewis's relationship with women in general, and in particular why he decided to marry Gresham rather than Pitter, exists.[2] While this is not the place for an exhaustive study, I do want to bring to light a heretofore untapped source of information regarding Lewis's relationship with Gresham and Pitter: the love poetry of each woman. Readers of Lewis have long wondered why it was that Lewis fell in love with Gresham, while those who also know of his prior relationship with Pitter are frankly puzzled that he chose to marry Gresham rather than Pitter. In short, I believe Gresham "won" Lewis because of her passionate, aggressive, winner-take-all attitude toward romantic love, as revealed in her love poetry, while Pitter "lost" Lewis because of her dispassionate, reserved, you-must-win-me attitude toward romantic love, as revealed in her love poetry.[3]

While it is impossible to document how often Lewis and Pitter met before Gresham came on the scene, such meetings ranged in the neighborhood of several dozen. Indeed, in part because of these frequent meetings, many of Lewis's friends believed he was attracted to Pitter. For example, in his biography of Lewis, George Sayer recalls:

> Ruth Pitter was one of the very few modern poets whose work [Lewis] admired. His writing to her of his appreciation developed into a witty and profound correspondence and occasional meetings between them. . . . I [drove him to see Pitter] three times between 1953 and 1955. . . . It was obvious that he liked her very much. He felt at ease in her presence—and he did not feel relaxed with many people—and, in fact, seemed to be on intimate terms with her. The conversation was a mixture of the literary and the domestic. . . . Each suggested amusing and improbable books for the other to write. Herbs were pinched and tasted in the cottage garden.

Homemade drinks were sampled. She asked for the recipe of my moselle-like elder-flower wine. Jack did not contribute much to this domestic conversation, but it was clear that he enjoyed it. . . . After one visit in 1955, he remarked that, if he were not a confirmed bachelor, Ruth Pitter would be the woman he would like to marry. . . . [When I said it was not too late, he said,] "Oh yes it is. . . . I've burnt my boats."[4]

Lewis's friend Colin Hardie was insistent that Pitter would have been a better match than Gresham for Lewis. According to Walter Hooper, during one of his visits to Colin and Christian Hardie the subject of Gresham came up:

Rather interestingly, I had never heard them speak of Joy Davidman before. During this visit Christian told me about a luncheon party at which Lewis introduced her to Joy, hoping, Christian thinks, that she would take her under her wing and become friends. I asked what came of it, and Christian confessed that she felt such a strong dislike of Joy that she couldn't bring herself to be nice to her. Colin, who had sat listening to this conversation, suddenly burst out with: "Jack should have married Ruth Pitter"—and nothing more was said about Joy.[5]

Other friends of Lewis's found his marriage to Gresham odd as well. For instance, J. R. R. Tolkien allegedly consistently referred to Gresham as "that woman."

Be that as it may, whatever Lewis's feelings for Pitter, they were not powerful enough to cause him to pursue her. Instead, once Gresham came on the scene, Lewis was drawn to her. Perhaps naively, Lewis hoped the two women might become friends, and so he arranged for the luncheon at the Eastgate Hotel. In her most terse, clipped journal entry, Pitter writes: "It was at this luncheon that I met Mrs. Gresham for the first and last time."[6] In spite of Lewis's best intentions, there is no evidence the two women he most cared about ever warmed to each other. The icy relationship between Gresham and Pitter is not surprising. Indeed, in the Bodleian Library there remains sealed correspondence between Pitter and Hooper that may reveal further evidence of Pitter's disaffection for Gresham; however, this correspondence may not be opened until the death of Gresham's sons, David and Douglas Gresham.[7]

His friendship with Pitter notwithstanding, Lewis fell in love with Joy Gresham and married her . . . twice. Why? I believe part of the answer is revealed in the love poetry written by each woman. As we have seen, Pitter came to sexual maturity during the height of World War I, and the devastating effect of the war on an entire generation—the decimation of the pool of marriageable men—caused Pitter and O'Hara, like many British women of this era, to give up thoughts of marriage. Yet Pitter occasionally did write about romantic love in

poems such as "Early Rising," "Weeping Water, Leaping Fire," "True Love's not
Told," "Fair Is the Water," and "As When the Faithful Return" from *A Trophy of
Arms;* "If You Came" from *The Spirit Watches;* and "The Swan Bathing," "But for
Lust," "Lament for One's Self," and "Vision of the Cuckoo" from *The Bridge.* "If
You Came," already discussed, best reveals her overall attitude toward romantic
love: while beautiful, intense, and desirable, it was a threat and an ultimately
unfulfilling alternative to her devotion to poetry.[8] Moreover, she would never be
the pursuer; if a man wanted her, he would have to seek out the secret places of
her heart, loving her for the things she loved. Her past disappointments in love
gave her a circumspect view of the possibility of passionate love. Although she
did have friendly relationships with several men throughout her life, including
Orage, AE, and Orwell, and was probably sexually involved with several others,
she also had a powerful sense of self-protection—both against a broken heart and
for her fiercely held muse. If a man could win and woo Pitter only by pursuing
her heart, Lewis was neither by nature nor inclination given to such pursuit. As
he told Sayer, he had burnt his boats. He would never be the pursuer.

     An important point to note here is that after *The Bridge* Pitter did not publish
any more love poems. This is significant because *The Ermine* contains poems
written between 1942 and 1952, the very years when her friendship with Lewis
began and was maturing. Why are there no love poems? I suggest several possibilities. First, given her desire to be the pursued, not the pursuer, Pitter would
never tip her hand through her verse; accordingly, in her poems she would not
indicate in any way whether she was excited or frightened by the possibility of
romantic love—not with Lewis or any other man. Second, given that *The Ermine*
is something of a poetic journal of her spiritual pilgrimage toward Christianity,
its concern is with agape rather than eros. Third, given that Pitter was fifty-six
when *The Ermine* was published, she may have tired of investing her muse in
poems about romantic love; a sore heart can as easily dampen the desire to write
about love as it can ignite it. Fourth, if she believed Lewis might be in love with
her, why risk putting something in print that might frighten him away? Finally, if
Lewis was not in love with her, why embarrass the two of them by writing about
it like a schoolgirl? Moreover, we need to keep in mind as well the stereotypical view that the English, particularly those of the era of Lewis and Pitter, were
circumspect about feelings—after all, it was seven years before they even started
using each other's first names in their letters. Lewis and Pitter did not wear their
hearts on their sleeves; matters of the heart were best kept private.

     If, therefore, Pitter was both personally and culturally prone to holding back
with regard to matters of romantic love—waiting, indeed, to be pursued—
Gresham was both personally and culturally prone to reaching out with regard
to such matters. Even before her marriage to William Gresham, she had been
sexually active; no doubt she had been pursued on many occasions.[9] However,

she was also used to being the pursuer; after her marriage to William Gresham fell apart and once she fell in love with Lewis, she pursued him with single-minded devotion. In saying this, I am in no way criticizing her. As Chaucer says, "Love is a mighty Lord," and a strong-willed person such as Joy would have been even more given than some to winning the love of the man she most admired. Accordingly, after her rejection of communism and after her conversion to Christianity, in which the writings of Lewis played no small part, she decided to seek out a relationship with him.[10]

After the American literary critic Chad Walsh published the first critical study of Lewis in 1949, C. S. Lewis: Apostle to the Skeptics, Gresham sought him out; a friendship resulted, and through Walsh Gresham began corresponding with Lewis in January 1950. A lively correspondence developed, one enjoyed as much by Warren Lewis as by his brother.[11] And as Dorsett shows in And God Came In, by the fall of 1952 Gresham had sailed to England and invited Lewis to meet her at a luncheon in the Eastgate Hotel in Oxford. Lewis, who obviously enjoyed being with Gresham, reciprocated and invited her to luncheon at his rooms in Magdalen College, much as he had done previously with Pitter, and then followed this up with the very unusual invitation for her to spend Christmas 1952 at his home, the Kilns.[12] Dorsett observes: "It is likely that Joy was already falling in love with C. S. Lewis. [Her cousin Renee] believed that [Joy] had fallen in love with Lewis's mind during their extended period of correspondence, and since Joy's marriage was a shambles, it does not require an overly active imagination to believe this. Lewis perhaps was growing infatuated with Joy; at least he delighted in her company, or he never would have continued the round of luncheons."[13]

Unlike Pitter, who published multiple volumes of poetry, Gresham had only one volume of verse, Letter to a Comrade (foreword by Stephen Vincent Benét), which won the Loines Memorial Award ($1,000) for poetry given by the National Institute of Arts and Letters (her co-winner was Robert Frost); this volume appeared in 1938, twelve years before she began corresponding with Lewis.[14] What can this volume possibly tell us about Gresham's romantic conquest of Lewis? Quite a lot. First, there is a definite, clear voice in these poems: focused, concentrated, hard, insisting to be heard, earnest, serious, determined, not suffering fools lightly, confrontational, zealot-like, insightful, and penetrating, yet at times needy, open, vulnerable, tender, and desperately longing for romantic love. This voice suggests someone who, once she knows what she wants, will move heaven and earth to obtain it. Second, while many of the poems reflect Gresham's communist agenda of the time, particularly her biting critique of American political, social, and economic policies, many others comment upon the nature of beauty, the certainty of death, and, ironically, the person of Jesus Christ. For instance, her haunting "Snow in Madrid" is a delicate poem of terrible beauty:

Softly, so casual,
Lovely, so light, so light,
The cruel sky lets fall
Something one does not fight.

How tenderly to crown
The brutal year
The clouds send something down
That one need not fear.

Men before perishing
See with unwounded eye
For once a gentle thing
Fall from the sky.[15]

And in "Againrising" Gresham offers a poem from the perspective of Christ on the cross. She takes us through the critical hours on the day of His crucifixion, beginning with "The stroke of six / my soul betrayed; / as the clock ticks / I am unmade," and ending with "The dawn great wide; / the clock struck five, / and all inside / I was alive" (81–82). This is a curious affirmation of Christ's resurrection, since Gresham's ethnicity as a Jew might have militated against such a view.[16] What all this suggests is someone who loves beauty and has an innate longing for spiritual connectedness—qualities shared by Lewis.

However, the most interesting thing about these poems is their exploration of romantic love. As a whole, these poems reveal a woman intent upon experiencing eros as comprehensively as possible—its joys, ecstasies, sensual delights, and soaring passions. Moreover, these poems reveal a woman pursuing with single-minded intensity a lover who will completely satisfy her—and once she finds this lover, she will never let him go. In many poems Gresham offers a hard-edged view of what it takes to survive as a woman. For example, her "To the Virgins" is nothing like Robert Herrick's "To the Virgins, to Make Much of Time." While the latter is a breezy entreaty for virgins to enjoy sexual activity within marriage as soon as possible in order to thwart time's effect on the body, the former is a steely-eyed warning to virgins to put themselves first and be wary of love: "Whatever arrow pierce the side / Or what confusion wring the mind, / Cherish the silver grin of pride / To stiffen your mouth in a whistling wind. /. . . . Love yourself / And show the pleasant world your teeth" (20). To Herrick's carpe diem Gresham counters with self-preservation. Similarly, her "This Woman" rejects traditional ideas of femininity: "Now do not put a ribbon in your hair; / Abjure the spangled insult of design, / The filigree sterility, nor twine / A flower with your strength; go bare, go bare" (54). Instead, Gresham says a woman should take on the hardness of a tree: "Branching from the broad column of your flesh / Into the obdurate and fibrous mesh / Stubborn to break apart and stiff to hew; / Lost at your core a living skeleton / Like sharp roots pointing downward from the sun."

Notwithstanding this hardness, many of Gresham's poems celebrate passion and the ecstasy of physical love. Sometimes she is a sorceress, chanting spells to bind her lover to her, as in "Sorceress Eclogue": "I for my lover / cook magic over woodfires to call him home. / . . . . This is magic made with a leaf and a leaf; / by this incantation his body drawn home" (58–60). Through her incantations she will pull him toward her so that "I shall kiss you with your mouth sticky with honey / your eyelids stuck together with sleep; / the summer shall enclose us in the heavy heat." Highlighting both sensuous and sensual details, in the end she will have him: "I shall put my hands over your hands / and feel the blood beginning in your arm / and run my hands over the hair on your arm." At other times she is helplessly driven to her lover, as in "Little Verse":

Do not speak of him
Lest I leave you
To flow like water
About his door step

Or like a moth
Touch his eyelids
With sleepy dust;
Or like a lover

Trouble his hearing
With sweet lust;
Or leave my body
Upon his doorstep. (77)

And at still other times she is lonely, looking for her lover to quell her melancholy through physical contact, as she suggests in "Il pleure dans mon coeur": "Only turn your lips to my lips and let your hair / lie in my hand or tangle in my hand, / and fall asleep, and let your body stand / between my sorrow and the weeping air" (50).

But most often she is a possessive, aggressive lover. For instance, in "Night-Piece" Gresham claims she will build protective rings around her lover:

I shall make rings around you. Fortresses
In a close architecture of wall upon wall,

Rib, jointed rock, and hard surrounding steel
Compel you into the narrow compass of my blood
Where you may beat forever and be perfect,
Keep warm. The blood will keep you warm, the body
Will curl upon you not to let the air
Sting you with ice. And you shall never be wounded
By your bright hostile business of living, while
I and my charitable flesh survive. . . .
. . . . Nor shall you
Suffer one touch of pain or recollection of evil
While you are in my bed. (42–43)

Gresham is determined to possess her lover; consider what she says about the multiple rings she shall build around him:

Now the first ring
Is the devious course of my blood going all around you
And you with a blind mouth growing in my flesh
In the likeness of a child. You cannot break free,
For I have locked a little of your life
Into my life; and the second ring to enclose you
My breast and arms; then a smooth round light
And a wall winking with sleek and brittle windows
With darkness cowering at them; the cold starry endless enemy
Crowding you in, crushing my arms around you
To keep off black terrors.

Her blood, her breasts, and her arms encircle and protect her lover, and her obsession for him culminates in the poem's final lines: "Keep warm, / My lover. Lie down lover. If there is peace / Arrested in any memorable fragment of time / I have shut you in with it and drawn a circle." Pitter could no more have written a poem like this than ice can form in a volcano. The energy, the passion, the aggressive desire to possess communicated by this poem certainly suggest something about Gresham's approach to romantic love. If she wanted a man, she would go for him. Unlike Pitter, who would wait for her heart to be found out, Gresham would not only seek her lover; she would build citadels around him, not so much to protect him from the outer world as to ensure that only she could have him.

A similar poem is "The Empress Changes Lovers," brilliantly written from the perspective of an empress's discarded lover.[17] Stung by her decision to throw him over, he warns her that she will not find it so easy to forget their passion:

You shall recall
Forever the tingle and flash of my body embracing you,
The way my strength came forth, the angles of my elbows,
The placing of my ribs, long clasps of thighs
And a flat back; you'll not obliterate
Any of my tricks of touching you to give you pleasure,
And worse for you you'll not forget your pleasure,
As thus and thus you prickled up your skin
And licked out with your rough dry catlike tongue
To which I tasted salt. Kill what you like;
You will not kill the antic of your own body
That remembers me, nor the words, the physical attitudes
And warm rooms, qualities of light, and secretive fabrics
That mean my name; the very smell of my flesh in passion.
But you'll remember, and you will regret
As long as flesh likes pleasant things, and the tenderness
By me created in you will absently come to haunt you
Without a name, and faceless, dumb, and eyeless
Ask for my body. (73–74)

Gresham's explicit description of and details about sexual love here suggest a frank-
ness akin to that of D. H. Lawrence. While we never learn why the empress has
decided to put him off, her former lover, mocking her future lovemaking sessions,
has the last word: "Never your special lust for me and its answer, / And the peculiar
and lovely delight you had in me; never / The pleasure your senses got from me
merely by wanting. / I'm saying you will not have me ever again." In this poem
love is reduced to animal passion—flesh, heat, sweat, climax, and a longing for
more and more. There is no holding back in this love; it wants what it wants when
it wants it, and no amount of self-denial can thwart the driving passion of such
erotic love. Once again, Ruth Pitter was incapable of writing a poem like this.

Yet in spite of the full pleasure and excitement of passion expressed by such
poems, Gresham also suggests in other romantic poems that the core of the
beloved—the essence of the person—cannot be touched by the lover. There is
a separateness, a distance that even passion cannot overcome. This is nowhere
clearer than in "Division." It begins by celebrating a rich passion that knows
sweet climax:

Behold how sweetly we have come together;
Rich night and air, the dark embracing air
And union of the ceiling and the floor

Enclosing passion; love, cool formal sheets,
And secret wool of blankets. And so sweetly
We come together; so the clasp, the spasm
Answer each other, suitably invent
Exhaustion sweeter than content. (78–79)

Recalling something of Maria's phrase "The earth moved" from Hemingway's
For Whom the Bell Tolls to describe the ecstasy of lovemaking, Gresham suggests
the soaring nature of the lovers' passion with the phrase "union of the ceiling
and the floor." She also deftly captures the orgasm of each lover in "we come
together, so the clasp, the spasm / Answer each other." Still, passion alone is
not enough: "Is there no more / To say? the body answering a body / In its own
fashion perfect as a flower; / Is there no more to say?" As she explores these questions and others, she wonders why the consummation of physical passion is not
enough to satisfy her deepest longings: "Shall I have of you / The lovely mud,
unreasoning, the flesh / Beautifully and unimportantly nourished, / While the
irrelevant brain stares off into space / At a blank wall; is there no more to say?"
    As close as physical passion brings them, it never satisfies the longing of her
soul to meet another soul "face to face":

I will not eat you; I desire of you
Not to devour your separate nature; never
Shall I suck out your soul. Let us keep lonely;
But I would see the eyes of loneliness
In your eyes meeting me; I would perceive
In this queer universe, life and the spirit,
And from the locked and isolated self
Salute the world outside.

And here is the poem's greatest irony: passionate lovers are nonetheless lonely,
unable to make deep soul connections:

I clamorous, I the imperative,
I the fond conqueror of your love, the lover,
The lion crying in the wilderness,
I conscious of your life, your thought, your soul
(Call it) now hold your body quite as closely
As one can meet another, and the body
Asks and is satisfied, complete, made perfect,
While the brain stares at nothing.

Indeed, the poem's opening ecstasy celebrating passion is undercut by Gresham's suggestion that her lover is just another object, another thing that has physical substance but no reality beyond that:

> You are not real.
> You are like wood and rock, like earth, like satin;
> You are a touch, a taste. You are the animal
> Gold rippling thighs of horses; or disturbing
> And twisting cats; you are the muscles of tigers,
> The objective eyes of owls. You are not life;
> I am life. I find your accidental body,
> I take you for my pleasure, and all's done;
> And I am sweetly fed. No more, no more?

While passion brings her some solace, her lover remains separate, distant, apart. Accordingly, only her interior life has meaning for her; it is only there she will find fulfillment. Yes, she will continue to enjoy her lover's body, but as the final question hints, there is "no more" she can expect from him. In addition, she will never turn away from physical passion since she could "no more" bear isolation than he. Finally, "no more" may be a plaintive query to the universe, asking in effect: Is there no more to life than sexual pleasure? Is there nothing beyond the physical, no transcendent reality that lovers can experience?

The last romantic poem to consider is "Yet One More Spring." Ostensibly about the springtime, the poem actually focuses upon death: "What will come of me / After the fern has feathered from my brain / And the rosetree out of my blood; what will come of me / In the end, under the rainy locustblossom / Shaking its honey out on springtime air / Under the wind, under the stooping sky?" (65–66). Gresham wonders rhetorically if she will be "voiceless" and "unremembered." In answer she provides one of her most powerful poetic passages:

> Out of my heart the bloodroot,
> Out of my tongue the rose,
> Out of my bone the jointed corn,
> Out of my fiber trees.
> Out of my mouth a sunflower,
> And from my fingers vines,
> And the rank dandelion shall laugh from my loins
> Over million-seeded earth; but out of my heart,
> Core of my heart, blood of my heart, the bloodroot
> Coming to lift a petal in peril of snow,

Coming to dribble from a broken stem
Bitterly the bright color of blood forever.

She will be no shrinking violet in death. The rich, concrete imagery of these lines suggests a vigor, a fierce sensibility, an intensity that indelibly mark Gresham's verse as uniquely hers. Every part of her will rise again through the natural objects that draw nutrients from her decaying body.

If the poem were to stop here, it would be a great success. Yet Gresham does not limit her legacy to mere reincarnation in nature. Where she will be best remembered is in the heart of her lover:

But I would be more than a cold voice of flowers
And more than water, more than sprouting earth
Under the quiet passion of the spring;
I would leave you the trouble of my heart
To trouble you at evening; I would perplex you
With lightning coming and going about my head,
Outrageous signs, and wonders; I would leave you
The shape of my body filled with images,
The shape of my mind filled with imaginations,
The shape of myself. I would create myself
In a little fume of words and leave my words
After my death to kiss you forever and ever.

Her promise to live on in the mind of her lover is striking, and anyone who has read Lewis's A Grief Observed will be struck by how these lines presage much of what he says about Gresham there. Indeed, if it were somehow possible, which I admit it is not, one would think that the final lines from this poem were Joy Gresham's prothalamion (a song celebrating a marriage to be) and epithalamium (a song celebrating a marriage just completed) to Lewis.[18] If ever a poet foresaw how her memory would affect her lover, it was Gresham in this poem. She could not have known, of course, that this lover would be Lewis, nor could he have had any inclination that he was being "pre-loved" by Joy Gresham with such intensity, but later events confirm the inevitability of their coming together as friends, companions, and lovers.

In the final analysis, what can we learn from the love poetry of Pitter and Gresham that might explain why Lewis chose as he did?[19] First, while Gresham was an active participant in matters concerning romantic love, Pitter was an observer, prone more to "lurk[ing] . . . in the undergrowth," as she put it, than pursuing romantic love.[20] Moreover, Gresham had numerous sexual relationships with men before Lewis; she was vastly more experienced than Pitter in matters of how to please a man sexually. Although Pitter had lived in the Bohemian ethos of London's Chelsea and thus was probably sexually active at times, she was almost certainly less sexually active than Gresham; she certainly was circumspect, since only in "The Swan Bathing" does she write about the sexual nature of romantic love, and even there it is veiled and implied. It is worth recalling also Lewis's already-cited comment to her after he first read A *Trophy of Arms:* "If the Lady in *Comus* had written poetry one imagines it wd. have been rather like this." The central theme of Milton's *Comus* is a celebration of chastity, as the lady, through the use of reason and her native innocence, fends off the aggressive sexual pursuit of Comus. For Lewis to make this kind of link between Pitter and the lady in *Comus* is striking and offers an indirect commentary on Pitter's reserve regarding romantic love.[21]

Second, Gresham, as an American, was culturally more prone to reach out for what she wanted; Pitter, as a Briton, was culturally more prone to hoping for what she wanted. Put another way, Gresham was bold, aggressive, and determined, while Pitter was shy, passive, and reticent. Gresham had the American penchant for wanting to know and get close to a celebrity; Pitter, while also thrilled at getting to know Lewis, exercised the reserve often associated with her countrymen. In addition, Gresham, though she had to earn a living as a writer, probably had more time on her hands than did Pitter. As an artisan, Pitter worked hard to earn a living, often twelve- to sixteen-hour days, six days a week. Gresham had the time to pursue Lewis; Pitter did not. Finally, Gresham was looking to escape from a terrible marriage; Pitter was living a happy if hard life free from reliance on a man. Put another way, Gresham needed a man, while Pitter did not.

But we are getting a bit ahead of the story. Pitter's friendship with Lewis did not cease after the February 1 luncheon with Gresham. Pitter does not even refer to Gresham's presence when she writes Cecil about the luncheon:

I had been plotting to have a little luncheon-party, thinking how nice it would be if after the end of term you [and Rachel] would drive the two Lewises over, but of course that will have to wait. . . . I lunched with him early in Feb., and was shocked to hear that they are almost frozen in college during bad weather, as they don't like to ask the scouts to carry up coals, this having long ceased during the worst shortage. This I think shows a craven spirit, and discounts perhaps the real affection and zeal the scouts are no doubt burning to show, perhaps. (March 13)

She also chats breezily in this letter about Dylan Thomas and Orwell. About the former, she says: "His power over words was uncanny, making other work look pale—rather like looking at other pictures after El Greco. . . . He was my betters, and I remember with compunction the queer shy way he used to look at me. For of course my little reputation was made before he was anybody, and he probably knew I should not think him respectable." Of the latter, she writes: "He was 17 when I first saw him, and apart from the curious heaviness of the jaw (a family defect) I thought him a very good-looking youth, and I have seen a photograph of the family where he, a child of 4 or 5, was almost too pretty, and his aunt, at the funeral, told me the same. My brother, not romantic at all, once shared a room with him, and said he thought him beautiful. The fact is, I think, that we can see spiritual beauty in others, but no one can see his own." Thinking about Thomas and Orwell leads her to offer an insight into her own frustrations and fears as an artist: "Oh, how I wish I had ever had the courage to go all out for being an artist. But how they can, when it means making others miserable and stealing by not paying one's way, I can't think. I suppose it is like an illness when genuine. Others have to bear it if we get smallpox, and real militant creativeness must be similar. Seek no further for the cause of women's minor capacity for art."

Now established at the Hawthorns, Pitter and O'Hara began to receive visits from their neighbors. Pitter's modest fame drew some, while others came out of traditional Long Crendon hospitality. At times Pitter was frustrated by the constant visits; she writes Cecil: "Till Monday week, I believe we are engaged in some way to every blessed creature in the place (they have hitherto refrained, but now there is a dam-burst). . . . We seem to have strayed into the most tea-party'd village in England. Waves of misery flow over me at the thought" (March 21). At the same time, Pitter urges friends such as Cooley to come over from the United States, noting that the Hawthorns is a much better place to host guests than was the flat in Chelsea. As winter gives way to spring, Pitter tells Cooley she looks forward to working her garden: "The slow, cold spring, is advancing, and we keep finding nice plants & shrubs. I am getting into a dream-like state as regards the outside world, and only wish I could spend all day in the lovely large garden where there is so much to do: I have got a good serious part-time boy, but K. heads him off the basic and turns him into a sort of bellhop with vague horticultural affiliations" (April 17). Furthermore, Lewis continues writing Pitter, offering an assessment of their mutual friend Herbert Palmer: "I had the increasingly pathetic Herbert Palmer here last term: now an old man in a rage like Oedipus or Lear. I'd give a lot to be able to tell him he was a great poet. But the sheer vigour of his rage is sometimes exhilarating (and, I hope, at least a momentary comfort to himself) as when he called Dylan Thomas 'a drunken, illiterate, leg-pulling, Welsh foghorn'" (460–61; Apr. 22).[22] David Cecil also kept Pitter apprised of what was happening with Lewis, sometimes offering a bleak view of his life: "I hear rather bad accounts of poor Jack Lewis.

They say he lives in such dreadful discomfort, like a bachelor in a story, in a house that is seldom clean and of which many of the windows are broken. In consequence, he never feels well. I do hope this is not true, because I see him as the sort of man who doesn't look after himself very well and is too good to bully other people into doing the work for him" (April 26).

Pitter, enjoying her move to Long Crendon, had put aside for the time being thoughts of writing poetry. However, on May 5 she was jarred out of her lethargy when she received a letter from John Patterson, the secretary of the Royal Society of Literature, that began: "Dear Madame, I have the honour to inform you that my Council wish to award you a prize on the W. H. Heinemann Foundation for Literature in respect of your work *The Ermine*. . . . I am directed to ask if it will be your good pleasure to accept this award. The prize is £100, which is not assessable for Income Tax." After winning the Hawthornden Prize in 1937, this was the second important critical affirmation of her status as a poet. Pitter quickly writes back: "In answer to your letter of the 5th May, I feel greatly honored that the council of the Royal Society of Literature should wish to award me a prize under the W. H. Heinemann Foundation, and I shall be delighted to accept this."

As summer and a visit from Cooley neared, Pitter decided to invite the Cecils and the Lewis brothers for a luncheon on June 12 at the Hawthorns. While enjoying their lunch, Pitter and Lewis engaged in a comic argument in which she one-upped him. She recalls:

> I asked C. S. if I might catechize him a bit about the delectable "Lion, Witch, and Wardrobe," in which I thought I had detected a weakness. Permission courteously given:
>
> R. P.: The Witch makes it always winter and never summer?
> C. S.: (In his fine reverberating voice) She does.
> R. P.: Does she allow any foreign trade?
> C. S.: She does not.
> R. P.: Am I allowed to postulate a *deus ex machina*, perhaps on the lines of Santa Claus with the tea-tray? (This is where C. S. lost the contest. If he had allowed the deus-ex-m., for which Santa gives good precedent, he would have saved himself).
> C. S.: You are not.
> R. P.: Then how could the Beavers have put on that splendid lunch?
> C. S.: They caught the fish through holes in the ice.
> R. P.: Quite so, but the drippings to fry them? The potatoes—a plant that perishes at a touch of frost—the oranges and sugar and suet and flour for the lovely surprise Marmalade Roll—the malt and hops for Mr. Beaver's beer—the milk for the children?

C. S.: (With great presence of mind) I must refer you to a further study
of the text.
Warnie: Nonsense, Jack; you're stumped and you know it.[23]

The humor and good spiritedness of this exchange say much about the nature of
Lewis's friendship with Pitter. While he may have been drawn to Gresham, he
nonetheless valued his relationship with Pitter and enjoyed being with her.

Not long after this, Pitter began a correspondence initiated by Arthur Wol-
seley Russell that continued until 1986. Russell (1908–1990) worked as a freelance journalist in London from 1930 until joining the BBC as a subeditor in
the empire news department in February 1935. He held a number of similar
posts before moving in 1951 into production on the program *London Calling
Asia*. In his capacity as producer, he would later work with Pitter on numerous BBC radiocast productions and become a close personal friend.[24] However,
what drew Russell to Pitter was her poetry, as letter after letter between them
illustrate. In fact, Pitter's reply to Russell's first letter indicates that he helped
push her to begin writing poetry again: "I remembered, soon after writing to
you, about the long poem I intended. Sorry to be so exasperating. I am vague
about a number of new poems as some are light & perhaps no good. You shall
see all [of them] when fair copied, and thanks for your interest. It's quite true
that I should not have written them but for you—you make me feel guilty. Social pressure will often work wonders" (June 24).

Cooley and her friend Dorothy Karl visited the Hawthorns in August on
their way farther north. In recalling the pleasure of having them there, Pitter
writes: "Well, now we are real acquaintances, though we have been friends for
a long time. I liked your coming here; there is something so old and real in
being able to welcome those who have done one good. I have a profound feeling about it, and always have" (Sept. 20). After over fifteen years of receiving
kindness from Cooley, particularly during World War II and afterwards, when
Cooley regularly sent care packages, Pitter was delighted to have been able to
extend hospitality to her. In this same letter, Pitter confides that she is almost
overwhelmed by her neighbors: "I get a bit mad now & then because the neighbours are so darned friendly, and it stops me from getting on, but apart from
that we are all right." Long anxious to retire to the country, Pitter wanted the
novelty of their move to Long Crendon to subside so that she could indulge her
private passions of gardening and writing. In a letter late in the year to Blackshaw, she offers a retrospective of their first year in Long Crendon as well as her
plans for the future:

[We] have been a whole year in our new house, and though the weather
has been a record for badness, I at least would not wish to be back in Lon-

don. It has been a big strain, all the business connected with moving, and having got the place about half-finished, we tend to call it a day and not to organize as well as we should. We have a large neglected garden and orchard with critturs in them—woodpeckers, hedgehogs, etc., and I aim at getting the effect of a bit of countryside that has had a shave and brush, for I shall never have lots of flower-beds, etc. for want of labour. However, undulating grass (motor-mower), a few big trees and nice shrubs, and the feeling of space, give quite a good effect. I have broken up a bit for vegetables out of sight, and am already independent of the market for potatoes. Apples and pears we have by the orchard—we take the best and leave the rest, and people who want any can fetch them. The blackbirds, thrushes, and fieldfares clear up the leavings. (Dec. 1954)

Clearly Pitter is quite happy at the Hawthorns and looking forward to cultivating the grounds for many years to come. She is finally able to live the dream she first had in Hainault Forest—living close to nature, working the earth, and reflecting upon larger workings of the universe.

Early in 1955 Pitter is excited over two developments. First she tells Cooley: "The new greenhouse has arrived, and the foundations are complete, but it looks like a holdup now, as we are deep in snow. However, we shall have it for the sowing season. Well, I do get out quite a lot really, only I want to be out all the time. Lately we had some calm weather, much drier than summer, and I got a lot of planting done and was in great spirits" (Jan. 4, 1955). Later in the year they added a lily pond, filled it with fish, and installed a small waterfall. She also says in the same letter to Cooley: "I know I spend too long painting, but I am so thankful I can get the work, and it takes such a lot to make ends meet now. I feel quite jubilant because I have good orders to start the year." The second event that excited her was the promise of a visit from May Sarton; she confides to Cooley in the same letter: "She doesn't have big sales, of course, but one way & another she succeeds in getting more & more time for writing, which is the great thing. K. may have felt jealous of her clothes, but did not actually try any piracy."

In addition, despite the infrequency of their visits once Lewis's relationship with Joy Gresham began in earnest, Lewis and Pitter continued to write. In one letter to Lewis she praises his new book in the Oxford History of English Literature series, *English Literature in the Sixteenth Century, Excluding Drama* (1954), and congratulates him on his move to Cambridge.[25] About the former Pitter recalls, "[It was] to me a work not only monumental . . . but dear and delectable, to read for enjoyment, for relaxation, for the sense of balance & just appraisal, bringing unction."[26] About the latter she asks if he is enjoying Cambridge and what he thinks his impact might be; Lewis replies that he is surprisingly happy, finding the small-town atmosphere enjoyable compared to Oxford. He adds that

"I am having an 'impact,' whether 'joyous' or not. If you have seen the 'Cambridge Number' of *The XXth Century* you'll see that the Orthodox Atheists are v. alarmed at this influx of Christians (Butterfield, Knowles, and C. S. L.)" (577; March 5). Two weeks later Lewis offers her lavish praise for a jar of homemade marmalade she had sent him and Warren: "This morning . . . I flashed my teeth in your gold and amber gift. It is delicious; a proper gift for a poetess, to show that you can imprison sunlight in other snares than words" (585; March 19). In the same letter he confides that he is having trouble writing poetry: "It is a long time since I turned a verse. One aches a little, doesn't one? I should like to be 'with poem' again." Good food was a common liking, but at least on one occasion Lewis scrupled to eat a pork pie Pitter had prepared especially for him. Pitter says: "I remember taking great pains to make a Raised Pork Pie, whose goodness surprised even myself, when Lewis was coming to lunch, only to find that he was reluctant to eat meat on a Friday (I had forgotten) and would hardly do more than taste it."[27]

Life at the Hawthorns gave Pitter more time to reflect upon writers and literary matters. In response to a query from Cooley about W. B. Yeats's relationship with Dorothy Wellesley, Pitter responds:

Yes, you are right about Yeats' letters to D. W.[28] They weren't lovers, you know; perhaps it would have been better if they had been. But they were both such towering egotists, and he such a filthy snob—she too, in her way, which wasn't as bad as his—that the whole thing is a monument to the peculiar romanticism of the twenties; as typical as cloche hats and early jazz. It must have been a scream to the onlooker. They used to fight horribly. Of course D. W. fights everyone, for that matter. But I think the impact of Yeats bowled her over, and she's never got over it. Just fancy—such whole-hearted praise, out of the blue, from a man of that prestige, to one who has always felt herself, and really is, an amateur. (May 1)

But even as Pitter writes about other writers, she is receiving more and more letters from admirers of her verse. None was more celebratory than one that began: "This is a letter of love and worship. When Theodore Roethke[29] read me 'But for Lust' a year ago, I knew, as he does, that it is one of the great lyrics of this or any time" (May 10). The writer, the American poet Carolyn Kizer,[30] while breathless in her own admiration, is equally revealing about Roethke's high regard for Pitter: "As Theodore said the other day, 'You can learn *everything* from her; it's all there, it's all transparent and pure.' I went to hear him lecture his class of practicing poets the other day. It was a wonderful thing. . . . He talked of you and read you, for the hour. . . . [He] says 'She has never written a poor poem or a faulty line.'" Kizer is effusive in her praise of "A Solemn Meditation," calling it "a landmark in the poetry of this century." About the line "Then Alleluia all my gashes cry" Kizer exclaims: "Muscular, powerful, brave—and a woman. My God!" She goes on to lavish praise on Pitter for her use of the caesura, her control of emotion, her rhetorical cunning, and her verbal felicity. About "The Swan Bathing," a poem she reads "over and over again," Kizer says it is "a piece of descriptive writing that is a model of its kind, yet with so many, many nuances and implications handled with such subtlety and finesse." Having for years felt isolated as a poet, Kizer glories to find "Ruth Pitter in the world—beautiful and brave and pure, a blood relation of the mind." Kizer's devotion to Pitter would later find expression when the journal she edited, *Poetry Northwest,* published several new poems by Pitter in 1960. Pitter's delight in such a letter can hardly be imagined; although it has taken many years, she is now experiencing on a regular basis the kind of recognition a writer lives for.

Moreover, because of the Heinemann Award she won for *The Ermine,* she became something of a minor celebrity. Producers from BBC radio begin to contact Pitter about participating in various programs. For instance, on May 17 she appeared on BBC radio and discussed the mystical characteristics of her poetry: "The chief source and origin of the poetry I have been trying to write for so many years is simply a strong natural mysticism. In nature . . . there is for me . . . a visiting spirit of delight, felt with great force and yet like all mystical experience, supremely difficult to communicate. This numinous experience al-ways seems to be good, absolutely good, good without reference to evil; it gives unique delight, or rather it is delight."[31] On the same day, BBC producer Mary Ann Sands wrote Pitter and invited her to participate in the series *Personal Call,* in effect asking Pitter to provide "really a fragment of autobiography" in-tended "to show something of the British character and way of life," targeted primarily at audiences of South and Southeast Asia and the Far East. Pitter happily accepted the invitation, and so on June 24 Sands, her production team, and Stephen Black interviewed Pitter at the Hawthorns.[32]

In the interview Pitter recounts the details of her early life and her earliest efforts at verse. She admits that her early success as a poet due to the attentions of Orage and Belloc may have been counterproductive: "I have been taken a good deal of notice of, because other things being equal, what a woman does is always news, and my first poems which were not at all good, I think, had a very good press, considering. I am afraid I didn't write any mature work, though I have been writing for so long, I certainly didn't write anything mature until I was well past 30. I am afraid until I was at least 25 I believed in fairies." Of special note are her reflections on writing poetry. In response to Black's question about how she gets an idea for a poem, Pitter says: "[What] one used is an idea which has lain dormant in one's mind for a long time. In my case, I feel that poems are concepts which have entered perhaps very many years ago, have lain in the unconscious mind for a long time, and at the touch of some stimulus will suddenly emerge as a poem." Then she adds: "A poem is, as it were, an explosion at the center of one's being which expresses itself in ripples which gradually reach the periphery. . . . The rhythm is decided by the explosion at first, and the tempo of the ripples which are set up from it. It hits one like some energy. In fact it sometimes, in my youth at least, it used to hit me so hard, that my eyes watered as though I had been hit on the nose." She also admits to being careful about writing: "I don't believe in putting down everything that comes into one's head. I think that when poetry does not do good it does harm and one should be very careful about writing it down. There's too much facile, undigested poetry written nowadays, and so I am very careful about it. I feel a kind of stage-fright in the presence of poetry. I feel I am taking up the weapons of the mighty, and they must not be dishonoured."

This interview, the first of dozens, is significant for several reasons. First, her success as a poet, now recognized, means she is sought out as an expert and given the opportunity to be an arbiter regarding poetry and poetic inspiration. This gives her a platform from which to critique modernist poetry, and while she rarely does, when she does, it is with the voice of some legitimacy. Second, this interview brings Pitter before the public in a way that none of her volumes of verse had, supplementing the modest fame brought her way by the Hawthornden and the Heinemann prizes. Pitter's appearances on the BBC radio further increase in frequency during this period. Many who heard her were struck by her common sense, her passion for poetry, and her winsome, modest assessment of her own poetry. Finally, this interview sets into motion later events culminating in her appearance on the BBC television program *The Brains Trust*.

Given the BBC's newfound interest in Pitter, she must have felt that her many years of laboring in relative obscurity as a poet were finally being rewarded. However, she could never have imagined the next honor to come her way. On July 6 she received the following letter from the poet laureate, John Masefield: "It is my happy fortune to have the honour & pleasure of telling you that Her Majesty, the Queen, has graciously approved the whole-hearted recommendation of the committee of judges that you should receive the Queen's Gold Medal for Poetry for this year.[33] I am so very glad that it falls to me to tell you this. With my greeting to Miss O'Hara & to you, & with our glad congratulations." Pitter's deep pleasure upon receiving this letter, especially since Masefield had always been a favorite of hers, is only partially reflected in her reply: "The honour which I am to receive at the hands of Her Majesty the Queen will be the greatest delight and consolation to me, all unworthy as I know myself, and I have to thank you very greatly for your most kind and courtly manner of announcing this good news to me" (July 7). In the flurry of correspondence between Pitter and Masefield that follows, the question of who will present the gold medal to Pitter is discussed, since only rarely had the monarch personally presented the award. In his July 13 letter to Pitter Masefield quotes from a letter he had just received from Dudley Colles, the Keeper of the Privy Purse: "Her Majesty will be graciously pleased to present personally the Gold Medal for Poetry for 1955 to Miss Ruth Pitter in view of the fact that Miss Pitter will be the first woman to receive the Medal. As Her Majesty is the donor of many other prize medals, it is not normally possible to present awards personally other than in exceptional circumstances, as in the case of Miss Pitter."

It is not hard to imagine Pitter's excitement at this news, and it is reflected in her reply to Masefield:

It was with great delight that I learned from your letter of yesterday that Her Majesty the Queen will herself present the Gold Medal for Poetry. I shall feel that this award, made by the Sovereign in person, is the greatest and most apt honour (undeserved as I must feel it) that could be offered to one who for over half a century has endeavoured to write English poetry for pure love of it. . . . I hope very sincerely that if there is any detail I should be likely to overlook, or if there is any action on my part that could add a grace to the occasion, you as the head and court representative of our English living poetry will advise me as a father. I know one *is* advised as to the ordinary deportment, but I mean from the poetic point of view. (July 14)

Once Pitter learns from Colles that the Gold Medal will be awarded on October 19, she looks forward to the day with excitement. To be recognized with such an award was one thing, but to have it presented personally by Her Majesty was an unexpected honor. Indeed, for Pitter's generation the person of the queen was greatly respected and few people could ever expect actually to meet her face to face. Out of love for her friend, Pitter arranged for O'Hara to accompany her to Buckingham Palace on the day of the award.

In winning the Hawthornden and Heinemann prizes and now the Queen's Gold Medal for Poetry, Pitter's public star reaches a zenith. BBC radio again approaches her, and on July 19 she appears on the broadcast "Ruth Pitter Talks about Her Own Poems." During the broadcast she is recognized for having won the Gold Medal and then is asked to talk about her poetry. When asked to describe herself in relation to other poets, she says: "Modern critics distinguish in English poetry of the past what they call the 'golden' and the 'drab' approach.[34] The 'golden' poets are those who find in the life about them a glory, a beauty, and a satisfaction which almost excludes the necessity for violence or despair as elements of art. I like to think of myself as a poet of this kind." She recounts how her parents had supported her development as a poet by encouraging her to memorize verse as a small child; in addition, she reflects upon her own sense of poetic rhythm: "But I soon went beyond the very regular forms, lured on by the fascinating echoes of unusual poetic rhythms that haunt our everyday speech. Over and over again a phrase would come up from the unconscious mind, clothed in a lovely rhythm, full of undertones and overtones, and 'trailing clouds of glory' in the way of associations, and I could not use it because it would not fit into the syllabic forms—I mean the conventional verse forms used for centuries in English."

This, she says, led her to experiment with Old English alliterative rhythms and to try to break her reliance on established verse forms: "Our conversational speech only fits into [most poetic forms] by accident or by skillful selection. In using them we tend, therefore, to drop the living rhythm, to the detriment of the work—to become enslaved to the mechanical beat of an unvarying metre. No wonder I felt these forms to be restricting." While she appreciates therefore the virtue of conventional English poetics since they "give poetry an athletic strength which is admirably virile," Pitter says that "there is an opposite virtue—the virtue of getting lucid thought and music into the simplest verse. I think where this does happen it will usually be found that the syllabic metre happens to fit the ordinary speech-rhythm without distortion, so that it might be a child speaking, and yet it is poetry." She also offers an insight into how her love of gardening has had an impact on her poetry:

> The mystery of life other than human has always held me strongly, particularly the life of plants. I see in them something I have never been able to express, though I have often tried. They have music in their silence, dancing in their stillness, speech without concepts. They are organisms as we are, and in the same world, but utterly different and apart, except that we live on them and could not live without them. There they are, supplying our primary needs, even the oxygen we breathe, and bearing, for anyone who can see it, a strange mystical emanation as of truth perceived in vision or in dream.

As Pitter is sought out more and more, she reveals more about her poetic sensibilities and commitments. For example, in a follow-up letter to Russell about this interview, she says: "Without committing myself to agreeing with your classification of yourself & your charming wife as readers of middle intelligence, I think what I call the rank & file reader often a far better judge than the intellectual. The latter, in spite of his extra intelligence, has often a set of symptoms that would sink a battleship. No brilliance can make an egoist other than blind-hearted in the main, whatever intellectual gleams he has on occasion" (July 25). Moreover, Pitter adds: "Everyman, on the other hand, lives by the heart, and backs the heart with all he has. His head may be dimmer, but his heart is brighter. . . . Simple people still love real English poetry in spite of all the horrors."

In August Pitter was disappointed to have missed a visit, inspired in part no doubt by her achievement of the Queen's Gold Medal, by Lewis and George Sayer. Lewis writes: "George and I were both very disappointed but the one miss out of a thousand days that wd. have been hits certainly suggests Providence Herself, moving in a more than usually mysterious way. But K. was very kind to us" (635; Aug. 5). He also comments at length on having seen a neighbor woman wearing trousers, something new to him, and compliments Pitter on an epigram she had written him celebrating his move to Cambridge: "Lewis appears, the Trojan Dinosaur; / Eggs of ambivalence distend his Maur. /What meant the Fathers who convey'd him in? / I wish I knew the mind of those grave Min."[35] This is also the period during which the frequency of Pitter's correspondence with Russell accelerates considerably. Russell, wanting to promote Pitter much in the vein of Orage and Belloc before him, sent her a draft of an article he was writing about her that he hoped to place with an important newspaper. In her response, she is almost embarrassed that he would undertake such a project. This letter also contains ruminations about how the poetry of T. S. Eliot has, in her view, negatively affected English poetry:

The Eliot part is ticklish. Here is a man, not English by birth, coming from far and bringing what is to me a strange and great disaster to that English poetry which is the treasure of the humble and the spiritual flower of a very great people, taking it away from the common man (whom he quite unconsciously but quite evidently despises) and making it the province of the few, and the snobbish few at that. This is quite horrible, and yet here also is a man, a kind, good, and much afflicted man, who is my fellow-Christian and my old acquaintance, (for I have known him slightly, through Orage and "The New Age" after Orage's American period) for many years. The conflict in me is real and fierce. If he were no poet there would be no conflict, but he has the gift, and this fact makes the battle in me one of angels and demons. I truly think him wrong, and my own spirit of unforgiveness (my besetting sin) keeps me on the horns of the dilemma which only charity can resolve. When I accosted him at the bus-stop (on the one day of many months that I was in London) it was an act of contrition on my part as much as a gesture of high spirits. It was not a light thing to me at all, though I laughed at it, and his positively gay aplomb, courteous kindness, and lighthearted disregard of being in the crowded street, were all very good. When I lived in Chelsea I often met him at the early Communion service at the Old Church. Something is here for tears,

and I don't understand it yet. . . . I can't see that there is in him any perversity which could have been avoided, thus averting the disaster. Many
wrongheaded writers and artists seem deliberately and wickedly perverse,
certainly not Eliot. To me it is real tragedy. (Aug. 24)

She later ameliorates her view of Eliot, in part due to Masefield's reaction to
seeing a draft of Russell's article on Pitter: "I see that Dr. Masefield is grieved
that I should bite Mr. E. It is a bit hard after all these years that one shouldn't
be allowed a mouthful, but do you know I think he is right after all? I turn a
very heedful ear to all who advise greater gentleness and forbearance in human
relations; and perhaps it is invidious that one living poet should decry another"
(Sept. 10). Given Pitter's own native understanding of English poetry, she could
not appreciate Eliot's poetry, though it is clear she realized his talent.

As the day on which she would receive the Gold Medal from the queen
neared, Pitter grew more excited, telling Cooley: "Many thanks for kind congratulations on the Medal. I am to go to the Palace on the 19th October, and
actually to see the Queen. So do think of me at 12.20 on that day" (Sept. 11).
In a later letter to Cooley, Pitter recalls her audience with the queen:

We hired a village car & driver (not at all smart) and asked our ancient
boy friend [Raymond Barnett] to escort us. We all met at a friend's flat in
Chelsea, smartened up a bit, and drove off to the Palace. They don't stop
you at all—you just slow down & tell the cop at the gate your name, and
he waves you on—no doubt all the names are down in the day's orders.
We drove into the inner courtyard, and as we were a bit early, the door-
keeper told us to pull to one side & wait a bit, and we saw the Turkish
Ambassador & his suite arrive in state, 3 coaches, most gorgeous. Then
we were waved on, & drew up at red-carpeted steps with no end of foot-
men etc., and at the top of the steps an equerry in dress uniform that I
could have eaten, sword & all. He took us through a long gallery with
crimson carpet, cream & gold walls, & Winterhalter paintings. We were
joined by a Lady in Waiting and sort of passed on from group to group
through several rooms, then K. was left with a nice lord and I was taken
on by the equerry & the lady to an anteroom, where we waited a bit in
front of a good fire. I checked up on the drill with them. Then a pair of
large folding doors were opened, I went inside, alone, & there was the
Queen walking towards me. I curtsied at the door, walked to meet her,
and curtsied again. The Queen said, "How do you do" & I said, "Your
Majesty," then she took up the medal in its case from a table by the fire
& said, "I am very happy to ask you to accept this," & took it out of the
case & showed it me. I made my little speech of thanks, then the Queen

said "Won't you sit down"? & there we were sitting by the fire together
& talking for 10 minutes or so. The Queen asked about my writing, and
made some interesting remarks on modern tendencies. She asked about
the rest of my life too, and I suggested sending her one of my books and
a painted tray, which, she smilingly said, I might. The Queen is small, of
course, smaller than you might think. She has good eyes and a straight,
honest, shrewd look. She was wearing a simple printed silk dress in light
grey with a pink tinge and a darker grey pattern. I didn't notice any jewel-
lery, and her make-up was not at all pronounced. I think she wore a little
rouge, but royal ladies always do, I believe. Presently I sensed that it was
time to go. I took up the medal, the Queen rose, and I curtsied myself out,
to come face to face with Dr. [Albert] Schweitzer! He was waiting for an
audience, surrounded by several other gentlemen. I immediately curtsied
to him as royalty, and he bowed gravely. (Dec. 31, 1955)

After the excitement of receiving the Gold Medal from the queen, Pitter and
her friends met Mary Ann Sands and Russell at the BBC and heard the playback
of the July 19 interview, "Ruth Pitter Talks about Her Own Poems." She writes
Sands: "I thought it excellent. The editing and interviewing were so skillful that
the very most had been made of the material, and the recording was faultless.
Modesty apart, I do think this an outstanding programme, and it made a very
great contribution to what, for me, was a most memorable day. I had 10 minutes
alone with the Queen, and found her most sympathetic, very well informed, and
a most charming person, beyond anything one had expected" (Oct. 20).

Still capitalizing on her newfound fame, on October 26 Pitter is heard reflecting on the question "What is a poet?" on another BBC program, *Woman's
Hour*. We gain yet more insight into Pitter's poetic vision when she says: "A
poet is a person who has *seen* something—something unforgettable. Like anyone else who has been enormously impressed, he or she has got to tell someone
about it—to get it out of the system. . . . Of course this special *seeing* . . . isn't
just seeing with the eyes. It is also hearing, smelling, tasting, feeling, or just
sensing." Whether it is a special passage of music, the sound of another's voice,
or a rich scent or taste, each can stimulate the poet to see the world, and Pitter
is most satisfied when what she sees is realized by her readers. In addition, she
reveals her Victorian origins when she muses upon being a poetess: "We have to
do it [write verse] in spite of everything else—all the multifarious demands of a
woman's life, whether she is a wife and mother or not. . . . Like Jane Austen in
a corner with her bits of paper, which she slid out of sight when anyone came
in, we have to do our composing and writing at any time, just when we can."
Moreover, she says a poetess is not able to express her feelings as openly as a
male poet: "We have a natural instinct to hide our feelings, as a bird hides its

nest." She ends by sharing about her audience with the queen: "And something has just happened to me that might be straight out of a poem, only it is real. I have been to see the Queen of England in her palace, and she has given me a great gold piece, a beautiful medal." Pitter's almost childlike delight in recalling her meeting with the queen and her belief that a poetess sees the world and communicates her vision of life from a somewhat constrained perspective mark her very much as out of the mainstream of twentieth-century modernist British poetry. She never writes verse in order to shock, to provoke, to challenge; instead, hers is a poetry of mystic visions and profound musings.

Pitter could not have imagined a year earlier that she would appear three times on BBC radio within the space of a week. Russell, sensing the depth of interest in Pitter, seizes the opportunity to schedule her for another BBC program in which he plans to have her reflect upon her relationship with George Orwell. Pitter tells him she will "be incubating a script" (Oct. 27), and later she adds: "I have some notes, not much more, towards a possible Orwell talk. (This is a very busy time in my trade). I find my memories of him tend to be a series of snapshots with more reference to the man than to his books; would this be in the picture?" (Dec. 4). As the year comes to a close, she hears from Blackshaw, who congratulates her on the Gold Medal and wants to know if she has another book of poetry in mind. She replies:

> Many thanks for your friendly congratulations. It has been very exciting and glorious, of course, to get the medal, and to get it from the Queen's own hand, not at a big investiture, but alone with her Majesty, who sat talking to me for about ten minutes by the fire, and asked many questions about my life and work. She is very sensible, frank, and kindly, and in spite of the formality inseparable from official royalty I felt quite at ease. Of course anything to do with the Queen draws a lot of publicity, and I had to appear on radio and television, and got (for me) an overwhelming lot of silly letters—not from people at all interested in one's work, but old school friends and neighbours who only wanted to claim acquaintance. I did reply to nearly all but it was dreary work. All this was a severe interruption to my usual trade, etc. I wish I had got the makings of a new book or anything like it, but for years now I have had no chance to write. By the time I have earned enough to live and done my share of the chores the day is over. I can get an hour or two out of doors only by working at my trade all the evening. I have scores of ideas but no chance to use them. I won't grumble, because it is simply the result of war—my share of the disaster, which swept away our good business and reduced the value of the savings I thought I could retire on—I always meant to buy my freedom as soon as I had collected the smallest competence, but now I never shall.

Others lost their lives, their husbands, children, homes, limbs, etc.—I am let off lightly. There is a big element of nastiness in my attitude, I know. If I really meant to write I should do it and starve. (Dec. 12)

Although Pitter could not have known it, her writing lethargy would be lengthy since her next volume of verse, *Still by Choice*, would not appear for another eleven years. At the same time, her manuscript notebooks reveal that she was writing verse, even if it was hit or miss, and she does publish a handful of poems in journals before the appearance of *Still by Choice*.

In her last letter of the year to Cooley, Pitter reveals that her energies have been focused not on writing but on enjoying the modest fame that has come her way: "What a lucky year it has been for me, getting that medal. Quite independently, a nice producer on the London Calling Asia programme started to run my work a bit, and the news of the medal came in nicely. Then I was asked to go on TV, and have become quite a local celebrity, and earned quite a useful amount of extra money" (Dec. 31). Indeed, while three new volumes of verse and two collected works are still to come, Pitter's time from 1955 onwards is given more to radio and television broadcasts and various works of prose, including religious drama, book reviews, magazine articles, and personal essays, than to poetry. Ironically, while the move to Long Crendon was intended to free her up for writing poetry, the fame she was now realizing because of her earlier verse kept her from writing much new poetry. Still, her fame brought her unprecedented opportunities to reach a public that heretofore had barely heard of her. It is to this next stage of her career, particularly her BBC appearances, that we now turn.

~ NINE ~

Public Figure,
1956–1966

Pitter soon became a familiar voice on BBC radio, appearing more than forty times between 1956 and 1966, most often on *Woman's Hour*. While sometimes she read and discussed her poems, more often than not she delivered a scripted talk on a topic mutually agreed upon by Pitter and her producer. Although still driven to earn a living as an artisan, she found the extra income these talks provided a tangible comfort. She writes Russell: "I was brought up to be overanxious about money . . . and it gets me down; not that I am in want, oh dear no; I believe I could earn a living in a dozen ways, as long as I keep my health. . . . I have spent less than I earned all my life and always have a good bit in hand—though I have been so grateful for your jobs because they pay better than painting . . . and are so interesting too" (Jan. 9, 1956). Russell becomes increasingly important to Pitter, not only because he both arranged contacts for Pitter's talks and actually produced them, but also because he did all he could to promote her verse. Although lacking the stature of Orage or Belloc, in the end he did perhaps more than either to keep Pitter in front of the public.

A brief review of Pitter's BBC radio broadcasts illustrates her fertile mind as well as her wide range of experience.[1] In addition to her detailed memories of Orwell noted earlier, her talks offer reflections on topics such as beauty, romance, leisure, and children. One important cluster of broadcasts reminisces about her childhood experiences in Hainault Forest. "A Friendly Day" recalls a day in the forest when she and her sister, Olive, and her brother, Geoffrey, were left by their parents, who had to return to work. Pitter remembers: "[The cottage] was on the edge of a forest. The front windows looked across a green slope to the trees. The back window looked over lovely fields. At the bottom of the slope was a brook. There were no real roads to the cottage, only a few tracks; so if you wanted to get anywhere you just had to walk."[2] On that day, rather than bickering, the children, with Ruth as the leader, decided to enjoy the delights of market day at the local village. The vibrancy of her recollections is best reflected in her description of a candy maker: "There was a man making toffee. He'd boiled up a lot of sugar, and poured it into a thick rope; [then he threw] it over a strong hook fastened to his stall, and twisting and pulling and throwing it again, till it got quite light coloured and shiny and too hard to pull any more; then he cut it into pieces with a great pair of shears, and the pieces fell into a tin, and the next minute he was shoveling them into bags and handing them out to his customers." She also remembers purchasing a little onion hoe for her father and how at the end of the day the three of them had dinner ready for their parents: "We were all clean and fresh, there were piles of logs ready to burn, the kettle was singing, the sausages and potatoes were sizzling in the oven, a large plate of toast was keeping hot in the fender, and the first owl was hooting outside. We looked at each other. We didn't say anything, but I'm sure we were thinking, 'This has been one of the nicest days of our lives. I'll always remember it.'" She then ends the talk with a tender memory: "Dad was very pleased with the little onion-hoe. I've still got it. You can see where the blade is worn away at one side. No wonder. It's been in use for forty-five years."

In "Glory Is Real" she remembers another day when their parents left it to Pitter to get herself and her siblings to an inn on the other side of the forest, some five or six miles away, where they would meet for lunch. She took this responsibility seriously: "No infantry subaltern, taking his company out on his first route-march, could have been more concerned than I was. And like the subaltern, I was not preoccupied with welfare efficiency and morale exclusively. I had dreams of glory. The whole meaning of life was, and is, glory: an incomprehensible, but inevitable, supreme good. I had glimpses of it everywhere. It was very strong that day. And I was leading my Olive and Geoffrey to it."[3] At first all goes well, but then after a long "forced" march, her sister and brother begin to falter. Hot, thirsty, hungry, and tired, they could see no glory. However, Pitter, ever the wise leader, produces small glasses filled with lemon juice and, passing them out, preempts a rebellion. Later she provides them cold tea and a wet cloth to wash off the dust and grime of the road. When they reach their parents, the glory of the day takes on a new twist as they are unexpectedly taken for a ride in their uncle's new automobile: "This was magic. There could be no other name for it. . . . Glory was real. There was its angelic messenger, the motor-car. Hushed and transfigured, we three children climbed slowly into the heavenly chariot, sat down, already half etherealized, on the red leather, and were whirled away in a trance of wonder and delight."

When asked to reflect upon her greatest personal pleasure for *Woman's Hour*, Pitter readily did so: "My greatest personal pleasure is the very ancient and simple pleasure of growing a few things to eat. When I bring in a basketful of fruit or vegetables from my own garden, or almost better still, well-stored produce in the winter when good stuff is scarce and dear—many's the time I've gloated over a four-pound string of handsome onions when there wasn't a sound onion in the shops—that's the time when I feel on top of the world."[4] Recalling her affection for potatoes, she says she loves having her own homegrown ones nearby: "They may say what they like about potatoes being fattening. I only know for a good, cheap, heartening meal—why, the floury potato baked in its jacket, or the roast potato, so savoury and appetizing, or the enticing little new potato with its whiff of mint and sprinkle of parsley, are things I should be a whole lot worse off without." Homegrown tomatoes, asparagus, rhubarb, lettuce, and cauliflower also come in for great praise. But even better than vegetables, says Pitter, are homegrown fruits, including apples, strawberries, and grapes. About the last, she recalls the wonderful vines from Oak Cottage: "It was a great loss to me when we left that house. But we did have twenty years of homegrown grapes. I mustn't grumble. It's better to have loved and lost, than never to have loved at all. My hands remember those vines so well. I believe I could still go even in pitch darkness, and prune the vines accurately by feeling the buds. Talk about pleasure!"

Listeners were delighted by Pitter's simple, honest reflections, particularly her capacity to speak directly to their hearts and minds. While not exactly homespun, her view of life was obviously informed by love of the natural world and respect for the values of the past. Here was a famous poet who was also personable, accessible, and winsome. These qualities come through clearly in Pitter's most famous broadcast, "Hunting the Unicorn." Confiding that she has been trying to write good poetry all her life, she further reveals that her poetry "is founded on something . . . we know about in a sort of way, but something we haven't actually got. Something we only catch glimpses of."[5] For her all things have a "secret, . . . hidden treasure" that we are always trying to perceive. Citing examples as varied as the Holy Grail, the burning bush, and the unicorn, Pitter says our vision of these things suggests transcendence and then she recounts an example from her own experience, almost certainly from her early days in Hainault Forest:

I was sitting in front of a cottage door, one day in spring, long ago; a few bushes and flowers round me, a bird gathering nesting-material, the trees of the forest at a little distance. A poor place—nothing glamorous about it, except that it was spring in the country. Suddenly everything assumed a different aspect—no its true aspect. For a moment, it seemed to me, the truth appeared in its overwhelming splendour. The secret was out, the explanation given. Something that had seemed like total freedom, total power, total bliss—a good with no bad as its opposite—an absolute that had no opposite—this thing, so unlike our feeble nature, had suddenly cut across one's life—and vanished.

In her expansion on this epiphany, she suggests that most people have prob-ably had a similar experience at least once in life, often as a result of falling in love. "For many of us this makes life entirely different, at least for a time. . . . We are so amazed at the transformation, so astonished by what we see, at the differ-ent quality life can assume, that we go about in a dream. . . . I can remember, at no more than fourteen years old, seeing that altered landscape; looking at the very grass in the fields with stupefaction, because apparently it had changed its nature, and 'put on immortality' to quote St. Paul." She goes on to suggest that the feelings generated by romantic love, while open to abuse and heartbreak, are intimations of divine love:

But Love in his own person, I say, is lord of all, forever; and the glimpse of glory, so far as it goes, is the truth. I'd stake my life on that. I do stake it. . . . Whether the revelation comes by sexual love, or seems to be directed through the arts, through science, or through religion—and it can seem to be coming from every direction at once—in whatever way it comes, for any-one who has had such moments . . . from a single flash—[she] can determine the values of life and death. We are then, in the words of Scripture, "strang-ers and pilgrims, seeking a country." The ordinary pleasures and pains of life are not undervalued, but they are pleasures and pains by the way. The way is the thing; we can't be anchored to the world's values, or we shall begin to rot. We follow the gleam, hunting the thing wherever we can get news of it. Poor dying creatures, with sore feet and a bit of mouldy bread in a dirty old knapsack, we are our own policemen, obstinately moving ourselves on, along the muddy gutters and littered pavements of the world, past the shops and theatres and government offices and factories and palaces of the world. The world's goods, and the world's ills, are marginal, are secondary, because, far beyond, we have *seen* something.

The glimpses of transcendent truth further spotlight why earthly delights and pleasures do not give us what we want—be it money, success, or power—because they are all limited good. "And," says Pitter, "we want an unlimited good. We want that. Everything to be all right, in every way, forever." No temporary good is enough. Would we stake our lives upon earthly delights? "How could we, when we think—we believe—that we can be given a complete, limitless, timeless good? Who could take less?"

As she strives to penetrate ever deeper, she suggests such an unbidden ex-perience is nothing less than a divine intrusion: "Is it—could it be, after all—a hint of something *more real* than this life—a message from reality—perhaps a particle of reality itself? If so, no wonder we hunt it so unceasingly, and never stop desiring and pining for it." Pitter then wonders if these divine intrusions may be the result of the intuitive capacity of our brains to glimpse "pure meaning which haunts all language, sometimes invading words and concepts, making them live, sending a current through them until they are white-hot, what we call inspired." This pure meaning affects both mind and body: "Our bodies may shiver, may bristle, we may weep copiously, while our minds are filled with nameless longings and glorious intuitions." She ends by affirming "that anyone who has had a glimpse, anyone who has been so illuminated, could [never] take less, could [never] abdicate eternity to exist merely in time."

The broadcast of "Hunting the Unicorn" unleashed a minor flood of correspondence; so many listeners requested a script that Pitter "spent whole days copying & recopying for the (often very urgent) applicants."[6] Pitter answered each letter, telling her producer, Barbara Crowther: "I have had much kind praise for 'The Unicorn.' Many friends and correspondents say 'It was packed solid,' 'Real thought and feeling,' 'Not just competent time-filling', etc., and though the transcendental element was (even rapturously) accepted, I do like praise for giving good value, giving oneself—this is the only thing that makes broadcasting honest work, at least this kind" (Feb. 22). Other BBC radio broadcasts by Pitter also elicited favorable letters from listeners. For example, on September 4, 1963, the day her "Romance" was broadcast, a physician, Dr. T. Russell, wrote the BBC: "Dear Sir, [Re] 'Romance.' The first time I've heard the wind of honest to goodness horse sense in all the present day welter of absurd nonsense we have these days. . . . Some more of your philosophy & half my nervous list would disappear on the shot."[7]

In addition to her burgeoning radio work, from 1957 to 1960 she appeared eleven times on the BBC television program *The Brains Trust*, one of the first "talking heads" programs. Having begun as a BBC radio program in 1942, it switched over to television in the early 1950s. The weekly format changed little over time: viewers were invited to send in questions on virtually any subject, and the following week a panel of three or four guests, led by a "question master," would offer their personal answers to the questions. Generally the panelists were a diverse group, resulting in a lively interchange of views and opinions. On May 26, 1957, Pitter appeared for the first time along with the biologist and writer Julian Huxley, the logical positivist A. J. Ayer, and the poet and later poet laureate John Betjeman. The questions ranged from the value of a technical versus a classical education and the reasons for the quality of English poetry to the architecture of unembellished engineering structures, the essence of words, and the relationship between psychology and religion. As a foil to the three male intellects, Pitter more than held her own.

For instance, after the three men offer their opinion on the issue of education, Pitter adds: "If I hadn't been able to do things with my hands I think I should have been a very unfortunate woman indeed because I can sit and do things with my hands and think which the intellectually preoccupied person is less able to do; he's often preoccupied on a technical question . . . and he's not thinking of what he would choose to think of at all. But a craftsman or a craftswoman can think and for that I'm very thankful." Moreover, when the discussion turns to the issue of original sin, both Huxley and Ayer, while admitting individuals do sin, refuse to accept the idea that individuals are born sinful—that is, with a tendency toward doing evil. Pitter, on the other hand, politely argues "that is theologically quite clear surely, [that] the doctrine of original sin proves the doctrine of actual sin, so that the sin of the species was the sin of the individual." When Ayer challenges Pitter, an interesting exchange follows:

Ayer: For how much that is evil can you sincerely hold yourself personally responsible? I mean we've all of us undoubtedly done bad things, all of us feel conscience stricken for them, but for the really big evils, for wars and the diseases and for the suffering of innocent persons, the sufferings of children and so on, can you honestly really hold that you are responsible for this and if so why? What have you done that these people should suffer?

Pitter: I take refuge in the words of John Donne: "No man is an island." And for the twentieth century we can't contract out of it.

Ayer: But you hold yourself guilty for these things?

Pitter: I hold myself guilty but I should not be prostrate under that guilt because I have hope; while the three Christian virtues are faith, hope, and charity, any proposition which is without all three has a fundamental unsoundness to my way of thinking.

Pitter's affirmation of a central tenet of her faith is admirable, particularly given the public context of the discussion and the formidable intellectual reputation of Ayer. One viewer wrote Pitter afterwards: "Will you please allow me to tell you how much I enjoyed your standing up against [Huxley and Ayer], and your being, in your thinking, so much nearer to reality and common sense in every point that came up for discussion."

In subsequent programs Pitter appeared on panels alongside Marghanita Laski, Sir Ifor Evans, Alexander Kennedy, Sir Eric James, Sir John Maud, A. L. Goodhart, Alan Bullock, the Most Reverend Joost de Blank, D. W. Smathers, Lady Violet Bonham Carter, David Cecil, Sir Miles Thomas, James Fisher, Margery Fisher, Rupert Hart-Davis, Reg Butler, James Laver, John Newsom, Noel Annan, Leslie Weatherhead, Lord Halsbury, and Wolf Mankowitz.[8] While the topics of each show ranged widely, Pitter seemed especially apt at communicating winsomely on matters regarding religion and faith, often, though not always, in contrast to the views of other panelists. For instance, during her appearance on September 15, 1957, a viewer asked: "We read much of vice, adultery, divorce, and often forgiveness is asked for and given? What is forgiveness?" When asked her view, Pitter, who struggled all her life with forgiveness, said: "I think, as a Christian, that forgiveness consists in loving where we cannot like, and in doing good to one's enemies, as we are enjoined and commanded to do. . . . It is a heavy thing . . . the hard thing to do. . . . It seems a strange paradox to love where we cannot like. There is a region of the mind where, I think, love is always to be found, and where forgiveness can always be found." Before ending her reply, Pitter added: "[Forgiveness is] very difficult to describe, but a trick that the soul learns, and a kind of accomplishment which comes with long practice and perhaps long labour, but no one could call it an easy thing, and nobody could call it an uncostly thing. It's both hard and very costly, and it can be done." Pitter's words on forgiveness provoked numerous grateful responses; one viewer wrote: "Your words on forgiveness two Sundays ago when you spoke on *The Brains Trust* affected me deeply . . . because at the moment I am trying, and failing I am afraid, to make a great act of forgiveness towards my husband who has left me with a tiny baby. . . . Prayer does not seem to help. . . . It was not until I heard your words that I began to understand what is required of me." Confessing that her husband's betrayal had destroyed her compassion for him, the viewer thanked Pitter for reminding her "that forgiveness eternally lives in some set apart place in the heart," and for giving her "courage to try to rediscover that place."[9]

Pitter's public presence during these years was not limited to BBC radio and television. Her growing fame also provided her with opportunities to write regularly for two magazines. Mary Grieve, the editor of *Woman: World's Greatest Weekly for Women*, wrote: "I wonder if you would ever think about writing particularly for women? They say seven million women read *Woman* every week" (Aug. 5, 1958). After meeting, they agreed Pitter would write six articles on gardening, and her first essay appeared in October under the running head "The Flower of Peace: A Countrywoman's Diary." Grieve was so pleased with Pitter's work that she commissioned six more, and then another six; eventually the essays appeared weekly from October 25, 1958, through December 5, 1959. Not surprisingly, Pitter's enthusiasm for gardening comes through clearly. For instance, in anticipating planting for the next season, she writes: "I don't know whether you feel like me about this. I want to have all the delightful things we read about in the nurserymen's catalogues."[10] Cold weather is no deterrent to the avid gardener: "There's one thing the keen gardener can always do, however bad the weather may be—get things in order. Tidy the shed, put the tools right, take stock of materials."[11] The first sign of winter's thaw sends a thrill though Pitter: "St. Valentine's Day, and they're here! The snowdrops, I mean. Not in bloom yet, but pushing through the grass and dead leaves, looking rather like fairy size teaspoons in green cellophane envelopes."[12]

As we might expect, the articles tend to be seasonal, as Pitter tracks through the year of a gardener's life. On the eve of spring she writes: "By now the soil should be dry enough to sow a great many seeds, and we begin to have a sense of hurry."[13] At the height of warm weather she notes: "This is the most magical time of the whole year—midsummer, with its 'livelong summer days,' when there's hardly any night."[14] As the days wane, she reflects: "It really is autumn now. However fine the weather may be, the days are shorter, and the evenings and early mornings chillier."[15] Other articles lament or praise the weather; discuss the pleasures of various fruits and vegetables; muse on difficult soil conditions; propose various garden projects, including building fish ponds and greenhouses; and celebrate the many birds that visit gardens.

However, underlying all of Pitter's gardening thoughts is the sense of divine blessing and Edenic bliss:

A little Scotswoman with a heartbreakingly pretty voice once said to me, while we were talking about flowers, "Don't you miss the Garden of Eden?" Yes, that's just what I do miss. I miss it desperately. Think of it! To live in a paradise; in a perfect garden, in a perfect climate, where there is no sorrow, no sin, no suffering, no death. To live on glorious fruits and to see nothing but heavenly flowers and beautiful creatures, and to have divine Love itself dwelling with you! We all miss it, and we miss it all the time. But we are promised heaven, and that is more wonderful still. So I plant and tend my garden, and struggle on in spite of disappointments and failures; and every time I see some rich plant in bloom, or some beautiful, wholesome fruit ready to pick, I remember the beauty of that lost garden in the old, wonderful story with its deep meanings. And I look forward; forward to the promised place of bliss, with beauties and delights that no one can ever begin to imagine.[16]

Pitter's search for lost Eden urged on her gardening instinct. In spite of nature's fallen status, in the garden she could glimpse the kindness, goodness, and benevolence of God. While human relationships would always be complicated by sin, the promise of the garden and its paradisal vestiges drew Pitter to the beauties of the natural world.

However, eventually the essays came to an end. Grieve had written: "Dear Miss Pitter, I am now in the annual process of reconsidering the make-up of *Woman* and I have a feeling that we are getting rather heavily loaded on the country theme, so with great personal regret I feel I must suspend your column, at least for some time. I have greatly enjoyed having you as a contributor to *Woman* and I know that you have made a steady readership, even though a minority one. I hope through your contributing to the paper, many more people have come to know you, thus bringing more readers to your poetry" (Sept. 30. 1959). Early the next year she added: "There have been many comments here since your articles ceased appearing in *Woman* and I think you would like to know this. I am sending you a couple of the letters we have received" (Jan. 28, 1960).

Just as the articles in *Woman* were ending, Pitter began a second series of magazine articles, this time in *Nursing Mirror and Midwives Journal,* running under the title "In the Service of God." The article "Ears" was introduced as the "first in a series of articles on the use of our senses, by Ruth Pitter, poetess, artist, and broadcaster."[17] As in her articles in *Woman,* Pitter shares her common sense, her religious faith, and her eye for detail in these short reflections on the senses. Regarding the use of the ears, Pitter notes how the saying of Christ, "He that hath ears to hear, let him hear," has its modern equivalent in "You have ears. Wake up and use them." She then encourages nurses to listen carefully for "the smallest murmur from the helpless patient or the young infant" so as to be of immediate service. Later in the essay Pitter complains about the nuisance of loud noises and quotes her mother, who, years before, railed against the harsh, piercing sound of car horns by saying: "I'm not allowed to hit him in the eye. Why is he allowed to hit me in the ear?"

In "Eyes" she notes numerous biblical passages about the importance of seeing God's glory in the natural world and then affirms: "But the eyes God gives us must be turned to all His works; not only to the stars and the flowers, but to our fellow creatures in general; to our neighbours. It is there that the eyes have their most Christlike task—to see where help is needed, and how best to give it. This is not always easy."[18] About "Noses" Pitter cites examples of how good doctors and nurses have used their sense of smell to diagnose and treat patients, and she cites biblical stories where perfume plays a central role, particularly where Mary anoints the feet of Jesus with rich ointment and dries his feet with her hair. Furthermore, she celebrates the delightful scents of nature: "New-mown hay, honeysuckle on a June evening, wood smoke, bread baking, sweet, clean linen—it hasn't any actual smell, only that fine essence of cleanness, better than perfume. The scent of the thirsty earth, when at last the rain falls!"[19] "Hands" explores the wonders of touch, recalling the numerous times Jesus laid his hands on the sick, and then noting similarly how important a nurse's gentle touch is in the healing process: "The touch of the hand is a direct physical contact, often flesh touching flesh. Make it real. Put your heart into your hand, and let the living wealth of love come through. Do not mistake me—the touch need not be a caress, sometimes quite the reverse. One may have to hurt, unavoidably, or to restrain forcibly. But the contact . . . can be a deliberate act of controlled and directed love, a willed and conscious gift."[20]

Her last article breaks the pattern; rather than write about taste, Pitter writes on "Voices." Noting how a harsh, grating voice puts one off, while a kindly, gentle voice gives the hearer solace, Pitter urges nurses to use their voices to encourage their patients. She also points out how many times God speaks in the Bible—from speaking the natural world into being to the "still small voice" that called to the child Samuel to the command of Jesus, "Lazarus, come forth!"—and concludes the article and the series with a homily: "When we are trying to help anyone and, indeed, whenever we speak, we can remember that Voice of healing and forgiveness and love, and try to use our own for the same divine purposes. Then we can be very sure that our human voices will be, in the ears of others, 'the voice of the Beloved,' no matter what kind of voice we start with."[21] Given the religious orientation of the *Nursing Mirror and Midwives Journal*, Pitter's overt expression of her faith in these articles was welcomed by the editors. While she tended to be indirect and oblique about her faith in her verse, when given the opportunity in prose to discuss important issues underlying her faith, she did so without pretence.

Still other opportunities to share her ideas through prose came to Pitter during this period, as she was regularly asked to speak to civic clubs, school groups, poetry societies, and literary gatherings. A partial listing of these talks indicates both her popularity and her diverse interests: "Poetry in Various Moods," "The Reading of Poetry," "Woman, the Good Peasant, the Good Lady, and the Good Queen," "Concerning God," "Money Is Not Everything," "The Bible and the Imagination," "My Favourite Virtue, Frugality," "Quality," "Women Are Magic," "My Life as a Poet," and "Interesting People." In addition, Pitter was writing occasional book reviews. Given all this public activity—radio and television appearances, magazine articles, speaking engagements, and book reviews—Pitter had little energy left for poetry.

Yet Pitter's life was not taken up entirely by public appearances. One new friend who came her way was the poet Norah Cruickshank, who had moved to Long Crendon with her parents in 1956. She and her parents shared Christmas dinner with Pitter and O'Hara, and before long, by 1958, Cruickshank had become a regular guest for tea at the Hawthorns on Thursdays. In addition, although Pitter had to travel more than in the past and while much of her time went to making production arrangements with the BBC, she continued her friendships with the Cecils, Cooley, Russell, and Lewis. Pitter's letters to Cooley during these years are newsy and fill in details about her everyday life and relationships. For instance, in a letter to Cooley, Pitter comments on her "ancient boy-friend," Raymond Barnett: "Well, he is a queer man of 50 odd, whom we have known for many years through his liking my work. He is pretty neurotic and no weight-carrier, but has an unusual gift of moral perspicacity (not always acted on) and is a great amateur of old keyboard music and instruments. Not at all the marrying sort, but nice to have around when in a good temper, and you can be fairly frank with him" (Sept. 2, 1956). About their Christmas turkey, she tells Cooley: "I must say, we do appreciate the contemporary turkey you [Americans] have invented. The rangy brutes of our youth have disappeared, and in their place we find a creature practically all torso, with little stumpy legs—as our butcher gloatingly puts it, 'Lovely little American starl (style) hen turkeys, double-breasted, Fat as Moles!'—in Essex and London it's always 'as fat as butter,' but here in Bucks, 'fat as moles'" (Dec. 29, 1958). She also admits to Cooley she will miss the extra income generated by magazine writing: "I've done pretty well the last 3 years or so, with one thing and another, but the coming year will certainly be leaner, as my little gold-mine, the weekly article for *Woman*, is being stopped" (Dec. 14, 1959).

Sometimes Pitter answers queries from Cooley, as when the latter wanted to know about the poet Kathleen Raine: "She was born, like me, at Ilford, Essex, and her father, like mine, was a teacher; but at the secondary school, while mine was elementary—significant difference then, as now—and she went to college, I didn't. She lived round the corner from us in Chelsea for a good many years, but I only met her once, by chance, and she, I thought, registered dislike. We are at opposite poles, really. I expect, being about 10 years my junior, she heard too much about me as a Local Girl Making Good" (Sept. 16, 1959). Other times she confides in Cooley about weighty matters such as the passing of Sir Winston Churchill:

The news of Churchill's death is scarcely 3 hours old, as I write to you. . . . I wonder where humanity would have stood at this moment but for him? Massive and diverse as our troubles are, they might have been so incomparably worse but for that towering man. We remember so well the open, direct impact of his wartime broadcasts, which made us feel, not a suffering civilian population but people under fire, people on active service. But a flesh-and-blood hero, not an iron war lord. I've never forgotten, at the very worst time, his words of pity for "poor little typists, thinly clad, waiting endlessly at bus stops" in hard winter weather. And so grimly humorous—what a relish there was to that. (Jan. 25, 1965)

After receiving the terrible news of John F. Kennedy's assassination, Pitter writes Cooley: "We were all stunned for a time by the news of President Kennedy's tragic death. Of all the wicked, useless, wanton things—oh, how it does show the badness, the plain unreasoning, unfeeling evil there is in mankind. We are anxiously watching President Johnson, and wondering about the next election"

(Dec. 29, 1963). About the death of T. S. Eliot, Pitter remarks: "I noted that several commentators seemed to assume that only his early work would live. My word, when I think of the way people used to study & discuss. . . . [his poetry] & mull over the footnotes, which it now seems he only did to make a bit more copy for a very slim book! But—he had the gift, all right" (Jan. 9, 1965).

Pitter's letters to Arthur Russell almost invariably offer specific critiques of poems he has sent. On August 15, 1957, she writes: "[Your] little 'Truant's Song' is lovely. I would not have it different; it is like the midges' flight, so delicate, really more poetical than the manly exercises. There is enough rhyme to content the ear, and the rest is like a silk scarf softly waved." Pitter, however, does more than simply praise Russell's work, offering constructive criticism as merited. In a discussion of epithets, Pitter writes: "Your epithets are always highly aware and usually choice and exact. But I do wonder whether you are getting too technical" (Oct. 22, 1960). When Russell urges Pitter to write poetry, she answers: "As for a new volume—if God wills! But not to derive from the simplest alone—it wouldn't be worth while. I haven't enough even for the beginnings of a book, as it is. But if the tide turned I could get enough in a year or a bit more" (Dec. 29, 1961). Several months later she adds: "There has been nothing doing in my literary life, except the inevitable wodges of bad poetry now & then, but . . . I've been trying to write poetry by will-power. I doubt if it's any good: but Arthur! There's one thing about the mere trying: the stuff runs in your head so that at least you are engaged in it, and all the time it runs it's shedding various impurities" (March 19, 1962). Pitter's public appearances and attention to prose were curtailing her efforts at verse; while her manuscript notebooks from these years demonstrate that she was attempting some poetry, most of it was halting and imperfectly realized.

Other letters to Russell have a literary focus; often she would vent some of her frustrations with the direction of poetry publications. About difficulties Russell is encountering in getting his own poetry into print, Pitter reflects: "It's horribly depressing now, the way poetry has to sneak in unheralded. Oh, wasn't it lovely when all the toshing little books got their prompt review, and never a harsh word either. . . . 'Miss Pitter's dainty lays (or even fairy chimes) would make the most delightful Christmas present. . . . such value at $^3/_6$, too.' Now they lump us all together, a dozen in a ¼ column, six months late, if we're lucky. The thankless Muse" (Nov. 16, 1965). She also shares with Russell her reflections on various matters. About the death of Dorothy Wellesley on July 11, 1956, she writes: "Poor old dear, I do hope she went easily; I know she was afraid of it, but this so often changes as the time draws near. It is the close of a chapter indeed. I shall never see that lovely house, or those strange rocks and woods, any more" (July 15, 1956).[22] On the issue of "old maids," she writes: "Oh, well, about us old maids, you must remember that (as Thackeray said) any woman can get married unless she be positively a hunchback. The old maid has either lost someone, or never met the right one, or sacrificed herself for others. Some are of a cool temperament who have never found anyone exciting enough, others have needed rescuing & not been rescued. There are many sorts, with one thing only in common—(except for the poorest poor things, God help them)—mere marriage to just anyone is not good enough, & they prefer to face loneliness, etc. rather than that" (Jan. 27, 1957).

Still other letters offer detailed word pictures of events in her life. About one appearance on *Woman's Hour* she writes Russell: "I'm not surprised that I sounded brighter on 'Woman's Hour.' It *is* the Light Programme, and they do their utmost to keep it bright; rather too much, I think. Then their method, treating the day's programme rather like a big newspaper, getting everyone together for final rehearsal & lunch, & broadcasting everything live as far as possible—this means that everyone knows everyone else and rather a party atmosphere is developed. But also there is the fact that I'm getting more at home with the mike" (Oct. 17, 1956). Reflecting her persistent work ethic, she tells Russell: "My customers are frantic, June orders unfilled; this wet weather drives people into shops, and they see trade lost without quick repeats" (Aug. 15, 1957). After a fall in which she broke her left wrist, she had to pay regular visits to the Radcliffe Infirmary in Oxford, and she draws a vivid picture of the place: "I've been paying a weekly visit to Casualty at the Radcliffe; goodness, it is old-fashioned there still. One has to walk in past the mortuary, and coffins are whisked by quite briskly, owing no doubt to all the traffic accidents. The porter lounges on a bench, just like Hogarth's 'Gin Lane,' with one of the peculiarly acrid, gritty old Oxford whores draped round him in broad daylight; interns row over pinched blankets, etc., people are carried past moaning, and babies pee on the floor" (June 16, 1962).

After Pitter's first appearance on *The Brains Trust,* Russell writes: "We enjoyed your Brains Trust—never watch except when you're on; it's such a silly way of spending a fine Sunday afternoon, anyway! But you always make it worth while. The girls thought you looked rather horsey in your tweed and check shirt and tie; I thought the make-up girls hadn't got your wavelength as well as usual; they gave your face a slight air of a Chinese portrait. Your contribution as always delightful" (May 26, 1957). She responds two days later:

My first impressions of TV . . . are confirmed: at least it doesn't rattle me. How we do attract the very thing we fear—Original Sin cropping up with an atheist at my elbow! But everyone is human, so is he—our own abstractions are the things that terrify us. . . . Oh, thank you for saying I looked all right. The make-up is very skillful, of course—mine was a Light Street—and I had slept in a hair-net the night before, so I felt fairly assured—but you never know what the camera will do. I like B[ernard] Braden [the question master] no end. He has a lovely face close up, with an expression as though he were listening to lovely music. J[ulian] Huxley has got to the burbling stage—he did it at lunch—but I was glad to see him again for old times' sake. [John] Betjeman I know a little & love a lot. Prof. [A. J.] Ayer is reacting against Calvinism, he told me so, without seeming to realize the implications. . . . I say! What a fine effect the big TV studio has, with its cruel lighting & the camera & mike men & machines like a sort of sinister artillery: the deadly quiet & concentration of these tough types, and statuesque attitudes, make them seem like scientifiction satraps just waiting for the word of command to loose the death-ray.

Moreover, Pitter's public stature also led to requests that she record her poetry. Because Russell had now become something of a confidante, Pitter asked Russell to serve as the producer of audio recordings of her poetry that she made for Louis Untermeyer for the Library of Congress on December 20, 1960.

In addition, Russell was invaluable to Pitter when she was in hospital with a severe illness from April through July of 1965.[23] During this difficult time he worked with Cresset Press to see that her corrections to the galley proofs of *Still by Choice* were incorporated before the final proofs went to press. On July 23, 1965, she writes Russell from her hospital bed: "No, send the pp. proofs straight back to the Cresset, & as soon as possible: my mind is in no condition for them after the new op[eration] (for the abscess). Much obliged for service wh. I know I can depend on." Given the severity of Pitter's illness, it is remarkable that Russell persevered so faithfully in getting *Still by Choice* published. While Pitter served as a willing mentor and an excellent sounding board for Russell from 1956 through 1966, in turn he assisted Pitter by getting her regular work on the BBC; perhaps more valuable, he worked tirelessly to promote her poetry.[24] Norah Cruickshank worried that Pitter would never recover from the illness, particularly since a village nurse said she could not see how Pitter would ever get better, and O'Hara was worried both for her friend and for her own future since she was so dependent upon Pitter. Fortunately, after several months of recovery, Pitter regained her strength and even returned to riding her bicycle through the village.

Another new correspondent was Stephen Tennant, who first writes Pitter early in 1964. Tennant greatly admired Pitter's verse; moreover, they shared a mutual love of gardening. In many of her letters to Tennant she replies to his questions about gardening and comments on various plants each is trying out. Pitter also confides to Tennant her feelings of isolation in Long Crendon: "I do hope you have friends and neighbours to commune with. It is very lonely to be a poet with nobody else of that kind about. There is no longer a fashion (as in my youth) for getting together and gushing about aesthetic subjects, I mean among ordinary educated people" (Aug. 10, 1964).[25] When he tells her that he is working on two books, she replies: "How productive you are! Two new books coming! I shall look forward to them. My publisher keeps asking for a new book of poems—it is 12 years since the last—but I was always very slow; now I have almost come to a standstill. It is natural enough as one grows older, and ever more unfashionable" (Feb. 21, 1965).[26] A month later she refers to what would eventually become *Still by Choice:* "I have scraped up a few poems which are to be published—it will be a skinny affair. They keep turning comic. Strange discovery, that the profane is also sacred. I can't think how this will work out in heaven, except that I am sure mirth and glee abide there too—can't imagine felicity without them—but the comic? Someone said heaven is comedy, but comedy as august as the highest tragedy. This would do me very well" (March 28, 1965).[27]Other letters discuss the weather, flowers, and wine making.

Pitter's correspondence with C. S. Lewis during these years is sporadic. However, Lewis is quick to congratulate Pitter on winning the Queen's Gold Medal, adding:

It's also amusing that a few nights before getting your letter I dreamed that I was presented to the Queen, and found to my horror, half way through the audience, that I was wearing my hat. At the same moment a lady in waiting approached me from behind with the speed of a roller-skater and snatched it off my head with the words "Don't be a fool." I left the presence . . . and on my way through a great gallery, finding, without surprise, a photograph of myself on an occasional table, tore it to pieces and went on. I've never had the dream of appearing in public insufficiently dressed: but I suppose too much means pretty well the same as too little. (Jan. 31, 1956)[28]

In late April Pitter writes Russell and tries to give him spiritual counsel, using Lewis as a touchstone:

About *Screwtape,* it's the book C. S. L. is best known by, but not (I think) his best, brilliant as it is.[29] He is so copious & various that one really needs to have read him all. The three romances are (I think) wonderful.[30] "The Allegory of Love" & "XVI Cent. Eng. Lit." excluding drama (works of scholarship) are so much more than mere studies that (for me) they return to the virtue of the Middle Ages when philosophy was the background of all knowledge.[31] Arthur! You must not reject religion because the world is bad! It is bad because creatures with free will have chosen badness! To be sure, if one sticks to the argument that what we see destroys the idea of a loving God, there is not much to be said. C. S. L. deals with this faithfully in "The Problem of Pain."[32] (April 24)

Then in the same letter she mentions a recent luncheon with Lewis: "He was here to lunch last week, having actually suggested it himself! Unheard of! Tremendous honour! We got our Palace chauffeur to take him home afterwards—he gets about in the cheapest & most laborious ways—and my niece Mary and I went too, to get a glimpse of where he lives, and it looked pretty forlorn, I must say."

On another occasion when Lewis believes he and Pitter might be attending a garden party given by the queen, he tries to arrange for them to travel and dine together; he felt her experience as a traveler would give him great moral support: "You are an experienced courtier and it would give me great moral support to arrive in your company" (769; July 9). Pitter had not attended the garden party, and the whole affair was not very enjoyable for Lewis (he complained of tasteless metal flamingoes), only partly redeemed by his having met one person he knew. In a follow-up letter he says he was one of 8,000 guests but never saw the queen, and the crowd was like that at the Liverpool train station on an August bank holiday. However, he is excited to hear Pitter has given lectures on his Ransom space trilogy and invites her and O'Hara for lunch: "I am thrilled to hear that you were lecturing on my trilogy. Is there any day (not next week) on which you wd. both be at all likely to come into Oxford? If so it would be a great delight if you would both come and lunch with me somewhere in Oxford" (771; July 14).[33]

From this point forward, Lewis's correspondence to Pitter drops off markedly, no doubt in part because Lewis had secretly married Joy Gresham on April 23, although public notice of the marriage did not come until December 24 with an announcement in the *Times;* moreover, since she appeared to be dying of bone cancer, all of Lewis's spare attention was consumed in caring for his wife.[34] On January 28, 1957, Lewis writes Pitter about his wife's bone cancer and reports that it had been incorrectly diagnosed as arthritis in the hip. While things look grim, Lewis writes, the cancer has gone into remission for the time being and they live under the sword of Damocles. His wife is confined to lying flat, but she can still read and Lewis invites Pitter to write her a letter: "I am sure [Joy] wd. love a letter from you though, for the mechanical reason, she will not be able to scrawl more than 10 words in answer. Thanks very greatly for your letter and kind offer of a tray, which we'd both love—later, when, and if, we get her out of the [Mayfair] Wingfield [Hospital]. . . . Hope is the *real* torture. I try to hope as little as possible. Have us in your prayers—but I know you do."[35]

On April 15 Lewis writes and thanks Pitter for her offer of financial support: "How can I thank you? Not, anyway, by accepting your offered kindness. There's still a good deal in the kitty. But thank you again and again. Joy is home, doomed, and totally bed ridden. We have two nurses and much of my day is spent on the duties of a hospital orderly. But she is, thank God, without pain and wonderfully cheerful: at times even happy. I know we have your prayers" (847). Gresham does eventually recover for a time, and she and Lewis would enjoy three years of happiness together before the cancer returned and took her life on July 13, 1960. Accordingly, five years pass before Pitter and Lewis meet again. Pitter writes of having "had such a surprise a week or two back. I was putting soot and salt on the onion-bed, and was even dirtier than usual, when I heard voices, and it was Owen Barfield and C. S. Lewis—O. B. was staying with him and had motored him over. I was very glad, as it must be 3 or 4 years since I had seen either. C. S. L. is a good deal changed, and no wonder, but seemed very cheerful, and determined to face life still. He asked us to go over and see him, as he will be in Oxford most of the vac., and this I hope we shall do" (July 31, 1962).[36] Two weeks later Lewis invites Pitter for a visit: "This day week (Aug. 15) wd. do me fine. I am ashamed not to be able to ask you to a meal, but our domestic arrangements hardly make that possible at present. What I shd. like, if it suits you, would be that you should come about 11 in the morning—I can manage elevenses—and leave in time to be home for your own lunch" (1363; Aug. 8, 1962). Pitter did visit Lewis on the fifteenth and his last letter to Pitter recalls the day. It compliments her on "Hunting the Unicorn" and is filled with discussion of poetry and Coventry Patmore, the effect of drug-induced dreams, and domestic musings, ending with his acknowledgment of her visit: "Remember me most kindly to Miss O'Hara. Your visit was a great pleasure" (1365; Aug. 20, 1962).[37] Pitter never saw or communicated with Lewis after this, as he died the same day John F. Kennedy was assassinated, November 22, 1963.

It is tempting to speculate about whether Pitter ever fell in love with Lewis. On one hand, her love poetry never addressed a particular person. At the same time, according to Mark Pitter, his aunt almost certainly had romantic feelings for Lewis. Pitter herself is never so explicit. Yet several letters to other correspondents offer tantalizing hints about her feelings for Lewis. In a letter to her sister-in-law, Mary Pitter, on November 10, 1963, just days before Lewis's death, she laments: "Poor Jack! I am afraid he hasn't much left: it seems he is a semi-invalid. D[avid] Cecil says he could do with visitors, as he will now be fixed in Oxford, and I mean to go, if I can make sure of not being a nuisance." Unfortunately, that visit never occurred. On January 12, 1964, Pitter writes Mary after Lewis's death: "I have had C.S. Lewis's last book—'Letters to Malcolm' to review for the 'Sunday Telegraph' (can't think why they asked me) and have found it very solid—can't write about it without reading every word & thinking a lot. It has kept him in my mind so; I feel his death like a weight at the heart, but it will pass" (Jan. 18, 1964).[38] In the review itself, Pitter admits publicly both her gratitude for and trust in Lewis's lucid writing on matters spiritual and her sorrow over his passing: "With many authors, one sometimes feels an obscure comfort in the idea that they might be wrong; but with Lewis, the idea that he might be wrong can be intimidating, for on many of us the magic of his style operates at times an hypnotic spell. The knowledge that this book must be among the last we shall get of him is desolating."[39]

Much later, on January 13, 1969, in a very revealing letter, Pitter answers several questions about Lewis posed to her by Walter Hooper:

An interesting subject, Jack's views on women. His perceptions were very numinous here as elsewhere. I have thought that losing his mother (cruel loss at age 8, and horribly emphasized by circumstances) must have seemed a black betrayal. If he was mistrustful of women, it was not hatred, but a burnt child's dread of fire. There was something else later on, I believe, in early manhood—some further ghastly let-down. There is such a thing as being ill-fated in one respect or another. It is a pity that he made his first (and perhaps biggest) impact with Screwtape, in which some women are only too well portrayed in their horrors, rather like Milton's Satan—it is this perhaps that has made people think he hated us? But even here, the insight is prodigious: and in the strength of the 3 romances, and the children's books, I would say he was a great and very perspicacious lover of women, from poor little things right up to the "Lady" in Perelandra. I think he touched innumerable women to the heart here—I know he did me—one could sort of "home on" his love & understanding like an aircraft on a beam. As for Screwtape, I have wondered whether his experience with the "mother" he adopted [Mrs. Janie Moore] did not find a steam-vent here. The pressure once let off, and the success of the book being so great, the steam could be put to work less violently. Surely the shoals of letters he got from women (as he told me) must show how great was his appeal to them: nobody's going to tell me these were hate-letters.

On July 25, 1974, Pitter also writes Hooper, this time thanking him for a copy of his biography of Lewis:

Of course I find it enormously interesting. For one thing it portrays a man far more complex and untypical than I had realized—for after all I did not see very much of him, and of course nothing of his academic life and private concerns. His bluff and friendly exterior seemed to betoken a simplicity which was not there: or rather a genuine simplicity—the lucid directness of his writing speaks for it—which existed in its own right over depths in which there abode such conceptions as the awful Earth-beetles (which by the way I think he said he found in Keats!) and the noble Hnakra-hunt, awful too. It will be a long time, as I think I said before, ere humanity gets a full summing-up of the man. . . . [Your] book will be a treasure to me, to put beside my collection of Jack's work; nearly complete, I think. How fortunate I have been to know such a sequence of great men, Lewis and Orwell especially.[40]

What conclusions can we draw regarding Pitter's feelings for Lewis? Certainly she was a great friend to Lewis, and he genuinely admired her poetry. At a minimum she was thankful to Lewis for the broadcast talks that had helped her avoid the "slough of despond" she felt herself slipping into during World War II.[41] Furthermore, she thoroughly enjoyed their discussions about poetry, and she was flattered that he held her poetry in such high regard.[42] To this we must add that she honored the strength of his mind and the fertile wealth of his imagination. Even after his death she paid him a compliment by alluding to his *Perelandra* in her poem "Angels" from *Still by Choice*. It should also be noted that her warm friendship with Lewis argues against the charge often made against him that he was a misogynist; someone who despised women would hardly have spent the amount of time and energy he did in writing to and visiting with Pitter. As with Gresham, Lewis appreciated the lithe, quick, bright mind he found in Pitter and enjoyed their discussions, arguments, and musings.

That said, we should not try to make more of their personal relationship than the evidence merits. We can say with certainty that they did meet frequently, but generally in the company of others, and usually in the context of discussing religion, books, writers, literature, and, in particular, poetry. If we accept George Sayer's word, at one point Lewis may have entertained thoughts of marrying Pitter, *if* he had been the marrying kind. If we accept Mark Pitter's judgment, his aunt probably was in love with Lewis, at least at some point in their relationship. According to various of her friends, whenever someone commented that Lewis once said if he were to marry, it would be to Ruth Pitter, she only responded with a smile or a noncommittal remark.[43] In addition, Pitter's letters to her friends suggest a warmth for Lewis that was more than disinterested affection yet less than heartfelt romance. Perhaps wistful longing is the best way to describe Pitter's feelings for Lewis. Beyond such speculations, however, we are on shifting sand. All we can say with certainty is that they were linked by their shared love of poetry and religious faith—links untouched by time or death.

In the end only Lewis knew what drew him to Gresham rather than Pitter. He certainly was not naive. If Gresham "swept him off his feet," he was a willing participant. While he may have enjoyed Pitter's company, poetry, and cooking, her own reticence to push herself forward militated against Lewis being the pursuer. He was incapable, either by inclination or constitution, of pursuing a woman; it would have to come from her side. He had to be made to fall in love; otherwise, he would remain a bachelor. Of the two women, only Gresham knew how to do this. Pitter, on the other hand, wanted to be pursued. Fire and ice, Joy Gresham and Ruth Pitter. Lewis chose heat and light.

Still by Choice

While her many public appearances, forays into prose, and increasing correspondence left little time for verse, Pitter did manage to squeeze out a poem from time to time. Prompted and encouraged by Russell, Pitter eventually published *Still by Choice*.[44] In order to show thanks to Russell for his many years of friendship, she dedicated the volume to him. The title suggests several things. First, Pitter intimates that her "stillness" or apparent poetic inactivity (it had been thirteen years since *The Ermine* appeared) was more a matter of choice than circumstance. Given that her letters reveal she was having a difficult time writing verse during her years of public prominence, such a pose may have been disingenuous. Nonetheless, such a reading of the title suggests the poems are a result of long, thoughtful incubation. Second, Pitter may be suggesting that she is "still" a poet, albeit one who has become very selective in the presentation of her poetry; that is, the title suggests that while the demands of her public appearance have taken a toll, she remains essentially a poet, not a broadcaster, television personality, dramatist, or essayist.[45]

Whichever way we read the title, what is certain is that this volume, while containing many memorable poems, lacks the thematic organization of her volumes from *A Mad Lady's Garland* through *The Ermine*. For instance, there are no groupings of poems around the natural environment, love, or even God. While some of the poems touch on these and other ideas, they are considered in relative isolation, suggesting perhaps something about the way in which many of the poems in *Still by Choice* were conceived—that is, individually, as the result of intense intermittent musings.[46] While it may seem too convenient to link this kind of poetic creativity with old age, it has to be admitted that Pitter no longer brought a concentrated muse to the writing of verse. She knew that her best days as a poet were behind her, yet the old urge to write still surfaced from time to time and she still "ached to be with verse" as these occasions occurred. Accordingly, the poems in *Still by Choice* tend to stand alone—reflections, recollections, or statements about the human condition.

"The New House" is much more than a panegyric about the Hawthorns. In fact, it is not sentimental at all. Instead, Pitter's warm affection for her home in Long Crendon is placed in the context of human mutability. The "strong new house" only appears to be a citadel against the ravages of time, for it "is nothing but desire and fear forming and dissolving, / With the wind streaming, with the world revolving."[47] Recalling how strong houses eventually vanish "and leave but the bare heather," she then observes that "we and the house are vanishing altogether." Yet as house and humans vanish, something does endure: "Save for the love that life always remembers, / Telling the tale over the winter embers; /

Save for the love moving this hand over the paper, / Hand that must soon vanish to earth and vapour." While human life is transient and passing, the love
that gives Pitter the capacity to write this poem endures and is realized every
time a future generation reads her poem. All life may fade, even its strongest
houses, but human love is a fortress against time.[48]

"In the Open" is a bald admission that one must flee self-protection and embrace exposure: "Move into the clear. / Keep still, take your stand / Out in the
place of fear / On the bare sand" (2). Such an act, while momentous, will reveal
what a "small thing" it is that we are protecting, and only through such an un-
veiling can that small thing "be killed." While Pitter never directly says who or
what does the "killing," she implies that it is God: "Look up and try to say, / Here
I am, for you called. / You must haunt the thin cover / By that awful place, / Till
you can get it over / And look up into that face." This affirmation of the necessity
of bringing before the inexorable sight of God whatever "small thing" it is that
needs to be killed has affinities with Christ's admonition: "And if thy right eye
offend thee, pluck it out, and cast it from thee. . . . And if thy right hand offend
thee, cut it off, and cast it from thee: for it is profitable for thee that one of thy
members should perish, and not that thy whole body should be cast into hell"
(Matt. 5:29–30). While Pitter's poem and the biblical admonition are harsh, from
Pitter's perspective, particularly since this poem is essentially addressed to herself,
she is saying that she is no longer willing to coddle whatever "small thing" it is
that needs God's cleansing and healing look. Not that self-revelation is easy or
comfortable—quite the contrary. It is terribly frightening. At the same time, however, self-revelation before one's Maker is absolutely necessary. Otherwise, Pitter
intimates, we remain prisoners in our tiny, safe, selfish little worlds.

Pitter, who often worked on her paintings late into the night, offers a fascinating poem in "Moths and Mercury-Vapour Lamp." As she looks up from her
work, she observes a scene that many have witnessed, yet only a poet's eye for
detail can bring it to life:

> Some beat the glass as if in agony,
> The pattern never still enough to see;
> In the unearthly strong cold radiance
> Eyes glitter, wings are flourished, weapons glance,
> Furs, metals, dyes; duellers with flashing foils
> Glitter like fire and struggle in the toils
> Of potent light, as deep-sea fish are drawn
> From profound dark to anguish and the dawn. (7–8)

While some of the moths flail unceasingly against the glass, what draws Pitter's
attention are those that cling to the window, the elaborate patterns on their

wings and bodies like messages from "sidereal regions": "What? Why? Who sends? and what is said to me / In urgent characters that I can see / And wonder at, yet never read the tongue?" Every night these silent messengers come and press themselves against Pitter's window, so she wonders if she is to read eternal truths in the emblematic patterns of the moths: "With eyes of night or diamond turned my way, / Upright, as crucified upon the glass, / That strong invisible they cannot pass, / For ever watching at the terrible gate, / Until the writing shall be read, they wait." Are the moths, in their frantic attempts at living, symbols of human beings who struggle to find meaning and to understand their place in the universe? Do humans, like the moths, crucify themselves against "that strong invisible" they cannot pass—the issue being whether or not human existence is meaningful? And what is it that humans are waiting for as they watch "at the terrible gate, / Until the writing shall be read"? Pitter leaves it for us to ponder such questions, but this poem offers tantalizing intimations via the emblematic patterns on the bodies of the moths.

Another introspective poem is "The Heart's Desire Is Full of Sleep," a work that considers two kinds of people: those contented by earthly experience and those longing for more than the merely temporal. The first sort believe their heart's desire has been met by earthly contentment, unaware they have "gained a good they cannot keep." Accordingly, they "must go down the hill, / Not questioning the seas and skies, / Not questioning the years; / For life itself has closed their eyes, / And life has stopped their ears" (10). Ironically, what they think to be their heart's desire blinds and deafens them to any longing for more. The second sort, among which Pitter numbers herself, are "true emperors of desire, / True heirs to all regret, / Strangers and pilgrims." These "enquire for what they never get." As strangers and pilgrims, they recall the biblical passage quoted earlier, Hebrews 11:13–16, and its focus on others unsatisfied by earthly experiences, who long to find their heart's desire in another place. Like the biblical strangers and pilgrims, Pitter's are certain that "what they know is not on earth," so "they seek until they find." And while "they cannot see love's face / They tread his former track; / They know him by his empty place, / They know him by their lack."

The realization that no thing in the wealth of earthly experience can sate the deepest longing of those who have once realized divine love recalls a memorable passage by C. S. Lewis: "If we consider the unblushing promises of reward and the staggering nature of the rewards promised in the Gospels, it would seem Our Lord finds our desires, not too strong, but too weak. We are half-hearted creatures, fooling about with drink and sex and ambition when infinite joy is offered us, like an ignorant child who wants to go on making mud pies in a slum because he cannot imagine what is meant by the offer of a holiday at the sea. We are far too easily pleased."[49] It is with such strangers and pilgrims that Pitter takes her place: "I seek the company of such, / I wear that worn attire; / For I am one who has had much, / But not the heart's desire." Pitter will have her true heart's desire only—and that is beyond the earthly. While it may be arguing too much to say that Pitter is offering support for the idea that one proof of God's existence is the argument from desire—our desire that nothing earthly can satisfy points to a transcendent Creator who can fulfill that desire—it is nonetheless clear that Pitter believes her personal longing to realize her heart's desire can never be realized on earth. It can be realized only by something other and outer.

"Exercise in the Pathetic Fallacy" was intended by Pitter as a simple descriptive exercise, as she indicates in the footnote appended to the poem: "The subject is an open can of white plastic paint, on the surface of which several spots of similar paint in various colours have been accidentally dropped. Under the influence of local forces (electrical induction and discharge, surface tension, convection currents?) these spots first expand, become more complex and mutually involved. Then they contract, 'de-differentiate,' and disappear" (14).[50] Written in terza rima, the poem is a careful description of how four drops of gold, yellow, red, and blue paint gradually subsume into the larger can of white paint. At times the drops reflect human propensities, including pensiveness, jealousy, rejection, cruelty, and desperation, particularly as they strive to remain individual spots. Soon, however, the futility of such effort becomes apparent: the gold spot "does not see that it has started shrinking; / So have the bloodseed and dark sapphire sun. / Something has changed, the space about them drinking / Their life, not giving it. All slide, all run / Together like mad enemies or lovers" (13–14). As the drops are finally absorbed into the white, Pitter wonders: "Look, now it writes a cipher—meaning sleep? / Breaks to a wisp, rolls to a seed of umber, / And sinks in the unblemished virgin deep. / Choose for yourself if this is death or slumber." The reader is invited to ponder the greater meaning of this rather mundane event. Among many possible implications of this is the literal sense in which the four small drops of color invariably tint the white paint, even if imperceptibly. Is this similar to the way in which fragments of truth affect the soul? Is this similar to the way individual lives affect the mass of humankind? Is this similar to the way human lives have an impact on the universe?

Like "The Bush-Baby" in *The Spirit Watches*, "Sweet Other Flesh" illustrates Pitter's longing for deep kinship with other organisms: "Sweet other flesh; mind claims it all, / Steps in unasked, but undenied; / Feels big on mountains; stooping small, / Walks in the lily's lofty hall, / Sharing an architectural pride" (18). As she considers other animals, she yearns to explore them in greater detail: "What seeking? See it search and pry, / Turn leaves, tap shoulders, reach and bend; / Start at a voice, stare in an eye, / Hold the soul still to read it by, / And realise there is no end." Indeed, there is "no end in flesh, sweet other breed, / That lets mind search, mind dwell upon / Chaste palaces within a seed." The potential meaning of every living thing fascinates Pitter, and this leads her to sense her connectedness to the natural world: "So faithfully before the mind / Flesh holds the truth, mortality; / Its suffrage being the law of kind, / It melts to leave me unconfined, / Declines, dissolves, dismisses me." Although death is the common fate of all, Pitter intimates it is also the vehicle that will join her to the natural world in a way she cannot understand while she is alive.

"Morning Glory" celebrates the simple, pristine beauty of one of springtime's showiest flowers: "With a pure colour there is little one can do: / Of a pure thing there is little one can say. / We are dumb in the face of that cold blush of blue, / Called glory, and enigmatic as the face of day" (23). As she gazes into the brilliant blue, she notes various optical illusions, seeing on one hand "delectable mountains," and on the other hand "a firmament, a ring of sky, . . . a universe." Playing on the flower's name, she reads in it a transcendent glory: "But it calls to mind spirit, it seems like one / Who hovers in brightness suspended and shimmering, / Crying Holy and hanging in the eye of the sun." In fact, the flower is a promise, "a prescient tingling, a prophecy of sound," assuring humankind of God's blessed hand upon the earth. "Morning Glory" considers the ineffable beauty of this favorite flower of Pitter and by extension is a gloss to God's mysterious, wonderful, blessed glory—a glory that is just beyond the ability of words to communicate.

"A Dream" has a surreal opening: "This is a strange, twilit country, but full of peace. / Faintly I hear sorrow; she sighs, moving away. / She goes, and guilt goes with her; all is forgiven" (26). All is calm in this place "more like the elysian fields than the fields of heaven." In the second stanza Pitter abruptly tells us that no one inhabits this place "but I and this silent child." Because the child needs to sleep, Pitter carries "her through the dim / Levels of this long river's deliberate mazes." No one else appears, and even other creatures are absent. In the final stanza we can see multiple levels of meaning:

She spoke so strangely that once, but she speaks no more.
Leans her head down in my neck, and is light to bear.
I think she walked here over the twilit stream.
I must find the tree, the elm by the river-shore,
Loosen her little arms and leave her there,
Under the boughs of sleep and the leaves of dream.

One reading of this last stanza is that it is a dim recollection of Pitter's childhood days in Hainault Forest; the poem expresses Pitter's long-held affection for the cottage and its environs. A second reading of this last stanza is that it is a suppressed expression of Pitter's longing to have given birth to a child; her protective care of the child as she carries her through the twilit world and the tenderness with which she allows the child to lean her head on her neck supports such a reading. In this case, the poem suggests Pitter's hidden, veiled mother self. A third and more controversial reading of this last stanza is that it is about an aborted child; if so, the last lines, where the speaker loosens the child's little arms that cling to her and leaves the child under the elm tree, "under the boughs of sleep and the leaves of dream," are poignant, revealing a grief beyond the measure of words to express. Although I have seen no evidence to suggest Pitter herself ever experienced such a traumatic event, the poem expresses her ability to communicate the crushing sorrow a mother has over her lost child.

Two poems contrast female perspectives on the larger world. "Charity and Its Object" verges on the comic: "Of one thing Mrs. Crow was sure; / She knew for certain she was poor. / It therefore followed with perfect clarity / That she was eligible for charity" (6). We can almost imagine Mrs. Crow going about her errands with a wry smile: "She did not beg; she did not whine; / She only took a reasoned line; / She followed what she had been taught. / She knew that richer people ought / To help God's good deserving cases, / And so she told them to their faces." Mrs. Crow has learned to be content in her needy circumstance, confident of God's provision. In fact, she believes her want brings spiritual blessings to her neighbors: "Firm in religion, there she stood, / And helped her neighbours to be good." At the other end of the spectrum is the woman of "Yorkshire Wife's Saga." If Mrs. Crow takes the perspective that "if God so clothe the grass of the field, which to day is, and to morrow is cast into the oven, shall he not much more clothe you" (Matt. 6:30), the Yorkshire wife takes the opposite: "War was her life, with want and the wild air; / Not for life only; she was out to win" (32). Along with her husband and seven sons, she works hard and scratches out a living. While her husband and sons labor in the mines, she does the rest: "Fierce winter mornings, up at three or four; / Men bawl, pigs shriek against the raving beck. / Off go the eight across the mile of moor, / With well-filled dinner-pail and sweat-ragged neck." In the end, though she is physically worn out, her tenacity is rewarded: "Of course they made it; what on earth could stop / People like that?" Her sons leave and marry, and their mother "could look about and feel she'd won." She spends her last days visiting her sons at their homes: "She liked going by bus / Or train, to stay a bit in those snug homes. / They were her colonies, fair glorious." Pitter's poem is a testimony to endurance, and in the Yorkshire wife Pitter may be celebrating her own commitment to hard work and success.

"Leafcutter Bees" lacks the seriousness of "Burning the Bee-Tree" in *The Spirit Watches*. Instead it is a light-hearted account of how a swarm of bees takes over an abandoned wren's nest and then wreaks havoc. After the swarm is initially discovered, consideration is given to destroying it, but someone says: "Oh the little darlings. . . . Leave them alone, they're only leaf-cutters, / They won't harm your potherbs or your posies, / Only cut round holes in the leaves of the roses" (33). The swarm is spared, but then something worse than cutting holes in rose leaves occurs—at least worse as far as Pitter is concerned: "Huh! They by-passed the roses as if they'd been nettles. / They wrapped up their eggs in geranium petals. / They took a dead set at a thing that really matters, / They cut the flame geraniums into shreds and tatters." Although she is clearly angry and "could have gone at night / And done them all in and served them all right," Pitter desists, in part because of the sentiment previously expressed in "Sweet Other Flesh"—there is a kinship between her and other living organisms that should not be trumped by anger over a few shredded flowers. Anger turns to forgiveness: "But we could not penalise them for their childish folly, / Any more than little girls who want to dress their dolly, / Who take their little scissors and with uncertain / Snips cut a great piece from your red silk curtain."

The urge to grow, to burst forth, to drive forward, to breed, and to thrive informs "Strongest in Spring": "Strongest in spring, the dream that drives, / To beasts afield, to little lives, / Blest bird aloft, blind man below, / Passes the word to groan and grow" (34). As nature awakens in spring, so awakens the spirit of man—to love, to venture outdoors, to leave off everyday work, to embrace life anew. While children scamper and scream and schoolgirls giggle, others set themselves to more serious tasks. Fathers "furiously dig . . . to salvage in a day / Time a whole winter stole away," while a "poor mother stands and hates the place, / Foreboding more than anything / A tiger's spring, a tiger's spring." The ambiguous ending suggests several things. First, the mother may fear that the fierce urges produced by springtime will lead her children and her husband to do unwise, destructive things. Second, she may fear how springtime affects her, awakening her to her dull reality and urging her to abandon it for something more. Third, the pun suggests that the dreams of springtime are about to pounce like a tiger, catching unaware all who have them and leading them to leave off productive if mundane lives in hopes of finding better, more meaningful, yet more uncertain lives.

"Angels" speculates about the real character of an angel: "And if you entertain one there, / What angel haunts your mind; / Terrible, tender, or severe?" (24–25).[51] She wonders if angels are like blinding lightning; tender watchmen; instruments of divine vengeance; youthful, gentle messengers; or stern heavenly warriors. In a tip of the hat to Lewis's Ransom trilogy, she wonders if angels are more like his *eldila:* "Or likelier, now we dream of space, / Lewis's dread sublime / Pillars of light, no limbs, no face, / Sickening our space and time?"[52] Pitter then admits that her own image of an angel is Victorian: "From some forgotten painting, I / Retain most clearly mine: / He seems a lively half-grown boy, / All tricked and flounced and fine." In her mind's eye she sees the angelic boy kneeling and speaking to something beyond her ken: "I cannot see the thing he sees, / The end of all desire; / Only a creature on its knees, / Mantled with love like

fire." The disconnect between Pitter, the angelic boy, and the object of his gaze
is heightened when we read:

> I see his rapture, see the storm
> Of bliss, the level calm,
> The huge surprise that fills his form,
> The passion of his psalm.
>
> As the clear crystal prism refracts,
> He flings across my days
> Drops from his fiery cataracts
> Of sempiternal praise.
>
> Cold, cold and dark behind the wall,
> The wall that I have made,
> I stand at my own funeral
> And weep and freeze and fade.

However, the vision of the angelic boy pulls Pitter out of her self-imposed exile,
especially as she realizes the magnificence of the object of his gaze: "But see the
living thing rejoice, / By freest love constrained: / Great-winged by nature, still
by choice, / Supremely entertained." The angelic boy, who has made a conscious decision to "be still" in the presence of Love Eternal, is delighting in his
state, entertained by the Creator of all. Clearly the implication is that angels
can draw us to a greater awareness of God's love.

Still by Choice received overwhelmingly favorable reviews. Richard Kell
praised Pitter for writing "firmly structured poems that attempt to communicate
sometimes difficult things with precision and clarity, . . . [searching] beyond appearances with the eye and mind of a visionary."[53] He also admired her "trans-
mitting of a strong personal vision in an artistic way." Maurice Wiggin was even
more complimentary: "Wordsworth would have been green with envy at some
of her unpretentious and almost perfect poems."[54] Wiggin also offered an in-
sightful comprehensive evaluation of Pitter's poetry: "The autumn of Ruth Pitter is more glorious than the spring. She is serene but not mawkish, shrewd but
not bitter; she sees through the blarney and writes like the angel she deserves
to be, celebrating the downs as well as the ups." Another reviewer added: "The
strength here lies in that finished, luminous precision of observation which give
extra weight to both themes and treatment."[55]

That Pitter was approaching seventy when Still by Choice was published is remarkable; that the poems are as good as they are is even more remarkable. That
is, while Pitter was slowing down her production of poems, the ones she writes

are as effective as ever. She continues to rely on established meter (iambic trim-
eter, tetrameter, and pentameter) and rhyme schemes (rhyming couplets or alternate line rhyme), but this is no fault, given the precision and expertise of her
lines. She is not stifled by tried and tested poetic forms; instead, they liberate
her to peer deeply into the human condition and write poems of penetrating
mystical exploration. And while her religious faith undergirds her vision of the
world, she explores issues of faith obliquely and indirectly. She was not about
to turn preacher; clubbing her readers with a spiritual cudgel would have been
anathema. Perhaps the greatest irony regarding *Still by Choice* is that it was
many readers' first encounter with Pitter's verse; that is, her poetry was made
popular because of her public prominence as broadcaster, television personality,
magazine writer, and lecturer, not primarily because she was a well-known poet.
Be that as it may, Pitter's creative fire, while waning, was still burning, and it
remains for us to explore the final flickering of her poetry in the next chapter.

TEN

Flickering Fires,

1967–1992

When *Still by Choice* was published, Pitter could never have imagined she had more than a quarter of her life yet to live. While her final years marked the end of her career as an artisan, she enjoyed continuing fame as a poet. Moreover, she was still sought out for BBC radio broadcasts. She also continued her correspondence with old friends, began pen friendships with several new admirers, and was active in the affairs of her parish church. Although she wrote poetry sporadically, two volumes of new verse as well as two collected volumes and a festschrift were still before her. Yet time gradually eroded her health and took away the most important people in her life. Indeed, outliving her best friends was disheartening to Pitter, yet she never sank into depression or self-pity, even after she lost her eyesight. Her mind stayed nimble and curious, and she took an interest in the affairs of the world until the very end.

Her letters after the publication of *Still by Choice* reflect her concerns with her garden, especially varieties of new plants she wanted to try growing; her family, particularly her sister-in-law, Mary, and nephew, Mark Pitter; and her health and that of Kathleen O'Hara. She is also thrilled when David Cecil asks if he might dedicate one of his books to her; she writes Cooley: "Oh, I have been so touched & delighted. Lord David Cecil, who did a series of lectures . . . on Samuel Palmer (cheers) and Burne-Jones (boos), has made them into a book . . . and asked if he might dedicate it to me. I really did shed a silent tear" (Jan. 6).[1] At about the same time Mark Pitter, who had always been the family member most keenly interested in Pitter's poetry, began making audio recordings of her reading her poetry.[2] After one of these sessions Pitter writes Stephen Tennant: "I have had a nephew, 16 & charming . . . for a few days. The creature was keen to record my reading. I find that generation knows my work quite well, unlike my own & the next, owing to its being in so many school anthologies. He was pale with attention, a thing I love to see" (Aug. 24).[3] A week later she tells Tennant: "A nephew & I have been recording as much as we could in the last few days—in case posterity should be interested!" (Aug. 31).[4] In the fall she writes Tennant about her new editor: "My publishers have been taken over by a larger firm, and whereas for over 30 years they took no notice at all, beyond doing a very good job on the books themselves, I now find a man who actually likes my work and says so! I hardly know where to look, like a yard-cat which has never been stroked" (Oct. 14).[5]

Pitter also decided in January 1969, in part at the urging of Walter Hooper, to give her correspondence from Lewis to the Bodleian Library. Because Lewis was notorious for not keeping letters written to him, in April 1969 she sent the Bodleian her recollections of what she had written to Lewis in her letters. In fact, many of the important events of Pitter's life through the end of the 1960s were literary. For instance, her first collection of verse since *Urania* appeared with the publication of *Poems 1926–1966* in 1968.[6] One reviewer lauds Pitter's "pure lyrics,"[7] while John Wain offers a more comprehensive review. He links Pitter's life as an artisan to her poetry: "This is the poetry of someone accustomed to working at a craft. Ruth Pitter does not merely string words together, or throw them up in heaps: she shapes them."[8] Then he adds:

Everywhere in her work, one sees the marks of a sensibility formed by the struggle with real materials: with wood, with paint, with soil and water and tendrils and leaves. This kind of work cannot be produced by someone whose life has been lived among abstractions, who knows only those realities that can be theorized into being. When Ruth Pitter goes to her desk to write a poem, she is motivated by love—not only by love of created life, but by love of language, of rhyme, of the matching of texture and weight and pace against what is to be said. She does not make, and does not allow her readers to make, the mistake of imagining that it is possible to love the soul of poetry without also loving its body.

Wain admires Pitter "best when she is putting on singing-robes . . . [in] the high style," but he also enjoys her pieces "streaked with irony: or, if not exactly irony, then with something intellectual and self-mocking, something powerfully at work to assimilate the doubts and hesitations it cannot help encountering, even generating it. It is this side of her work that aligns her with Donne."

Wain's thoughts on Pitter's poetry offer an important corrective to those who might dismiss her since she is not in the modernist line of Eliot, Pound, and Auden. In fact, Wain says that to devalue Pitter is to devalue "the best of Yeats, virtually all of Dylan Thomas, the love poems of Theodore Roethke, [and] the most urgent and compelling of Robert Lowell's poems." In the preface to *Poems 1926–1966*, "There Is a Spirit," Pitter expands upon the qualities of her verse extolled by Wain:

My purpose [as a poet] has never varied. . . . It has been simply to capture and express some of the secret meanings which haunt life and language: the silent music, the dance in stillness, the hints and echoes and messages of which everything is full; the smile on the face of the tiger, or of the Bernini seraph. The silent music is within oneself too, or it would not be detected elsewhere. In the face of mundane joy it says " . . . but all the same"! and in the face of horror " . . . but all the same"! As though the normal targets of consciousness were somehow unreal; life, bursting with its secret, sits hugging itself until we have read the riddle. (xi–xii)

She shares her conviction that a poem "begins and ends in mystery," and it is the poet's task to give it the most effective shape, form, and substance. Her poetry is meant to take us beyond the common realms of human pain and delight: "The summits of poetry are mysteries; they are shiftingly veiled, and those who catch glimpses see different aspects of the transcendental; but they have *seen something,* and they come down with the glory lingering on them" (xii).[9]

The second important literary event of these years also involves John Wain, since he interviewed her for a BBC radio broadcast that aired on October 31, 1968. In the interview Wain queries Pitter on the influences on her verse but then gets her to discuss her own poetics. At one point she says that form is "the whole art and perhaps the whole gift of poetry—to be able to express a thought, and perhaps a very recondite thought, in close form without distorting either the form or the thought. This is the glory of poetry, and it's the pieces that do this which are remembered."[10] Later she adds: "The rhythms inside oneself are more fundamental than the artificial rhythms we try to follow. And I frequently find—I find them more as I get older—that these tend to take over. It's harder to pursue the normal metre and easier to rely on the rhythms that come from one's own internal consciousness. And I think that is a case in point. I never really stopped to think what rhythm or what metre I was writing in at all." She also reveals how important the natural world has been to her verse:

We had a little house [Oak Cottage] in Essex for about twenty years, and it had one great peculiarity. It was only a little house, but it had an enormous vinery tacked onto it which we furbished up and got to grow the grapes very well. And I found this a wonderful occupation because pruning and training vines is a work of great precision. Every bud matters. And I think I could go back again and do it in the dark, simply by feeling the buds. And to have produced beautiful bunches of grapes, and these leaves alone are so beautiful, and the scent of the flowers is so beautiful. And the amount of judgment necessary to discriminate between one growth and another is so civilized, if you like, and I found it most absorbing. And it was one of the things in my life that I was sorriest to leave behind. . . . I find these contacts not only with plants, with animals and even more with human beings, the most powerful experiences of my life.

Pitter was pleased with the broadcast, writing the producer, Hallam Tennyson: "Many thanks for the programme, which (I could not help thinking) was really good, though I say it myself. It was so clever on your part to have found out that John Wain liked my work. He has rare qualities, I think; the best perhaps being his complete independence of thought. . . . This has been quite an event in my life" (Oct. 31, 1968).

The third literary event of these years may have been the most satisfying: the publication of the festschrift *Ruth Pitter: Homage to a Poet*. Originally the idea of Russell, who served as the general editor and wrote a biographical essay, the book contains over two dozen brief essays by Pitter admirers. David Cecil, who writes the introduction, says: "She is the most moving of living English poets, and one of the most original."[11] John Arlott refers to her as "a poet's poet" (43), while Thom Gunn notes she "is the most modest of poets, slipping us her riches as if they were everyday currency" (64). Richard Church believes that her poetry "will endure for a long time. It is non-fashionable, like all permanent things such as bread, and water, and a well-made kitchen table" (49). Kathleen Raine is the most lavish in her praise: "I now see her as one of the poets whose best work will survive as long as the English language, with whose expressiveness in image and idea she has kept faith, remains" (106). Other writers who praise Pitter in this volume are Edmund Blunden, Andrew Young, John Betjeman, Roy Fuller, Mary Grieve, Elizabeth Jennings, Carolyn Kizer, Dame Ngaio Marsh, Robin Skelton, Hallam Tennyson, and John Wain. Although the festschrift was long on praise and short on analysis, it was a welcome and well-deserved recognition. Pitter's only regret was the portrait of her done by Norman Garner. She writes Cecil: "Oh dear, that portrait!! But then, nowadays if we are no longer glamorous, they make us hideous" (Sept. 30, 1969).

Her regular letters to Russell were filled with her commentary on poems he sent for critique. She was managing to write the odd poem here and there, even receiving remuneration on occasion, as she tells Russell: "Well, I did finish another fairly long bit after the lily, pearl, etc. one, and sold them both, with 2 old dug-outs, to an American review in the Deep South which asked to see some poems—got £87!" (July 8, 1970).[12] In addition, she was being regularly invited by Walter Hooper to annual summer meetings of Lewis's friends. She was also still doing BBC radio work; "The Pleasures of Old Age" is typical of her appearances during this period. It begins slightly tongue in cheek: "Well, for a start, the biggest pleasure in being old . . . is *not to be young*. Oh, what a treat to have so many anxieties behind one! All over and done with. Getting a living. Making a

career. Love-troubles, ambitions, the two world wars. . . . It's sad, of course, not
to have descendants; but there again a lot of worry is saved."[13] She also cites as
positive pleasures being able to maintain her peace of mind in the midst of daily
crises, being able to drop off in sleep (even in the presence of other people), and
finding answers to lifelong queries. However, her greatest pleasure in growing old
is that she can now have "real men friends at last." She says:

> There's still the natural attraction between the sexes, as inevitable as the
> force of gravity; but now we can use it instead of it using us. Men have
> a great capacity for friendship with women; only love does muddle it so.
> With an old woman, a man can speak his mind, and she can speak hers.
> She's free to express great affection without the fear of being misunder-
> stood. In a way it's like returning to the frankness and confidences of
> childhood. Now we're on the doorstep of eternity, this is the time to talk
> about the soul, about time and space and all the mystery.

Other broadcasts return to childhood memories of Hainault Forest, while others, for example, "I Know That My Redeemer Liveth," which aired during Holy
Week in April 1971, are spiritual reflections.

Yet she also felt the press of time's "winged chariot." O'Hara's medical condition was tenuous and Pitter herself was taking medications to control angina.
She found comfort in her friendships with David and Rachel Cecil in spite of
the fact that they had moved away from Oxford after his retirement. In one
letter to David she reflects upon another benefit of old age: "As for thinking
more about oneself when getting older, isn't this 'making the soul'? For the
first time one has leisure & liberty to meditate on one's own personality and
its path through life. The weaknesses may not have diminished, but we know
more about them, and (to use a cricketing metaphor) we know better how to
place our men in the outfield to catch them" (Nov. 29, 1970). After Cecil's
Visionary and Dreamer appeared with the dedication to her, Pitter tells Cecil:
"I've just found the dedication, and it has touched my heart afresh. How generous you are, so much more so than authors usually are to their fellows. Really I
have a very great deal to be thankful for. I wish I could express my deep sense
of your kindness & affection. It was so delightful to see you and Rachel again,
both looking so young and well—it made the idea of your being retired quite
ridiculous, and in any case you are still in full cry as an author" (March 14,
1971). Pitter also tries to encourage other friends who are aging but with less
grace than she. For example, she tells Richard Church: "I am sorry you feel so
deflated: you ought not to. What a sense of hope and glory we had—the young
do not have it now. The country was the country in our time, when we could
get there: food and clothing were genuine, what we could afford of them. Our

morals, etc., were lovely and of good report, and our inner lives would be the envy of any who could now perceive them. That we are ignored now is no great wonder: things have been Taken Over, we are Occupied: but the end of our pilgrimage is in sight" (June 4).

References to O'Hara's poor health appear with increasing frequency; several episodes involved lengthy stays in hospital. Pitter writes Cecil on May 2: "I think I told you K. had broken a shoulder—just chips off—and she has recently returned after a month in the Cottage Hospital, and thankful we were to get her into this, only 2 miles away and very kind & good. She still has a good deal of pain, poor thing, and the mishap hasn't done her any good, at 85." Even O'Hara, however, brightened with the arrival of the new parish priest, Stanley Young. Pitter confides to Cooley: "We have had a wonderful stroke of luck here in getting a most exceptional new vicar; piety, learning, and manners all together. A middle-aged but very youthful bachelor. Knew my work and said he lived on it! Tableau! It seems a bit hard that after my sizzling bohemian career, I should finish as an aged village spinster doting on the vicar, but we are all doting on him, even the other denominations" (July 3). This letter also reveals that Young was in part the catalyst for Pitter's writing of religious drama: "He wants to get up some of the mediaeval religious dramas to be done by the real locals, to go on for ever like Oberammergau; has already done it in a previous parish, where it has quite transformed the life of the place." In a later letter to Cooley, Pitter says that the new vicar "has succeeded in starting a production of part of the York Cycle of mystery plays—my great love. I never thought to see any of it produced on my own doorstep. I have already done a version of 'The Harrowing of Hell' that will be readily intelligible to all & sundry, and I gather that I shall be expected to do this eventually for all of the 6 episodes of the Cycle that we are doing" (Nov. 27).

In addition to *The Harrowing of Hell*, Pitter did eventually write five other adaptations of the York Cycle: *The Resurrection, Mary Magdalen at the Sepulchre, Doubting Thomas, The Road to Emmaus*, and *The Ascension*.[14] Once the productions began, Pitter was fully engaged, as she tells Cooley:

In this village we are beginning to be very busy with our forthcoming production of part of the York Cycle of mystery plays. The drill is to get villagers in and keep residents (especially older ladies) out. The plays would have been performed by men only originally, and our Drama Group ladies seem not to be aware that none of the Apostles, for example, were aged females, and that it is better to have young men for angels, rather than frumps. The younger ladies, eager to show their charms, see no reason why Pilate and the Chief Priest should not be discovered in the hall of judgment watching Oriental-type dancers, while their seniors contend that this is something those gentlemen could not afford to be known to do. A portentous professionalism is very general, especially among those with the smallest parts, and advice on interpretation has to be very tactful. The Harrowing of Hell is great fun, and always was; devils have always been much relished, down the ages. I hope there will be a sufficiently frightful noise when the Gates of Hell are bust wide open. I say we should take the great Bible and drop it on one of the slabs in the pavement where some-one is buried; it might give a very grand boom. But it is doubtful if this would be countenanced. A frightful bang I must have. (Jan. 13, 1972)

To Stephen Tennant she confides that the older women are complicating the rehearsals: "There shouldn't be any women, of course, but my goodness, how to keep them out! Especially as angels. You know as well as I do that angels are not frumps, haybags, or old trouts: they are awful, upsetting, sort of electric things—I wonder at the old girls" (Feb. 8). The plays were performed to great acclaim during Holy Week, and she tells Mary Pitter that they "went magnificently. We could have filled the church 3 times over. As a spectacle it was astonishingly good, but from the poetic point of view left a good deal to be desired. . . . The impact was deeply felt. Some people went away without speaking a word. The devils were prime: they had horrible costumes, with snouts, horns, & tails and some of them (in their leisure time) took to popping in & out of Public Bars thus attired, with edifying results" (July 8). In subsequent years the plays were regularly repeated to local acclaim.[15]

With the death of C. Day Lewis on May 22, 1972, Pitter's name was men-tioned in the debate concerning who should succeed him as poet laureate. Al-though flattered, Pitter knew she was not a serious candidate, writing Cooley: "I was tipped in some of the papers for the Laureateship, but this was due to a friend of mine who wrote to the P. M. and suggested me—had a very civil answer, too. I couldn't have accepted it, even had it been offered—no London base, no car, no secretary, no money or clothes, too old, etc. No, [John] Betjeman is the right person, I've always thought so" (Nov. 17). Then she adds whimsically: "But I could not help thinking that if I were Laureate, I would insist on wearing the laurel on ceremonial occasions. With it, a dress of real Genoa velvet the colour of mouldy cheese (beautiful colour) made on mediaeval lines."

Pitter's work on the mystery plays kept her busy, but it also wore her down. In fact many of her letters of this period reflect a growing fatigue and make mention of the continuing decline of O'Hara. She tells Cooley: "We are really getting old now. K. is poorly, and spends most of her time in bed, and just lately both our good faithful helps have been laid up. You can imagine! The only thing I really mind is when I can't get out, as the open air is the one thing for me" (Dec. 21). In the same letter she reports other unhappy news: "It's been rather a sad year here, with disagreeable weather and many more deaths than usual: mostly the old, but some untimely—accidents & illnesses—and several very useful & nice people leaving: we feel there are real gaps in our ranks. My only brother has Parkinson's disease, I fear. It does seem as if things & people go on steadily for quite a long time, and then suddenly everything starts dropping to pieces." The end finally comes for O'Hara on March 18, 1973, and Pitter writes the Cecils that O'Hara had been so full of pain and misery that she was very ready to go. After the funeral she thanks them for attending and for their flowers: "I was glad too that you both had kind old memories of K. in Chelsea, etc., and indeed it is many years since we all met first. I note that David is saddened by life's drawing to a close—near to its close—for us as for everyone in the end. . . . But for me, I am a bit like Oedipus at Colonus, feeling that inasmuch as life is grievous, death is propitious. It was so with K., who had so many years of multifarious ailments, and whose end was so painless and so summary—less than 3 full days from the onset to the end" (March 25).

At first Pitter was so busy arranging for O'Hara's funeral and related events that she did not have time to begin the grieving process. She tells Mary Pitter: "I have only just started to miss K. There has been so much to do. But now I do begin to feel rather low and empty. I should have been sorry not to feel so at all, but I took her death & funeral so much in my stride that I wondered. But really, so quick & easy a death after such years of ill-health, did seem a boon, and I knew she was longing to go" (Apr. 2). Almost a month later she adds: "I am in a muddle. I kept my steering quite steady during K.'s last illness, and for nearly a month after, but now I begin to feel confused and uncertain. Not sorrowful or lonely, but unsystematic, as it were. Well, it would have been rather inhuman not to have any kind of reaction" (Apr. 27).[16] While deeply saddened by the death of her friend and business partner for over fifty years, Pitter did not slip into depression. She saw O'Hara's passing as inevitable, and so she tried to be content with whatever came her way.

She continued doing BBC radio work and kept as active as she could, both mentally and physically. While it was increasingly difficult for her to garden, she managed a bit here and there, especially with the help of hired workers. Pitter was frequently visited by neighbors such as Norah Cruickshank and other village friends who cared about her well-being.[17] She was appreciative, although sometimes she was more tired and put out by such visits than helped. Perhaps more than anything she wanted to maintain her independence as long as pos- sible; even old age and its infirmities she wanted to overcome. In one letter to Cooley she recounts episodes that illustrate her pluck and independence:

Lately I've been having trouble with the water-heating; it was circulating the wrong way, and none of the local geniuses could think why. Recalling the fact that water, like air, rises when heated, I finally drew the fire, let the whole thing get stone cold, then stoked up strongly, and it is going right again. Similarly, a worn-out heating stove was almost useless (the new one has been ordered for nine months, and sitting on the porch for six weeks, for want of someone to put it in). So I got some fire-cement, and stuck back all the bits of iron that had fallen off, and I've just lit it up—a very comfortable little fire on this wet cold and windy day. I then twirled an imaginary moustache, thinking myself very wonderful. (Nov. ? 1973)

Pitter's sense of worth was further heightened when her publishers, Barrie and Jenkins, asked for another volume of poetry. With some excitement she writes Cooley: "I didn't expect this. So I am doing the old poet's trick of sweeping up all the bits and seeing what I can do with them" (Dec. 21). Similarly she tells Stephen Tennant: "I have been exercising my own cunning in trying to finish all the old pieces I can find in my rough books, in order to scrape up one small volume more. . . . It does seem to me, rather to my satisfaction, that as inspiration fades, cunning increases, so that many a reject can now be turned to account. But mind you, I am not saying these have the freshness of the more spontaneous!" (Jan. 11, 1974).[18] Furthermore, she is encouraged when she receives an official letter informing her she has won yet another national recognition for her poetry. She replies: "I am gratified by the unanimous vote of the Council of the Royal Society of Literature in offering me the honour of Companion of Literature, and I have much pleasure in accepting" (Feb. 18).[19] In her typical self-effacing manner, she downplays the award, writing to Russell: "The Royal Literary Society says it has decided to offer me the award of Companion of Literature. No one should be taken in. I daresay you know the Society—ancient & respectable, certainly, but it consists of the bumbling has-beens & the desperate would-be's. I remember it well from my London days. No live writer would be seen dead there. I can't refuse, because old Rab Butler is the President, and I don't want to be rude or unkind to him. As for the honour, a few kids playing at King Arthur's Knights could do the same" (March 8).

End of Drought

Pitter worked diligently on galley proofs throughout the fall of 1974 and was rewarded when *End of Drought* appeared early the next year; it is primarily composed of independent poems culled from old manuscripts or from previously published but uncollected pieces. Many are notable for prosody, including "Planting Mistletoe" for its internal rhyme—"Let the old tree be the gold tree; / Hand up the silver seed: / Let the hoary tree be the glory tree, / To shine out at need"[20]—and "Raspberry Nectar" for its alliteration—"Why do you clash your lush plush bums together, / Rustle your sable capes and silver-banded wings, / Wild bees, tame bees, hoverflies all of dither, / Worthy hardworking females, drudging things" (44). Other poems, such as "Victory Bonfire," with its description of burning a gigantic haystack to celebrate the defeat of the Nazis, evoke powerful visual images:

> A pause, a crackle, a roar!
> Sheets of orange flame in a matter of seconds—
> And in a matter of minutes—hypnotised minutes—
> Vast caverns of embers, volcanoes gushing and blushing,
> Whitening wafts on cliffs and valleys of hell,
> Quivering cardinal-coloured glens and highlands,
> Great masses panting, pulsating, lunglike and scarlet,
> Soaring up like balloons, formal and dreadful,
> Threatening the very heavens. (5–7)

"Swifts" recalls the sand martins from "Freemasons of the Air" in *The Bridge* and is a precise word picture capturing the energetic flight of the swallows and chimney swifts Pitter observed in and around the Hawthorns: "Low over the warm roof of an old barn, / Down in a flash to the water, up and away with a cry / And a wild swoop and a sharp turn / And a fever of life under a thundery sky, / So they go over, so they go by" (12). "So Good of Their Kind," with its celebration of slug mating, can be linked to earlier poems where Pitter found affinity for other living creatures, including "The Viper" in *A Trophy of Arms*, "The Bat" in *The Bridge*, and "The Captive Bird of Paradise" in *The Ermine*.

There are also comic poems in the vein of *The Rude Potato* and *On Cats*, especially "Fruit-Fly and Drop of Honey," "Rhubarb, Rhubarb," "Our Best Stoker," and "The Plain Facts." "Pot-Bound" may be the most effective of the comic poems since it offers a metaphor for the human condition; that is, though we smile as we read of the plant's struggle against being confined by its pot—it longs to be repotted so that its roots may reach out and it can grow—Pitter invites us to compare this to what might happen to a constricted human life that is similarly unbound:

> A long-retarded Plant, when thus relieved,
> May grow so swiftly, and so thickly leaved
> And richly budded, that its bright Ascent
> And Blossoming are an Astonishment:
> O give me leave thus to aspire and blow,
> And come at last to the great Flower-show,

Where every past Despair and bygone Grief
I'll sublimate in each transcendent Leaf;
The bitter darkness of that former gloom
Will write in all the brilliance of a Bloom. (45–46)

Some poems muse on things spiritual, such as "Holiday in Heaven," which celebrates heaven's bliss; "A Happy Christmas—Love to All," which invites us to
embrace God's love; "Lame Arm," an ironic piece that gently rebukes God for
human aches and pains; "Line Engaged," which suggests that our frantic pace
of living blocks us from learning what it is God wants us to know; and "The
Penny Chick, or The Triumph of Faith," which explores how simple faith is
surprisingly rewarded.

Other poems are memorable because they capture a compelling slice of life.
For example, in "To a Lady, in a Wartime Queue" Pitter is struck by the patience of a young girl who is forced to stand in line with her mother in bitter
cold and freezing slush: "I thought 'She cannot choose but wail'; / I erred, for
you were not so frail. / You were determined not to cry" (4). "A Crownèd A"
also concerns a child, this time what appears to be an overdressed, spoiled,
and pampered boy who surprises two petty onlookers when he pauses outside
the butcher's shop: "And gorgeous Ted dismounts, to kiss / The butcher's cat,
a friend of his. / He kneels before her, as he tries / To read her enigmatic eyes"
(40). His tender compassion is seen as well when "he lays his cheek upon her
head." In brief, "he wipes the sawdust from her fur, / As if he really felt for her. /
. . . The case is plain. / The child is loved, and loves again." "Gosling" is a tender
encounter between Pitter and a delicate gosling; she delighted in rubbing her
chin on the fine down covering his body, and he rewarded her by rubbing her
back: "Instead of striking with hiss and quack / With love and liking he paid me
back" (34). "February Walk" recounts a day in which winter is cheated by unexpected warmth: "One winter morning we set out. / By midday it was spring."
Although the walkers try to convince themselves that winter has really gone,
they "did not incline / To wade in brooks that day." And so the warm day fades
and the truth of the season returns: "And early a vermillion sun / Went down
a purple wood: / And so the day that had begun / Cold, now declined a wintry
one, / In northern solitude" (8–9).

Other significant poems include "They Have Murdered My Village," a lament
against progress: "They have murdered my village, / My tree is cut down. / Over
the tillage / Advances the town" (11). "Bad Child Left Behind" is a modern
parable with faint echoes of the story of the Prodigal Son. In Pitter's version,
in which she uses Old English alliterative meter, a willful young boy refuses his
father's kindly guidance—"He would have his way: he chose his own woe"—and
so "he was left there to learn what loneliness may teach" (19). Foolishly, the boy

looks for fruit in brambles, finding thickets of thorns blocking his way. Undeterred in his stubbornness, he plunges into the cutting branches: "With piteous face, / Wry and rueful, he ravaged the clusters, / Shuddering for the sharpness: with shame wretched, / Desperate he dared them, for his dear will." When he finally has enough, he cries out: "'Oh help me, Father!' / Emptiness answered, and his own echo." The lack of grace marks this as a poem in which Pitter considers the inevitability of poor choices. Consequences dire and painful follow from living willfully and from rejecting wisdom and reason. "One Does Get Old at Last" warmly embraces the aging process, admitting that one gets "stiff about the knees, / Mind and eyes a bit dim." From this it follows, for Pitter, that "it's time we turned to Him. / For there is something in us willing to go, / Something that knows its time." The wisdom of age affirms it is "easier far now than it was at first, love, / No more to be possessed, / Or to possess ourselves, or things; the worst, love, / Is over, not the best" (24).

In contrast, "Red Boy" communicates the boundless enthusiastic energy of youth as it portrays a conversation between an older speaker and young redheaded boy planting a vine—"a real vine, / With juice like blood! / Look, red as wine / Where I scrape the wood!" (33). The boy is bursting with his knowledge of the vine, exclaiming: "Here's a good hard bud, / For when time's fit, / And a tall strong rod / Will grow from it." The poem's last stanza best captures the never-say-die, optimistic, sunny disposition of youth: "What do you want to learn, / You in your hot spring? / He answered, brief and stern, / 'Everything.'" "End of Drought" is also optimistic in its deft description of a long, emotionally dry period: "Drought breaks. Like iron icefloes feeling / Groundswell and rising tide, relent / Air, earth, and mind: veering and wheeling / A full half-compass, the wind's sent / Round to fetch back the spice and bloom, / Half round the world to fetch love home" (23). Just as rain brings new life to the earth, so love renews the parched soul: "Your old love laughing runs to kiss you: / New love consenting clasps him too: / Fluttering with shreds of silver tissue / From the washed sky they have been through: / From a rich cloud, in a warm rain / New love and old come home again." Although *End of Drought* attracted little critical comment, perhaps because it was seen as "picked over pieces," it does illustrate Pitter's lingering poetic sensibilities. Undoubtedly she was past her best work when *End of Drought* was published, yet it retains glimpses of a poet in love with language and the human condition.

The last seventeen years of Pitter's life were comfortable, though she was somewhat restricted by her failing health, particularly by the gradual loss of her eyesight due to cataracts and macular degeneration. During the years when she could still read, she devoured books and enjoyed watching television, especially science and nature programs. She never tired of learning more about the natural world, as such knowledge augmented her own early love of nature in Hainault

Forest. She still enjoyed her garden, though now primarily as an observer. For example, regarding the return of spring, she writes Russell: "Toads mating in ponds; you could see them coming through the undergrowth, their eyes shining, waiting till there were no humans about. They get very ratty if one interferes—I've seen them get up on all fours and rush at one, croaking desperately" (April 26, 1975). She was also blessed to be living in a village inhabited by people who cared so much for her. Among her favorites was Stanley Young; she writes Russell: "He is a truly remarkable and most lovable man, who activates things and people most exceptionally. . . . It was a great piece of luck for me to come across him. . . . Yes, it is quite true that he came here knowing my work and possessing my books; he says he cannot remember when he first discovered me" (Nov. 6, 1976). At the same time, Pitter enjoyed being by herself. In a 1977 BBC radio interview with Hallam Tennyson she says:

> I think I'm rather canny in looking after myself. But being alone is what I always liked. In fact, my most delightful moments have always been in solitude at a cottage in the forest. In my youth, why I know not, it was to weep with pure felicity in that place, and I don't think I should have ever have done that in the presence of anyone else. But, of course, the position is basically untenable, but I don't mind. I don't try to plan about it. There's a [rest] home up the road I can go to if I become helpless, and my neighbours keep a very strict eye on me. If the lights don't go out at the proper time or anything like that, they would take action, so that I don't feel insecure.[21]

On her eightieth birthday a grand party was held for her, hosted by Young. Pitter gives a good account of it to Cooley: "I had such an 80th birthday! The folks got up a splendid party, in the Vicarage dining-room. . . . There was a great cake made by some wonderful catering ladies, all over symbols of poetry & gardening, with a book in the middle made of almond paste but really resembling antique calf, an almond-paste wheelbarrow, and sugar flowers & vegetables galore" (Dec. 11, 1977). She also describes the events of the day: "Somebody wrote and read a complimentary poem; there was beautiful wine, too. The old chaps had their 1914–18 medals on. I kissed all sorts, including the Catholic priest, and made a speech of my own, telling them of the great day in 1955 when I went to see the Queen, and about quite a few of the comic incidents of that great day. What a lucky old baggage I have been!"

Pitter was also enjoying sage-like status among her new admirers. One correspondent was Canadian John Adams, who first wrote Pitter in September 1970. He was a great admirer of Pitter's poetry, and soon they developed what would be a lengthy and regular correspondence. In her letters she responded to his queries about her life, her favorite poem of her own composition (she would not choose one), world events, where he could find all her books, writing, and their shared faith. After many years of friendship, Adams asked her advice about marriage. Pitter replies:

> I am sure you must have been wishing for an early reply to your very interesting letter, but I took time to think, because the subject is obviously so important to you. I do feel qualified to say something about it, because like yourself I have not married (so far) and because your liking for my work is a bond, and an evidence of similarity in nature. I do feel that as a sincere Christian you are committed to making a Christian marriage, if and when you do marry. This means, of course, that you will not form irresponsible sex relationships, and that you accept the hard rule that there is only one correct sex relationship, the uniting of two persons into one mysterious unit according to the rules. It is still done, in spite of the state of the world. Now, I am sure you know about the two departments of the brain. I think that many people live largely in the cerebellum, which controls the muscles and I believe the primitive urges. They will get on with their sex-life early—helped by modern permissiveness—to them it is an obvious priority, whatever the pitfalls. . . . If however one lives largely in the world of ideas, the world of the cerebrum—and that you yourself live there very largely your Christianity and your love of poetry prove—this means that you are not dominated by the department of primitive urges, and that you can take time, and make sure—reasonably sure of a real marriage with your true love. You will know her all right when she comes along, and (to be a bit worldly), if by then you have that good job, you will be in a favourable position to marry, and good luck to you. In my own case, I have felt dedicated to trying to write poetry since early childhood. I had a vocation which has been my obvious, inescapable priority. I have often been in love, but if the man, however delightful, regarded this vocation as marginal, then he was marginal to me. I feel bound to add that these chaps were apt to be very gifted and interesting, but Bohemians—security very doubtful! I never lacked common sense. (April 10, 1978)

In addition, she continues her warm correspondence with Russell and Cecil. After receiving one encouraging letter about how her poetry has always affected him, she writes Cecil: "How can I thank you for your beautiful letter, which comforts, justifies, and consoles me so amply that I feel I have not lived in vain? How fortunate I have been in pursuing the tenuous, remote intuitions through the thickets, to get even an occasional glimpse or waft of them which others—one here & there—will recognize and acknowledge, setting the seal now & then with a tear or two! And from you above all this is most valuable (justifying me to myself) since you are so excellent a critic" (Dec. 28, 1978). Later in the letter she adds: "Oh, does your sense of the unearthly fade? For you yourself are not very earthly, at least to me and I am sure to many others. I could feel you about long before I knew you—in adolescence was sure there was something—someone—a child? not very many miles to the north." Several years later she writes Cecil and tries to encourage him in his ol[...]k forward to much in this life as we are now, b[...]s delight, edification, and instruction by your[...]d invaluable encour- agement—you are alway[...]ur standard" (Jan. 8, 1980). Then she reveals[...]For my part, I set out to write a line or two w[...]lieve that a few lines of mine may last—one a[...]ph—'Ephphathah.'22 Every creative person kr[...]its confronted by the Inexpressible, and perha[...]may be opened, and the string of our tongue l[...]'"

Pitter's final national[...]etter from 10 Down- ing Street: "The Prime[...]you, in strict confi- dence, that [Margaret Th[...]it your name to The Queen with a recomme[...]e graciously pleased to approve that you be[...]Order of the British Empire" (May 24, 1979)[...]ublic, Pitter was sur- prised at how much congratulatory correspondence she received. While she had downplayed being named a companion of literature, she celebrates being named commander, writing Russell: "I never thought that this was recognition at national, rather than literary, level, but now [that] I do, I am duly gratified. I am so glad, too, that I am a Commander (so gallant) rather than a Dame (all petticoats) although I believe Dames are above Commanders" (July 6, 1979). And she confides in Russell how she is glad that her poetry, while now hard to find, still brings pleasure to some: "I am now a poet of the past, as my books are all O. P., jobbed off, remaindered. But I still get letters of thanks for the consola- tion. What a wonderful thing, to have lightened the burden of life for some few people" (Nov. 22, 1980).

The early 1980s were years marked by the appearance of several new friends. Chief among them was a Welsh woman, Mary Thomas, who, having come across a typed version of "The Heart's Desire Is Full of Sleep" stuck between the pages of a poetry anthology, spent two years tracking down the author and eventually wrote Pitter. In her first letter to Pitter, Thomas speaks for many in describing what drew her to Pitter's verse: "[I like your poems] partly because they seem aware of the natural world as being there in its own right, & not merely for hu- man pleasure & convenience. I like them also because they are very disciplined

& exact, but also full of grace & feeling. They recall or recreate for me experiences of my own & also open my mind to other aspects of experience which I was not aware of. I am astonished in some of them to find my own inner feelings so completely stated by another person" (Jan. 29, 1981). Pitter was touched by Thomas's lengthy search to find her: "Your description of the effect of my verses on your own mind recalls an image I have long held—the analogy with the maritime depth-sounding apparatus. The signal is sent out, and is echoed from far down or far away" (Feb. 3, 1981). A lively correspondence developed, a warm friendship ensued, and soon Thomas was coming to the Hawthorns for occasional visits. The correspondence between them touched on many topics, including gardening, new scientific discoveries, and literature. At times Pitter also expressed wonder that she was still living while many of her friends were already dead: "The other day I said to our Vicar . . . 'I can't think what the dear Lord means by keeping me hanging about so long—I've done what I set out to do, and I'm tired after the long day, and waiting for the last bus to get home & get my head down.' Correctly, he raised against me the forefinger of reproof. 'We are not to question God's will.' But so lovingly" (Feb. 9, 1983). Along the same lines, she writes Russell: "I am really . . . pretty well and comfortable, I do not know why the dear Lord keeps me waiting so long for the last bus. I have said my piece, and there is no more poetry left in me. Nearly all my friends, and all but a few natives, are dead, or living far away" (Feb. 19, 1983).

Both Pitter and O'Hara had used hired help to assist them in running the house, and this had become more necessary after O'Hara's passing. Increasingly feeble and poor of sight, Pitter now had to rely extensively upon hired helpers. On one occasion she writes Thomas: "I have at present a temporary housework help (while one is laid up) who is absolutely frightening in her thoroughness. [For example] a canister of whatsit powder for use after the bath, which has never had its sprinkler top reversed to close the perforations in the six or eight years we've had it, has now been closed. Etc. Poor spiders—poor microbes!" (Nov. 11, 1983). However, helpers could not always be present, so Pitter was often left on her own. Unfortunately, one evening in late October 1984 on her way to empty a bucket of ashes, she fell on hard concrete and suffered serious bruising and scraping. Confined to bed for a week, Pitter slowly recovered; after this fall she became less active and her limited mobility kept her confined primarily to the downstairs of the Hawthorns. In part because of Pitter's fall, Thomas began to visit three or four times a year, usually staying a fortnight or more. At about this time John and Ellen Rixon moved directly across the street from Pitter, and the entire family befriended her. Ellen and her oldest daughter, Rachel, became very loving, helpful neighbors. Good fortune followed when yet another new resident of Long Crendon, Muriel Dickinson, befriended Pitter, eventually coming almost every evening to read to the nearly blind poet.

As the decade passed, Pitter lost more friends. When David Cecil died on January 1, 1986, she wrote Russell: "Yes, David Cecil's death was a blow but one cannot complain, as he was 83, and had been a very delicate child. It was a very great pleasure & privilege to know him"; about her own aging she adds: "I can't complain. I have had a great time, but I would be glad to be gone now: 89 is too long to be hanging about—and I suspect I have become an awful old bore" (Jan. 28, 1986). Reflecting on the passing of her old friends, she tells Norah Cruickshank: "My friends who are dead far outnumber those who are alive . . . and somehow those who are alive seem so much less lively and interesting than those who're dead. . . . I've known so many famous and brilliant people: Lewis, George Orwell, James Stephens, and David Cecil" (Sept. 18, 1986).[24] As she became less able to care for herself, she gave power of attorney to her solicitor, Ian Taylor. Taylor arranged for Pitter to have full-time caregivers, and while most of these women were kindly and caring, Mary Thomas worried that Pitter was occasionally neglected.

By 1987 Pitter was effectively blind. Unable to read, Pitter was discouraged, but her spirits were partially lifted when an enthusiastic American devotee of her verse, Thomas McKean, who had first begun to correspond with Pitter in July 1983, wrote and asked if he might visit. Several visits and letters followed over the next few years. In one letter Pitter thanks McKean for his gift of maple syrup and notes how its scent reminded her of an event from her childhood:

> It gives me much the same feeling as the earliest Christmas I can remember. . . . It would be 1898, when I was about 1 year 2 months. There was a little Xmas tree in a pot on the kitchen dresser—little candles burning, a strand or two of tinsel. Someone, no doubt Mother, held me up to see it close. But what I remember best was the scent. . . . I am sure of this experience because we moved out of there very soon afterwards, and I could still draw a plan of room, dresser, door, window—all distinctly differently placed from those in new home. But that scent—for me, all my life, the smell of magic festivity! Deo gratias. (Dec. 17, 1983)

In 1985 McKean asked if he could make a visit in order to see if there were unpublished poems among her papers that he might bring out. Pitter was flattered by such attention and agreed. Like Orage, Belloc, and Russell before him, McKean became an advocate for Pitter's poetry. Eventually McKean compiled and secured a publisher for Pitter's last volume of verse, *A Heaven to Find*, to which he also wrote the introduction.

A Heaven to Find

With the exception of "Cricket Match, 1908"; "Close, Mortal Eyes," which is an expanded version of the same poem first published in A *Trophy of Arms*; and "Lewis Appears," which Pitter had sent C. S. Lewis in August 1955, the poems in A *Heaven to Find* were written in the 1970s or early 1980s.[25] As such they are the final harvest of her verse. "High Summer" complains of a year when summer never seemed to come: "Last winter was so long and cruel / We thought it would never be done."[26] "For Unhappy Lovers" chronicles how passion gives way to unrequited, thwarted love, leaving the lover "to weep alone, and wander / At random in the cold, orphaned and aching / . . . / Bankrupt and sick, with no life worth the taking: / Knowing that fleshly pain of the heart breaking." While the poem has connections to Pitter's love poetry of the 1930s and 1940s, what marks this as a later poem is the conclusion, in which she finds heavenly solace: "For broken hearts derided, / For widowed bodies in the midnight burning, / For fast-locked loves divided, / Only one sleep can still their endless turning, / Only one Remedy assuage their yearning."[27] "Valediction (for Milton's Tercentenary)" is Pitter's panegyric farewell to the "poet of paradise, poet of heaven and hell, / Peerless, next to our William [Shakespeare]." "The Ploughboy's Plea" celebrates the tender relationship between a young boy and his loving mother; as he goes out to plough in the early morning fog, he entreats her to keep a fire burning in the hearth by which he can warm his hands in the morning and the light of which he can use as a beacon to guide him when he comes home at night.

"Main-Road Lighting" is the most effective poem in the volume; its opening is particularly visually evocative:

Seen from a cold upper window in middle night
Over dark country, thick trees, some two miles away,
Main-road lighting, shivering glow-worm light,
A long necklace trembling continually, as may
Emeralds flash on the neck of the forsaken,
So by air-flows interposing they seem shaken.[28]

After noting the connections between the headlights of cars off in the winter distance and her memory of summer glow worms, she wonders if the headlights are shaken "by any trouble I know?" As she ponders that question, it reminds her of the mystery of the light of glow worms: "It is a secret still how those beetles glow, / Summoning love in summer with their green shine; / But it is winter now, and of love no question, / Only benighted trembling, cold sugges-tion." The dissonance between man and nature is then deftly captured in the poem's conclusion:

The lamps are man-made, yet they speak only
Some grief we cannot track down, nor find in nature:
Not of earth, not of heaven nor hell, but of the lonely
Sorrow to which we can give no form nor feature,
A wandering on that middle road, the merely other,
Where they who have lost this universe may gather.

Pitter's dispassionate musing on the essential loneliness of the human condition
is the result of a lifetime's loneliness, and the death of Cecil may have exercised
an influence on the poem as well. Regardless, "Main-Road Lighting" illustrates
that Pitter was capable of writing finely crafted pieces into her late seventies;
though fading, she still had the gift.

Not surprisingly, several poems focus upon her faith. "The Half-Remembered Tune" suggests that just as we can faintly recall the sweetness of a tune
that eludes us, "so in the central void of mind / Where sense is empty, thought is
blind, / Both omnipresent and alone / We feel the music of the One." "Rogation
Hymn," one of Pitter's few poems indicating her awareness of the church calen-
dar, is set sometime during the three days before Ascension Day. In recognizing
the inexorable link between the earth and human life—"This Planet is our
mother: / Our bodies and our sustenance we owe / To You through her"—the
poem is a plea for God to continue blessing both the harvest of the current year
and the sowing to follow in the spring so that His Love will be apparent to all:
"Not for our own need merely / We ask: but for the poor (who like Your son /
Live, if they live, so barely, / Yet dear to You, each one) / Something to spare,
that Love's will may be done." "Chorus" affirms that we "can't forget / The pull
of God, the ache, the call. / Our hearts know Love makes up for all."

However, the poem that best communicates her faith is the first one in the
volume, "Good Enthroned":

Absolute good sits throned in the middle of the mind.
There must be—I know there is—a heaven to find:
Our final bliss, perfectly passionate, perfectly kind:
It is our first love, long since left behind.

We need no more than one look to know our own.
Turn a page. In place of the print, an image is shown:
Then broken and healed, created and overthrown,
We fall at the feet of the New we have always known.[29]

In effect, Pitter insists that all innately know that "absolute good sits throned"
in the middle of our minds, a Platonic affirmation. Although awareness of this

knowledge sometimes fades—either through familiarity or disinterest—old age and the certainty of coming death shock us back into this final realization: "We fall at the feet of the New we have always known." Earlier in her faith journey Pitter would not have published such an overt confession of faith; now, however, as she faces the coming moment of her own death, she no longer feels the need to be oblique or to use indirection regarding matters of faith. God is a certainty, so it is natural and fitting that she give poetic utterance to her faith—it is indeed "a heaven to find."

McKean's preface to the book provides a helpful overview:

> The poems in this volume, culled from Miss Pitter's manuscript notebooks, give a good idea of the range of [her] work. One thus finds everything from humorous pieces ("Potting Shed Tutti-Frutti"), to spiritual observations ("Good Enthroned"), to poems expressing her abiding love of Nature ("Brambleberries, Blackberries") and to moving expressions of religious faith ("Rogation Hymn"). Some of these poems—for those well-acquainted with the author's work—reveal a darker side of the poet. In this regard one notes "Main-Road Lighting" and "High Summer." But no matter the content, binding all these pieces together and making them one, are the love and care Miss Pitter takes in transforming inspiration into words.

Pitter was very pleased with *A Heaven to Find*, writing McKean: "I have been so delighted with the news about the new little book, and I was kept busy signing what appeared to be an entire edition. . . . It was strange to me to meet again so many lines which I had quite forgotten. I do feel grateful and indebted to you for your efforts, including the excellent preface. Technically it is a handsome little book which I feel does me honour" (July 5, 1987).

While *A Heaven to Find* was Pitter's last new volume of verse, another literary accomplishment—perhaps her crowning achievement—occurred when in 1990 Enitharmon Press published her *Collected Poems*, a compilation of her best work from *A Mad Lady's Garland* through *A Heaven to Find*, with an introduction by Elizabeth Jennings. On August 12, 1990, Stephen Stuart-Smith, the editor of Enitharmon, arranged for a party at the Hawthorns, where he presented Pitter a copy of the new book prior to its official launch. Surrounded by friends and admirers and toasted for her health and the book's success, Pitter was delighted, and she charmed the assembled group by quoting from memory her poems, as suggested by those present. Norah Cruickshank reported that Pitter was "chatty and jolly." Pitter was also honored on October 11, 1990, when the Poetry Society of London sponsored an evening program that featured her poetry. Hosted by Peter Dickinson, composer, performer, writer, broadcaster, and son of Muriel Dickinson, the program celebrated Pitter's contributions to English poetry in the twentieth century and coincided with the official publication of *Collected Poems*. In offering a review of Pitter's poetry after the appearance of *Collected Poems*, Selena Hastings writes: "In her day [Pitter] was as popular as Betjeman and Larkin are now; loved, particularly during the war, for her Englishness, the clarity and innocence of her vision, and for her apparent unawareness of the modern technological age. She never wrote of aeroplanes or electricity; there are no pylons in Miss Pitter's poetry."[30] In underscoring Pitter's midcentury popularity, Hastings adds: "In 1950, when R. A. Scott-James brought out his *Fifty Years of English Literature*, John Betjeman was allotted three sentences; Ruth Pitter was given nearly three pages." Such remarks delighted and bolstered Pitter, reaffirming her deserved place in the center of twentieth-century English poetry.[31]

Pitter's last two years were quiet and uneventful; though she could not read, she often kept her mind active by reciting from memory her favorite Shakespeare, Milton, Wordsworth, Keats, and Tennyson poems from the book that meant so much to her poetic development, Palgrave's *The Golden Treasury*. The last of her great friends, Arthur Russell, died on November 21, 1990, and this saddened but did not depress her. She slept more and more under the kindly eyes of her caregivers. While she had been comfortable on February 24, 1992, the next day she suffered a mild heart attack. Over the next two days she was drifting in and out of consciousness. By Thursday, according to Mary Thomas, Pitter was distraught about something, so a doctor came and gave her a shot of morphine. Another shot was required the next day. During the early evening Ellen and Rachel Rixon, Muriel Dickinson, and Norah Cruickshank sat with her. Saddened by her rapid decline, Stanley Young came and stayed with Pitter through Friday night and into Saturday morning. At 3:00 A.M. on February 29, 1992, Pitter died peacefully, probably unaware that her death in wintertime fulfilled the imperative of "Call Not to Me" from *A Trophy of Arms*:

> Call not to me when summer shines,
> Death, for in summer I will not go.
> . . . .
> But I will hear you when all is bare;
> Call and welcome when leaves lie low;
> When the dry bents hiss in the raving air
> And shepherds from eastward smell the snow;
> When the mead is left for the wind to mow,
> And the storm is woodman to all the sere,
> When hail is the seed the heavens sow,
> When all is deadly and naught is dear—
> Call and welcome, for I shall hear,
> I shall be ready to rise and go.[32]

Her funeral, conducted by Young, was held in Long Crendon on March 5, 1992. During the service Rachel Rixon read one of Pitter's favorite biblical passages: "And Ruth said, 'Entreat me not to leave thee, or to return from following after thee: for whither thou goest, I will go; and where thou lodgest, I will lodge: thy people shall be my people, and thy God my God: Where thou diest, will I die, and there will I be buried: the LORD do so to me, and more also, if ought but death part thee and me.' When she saw that she was stedfastly minded to go with her, then she left speaking unto her. So they two went until they came to Bethlehem" (Ruth 1:16–19). Pitter's journey of faith to Christianity was long, but once she affirmed it, she held on to it tenaciously, for it offered her meaning, purpose, and comfort.

Her death was widely hailed as a great literary loss. One writer called her "one of the truest and most dedicated poets of her time; and it is a standing rebuke to English letters that her voice—clear, precise and unflustered amidst unfathomable depths—should have only lately sounded in the wilderness. . . . Pitter's beautifully contrived utterance calls her readers to attention; her seamless simplicity holds them transfixed. In her ordered scheme neither obscurity nor banality had any place."[33] He also added perceptively: "Her poetry combines grit and tenderness, hardness and fragility, sensual experience and intellectual vision. Yet somewhere behind these multiple antitheses, she would hint, there lies the single unattainable truth." Another said: "She came to enjoy perhaps the highest reputation of any living English woman poet of her century."[34] He also noted her isolation from the modernist poetry of her day: "Few who took the trouble to read her came away unimpressed by her Traherne-like dedication to Christianity or by her refusal to write except in her own voice. Her poetry behaves as if all the literary movements of the past century, from Georgianism to Concrete Poetry, had simply never happened. . . . In this, as in her wholly genuine modesty and disregard for fame, she was unique among her contemporaries. She was concerned only with verse." Ann Margaret Ridler affirmed that Pitter's "whole life was devoted to her craft, her writing grounded in the natural world, in common things and people portrayed with love and a painterly clarity."[35] Ridler went on to say that Pitter "celebrated a triumphant faith in an all-pervading divinity. Though at times she conveys a profound desolation, again and again she affirms the miracle of rebirth. . . . Her finest work reveals a strong certitude of visionary splendours within, through and beyond the natural world, and in this respect she was a true modern metaphysical."

In offering a final consideration of Ruth Pitter's poetry, it is germane to note the key characteristics of her verse as well as the writers who most influenced her. Carolyn Kizer argues that Pitter's deft use of the caesura, her control of emotion, her rhetorical cunning, and her verbal felicity mark her as a great poet. She also says Pitter's use of poetic devices, including inversion, repetition, rhythm, and pace, as well as poetic forms such as sonnets, quatrains, sapphics, couplets, tercets, terza rima, and unrhymed hexameters is masterful.[36] When we consider as well her precise diction and deft use of sound, we have in Pitter a poet of great ability following in the tradition of the poets she so admired. Her debt to Edmund Spenser is clear in her regular use of the stanza named after him as well as her deliberate archaisms and inversions. Thankfully her fascination with fairies, archaic speech, and impersonalized emotion were largely confined to her earliest volumes, and beginning with A Mad Lady's Garland a distinct, clear poetic voice started to emerge. As she matured, she began to write one powerful poem after another, often exploring the sense of something behind or above the natural world. It is this bent that has caused some to link her to the seventeenth-century religious poets.

When we consider specific influences, two poets stand out: George Herbert and Thomas Traherne. For example, in Herbert's "The Windows" he muses upon how the stained glass window of a church may be compared to a preacher: "Lord, how can man preach thy eternal word? / He is a brittle, crazy glass: / Yet in thy temple thou doest him afford / This glorious and transcendent place, / To be a window through thy grace."[37] He then suggests that just as heat is used to burn color into the stained glass, so the suffering of a preacher (and by implication the suffering of Christ) is used to "color" or to bring meaning to Scripture: "Doctrine and life, colours and light, in one / When they combine and mingle, bring / A strong regard and awe." Herbert's intense spiritual reflection is similar to Pitter's in "Spectrum" (from End of Drought), a poem that came to her after she saw a glass of water in the vestry of her parish church in Long Crendon: "A little window, eastward, low, obscure, / A flask of water on the vestry press, / A ray of sunshine through a fretted door, / And myself kneeling in live quietness: / Heaven's bright- ness was then gathered in the glass."[38] The simple, terse diction of these lines invokes a sacred moment as Pitter enjoys how the sun "made his dear daughter Light sing her own praise, / . . . Counting her seven great jewels." As she wonders at the beauty of the seven refracted colors—violet, indigo, blue, green, yellow, orange, and red—she also wonders how, from a different visual angle, "those rays / Remerged in the whole diamond, total sight." In this moment of seeing how "wa- ter and glass obeyed / The laws appointed," Pitter humbly worships: "With them, yet how far / From their perfection, I still knelt and prayed." This divine encoun- ter, this sacramental vision of seeing how the natural world obeys its God-given laws, forges in Pitter a desire to do the same. It would be too much to say that "The Windows" directly influenced "Spectrum"; however, it would be accurate to say that Herbert's sacramental vision of the world was one shared by Pitter.

Throughout the poetry of Traherne there is a preoccupation with the inno- cence of childhood; often direct encounters with the natural world transform this innocence into mystical experiences of joy. In "Innocence" Traherne explores his earliest childhood memories, affirming,

> No darkness then did overshade
> But all within was pure and bright,
> No guilt did crush, nor fear invade
> But all my soul was full of light.

> A joyful sense and purity
> Is all I can remember,
> The very night to me was bright,
> 'Twas summer in December.[39]

The poem climaxes with an epiphany, claiming that his sense of sin had been removed and replaced by the light of God's love:

> Whether it be that nature is so pure,
> And custom only vicious; or that sure
> God did by miracle the guilt remove,
> And make my soul to feel his love,

> So early: or that 'twas one day,
> Where in this happiness I found;
> Whose strength and brightness so do ray,
> That still it seemeth to surround.

> What e'er it is, it is a light
> So endless unto me
> That I a world of true delight
> Did then and to this day do see.

Traherne's mystical affirmation of God is found throughout Pitter's later work, most notably "Sudden Heaven" in A Trophy of Arms. Pitter combines a clipped, terse style with an incisive eye to create a poem of startling power about unexpected, unsolicited joy:

> All was as it had ever been—
> The worn familiar book,
> The oak beyond the hawthorn seen,
> The misty woodland's look:

The starling perched upon the tree
With his long tress of straw—
When suddenly heaven blazed on me,
And suddenly I saw:

Saw all as it would ever be,
In bliss too great to tell;
For ever safe, for ever free,
All bright with miracle:

Saw as in heaven the thorn arrayed,
The tree beside the door;
And I must die—but O my shade
Shall dwell there evermore.[40]

"Sudden Heaven" is filled with rich natural images, including "misty woodland's look," "starling perched upon the tree," and "long tress of straw." Yet its real power comes through Pitter's subtle infusion of biblical images, motifs, and allusions such as "suddenly heaven blazed on me," "bliss too great to tell," "bright with miracle," and "the thorn arrayed." Most impressive is her deft use of the tree as an image of both nature, where the starling perches, and the divine, where we envision Christ and his crown of thorns. Traherne and Pitter are among the best of mystical poets; they help us draw near the inexpressible through their powerfully realized poems.

In her introduction to Pitter's Collected Poems, Elizabeth Jennings praises Pitter's "acute sensibility and deep integrity"; Jennings claims that her poems "are informed with a sweetness which is also bracing, and a generosity which is blind to nothing, neither the sufferings in this world nor the quirky behavior of human beings."[41] Philip Larkin, who edited The Oxford Book of Twentieth-Century English Verse, included four of her poems.[42] He considered her poetry "rather good," high praise coming from one of the most respected twentieth-century English poets.[43] As I have tried to demonstrate in this study, Ruth Pitter deserves a wider reading and a more judicious critical appraisal. If she "enjoyed the highest reputation of any living English woman poet of her century," it is time that both her life and her art be given the exposure and recognition they so richly deserve.

Notes

Introduction

1. That she continues to be enjoyed by readers is evidenced by Fleur Adcock, ed., *The Faber Book of 20th Century Women's Poetry* (London: Faber & Faber, 1987), in which her "The Sparrow's Skull" and "Morning Glory" (77–78) appear; *More Poetry Please! 100 Popular Poems from the BBC Radio 4 Programme* (London: Everyman, 1988), where her "The Rude Potato" (101–2) appears; Sandra M. Gilbert and Susan Gubar, eds., *The Norton Anthology of Literature by Women: The Traditions in English*, 2nd ed. (New York: W. W. Norton, 1996), where her "The Military Harpist," "The Irish Patriarch," "Old Nelly's Birthday," and "Yorkshire Wife's Saga" (1573–77) appear; and Paul Keegan, ed., *The New Penguin Book of English Verse* (London: Allen Lane, Penguin Press, 2000), where her "But for Lust" (962) appears.

2. Ruth Pitter, "There Is a Spirit," in *Poems 1926–1966* (London: Barrie and Rockliff/ Cresset Press, 1968), xi.

3. Paul Schlueter. "Ruth Pitter." *An Encyclopedia of British Women Writers*. Ed. June Schlueter and Paul Schlueter (New Brunswick, NJ: Rutgers Univ. Press, 1999), 512.

4. "Ruth Pitter Obituary," *Times*, Mar. 3, 1992, 15.

5. BBC Radio, "Hunting the Unicorn," Feb. 17, 1961.

1. The Growth of a Poet, 1897–1920

1. In later interviews, she explains:

When I was young I used to brood upon it, till I was sure that once I began I could end. I would write it down like a shopping list after I had incubated it long enough. Very much surely as A. E. Housman's process in the *Name and Nature of Poetry*. The theme strikes you like a blow in the face. It comes up from the unconscious mind somewhere; you feel about until you can get some sort of phrase or something you can put down, and then if you can do that you can return to the mood at any time and with any luck the rest of the poem will crystallize out of it. ("The Poet Speaks," Mar. 24, 1964)

And I can remember the afflatus. I sat down and thought on my subject. I could feel a sort of oppressive feeling in my chest and a tingling in the throat, which presently mounted to the back of the nose; then my eyes filled with tears. I am persuaded this was the authentic afflatus of the poet, celebrated in ancient literature. I remember the subject, too. It was an old deserted windmill, of all things the most lifeless when it ceases to function and of all things the most alive all over when it is functioning. I think it was a good subject to start with, [but it] wasn't a good poem. (BBC Radio, "Ruth Pitter Talks to Hallam Tennyson," Nov. 7, 1977)

2. First published in 1861, Francis T. Palgrave's *The Golden Treasury: Selected from the Best Songs and Lyrical Poems in the English Language* (Oxford: Oxford University Press, 1964) was immensely popular and went through many editions and enlargements. In the preface he writes:

Like the fabled fountain of Azores, but with a more various power, the magic of [poetry] can confer on each period of life its appropriate blessing: on early years Experience, on maturity Calm, on age, Youthfulness. Poetry gives treasures "more golden than gold," leading us in higher and healthier ways than those of the world, and interpreting to us the lessons of Nature. But she speaks best for herself. Her true accents, if the plan has been executed with success, may be heard throughout the following pages: wherever the Poets of England are honoured, wherever the dominant language of the world is spoken, it is hoped that they will find fit audience. (xii)

The Golden Treasury is filled with the poetry of Burns, Byron, Campion, Cowper, Gray, Herrick, Keats, Marvell, Milton, Scott, Shelley, Shakespeare, and Wordsworth.

3. In "The Poet Speaks," Pitter recalls:

Both my parents were devoted to poetry, at a rather simple level. At some sort of *Golden Treasury* and Blake's *Songs of Innocence* level, my parents were teachers and they were devoted to the kind of poetry that means something to children, and I think with this experience I was imprinted with poetry at a childish level. And the sort of immediately comprehensible poetry and standard authors have always had a value to me, which nothing subsequent can quite have. . . . *The Golden Treasury* influenced me very much, but I have lived to realize you can have a bad case of *Golden Treasury* ear in later life and one gets sophisticated and guards against it. *The Golden Treasury* is really rather unbalanced, but for many years people didn't like to say so; it was so revered. And then Earnest Reece brought out a new *Golden Treasury*, which was in effect supplementary to the old one, and this included many more early poems, and those I fell in love with at once. [*The Golden Treasury*] was, I think, at the source; a young person would always find something pure and powerful to nourish and simplify. I mean such poems as "The Bailey Bareth the Bell Away," and "Alisoun" and "Lenten Has Come with Love to Town." Poems like that, they took possession of me, and "The Maid of the Moor."

4. The school building still stands at 31–33 Bow Road, London, E.3. In the early 1970s the Coborn School for Girls was amalgamated with the Coopers' Boys' School and moved to a newly built site in Essex. The Central Foundation Girls' School now occupies the old building on Bow Road.

5. My reconstruction of her experience in Hainault Forest draws from her letters, interviews, essays, and BBC transcripts. I am also indebted to Thomas McKean and an unpublished interview he conducted with Pitter in October 1985, in which she recalled many events connected with her early life. This interview is available in Pitter's uncataloged papers in the Bodleian Library.

6. The explosion may have been caused by one of the following. First, it may have been the result of the mild heat of an encapsulated fruit (a dry fruit pod-like structure) that structurally expanded and prompted the explosive eruption of seeds from the fruit. Second, one of the *Lycopodium* species produces a flammable spore. *Lycopodium* spores were a component of the flash powder used by photographers in the 1800s (the big flash and ensuing smoke from the thing resembling a mortarboard held by the photographer's assistant).

7. In G. Rostrevor Hamilton and John Arlott, eds., *Landmarks: A Book of Topographical Verse for England and Wales* (Cambridge: Cambridge Univ. Press, 1943), 3.

8. Pitter, "The Strawberry Plant," *A Trophy of Arms: Poems 1926–1935* (London: Cresset Press, 1936), 65.

9. Pitter's unpublished poem "The Cottage," written in 1926, also offers vivid recollections of her early days in Hainault Forest. See chapter 2, where I discuss this poem in connection with the death of her father.

10. She writes later that after her mother said this, "a frightful pang of love-killing jealousy and disillusionment shot through me. The whole world seemed to turn sick. And in one moment I was cured. Childish adoration was replaced by maidenly self-consciousness. Mr. Patterson, tweeds and all, shrank to his proper size. Just a neighbour, a little more interesting than the others—that was all." Sixty-five years after the event, Pitter remembers Patterson in "Piblett, 1910," published in *End of Drought* (London: Barrie and Jenkins, 1975): "He was enough for all our needs, / Old Piblett in his Harris tweeds— / Those tweeds so shaggy, peaty, nifty, / And Piblett the right side of fifty— / Piblett the superman, who knew / All it behooved a man to do" (41).

11. Mildred Jennings had first come to know of Pitter through her poems in the *New Age*.

12. From the company's *Catalogue of Painted Furniture* (1927). The catalog also offers the following "practical points":

1. All furniture is made of American White Wood or Satin Walnut unless otherwise specified. This does not apply to chairs, which are usually made of Birch or some equally hard wood.
2. The furniture is painted by hand, with three coats of specially hard durable paint which has a matt surface when dry. A good furniture polish is then used all over the surface, and the more this process is continued when the furniture is in use, the better it will wear.
3. The paint, not being enamel, will not chip at the edges.
4. Old painted or stained furniture can be somewhat altered and then repainted and decorated at a moderate cost with very happy results.
5. Estimates for a single piece or for several rooms of furniture are given free. All prices are kept as low as is possible, compatible with good workmanship and material.

Items listed for sale include beds, bookshelves, chairs, chests of drawers, china racks, cupboards, dressers, floor mats, hat and coat racks, hatboxes, mirrors, newspaper racks, stools, tables, toilet sets, umbrella stands, wardrobes, washing stands, and wastepaper baskets.

13. For more on this, see her poem "The Knightly Damoiseau," *New Age* 24, no. 9 (Jan. 2, 1919): 148.

14. Pitter, "The Poor Poet," *New Age* 21, no. 22 (Sept. 27, 1917): 462.

15. Pitter, "Song (The End of True Love Is to Sit and Mourn)," *New Age* 23, no. 7 (June 13, 1918): 112. The untitled poem beginning "True love's not told" in *A Trophy of Arms* that appears almost twenty years later has several verbal echoes to "Song." It is discussed in chapter 3.

16. Pitter, "The Consummation," *New Age* 23, no. 18 (Aug. 29, 1918): 289. In this regard, see also "The Companion of Youth," *New Age* 22, no. 6 (Dec. 6, 1917): 117, and "Felicity Seen from Afar," *New Age* 25, no. 11 (July 10, 1919): 188.

17. Pitter, "My Love's Cold," *New Age* 27, no. 26 (Oct. 28, 1920): 372.

18. The texts of the three chapbooks follow. "Light in Our Darkness": "I will help you, Mother, said Sara Forpoot. . . . So Sara began to help to peel the potatoes. Would you like some dinner she said. Yes, my good little Sara said Mother. So Sara gave Mother some dinner. Sara felt happy. In the afternoon Mother was well and Sara went to spend the wages she had earned by cooking the dinner and bought some lovely apples for Mother. Mother said, Thank you. Sara felt so happy all that afternoon. It was indeed a good thing for a little girl to do." "Days of Youth: William Noel": "William Noel was a little boy. . . . At first [I] thought that he was a man but he was not. He was a through [sic] little gentleman as well as always being clean and tidy. One day a little girl came by, and, as Willy liked her, he said, I like you. Will you be my sweetheart. Yes, I will she said. So they were married. It was a very funny marriage. Before the marriage they washed their faces in puddles. Each had a puddle for a bath. They were badly off for marriage. Goodbye children. Presented to Mother, June 25, 19[03?]." "Honeysuckle Fairies": "Presented to Mother. Fairies as I suppose you know are pretty little creatures. Some people don't believe in fairies, but I do. Do you? I like to believe in them, for when I have a sad or naughty feeling in my heart, I comfort me by drawing in my mind pictures of fairies. But these fairies belonged to honeysuckle. They smelt all over with honey suckle and everybody liked them and were delighted when they saw [them], when the fairies were dancing. They also ate honeysuckle berries which they enjoyed and what you would turn your nose up at. These honeysuckle fairies were dressed the colour of honeysuckle."

19. A. R. Orage (1873–1934) was the controversial editor from 1907 to 1922 of the socialist periodical the *New Age*, a weekly review of politics, arts, and letters. He also published her poetry in the *New English Weekly* when he served as editor (1932–1934).

20. Pitter, "Field Grasses," *New Age* 9, no. 2 (May 11, 1911): 29.

21. See her poems "Spring," *New Age* 15, no. 4 (May 28, 1914): 92; "The Debtor," *New Age* 25, no. 6 (June 5, 1919): 101; "Appraisement," *New Age* 26, no. 23 (Apr. 8, 1920): 363; "Sea-Herb," *New Age* 26, no. 25 (Apr. 22, 1920): 408; "Pastiche: In Praise," *New Age* 27, no. 1 (May 6, 1920): 16; "To the Beloved," *New Age* 27, no. 14 (Aug. 5, 1920): 220.

22. When "Song" was published in the *New Age* 11, no. 4 (May 23, 1912), "amorous" was replaced with "silently": "When I die, O joy! I shall shake off the heavy cold chain / Of the body: I shall speed over the wandering mist / That winds slow, slow, on the peaks all silently kissed / Into scarlet and gold by the sun—a cloud crowned train" (88).

23. Pitter, "Fairy-Gold," *New Age* 11, no. 8 (June 20, 1912): 184. It also appears in *First Poems* (London: Cecil Palmer, 1920), 3.

24. In total, over the next twenty years Orage published more than 150 of her poems. Others not appearing there were published in *First Poems*.

25. The poem to which he refers was later published as "Spring (Rondeau)," *New Age* 15, no. 4 (May 28, 1914): 92.

26. Pitter, "Fairy-Gold." *New Age* 11, no. 8 (June 20, 1912): 184; see also *First Poems*, 3.

27. Pitter, "To the People," *New Age* 9, no. 14 (Aug. 3, 1911): 332.

28. Pitter, "A Song of a Child's Happiness," *New Age* 10, no. 12 (Jan. 18, 1912): 268.

29. Pitter, "Spring (Rondeau)," *New Age* 15, no. 4 (May 28, 1914): 92.

30. Pitter, "The Earth and the Heaven, in the Evening," *New Age* 21, no. 21 (Sept. 20, 1917): 454.

31. Pitter, "Prayer for a Fair People," *New Age* 21, no. 23 (Oct. 4, 1917): 488.

32. Pitter, "Song (Grieve No More)," *New Age* 23, no. 15 (Aug. 8, 1918): 241.

33. Pitter, "Whom We Have Buried," *New Age* 25, no. 1 (May 1, 1919): 16. Later reprinted as "The Heavenly Love," *New Age* 26, no. 11 (Jan 15, 1920): 180.

34. Pitter, "Silence Shall Cover Thee," *New Age* 27, no. 6 (June 10, 1920): 83.

35. Pitter, "Of the Damned," *New Age* 27, no. 8 (June 24, 1920): 120.

36. Pitter, "The Debtor," *New Age* 25, no. 6 (June 5, 1919): 101.

37. Pitter, "The Oak Tree," *New Age* 23, no. 14 (Aug. 1, 1918): 221.

38. Pitter, "The Swan," *New Age* 23, no. 15 (Aug. 8, 1918): 244.

39. Pitter, "The Promised Rest," *New Age* 24, no. 10 (Jan. 9, 1919): 168.

40. Pitter, "Alone," *New Age* 26, no. 16 (Feb. 19, 1920): 260. Other of her poems in the *New Age* celebrating Hainault Forest include "Andante," *New Age* 26, no. 12 (Jan. 22, 1920): 196; "Be Dim, O Sanctuary," *New Age* 27, no. 7 (June 17, 1920): 109; and "Poverty Malcontent," *New Age* 32, no. 25 (Apr. 19, 1923): 403.

41. Versions of these fourteen poems appear in her manuscript notebooks covering 1912–1920.

42. "Recent Verse," *New Age* 26, no. 14 (Feb. 5, 1920): 225.

2. Artisan Poet, 1921–1931

1. In addition to Pitter's recollections of Orwell here, see Peter Stansky and William Abrahams, *The Unknown Orwell* (New York: Alfred A. Knopf, 1972), especially 221, 223–28, and 273–74.

2. BBC Radio, "Ruth Pitter's Personal Memories of George Orwell," Jan. 3, 1956.

3. Pitter's shorthand for Kathleen O'Hara.

4. Hilaire (Joseph Pierre) Belloc (1870–1953) was born in La Celle-Saint-Cloud, France, and later educated at the University of Oxford. He became a British subject in 1902, served in Parliament (1906–1910), and was a popular and prolific author. His early works include *Danton* (1899), *Robespierre* (1901), *The Path to Rome* (1902), and comic verse, including *The Bad Child's Book of Beasts* (1896) and *Cautionary Tales for Children* (1907).

5. *First and Second Poems: 1912–1925* (London: Sheed and Ward, 1927), 6; subsequent references in the text.

6. "A Classical Poet," review of *First and Second Poems: 1912–1925*, *Times Literary Supplement*, May 5, 1927, 316.

7. Gorham B. Munson, "Concerning Ruth Pitter," *Commonweal* 10 (Sept. 11, 1929): 472–75.

8. Richard Church, "Gold in the River Sands," review of *First and Second Poems: 1912–1925*. *Spectator* 144 (Apr. 5, 1930): 562.

9. Eda Walton, "A Seventeenth-Century Mind," *Nation* 131 (Oct. 8, 1930): 383.

10. First published in the *New Age* 28, no. 11 (Jan. 13, 1921): 132.

11. First published in the *New Age* 27, no. 1 (May 6, 1920): 16. Other blank verse poems are "The Human Spirit" (75–76), "To the Unknown Art" (77–78), "So Fair" (79), "Confusion" (80), "The Birds Mourning" (81), "The Unborn Ladies" (82), and "No Heroic Gestures" (83).

12. First published in the *New Age* 26, no. 25 (Apr. 22, 1920): 408. The other sonnets are "The Debtor" (84), "Sonnet" (86), and the three-sonnet sequence "Morning: Aphrodite" (87), "Noon: Demeter" (88), and "Night: Nameless" (89).

13. It is worth noting here that Orwell actually visited the cottage in Hainault Forest before Pitter's family stopped renting it. In "Ruth Pitter's Personal Memories of George Orwell" she recalls: "I have one memory of Orwell . . . at a place which he visited only once. This

was a small cottage in Essex which my family had as a week-end home for years. It was in the forest—there are considerable remnants of ancient forest in Essex, which of course are now piously preserved. The party consisted of Orwell, my brother, myself, and I think my mother. It was fine spring weather, and there were plenty of flowers; I think we were all happy.

14. She goes on to say in "Ruth Pitter's Personal Memories of George Orwell":

By this time Orwell had had several bouts of pneumonia, and I knew very well that he would never make old bones. I remember one perfectly horrible winter day with melting snow on the ground and an icy wind. Orwell had no proper overcoat, no hat, gloves, or muffler. I felt quite sure he was in what is called the pre-tubercular condition. And here he was, exposing himself to such weather in totally inadequate clothing. It wasn't just poverty. It was suicidal perversity. More than once I made an open attack on him, trying to get him to take proper advice and attend to his health. All in vain. He would never face the facts. On one occasion he *was* tested for TB, but the result proved negative, or so he said. He never had proper treatment until it was too late.

My mind is full of pictures of him on these various outings. There he is, sitting on the canal-bank, fishing, but shaking with silent laughter at something he has over-heard, as two woman pass behind him on the towpath. He leans in the twilight on the parapet of Chelsea Embankment, and says that the trees in Battersea Park, over the river, look very like the Burmese jungle. Sometimes he looks well, young and gay, sometimes quite grey and desperate. In the bus, I sneak the money for our fares into his hand. Ah, today he *has* some money—we have lunch in a restaurant, and even a bottle of wine. Now he is penniless again, and I treat him to a dinner; he is furious, until I remind him that he is the younger person and must put up with it. He gets a poorly-paid school-mastering job, then pneumonia defeats him again. He is helping a bookseller out Hampstead way, and there is a man, or rather a boy, whom he has met in those parts—a young Welshman, a poet, who has just come to London and is rather interesting and his name is Dylan Thomas.

15. *A Trophy of Arms*, 39. A version of this poem appears in Pitter's manuscript note-book dated 1930.

16. "Ruth Pitter Reading Her Poetry," recorded by Lee Anderson for Yale University, Apr. 26, 1960.

17. William Wordsworth, *The Prelude* (1805), book 11, lines 258–68, 274–76, in *William Wordsworth*, ed. Stephen Gill (Oxford: Oxford Univ. Press, 1984), 565.

18. Letter to Herbert Palmer, Nov. 14, 1936.

19. BBC Radio, "Romance," Sept. 4, 1963.

20. BBC Radio, "Ruth Pitter Talks to John Wain," Oct. 31, 1968.

21. BBC Radio, "Ruth Pitter Talks to Hallam Tennyson," Nov. 7, 1977.

22. *The Spirit Watches* (London: Cresset Press, 1939), 23. A version of this poem appears in Pitter's manuscript notebook dated 1937.

23. "Ruth Pitter Reading Her Poetry," recorded by Lee Anderson. In an earlier interview she put it this way:

There is a deep instinct, a biologically sound one, I think, in women's hearts—that in love they must be sought out. They have a right of veto, but they mustn't make ad-vances, even if they are deeply in love. In fact, the proof of a true lover is that he knows this and will discover their feelings however well they hide them. If he isn't interested enough to find out their secrets, he cannot be accepted. In this poem "If You Came," the woman is saying that she will surrender completely, but only if the lover can find out her hidden heart, which she conceals as jealously as a bird hides its nest in the woods. (BBC Radio, "Ruth Pitter Talks about Her Own Poems," July 19, 1955.)

24. *Persephone in Hades* (Auch, France: A. Sauriac, 1931), 1; subsequent references in the text.

3. Critical Acclaim, 1932–1937

1. John Edward Masefield (1878–1967) was a British poet, playwright, fiction writer, and poet laureate (1930–1967). His *Salt-Water Ballads* (1902) illustrated early his penchant for stories in verse, and his narrative poems included *The Everlasting Mercy* (1911) and *The Widow in the Bye Street* (1912). He was also the author of more than twenty volumes of fiction, which included novels, books for children, and collections of short stories; in addition, he wrote several historical books and seventeen plays in prose and verse. Walter de la Mare (1873–1956) was a British novelist and essayist, perhaps best known for his poetry and verse for children; his works include *Songs of Childhood* (1902), *The Listeners and Other Poems* (1912), *Peacock Pie* (1913), a play entitled *Crossings* (1921), *Memoirs of a Midget* (1921), *The Riddle, and Other Stories* (1923), *Broomsticks, and Other Tales* (1925), *Stuff and Nonsense* (1927), *Poems for Children* (1930), *The Wind Blows Over* (1936), *Behold, This Dreamer* (1939), *The Burning Glass* (1945), *The Traveller* (1946), *Collected Stories for Children* (1947), *Inward Companion* (1950), *O Lovely England* (1953).

2. Australian Vance Palmer (1885–1959) was a prominent essayist and novelist whose early friendship with A. R. Orage and the *New Age* may have been Pitter's initial connection to him. His wife, Nettie Palmer, née Higgins (1885–1964), was also a prolific writer, and the author of *Modern Australian Literature: 1900–23* (1924). Their marriage has been widely hailed as the most significant partnership in Australian literary history.

3. To Belloc she adds a year later: "I am so sorry the slump caught you. We are doing pretty well by dint of working 12 hours a day for months on end: but the sanguinary dog-fight of commerce in these times has me heartscalded" (Dec. 8, 1933).

4. In her manuscript notebook for poems covering 1927–1934, she writes in August 1934: "But in these three years [1932–1934] I have written little and preserved less, except the poems in 'Mad Lady's Garland'—something, after all. Commerce is not merely a living death, but an earthly hell."

5. From 1922 to 1930, Orage was under the influence of P. D. Ouspensky and G. I. Gurdjieff, mystical spiritual gurus. Orage left London in 1922 to attend Gurdjieff's Institute for the Harmonious Development of Man in Fontainebleau, France. From 1924 to 1930 Orage was in New York to help Gurdjieff spread his work. Tiring of his work and somewhat disillusioned with Gurdjieff, Orage returned to England in 1930. For more on Orage, see Philip Mairet, *A. R. Orage: A Memoir* (London: Dent, 1936; New York: University Books, 1966); C. S. Nott, *Teachings of Gurdjieff: The Journal of a Pupil; An Account of Some Years with G. I. Gurdjieff and A. R. Orage in New York and at Fontainebleau-Avon* (London: Rout-ledge & Kegan Paul, 1969); and Louise Welch, *Orage with Gurdjieff in America* (Boston: Routledge & Kegan Paul, 1982). Just how much affection Pitter still retained for Orage is revealed in this excerpt from a letter to Nettie Palmer: "Mr. Orage . . . and his charming American wife, are neighbours at present, and we see them fairly often. They have a nice little boy of three. I don't know how Orage would strike me if I met him now for the first time, but having known him since I was 14, I have no objective consciousness of him, and take him for granted, like a Heavenly Body" (Nov. 28, 1932).

6. *A Mad Lady's Garland* (London: Cresset Press, 1934).

7. Perhaps influenced by Virgil's *Eclogae*, a series of short bucolic poems usually in the form of a dialogue. The mock tone of this poem is repeated throughout *A Mad Lady's Garland*.

8. First published in the *New English Weekly* 2, no. 10 (Dec. 22, 1932): 237. Reprinted in *A Mad Lady's Garland*, 5–6, and in *On Cats* (London: Cresset Press, 1946), 32–33; subsequent references to *A Mad Lady's Garland* in the text. The original version of the poem uses archaic spelling, perhaps to intimate authenticity; I use here (and for the other poems discussed below) the modernized spelling of the version published in *A Mad Lady's Garland*.

9. This letter is available in Pitter's uncataloged papers.

10. Belloc's quick liking for the poem suggests there was always something in Pitter's poetry that he admired, even when he did not know she was the author. On the postcard that Belloc sent Orage, who then forwarded it to Pitter, she appended the following at a later date: "This poem appeared over a pseudonym. My first profane piece. Jolly good, too. It was in 'Olde Englysshe' to make it funnier. You see? [Belloc] had no idea who had written it. People said Orage never printed a good poem. He did—this one."

11. Pitter was singularly fortunate to have both Orage and Belloc as advocates. About her distaste for promoting her own work, she wrote Nettie Palmer: "The books I have had published have only appeared through the good offices of Orage and Belloc, who push me along in a bathchair. I never do anything about it, having a squeamish horror of muscling in on the dirty racket. . . . My best line is to keep my head down. It sounds feeble, and I know I ought to fight, but I'm a calcium deficient: and so I've never been in a publisher's or newspaper office, but stay in the cold studio and suck the chilblains on my fingers" (Apr. 19, 1933). To Belloc, she added: "It seems to me that I am horribly lazy and selfish not to see about getting my own books published. After all, why should I spend all my time money-grubbing and expect my betters to do my dirty work? Honestly, I do know a little more about such things now, and as you are busy I very earnestly ask that you will return the poems and let me have a shot at the publishers myself. It's so bad for one to be spoon-fed like this: would you believe it. I have never been in a publisher's or newspaper office in my life?" (Dec. 8, 1933). In letters to Belloc leading up to the publication of *A Mad Lady's Garland* Pitter revealed that she did get more involved, corresponding with various editors and personnel at Cresset Press. Two items generated much discussion: first, whether the archaic spellings used in the *New English Weekly* versions of the poems would be reproduced in the book (Belloc favored this); they were not. Second was whether Pitter herself would provide illustrations for some of the poems; she did not, nor did any appear in the book.

12. First published in the *New English Weekly* 2, no. 18 (Feb. 16, 1933): 429.

13. A poem with a similar though less lethal persona is "The Matron-Catts Song," *New English Weekly* 3, no. 1 (Apr. 1933): 22–23. Reprinted in *A Mad Lady's Garland*, and in *On Cats*, 34–36. I discuss it later in chapter 6.

14. First published as "The Earwig's Complaint," *New English Weekly* 2, no. 13 (Jan. 12, 1933): 308–9.

15. First published in the *New English Weekly* 5, no. 11 (June 28, 1934): 252. Some readers may hear in this poem an echo to Andrew Marvell's "worms will try thy long preserv'd virginity" in "To His Coy Mistress."

16. The passage in 1 Corinthians 15:35–42 is worth quoting in full:

But some man will say, How are the dead raised up? and with what body do they come? Thou fool, that which thou sowest is not quickened, except it die: And that which thou sowest, thou sowest not that body that shall be, but bare grain, it may chance of wheat, or of some other grain: But God giveth it a body as it hath pleased him, and to every seed his own body. All flesh is not the same flesh: but there is one kind of flesh of men, another flesh of beasts, another of fishes, and another of birds. There are also celestial bodies, and bodies terrestrial: but the glory of the celestial is one, and the glory of the terrestrial is another. There is one glory of the sun, and another glory of the moon, and another glory of the stars: for one star differeth from another star in glory. So also is the resurrection of the dead. It is sown in corruption; it is raised in incorruption.

But there is no promise of resurrection in the poem. With a view limited to enjoying and consuming the flesh of the dead man, the philosopher worm cannot know whether the man will be raised "imperishable." He can only claim, and that without substantiation, that the imperishable part of the man will find peace from love. In fact, the soul of the man, his "imperishable part," is of little interest to the worm. For him it is all about flesh.

17. Christ is often linked to the phoenix, further enhancing the idea of never-ending love. For instance, according to Oliver F. Emerson, "The likeness of the Phoenix to Christ appears, perhaps first, in the Greek *Physiologus*." See his "Originality in Old English Poetry," *Review of English Studies* 2 (January 1926): 31.

18. First published in the *New English Weekly* 4, no. 23 (Mar. 22, 1934): 546.

19. First published in the *New English Weekly* 3, no. 24 (Sept. 28, 1933): 573.

20. A poem with a similar self-righteous persona is "The Pious Lady Trout" (59–60). Here a smug, vain, self-congratulatory trout brags of her happy state in the clear stream she enjoys, confident this means "Providence hath destined me the whole / Large kingdom and gay court of Paradise, / Meet for a lady beautiful and wise." In fact, her primary source of food is, for her, proof positive she enjoys the good favor of heaven: "How am I fed? . . . / [On the flies] those sinners of the air / That off this element presume to get; / So piously I purge the gentle sky / Of nasty atomies that dare to fly." A poem that is almost a companion piece is "The Mayfly" (61–62). There a slightly melancholic fly stoically notes that it only lives a day, as "yon greedy trout hath had / Ten [of us] with no labour." He calls upon his beloved to "love me while yet I shine / In my best feather, / And for grief's anodyne / We'll die together."

21. First published in the *New English Weekly* 4, no. 10 (Dec. 21, 1933): 236–37.

22. First published in the *New English Weekly* 5, no. 6 (May 24, 1934): 132–33.

23. If Pitter also had in mind political rescue, she could not have anticipated how ineffective the British government would be in dealing with the growing European threat of fascism and its most terrible face, Nazi Germany.

24. She writes Nettie Palmer:

Thank you, really and truly, for your quotation from T. S. Eliot on the distinction between "philosophic belief" and "poetic assent." My mind has been thirsting for it for years: hurrah! How can it be (says I) that while I could not assent to any dogmatic religion, I read the Bible with "trusting tears?" (Blunden). While I can admire "The Golden Bough" as a monument to the noblest sincerity, and yet can say "I *know* that my Redeemer liveth"? Have you ever noticed how human thought fetches up in complete paradox, insoluble paradox: the scientific versus the religious? Long since, I have thought this must be simply the result of the eternal duality of our consciousness: everything in pairs of opposites: life and death, night and day, good and bad, male and female: and then recalled the Bhagavad-Gita: "It is desire, it is wrath, born of the duality of opposites: the steadfast one marvelleth not thereat." So the poetic assent fits me: I shall not be numbered either with the cruel dogmatists or with the foolish unbelievers. (Apr. 19, 1933)

Later she tells Belloc: "I do not claim the Beatific Vision, but of its 'endless variety' there can naturally, I think, be no question, though it must simultaneously appear One and indivisible: it seems to me that at the summits of human experience there is always a Paradox: external truth probably shows thus in terms of our dualistic consciousness: as the certain knowledge of death versus the certain knowledge of immortality. I like St. Paul on this" (June 13, 1935).

25. John Masefield wrote an introduction to the American edition in which he noted Pitter's originality, her deft but gentle satire, and her delicate ear for cadence; in particular, he praised "Fowls Celestial and Terrestrial": "A serious poem of much beauty and delicacy, of the birds of the poets. . . . These four birds of romance are by her again touched with beauty and strangeness, so that they become alive in our imaginations and dwell with us as creatures of delight." See *A Mad Lady's Garland* (New York: Macmillan, 1935), viii. In a letter to Belloc on Apr. 9, 1935, she explains how Masefield got involved:

A week or two ago I had the happiness of receiving a very kind letter from Mr. Masefield, praising the "Garland." This led to my visiting him, and when he heard that no New York publisher would accept the book, he at once wrote to Macmillan's, who took it forthwith. Now as it is some months since the book was published here, Macmillan's say that to satisfy a point of law it must include some new material, and Mr. Masefield has offered to do a special preface for the American edition. Shall you mind? I related to Mr. Masefield the story of your unflagging championship of my work, a championship which must now be almost twenty years old, and he exclaimed "Good old Belloc!" with enthusiasm. They were rather taken aback to find I had never been to college (having regard to the classical tags in the book) but I hastened to explain that the "Garland" had about cleared me out of my Latinity, and would necessitate my laying in a fresh stock.

26. An Irish poet, painter, and playwright who lived from 1867 to 1935, AE, like his countryman and friend W. B. Yeats, was inclined toward the mystical and supernatural. One critic claims that "the key to AE's life is the fact that he had elected to be a student of esoteric wisdom, and that his interests in literature, in poetry, in painting and in practical affairs were all to a large extent rooted in this original impulse." See Monk Gibbon, foreword to *Letters from AE*, by George William Russell, ed. Alan Denson (London: Abelard-Schuman, 1961), xv.

27. This material appears in a promotional flyer for the volume; a copy is available in Pitter's uncataloged papers.

28. Pitter herself was heartened by the initial reviews. Writing to Belloc, she says: "Heartfelt thanks for your most kind and cheering letter. Do you really think the book has won though? The publishers have certainly been most energetic in pushing it, and I think it is a beautiful job of printing" (Oct. 5, 1934).

29. "Wit-Melancholy," review of *A Mad Lady's Garland*. *Times Literary Supplement*, Oct. 4, 1934:670.

30. Richard Church, "A Disciple of Aesop," review of *A Mad Lady's Garland*. *Christian Science Monitor*, Nov. 21, 1934:12.

31. Michael Roberts, "Satire Stays at Home," *Spectator* 154 (Jan. 25, 1935): 132.

32. William Benét, review of *A Mad Lady's Garland*, *Saturday Review of Literature* 13 (Nov. 30, 1935): 16.

33. D. G. Bridson, "An English Eccentric," review of *A Mad Lady's Garland*. *Poetry: A Magazine of Verse* 47 (Nov. 1935): 103.

34. Percy Hutchison, review of *A Mad Lady's Garland*. *New York Times Book Review*, Dec. 1, 1935:35.

35. The favorable critical success of Pitter's poetry even before the publication of *A Mad Lady's Garland* led to invitations to contribute some of the poems to contemporary anthologies. To such an invitation from Alida Monro, Pitter wrote: "I am sending under separate cover all copies of 'The New English Weekly' containing anything of mine, with the exception of 'Matron Cat' and 'Portrait of a Gentleman.' . . . I am afraid the affected archaic style won't be much to your purpose, but I have not ventured to make any selection myself. . . . With many thanks for your kind notice, and assuring you that I shall be flattered to appear in your anthology" (Sept. 23, 1933). See Alida Monro, ed., *Recent Poetry, 1923–1933* (London: Gerald Howe and the Poetry Bookshop, 1933).

36. Although Pitter dates this letter July 14, 1934, she must have made an error since in the letter itself she tells Belloc she is going to visit AE on "1st July." Accordingly, I date the letter June 14, 1934.

37. The details of this recollection are available in Russell, *Letters from AE*, 239–40.

38. Russell, *Letters from AE*, 212–14. Later she wrote a poem honoring AE that appears in her manuscript notebook for 1934–1944, "A. E., The Apple-Tree; written Nov. 1934." It was later published as "The Apple Tree" in *A Trophy of Arms*, 66.

39. On December 27, 1934, Pitter writes Belloc about her visit:

He is a cloud-cuckoo too, but a very charming one, and it was prime to "go down to the strand and wade in the tide" with him, or to sit over the turf fire in the twilight and to be *almost* carried away by the enchantment of his Druidic voice. Never quite carried away—my 50% and more of French blood rejects enchantment as the last impertinence, and just when my Irish blood is mounting strongly towards Cloud-Cuckoo-land, the former hisses in my ear *"un tas de vicilles pommes cuikes!"* [a pile of old cooked apples] and Deirdre & Co. are done for. It is very sad, really, not to be able to get intoxicated on the Heeroes, the Champeens, the Goold, Jools, Chawyots, and other trappings of Celtic magnificence. God forgive me, for I love AE. dearly for the good decent man and the Sage that he certainly is. And I shall go again if I get the chance, like a shot!

To Nettie Palmer she adds:

I spent a fortnight with AE in Donegal last summer, and got petrified with his talk. I never knew anyone else who could talk for sixteen hours at a stretch, and yet never talk nonsense. . . . But don't think that anything will keep me out of Donegal, all the same! What a rocky coast, what air, what colours! I have to pull AE's leg about the Celtic twilight, but he says he'll have me seeing fairies yet. You see, I over-indulged in them when young, and now find them repulsive. . . . If you come to London we are sure to meet. AE says the right people always meet by spiritual gravitation. (Mar. 4, 1935)

40. Pitter writes Belloc on Apr. 9, 1935: "The Garland is getting on for the end of the first 1,000." A month later she adds: "I believe the Cresset Press intends (eventually) to publish my collected poems, including 'First and Second' and 'Persephone'" (May 14, 1935). Cresset did not.

41. In her manuscript notebook for 1934–1944, the poem is titled "A. R. Orage, died November 6, 1934."

42. In later letters, she writes about her feelings for Orage:

So many brilliant people loved to work for him for nothing. It was because they loved him: and they loved him because he made everyone feel of some importance & significance—listened as though one's words were worth listening to, and put just the right questions. Many loved him too much, so that it distorted their lives. His women did him no credit, but that was because he was so attractive that they got perfectly senseless about him: he was never free to choose: the most ruthless one got him, until knocked off by one still more implacable. I simply pined with love for him from the age of 14 to 18, but no one ever suspected it. (Letter to Nettie Palmer, May 15, 1946)

My first impression of Orage was that he was the possessor of a devastating charm. I was only fourteen, and it quite bowled me over. What a sophisticated person might have thought, I cannot say. . . . As I became adult, I grew more and more doubtful, without losing any of the admiration and affection I had felt at first. I came to think it one of those cases where a man misses and falls short solely for want of material, relevant material: the technique of reference, the actual connections with better-informed persons, the mere sophistication that a university and a wider acquaintance with the world might have supplied. Of his ability there could be no doubt; but the plant needed a bigger pot. Mind you, I say all this from the standpoint of the under-privileged, not having been properly educated myself; and without grudging any of the very great gratitude I felt and still feel. (Letter to W. Martin, Feb. 28, 1960)

Later she recalls:

Orage was very good at publishing young writers. He encouraged many of us to go on and think it worthwhile to go on. . . . And my father—as a cat will take a kitten in its mouth and exhibit its kitten to its owners—my father took me and exhibited me to Orage, a not at all discreet thing to do. But . . . Orage was so kind and good and my mother took me down for a weekend to where Orage was living in the country. Dear me, with a lady [Beatrice Hastings] he wasn't married to. My poor mother! And such an exciting lady too, so exotic in her dress and ways. I was struck all of a heap. I think I was more struck than the lady and the gentleman, and they said could I go and stay with them in the holidays. My mother said no quite firmly. It was my first quarrel with my poor, dear mother. (BBC Radio, "Ruth Pitter Talks to Hallam Tennyson," Nov. 7, 1977)

In still another letter to Nettie Palmer she says:

As to Orage, he is rarely heard of since his death. None of his friends are now in the swim—all our fashionable writers are of a different provenance. Of course his own origins partly explain this: I mean that a man who goes through the schools & universities is automatically orientated to current thought, & Orage was never brought in that way. I think, too, that philosophically he was an end product of that liberal humanism which has now gone down the drain. I'd like to know how he would have reacted to the strong & growing present tendency towards orthodox Christianity. The last 15 years have seen an unbelievable change there: and when I think of his many & various excursions after strange gods, I wish he hadn't died so soon: Social Credit was no tune to march out to. Some of us called him our catalyst. He brought out the best in others, without himself producing (I think) one work of importance. (Jan. 22, 1946)

43. In a telling letter to Nettie Palmer, Pitter contrasts herself with Pamela Travers, the pen name of Helen Lyndon Goff, the author of *Mary Poppins* (1934), whose early poetry had been published by Orage in the *New Age*:

She is a most warm-hearted creature, swift in all feeling, and a good poet too. There is a very great difference between us, though. She is purely good natured, while I (to quote AE) am the best-natured ill-natured woman on earth. This means that in matters where Pamela is starry with conviction and bright with a brave joy, I am inclined to murmur *surtout point de zéle*. It's the difference between her Leo and my Scorpio, her sun and my Saturn, her Irish blood and my French, her constitution (inclined to T.B., living in the moment) and mine (subnormal temperature, non-impulsive, great tenacity of life). I think I repel her a little at times. She worships a lovely duality, I an eternal unity. She sees the full beauty of life in its dazzling changes: I see it where "there is no change, neither the shadow of turning." For her, birth is the divine comedy, and death the eternal tragedy, while I delight not much in the one, nor am dismayed at the other. But I envy her, as I envy all warmth and brightness. She has more courage in her little finger than I have in all my dense body. (Mar. 4, 1935)

44. To Belloc she confides:

I have tried not to dry up, especially as the Cresset Press wants to publish my Collected Poems next—I don't know when. This is some inducement to write, but it *is* hard, with Atra Cura digging her hatpins into one all the time, as she does to all who are engaged in trade. A paid job, even a mean one, even where one is oppressed, is really less worrying, I think. I should like it to be written on my tomb that I worked an average of at least ten hours a day and paid my debts with rigid punctuality, as I feel that this is my chief claim to honour among mankind: but if only one had not to be so preoccupied with it! It shuts one out from the land of the living. But I am equal to it. (Dec. 27, 1934)

45. Pamela Travers, also a friend to AE, writes Pitter: "He is dead. He died last night soon after eleven o'clock. . . . The night was beautiful, full moon, that always affected him so strongly and his own planets, Jupiter and Venus so high and full and the sky so lofty over the sea. Such a night to set out! All my good has come from him. I feel in a way lost and orphaned as one never was by parents. But at the same time so humbly proud to have known such a soul" (July 18, 1935).

46. In an interesting series of letters, Pitter asks Belloc to assist her in getting a meager royalty payment for *First and Second Poems* from Sheed and Ward. It soon becomes obvious that Belloc had actually borne the cost for publishing the volume. He graciously offers to give her a check for approximately £32 that he had received from Sheed and Ward covering what he assumed were some of the costs he had incurred in financing *First and Second Poems*. She writes him on September 14, 1936:

It was infamously done to send me this money, and I think you ought to ask my pardon. I said quite plainly in my letter that there was no self-interest in my enquiry, and I repeat that my concern was solely that you should be reimbursed as far as possible for your outlay in so generously financing the publication of the book. You promised to let me know whether S. & W. had made any kind of settlement with you, and after the lapse of some months I took the liberty of reminding you. I felt your expenditure as (in a way) a personal debt owing from me to you, and was anxious, on account of this sense of financial indebtedness. I don't suppose for a moment that the amount of the cheque covers your outlay, let alone showing a profit. But I am glad that some repayment was made to you. How could you!

47. It appears Pitter did send Belloc poems and prose for *G. K.'s Weekly* but he deemed them not useable because of space constraints.

48. *New English Weekly* 1, no. 12 (July 7, 1932): 279. Reprinted in A *Trophy of Arms* (London: Cresset Press, 1936), 41–42; subsequent references in the text.

49. After describing how he will go to Innisfree and build a small cabin "of clay and wattles," Yeats ends his poem: "I will arise and go now, for always night and day / I hear lake water lapping with low sounds by the shore; / While I stand on the roadway, or on the pavements grey, / I hear it in the deep heart's core."

50. See Thomas H. Johnson, ed., *Final Harvest: Emily Dickinson's Poems* (New York: Little, Brown, 1961), 229. "The Viper" was first published in the *New English Weekly* 4, no. 12 (Jan. 4, 1934): 276.

51. First published in the *New English Weekly* 1, no. 12 (July 7, 1932): 279.

52. First published in the *New English Weekly* 4, no. 12 (Jan. 4, 1934): 275.

53. First published in the *New English Weekly* 1, no. 18 (Aug. 18, 1932): 425.

54. Some readers may hear an echo to George Herbert's "Easter Wings" in Pitter's phrase "swift fall wings the ascent."

55. First published in the *New English Weekly* 1, no. 12 (July 7, 1932): 279.

56. Also explicitly religious is "My God Beholds Me," 69–73. Subtitled "Hymns to the Noumenon," this poem traces Pitter's movement from disgust with those who either abuse or reject the idea of God to affirmation that none will be rejected by God. She employs biblical motifs, ideas, and phrases, but the unifying idea is that God beholds all and is ultimately benevolent.

57. First published as "Silence," *Atlantic Monthly* 144 (July 1929): 38.

58. First published in the *New English Weekly* 8, no. 3 (Oct. 31, 1935): 51.

59. First published in the *New English Weekly* 1, no. 7 (June 2, 1932): 169.

60. Perhaps appropriately, Pitter died on February 29, 1992.

61. Stephens, an Irish poet and fiction writer (1882–1950), had his first volume of poetry, *Insurrections*, appear in 1909. Later volumes include *Songs from the Clay* (1915) and *Kings and the Moon* (1938). He is best remembered for his prose writings in which he celebrated Irish legend and folklore, including *The Crock of Gold* (1912), *The Demi-Gods* (1914), *Irish Fairy Tales* (1920), *Deirdre* (1923), and *In the Land of Youth* (1924).

62. John Gawsworth, review of A *Trophy of Arms*, *New English Weekly*, Sept. 24, 1936.

63. Hilaire Belloc, "Two Poets," review of A *Trophy of Arms* and A. E. Housman's *More Poems*, *G. K.'s Weekly*, Oct. 26, 1936:146. He continues: "But the artistic mood of the day is not on that side, any more than it is on the side of gaiety, which is the natural fruit of the old religion. It is on the side of fatigued negation."

64. Eda Walton, "Miss Ruth Pitter's Poems," review of A *Trophy of Arms*, *Times Literary Supplement*, Oct. 3, 1936:784.

65. Dilys Powell, "Ruth Pitter's New Poems," *London Mercury*, 34 (Oct. 1936): 559.

66. Michael Roberts, "The Eternal Fog," *Spectator*, 157 (Oct. 16, 1936): 652.

67. Siegfried Sassoon, "Two Poets," review of *A Trophy of Arms*. *New Statesman & Nation* 12 (Dec. 19, 1936): 1034. In earlier letters to Pitter, Sassoon is highly complimentary. In a letter of October 22, 1936, he writes: "Please allow me to congratulate you on your beautiful book of poems. Until I bought 'A Trophy of Arms' I was entirely unaware of the existence of your exquisite work; but when I read 'Sudden Heaven' I felt so grateful to you that I hasten to thank you. . . . Hoping that this letter will give you a little pleasure." Two months later, after his review of *A Trophy of Arms* appeared, he writes: "It was a great privilege to be able to praise your poems in print—a proud & pleasant privilege, in fact, to continue the alliteration! Your poems have qualities which I admire so deeply & gratefully. What I wrote about them was like a well meaning elephant in a garden. . . . I only hope that my review has helped to make you more widely appreciated. . . . I very much hope to meet you one of these days" (Dec. 22).

68. Dallas Kenmare, "The Triumph of 'Pure Poetry,'" *Poetry Review* (1937): 373–80.

69. Edward Christian David (Gascoyne) Cecil was a fellow of Wadham College, Oxford, 1924–1930; a fellow of New College, 1939–1969 (emeritus fellow 1970–1986); and Goldsmith Professor of English Literature (1948–1969).

70. Along with her husband, Philip E. Morrell, Lady Ottoline Violet Anne Morrell (1873–1938) was patron to a circle of notable intellectuals, artists, and writers that included Bertrand Russell, D. H. Lawrence, and W. B. Yeats.

71. Herbert Edward Palmer (1880–1961), an earnest if unappreciated poet, often wrote Pitter about his frustrations related to getting his poetry published and recognized. She writes him on November 14, 1936: "As for selling yourself: have we any right to expect this? We write because we must, but the public owes us no obligation, and any praise or reward we reap is a gift from Heaven, not our just due. . . . Do not be discouraged that you are tired, and feel insufficiently recognized. You are widely known: and there is no stage of life at which a blessed expansion and fulfillment are not possible."

72. Edward Shanks won the initial award in 1919 for *The Queen of China*. Later winners included Edmund Blunden for *The Shepherd* (1922), Sean O'Casey for *Juno and the Paycock* (1925), Virginia Sackville-West for *The Land* (1926), Siegfried Sassoon for *Memoirs of a Fox-Hunting Man* (1928), Lord David Cecil for *The Stricken Deer* (1929), James Hilton for *Lost Horizon* (1934), Evelyn Waugh for *Edmund Campion* (1936), David Jones for *In Parenthesis* (1938), Graham Greene for *The Power and the Glory* (1941), and Ted Hughes for *Lupercal* (1961).

73. Hassall won the award himself in 1939 for *Penthesperon*.

74. Cited in Peter Dickinson, "Ruth Pitter," *Canadian C. S. Lewis Journal* 79 (Summer 1992): 1–3.

4. War Watches, 1938–1941

1. Pitter kept a journal notebook during this holiday. Even though the notebook containing these notes indicates the trip was taken during August 1937, Pitter's stamped passport confirms this trip was actually taken in August of 1938.

2. Walter de la Mare, *Behold, This Dreamer!* (London: Faber & Faber, 1939).

3. De la Mare included "The Unicorn" (658–59) and "Sudden Heaven" (655–56).

4. *Virginia Quarterly Review* 15 (1939): 246–48.

5. *The Spirit Watches* (London: Cresset Press, 1939).

6. *The Spirit Watches*, 10–11; subsequent references in the text.

7. "The wind bloweth where it listeth, and thou hearest the sound thereof, but canst not tell whence it cometh, and whither it goeth: so is every one that is born of the Spirit."

8. First published in the *London Mercury* 39 (Mar. 1939): 512–13.

9. First published in the *London Mercury* 35 (Feb. 1937): 358–59.

10. First published in the *London Mercury* 37 (Nov. 1937): 8.

11. First published in the *Virginia Quarterly Review* 15 (1939): 247.

12. Other divine agents she might have used here are Urania (the queen of the Muses) or Mercury (the messenger of the gods).

13. First published in the *Virginia Quarterly Review* 15 (1939): 248.

14. *Norton Anthology of English Literature*, 8th ed. (New York: W. W. Norton, 2006), 2:92.

15. Stephen Spender, review of *The Spirit Watches*, *New Statesman & Nation* 18 (Dec. 9, 1939): 834. Pitter expressed her pique upon hearing about Spender's review to Herbert Palmer: "I have not seen Spender's review in the Statesman, but I am told it is very hostile, and gives a list of those who like my work, as if these names alone were enough to render it contemptible. I begin to think that these Reds are *paid* to attack anything which attempts to glorify God" (Dec. 20, 1939).

16. Desmond Hawkins, "Recent Verse," review of *The Spirit Watches*, *Spectator* 163 (Dec. 15, 1939): 876.

17. "The Watching Spirit," review of *The Spirit Watches*, *Times Literary Supplement*, Dec. 23, 1939:746.

18. Eric Forbes-Boyd, "Two English Poets," review of *The Spirit Watches*, *Christian Science Monitor*, Feb. 24, 1940:11.

19. Louise Bogan, review of *The Spirit Watches*, *New Yorker* 16 (Apr. 20, 1940): 92.

20. Review of *The Spirit Watches*, *Christian Century* 57 (Apr. 24, 1940): 547.

21. Louis Untermeyer, "Exquisite and Stern," review of *The Spirit Watches*. *Saturday Review of Literature* 22 (July 20, 1940): 10.

22. May Sarton, "Two Poets: W. B. Yeats and Ruth Pitter," *University Review (Kansas City)*, Oct. 1940:63–65.

23. Other generally positive reviews include that published in the *Catholic World* 151 (Aug. 1940): 630; Lawrence Lee's "The Extension of Poetry in Time," *Virginia Quarterly Review* 16 (Summer 1940): 481–84; and Roberta T. Swartz's review in *Poetry: A Magazine of Verse* 56 (Sept. 1940): 334–37.

24. These journal notes cover Saturday, Mar. 9, through Wednesday, Mar. 20, 1940, and appear in a thin olive-colored notebook.

25. Illustrating the character of their friendship, Pitter ends the letter: "Kathleen O'Hara sends kindest regards to you and to the family. When the days are longer we should dearly like to run down to Oxford and see you all. It must be exciting to have the child speaking. Please give my greetings to your wife."

26. *The Rude Potato* (London: Cresset Press, 1941).

27. On Apr. 16 she had written to Cecil: "What sounds like a large bomb has just gone off fairly close, and the news is fierce and implacable. But I have sown my onions and dug up hundredweights of weeds, and am well forward with the greenstuffs (what an extraordinary number of varieties there are in the cabbage family!) so I shall sleep in spite of all."

28. She writes Cecil on July 17: "I had a day out last Saturday . . . reading to the local branch of the Poetry Society (This body makes me feel uncomfortable. It is by far the largest organization devoted only to poetry: it is all alive-o, and holds its competitions, and runs its journal, through thick and thin: but it breathes a parochial rather than a Parnassian air, and I would rather have the twelve most crabbed of all our dons, and critics, and writers

combined into a society to castigate me, than all the laurels of this great concourse: but it has to be reckoned with.). I must say I enjoyed myself, as I always do when I can get anyone to listen to my stuff."

29. Pitter later arranged for the following inscription to be cut into her mother's oak tombstone in the churchyard of Black Chapel, the church near Oak Cottage:

Louisa Rosamund Pitter
Widow of George Pitter
Died 7 October, 1941, aged 71
A Seeker After God
And he shall be as the light of the morning, when the sun riseth, even a morning without clouds; as the tender grass springing out of the earth by clear shining after rain. 2 Sam. XXIII.4

Although the cost of this inscription was great, Pitter explained: "As my mother chose the text before her death, I feel that it would not be right to change it" (letter to Brown & Son, June 13, 1950).

30. *The Rude Potato*, 1; subsequent references in the text.

31. If but some vengeful god would call to me
From up the sky, and laugh: "Thou suffering thing,
Know that thy sorrow is my ecstasy,
That thy love's loss is my hate's profiting!"

Then would I bear it, clench myself, and die,
Steeled by the sense of ire unmerited;
Half-eased in that a Powerfuller than I
Had willed and meted me the tears I shed.

But not so. How arrives it joy lies slain,
And why unblooms the best hope ever sown?
—Crass Casualty obstructs the sun and rain,
And dicing Time for gladness casts a moan. . . .
These purblind Doomsters had as readily strown
Blisses about my pilgrimage as pain. (*The Norton Anthology of English Literature*, 2:1868)

5. Crossing Over, 1942–1946

1. She adds: "I hear that Sir R. Storrs had the temerity to read 'The Weed' aloud to the Princess Royal. It comforts me a good deal that you do not seem to think the 'Potato' nasty."

2. In this letter she also congratulates the Cecils on the birth of their second child, Hugh. She ends her letter by thanking Cecil for his unflagging support: "Believe me, I am very grateful for your continual advocacy of my work, a kindness I cannot repay. I can only call down blessings on the heads of you and yours, and hope you will realize your own inmost wishes."

3. BBC Radio, "Ruth Pitter's Personal Memories of George Orwell," Jan. 3, 1956.

4. Dorothy Violet Wellesley, Duchess of Wellington (1889–1956), published selections of her poems beginning in 1913. *Early Light*, her collected poems, appeared in 1955.

5. Lewis's broadcasts began on August 6, 1941, and continued on and off until Apr. 4, 1944. Generally given in a fifteen-minute format, there were actually four series of talks: "Broadcast Talks" (Aug. 1941), "The Case for Christianity" (Jan.–Feb. 1942), "Christian Behavior" (Sept.–Nov. 1942), and "Beyond Personality" (Feb.–Apr. 1944). For complete information on the talks and their relationship to Mere Christianity, see Jeffrey Schultz and John West, eds., The C. S. Lewis Readers' Encyclopedia (Grand Rapids, MI: Zondervan, 1998), 270–73.

6. While it is not possible to date this reference precisely, I suggest Mar. 1943, when Pitter confessed being at her "lowest ebb" to Cecil.

7. BBC Radio, "Ruth Pitter Talks to Stephen Black," June 24, 1955.

8. "The Poet Speaks," Mar. 24, 1964.

9. BBC Radio, "Ruth Pitter Talks to John Wain," Oct. 31, 1968.

10. BBC Radio, "Ruth Pitter Talks to Hallam Tennyson," Nov. 7, 1977.

11. The Bridge: Poems 1939–1944 (London: Cresset Press, 1945).

12. The Bridge, 7; subsequent references in the text.

13. For example, see Romans 6:3–5: "Know ye not, that so many of us as were baptized into Jesus Christ were baptized into his death? Therefore we are buried with him by baptism into death: that like as Christ was raised up from the dead by the glory of the Father, even so we also should walk in newness of life. For if we have been planted together in the likeness of his death, we shall be also in the likeness of his resurrection."

14. Since France surrendered on June 22, 1940, we can reasonably date the poem to the early days of the war, sometime shortly after this catastrophe. Pitter's MS notebook gives the date of the poem as 1940.

15. First published in the Virginia Quarterly Review 16 (1940): 380.

16. First published in the Virginia Quarterly Review 16 (1940): 381. While I do not deny this poem can be read as simply a wonderfully detailed description of a swan bathing, I suspect something else is also at work; that is, Pitter is exploring via her poem the sensual relationship of two lovers. While she would never write explicitly about this, in her verse she can offer veiled commentary on a physical relationship between a man and a woman.

17. First published in the Poetry Review 32, no. 2 (Mar.–Apr. 1941): 75–76.

18. "From Death to Life," review of The Bridge, Times Literary Supplement, Apr. 7, 1945:164. In his Four Living Poets (Santa Barbara, CA: Unicorn Press, 1944), Rudolph Gilbert had anticipated this reviewer, calling Pitter "the poet of purity" and noting, "What the poetry reader values most in Pitter's poems is her eloquence. . . . In Pitter one almost looks through the language, as through air, discerning the exact form of the objects which stand there, and every part and shade of meaning is brought out by the sunny light resting upon them. . . . She has a first-rate intuitive gift of observation, a control of poetic language and magical perception that is always to be found in great poetry" (48–49, 52).

19. Wilfrid Gibson, review of The Bridge, Manchester Guardian, May 23, 1945:3.

20. "Two Contemporary British Poets Who Build Bridges," review of The Bridge, Christian Science Monitor Weekly Magazine Section, July 7, 1945:15.

21. Review of The Bridge, Kirkus 13 (Dec. 15, 1945): 552.

22. G. W. Stonier, review of The Bridge, New Statesman & Nation 29 (Apr. 28, 1945): 276.

23. Review of The Bridge, New Yorker 22 (Feb. 23, 1946): 91.

24. Randall Jarrell, review of The Bridge, Nation 162 (May 25, 1946): 633–34.

25. Christopher Morley, "Testament against Terror," review of The Bridge, Saturday Review of Literature 29 (Mar. 23, 1946): 12.

26. Frederick Brantley, "Sparrow's Skull," review of The Bridge, New York Times, May 5, 1946:8.

27. Babette Deutsch, "Delight and Dismay," review of *The Bridge*, *Poetry: A Magazine of Verse* 68 (May 1946): 103–6.

28. Theodore Maynard, review of *The Bridge*, *Catholic World* 163 (July 1946): 373.

29. "The Swan," *New Age* 23, no. 15 (Aug. 8, 1918): 244. Reprinted in *First Poems*, 5, and *First and Second Poems*, 17; "The Birds Mourning," *Illustrated Review* 1, no. 2 (July 1923): 74. Reprinted in *First and Second Poems*, 81.

30. BBC Radio, "Alexander Pope," Jan. 26, 1946. Pope's influence on Pitter is most noticeable in *A Mad Lady's Garland*, so it is not surprising she could speak about him with admiration and sympathy.

31. Eugene Walter was born in Mobile, Alabama, in 1921. He traveled to New York in the late 1940s after having served as a cryptographer during World War II in the Aleutian Islands. He was a part of the Greenwich Village art scene and won the Lippincott Prize for fiction for his first novel, *The Untidy Pilgrim*. After moving to Paris in the 1950s he was a founding member of the *Paris Review*. When he became editor of *Botteghe Oscure*, a literary journal, he moved to Rome and joined Federico Fellini as an actor and assistant. He enjoyed a fabled career as an entertainer who opened his house and table to some of the most famous people in the world during the 1960s. Walter returned to his native Mobile in 1979 and continued writing for a number of publications until his death in 1998.

6. Friendship with C. S. Lewis, 1947–1949

1. Pitter never specifies the church or its precise location.

2. The complete text of Lewis's December 15, 1945, letter to Palmer is available in Lewis, *Books, Broadcasts and War, 1931–1949*, vol. 2 of *The Collected Letters of C. S. Lewis*, ed. Walter Hooper (London: HarperCollins, 2004), 683–85.

3. To another friend she writes: "Oh, I say! Do you read C. S. Lewis at all? Try at least to get the trilogy 'Out of the Silent Planet,' 'Perelandra,' and 'That Hideous Strength': and also (quite different) 'The Allegory of Love'" (Mar. 27, 1946).

4. In Lewis's letter to Palmer of Apr. 9, 1946, he invites Palmer to visit him and sleep over at Magdalen College on Friday, May 17, 1946. See Lewis, *Books, Broadcasts and War*, 705.

5. Palmer adds: "His exact words are: 'My duty to Miss Pitter. She can know me when she pleases.'" The complete text of this letter is available in Lewis, *Books, Broadcasts and War*, 718.

6. Lewis, *Books, Broadcasts and War*, 718; subsequent references in the text. While Pitter's letters to Lewis have not survived, when she gave her letters from Lewis to the Bodleian Library in the mid-1970s, she provided a journal in which she tried to recall the nature of their correspondence. This journal (hereafter Pitter journal) is available in the Bodleian Library, MS. Eng. lett. c. 220/3. In her journal recollection for July 13, 1946, she writes: "My first letter to Lewis began 'God bless you.' I had scraped acquaintance through poor Herbert, who at that time was determined to 'bring out' Lewis as a poet, and who was, I am afraid, very trying in his visits, etc. Palmer knew how much I loved Lewis's work, and wrote asking if I would like to know him. I replied that I would do any honest thing to this end, and duly encouraged by Palmer, I wrote and asked if I might come to see the great man. The trepidation was the usual feeling (perhaps not so usual now) of sensitive nobodies encountering greatly gifted persons. (It must be awful at the receiving end.)" Pitter journal, MS. Eng. lett. c. 220/3, fol. 18.

7. I surmise these are *The Spirit Watches* (inscribed on the inside cover in Pitter's hand is "To C. S. Lewis from Ruth Pitter, July 1946"), *A Mad Lady's Garland*, and *The Bridge*

(inscribed on the inside cover in Pitter's hand is "To C. S. Lewis from Ruth Pitter, July 1946"). Also Pitter gave Lewis a copy of *A Trophy of Arms* inscribed with: "To C. S. Lewis from Ruth Pitter, 55A Old Church St." Lewis's copies of Pitter's books are available at the Marion E. Wade Center, Wheaton College, Wheaton, IL.

8. This is the only letter by Pitter to Lewis that is known to have survived. I discovered it on Apr. 11, 1997, stuck between the pages of Lewis's copy of Pitter's *The Spirit Watches* in the Marion E. Wade Center.

9. The poems that he includes are "The Birth of Language," "To C. W.," and "On Being Human." Hooper prints these poems in Lewis, *Books, Broadcasts and War*, 725–28. Versions of these poems are also available in C. S. Lewis's *Poems*, ed. Walter Hooper (New York: Harcourt Brace Jovanovich, 1964).

10. Pitter journal, MS. Eng. lett. c. 220/3, fol. 23.

11. On August 6, 1946, Pitter also writes Theodore Maynard about this meeting:

I had an adventure recently. I have been struck all of a heap by the writings of C. S. Lewis, but should never have thought of trying to make his acquaintance: but it came about through a friend, quite without my own volition, and I went down to Oxford and sought him out in his study at Magdalen. It was a great success from my point of view. He only knew about my work vaguely, but I sent him the "Trophy," and he was quite enthusiastic. He has sent me some MS poems of his own—he calls himself a "failed poet"—but such metrical skill without the slightest distortion of profound thought I never did see—didn't think English (or any tongue) capable of it. He doubts, however, whether it's true poetry. It would be glorious to find out where he's sticking, either in the work or in his estimate of it, and I mean to try—sadly hampered as I am by want of the analytical faculty. (Special Collections Division, Georgetown University Library)

Later on September 4, 1946, Pitter writes Maynard: "I'm so glad you know C. S. Lewis's works. All denominations seem to agree on this—the Abbot of Buckfast told me he thought Lewis particularly good at devils!"

12. Warren Lewis confirms Pitter's attendance in his *Brother and Friends: The Diaries of Major Warren Hamilton Lewis*, ed. Clyde S. Kilby and Marjorie Lamp Mead (San Francisco: Harper & Row, 1982): "Thursday 10th October: Yesterday J gave a mixed lunch party in the New Room, at which I found myself sitting next Ruth Pitter, the poetess; inter alia she told me of how in her youth she had known AE" (195–96). Pitter found Oxford in general to be fascinating. She writes Herbert Palmer on February 18, 1947: "I heard from Lewis about your having been there [at Magdalen College]. Lord, what a hampering thing it is to be a woman—how I shd. like to pop in & out of colleges: but Herbert, I don't think it at all likely that bachelor dons are allowed to harbour females, and anyway I can stay with the David Cecils close by if I need a billet."

13. Pitter journal, MS. Eng. lett. c. 220/3, fol. 30.

14. In her journal recollection of January 4, 1947, she writes: "'A Voyage to Arcturus' had been serialized on the radio, and I was quite indignant, thinking it was a plagiarism of Lewis, instead of vice versa (not that it could really be called so—the spirit could hardly be more different. The 'Voyage' is a very strange, painfully unhallowed book). I had so fallen in love with 'Perelandra' that I could not bear to think it would be different on Venus if one could get there. And I so loved the *Hrossa* and the *Sorns* in 'Out of the Silent Planet' that there was a pain in my chest for them, as when one is in love at 20. It was this world, our world, that seemed unreal to me then, not theirs." Pitter journal, MS. Eng. lett. c. 220/3, fol. 34.

15. Pitter journal, MS. Eng. lett. c. 220/3, fol. 38.

16. Pitter journal, MS. Eng. lett. c. 220/3, fol. 41. Then she adds: "But then he was a critic if ever there *was* one. (His 'Eng. Lit. in the 17th [sic] Cent. in the Oxford UP series I can read and re-read for simple refreshment, for the real exhilaration of feeling the scales sway so level). No one is infallible, but I have a strong feeling that Lewis was not fallible in any way that self-discipline could remedy."

17. Sir Ronald Storrs (1881–1955) was an English diplomat and historian. He served a variety of diplomatic positions in the Middle East.

18. Pitter recalls in her journal: "I had been transcribing the paean of praise towards the end of *Perelandra* into irregular Spenserian stanzas simply as a mnemonic: I wished so much to have these enormous transcendental ideas in a form I could memorise & use wherever I happened to be." Pitter journal, MS. Eng. lett. c. 220/3, fol. 52. For a complete discussion of their correspondence and the Spenserian transcriptions, see my "The Poetry of Prose: C. S. Lewis, Ruth Pitter, and *Perelandra*," *Christianity and Literature* 49 (Spring 2000): 331–56, and *C. S. Lewis, Poet: The Legacy of His Poetic Impulse* (Kent, OH: Kent State Univ. Press, 2001), 14–16, 224–37.

19. Pitter's excitement as the luncheon nears is reflected in her datebook recording for July 16, 1947: "Lunch with Lewis? Yes. 1 p.m. Mdln [Magdalen College]." Pitter's uncataloged papers.

20. Laurence Whistler (1912–2000) was a glass engraver, writer, poet, and architectural historian. For a review of this correspondence, see Lewis, *Books, Broadcasts and War,* 756–58. Whistler hoped to enlist support from Lewis as well as Pitter, T. S. Eliot, and Richard Church for this new journal.

21. The letter goes on:

C. S. L. says that G[eorge] E[very] isn't sinister, but one can always feel that *pull* towards something, which he says positively is the result of G. E.'s being a *converted scrutinizer,* and is something to do with F. R. Leavis. What this means I haven't the faintest idea, but there is no doubt that Lewis thinks the man all right, only rather tiresome & dirty. C. S. L. says further that if [John] Betjeman is editor [of the proposed journal and a former pupil of Lewis's], it may exclude himself as contributor, so thoroughly has B. slashed him in reviews: otherwise he says it is an excellent choice, and he likes him very much for himself, in spite of their differences, wh. as you know started during B.'s academic career.

In addition, in her journal Pitter recalls: "Neither [Lewis nor Storrs] would have noticed the drooping ghost of my girlish dream, of course (God help me—I was in my 50th year, not my 15th!)." Pitter journal, MS. Eng. lett. c. 220/3, fol. 46. Brother George Every (1909–2003) was a member of the Society of the Sacred Mission, an Anglican theological college, and author of numerous books, many focusing upon the schism between the Catholic and the Eastern churches. F. R. Leavis (1895–1978) was the well-known Cambridge literary critic and founder of the literary journal *Scrutiny* with whom Lewis disagreed. During John Betjeman's (1908–1984) brief stay at Magdalen College Lewis had been his tutor. He served as poet laureate from 1972 to 1984.

22. The poems were published as follows: "Donkey's Delight," *Punch* 213 (Nov. 5, 1947): 442 (N. W.); revised and reprinted in Lewis's *Poems.* "Dangerous Oversight," *Punch* 212 (May 21, 1947): 434 (N. W.); revised and retitled "Young King Cole" in *Poems.* "Vitrea Circe," *Punch* 214 (June 23, 1948): 543 (N. W.); revised and reprinted in *Poems.*

23. July 6, 1947. Pitter journal, MS. Eng. lett. c. 220/3, fol. 52.

24. It appears that Pitter gave Lewis his copy of *The Rude Potato* during the July 16 luncheon since the flyleaf of Lewis's copy of this volume has Pitter's handwritten note: "To C. S. Lewis from Ruth Pitter, 16th July, 1947."

25. In the meantime, knowing of Lewis's delight in grapes, Pitter sends him some from her own Essex vines; regrettably, he is away when the grapes arrive and they spoil by the time he returns. On September 26, he writes her an elaborate apology in mock Middle English. The complete text of this letter is available in Lewis, *Books, Broadcasts and War*, 879–80. Pitter recalls in her journal entry of the same date: "I had noticed that Lewis had a special feeling about grapes. So have I. Of all fruits they are the most wholesome, grateful, beautiful, various: the plant is '*de tonte béaute*,' the modest flower ravishing in scent: then there is wine. . . . And most of all, the sacred associations & imagery." Pitter journal, MS. Eng. lett. c. 220/3, fol. 60.

26. Pitter journal, MS. Eng. lett. c. 220/3, fols. 63–64. Reprinted in Lewis, *Books, Broadcasts and War*, 882.

27. This poem was never published during Lewis's lifetime. It appears in his *Poems* (38–40).

28. In her journal recollection of December 6, 1948, Pitter reacts:

"I sometimes wonder whether we know anything about poetry." Yes. I read somewhere recently that all the study of all "work-sheets" has shed no light. I am never sure myself that a reader, however subtle & discriminating, has taken my most secret meanings: there are layers, from the most obvious to the most intangible, and I watch like a cat to observe who has taken the latter, if indeed any such there be: for we must be prepared to admit that these very innermost things may be *chimaerae*. And of course there are meanings in our own work that we have never seen, and when others point them out we are quite astounded. (Pitter journal, MS. Eng. lett. c. 220/3, fol. 67)

29. In her journal recollection of December 11, 1948, Pitter says: "Beautiful letter, but he doesn't reflect that nowadays everybody has to do chores and is constantly interrupted—it is almost lyrics or nothing, especially for women. Taking to invalidism is an idea, but not so easy now: or to get oneself accepted as a Guarded Flame & be surrounded by stooges (horrible). Being in love, to be sure, does get one airborne, but only in hops of varying length, and is not to be relied on for much more than half a century: and even for this, the chores make everybody so careworn and unresponsive after youth is past. Never mind, poetry has perhaps always been done against odds." Pitter journal, MS. Eng. lett. c. 220/3, fol. 70.

30. Pitter later writes her friend Mary Cooley: "Somebody's just lent me C.S. Lewis's . . . very long poem called 'Dymer' published under the pseudonym of Clive Hamilton. It was published by Dent in 1926 & failed utterly, but (though I expected academic interest only) it is a brawny performance with the clear foundations of mature work, & ought not to have passed unnoticed—very imaginative too" (July 26, 1949). Lewis's letter to Pitter of August 19, 1949, contains his latest poem, an epigram that had been published as "Epitaph in a Village Churchyard," *Time and Tide* 30 (Mar. 19, 1949): 272. Retitled and reprinted as "Epigrams and Epitaphs, No. 16" in Lewis's *Poems*.

31. Specifically, her datebook shows meetings on July 27, 1949; August 22, 1949; September 20, 1949 (her entry for this day reads: "Finally, they did actually [come]. CSL &OB? Yes, hooray"); October 2, 1949; November 2, 1949; and December 26, 1949.

32. George Hamilton, *The Tell-Tale Article: A Critical Approach to Modern Poetry* (Ox-

ford: Oxford University Press, 1949). Pitter writes in her journal recollection for August 14, 1949: "Sir George Hamilton's "The Telltale Article" was a great eye-opener and comfort to me. It was salutary for my own work, and enabled me to rebel against the current modernism with a clear conscience & a good case. I find it surprising that it has not been much more widely recognized as a fine faithfully worked-out seminal piece of criticism: but there, it was against the prevailing current." Pitter journal, MS. Eng. lett. c. 220/3, fol. 78. Lewis's August 14, 1949, letter to Hamilton is available in Lewis, *Books, Broadcasts and War*, 966–67.

33. Barfield had written Pitter on September 18, 1949, about himself and Lewis finding their way to her flat: "You have a higher opinion of my staff work [?] than Mr. Lewis himself has. At least you profess one, while taking the wise precaution to make your instructions foolproof. Add that I am a Cockney born and bred, possess an A1 map of London in my office drawer and am on the No. 11 bus route—and the chances are that we shall find our way to No. 55A by 1.00 on the [Sept.] Tuesday 20th visit. At all events it will take a lot to keep us away."

34. It later appears in *The Ermine: Poems 1942–1952* (London: Cresset Press, 1953), 19–20.

35. *Paradise Lost*, book 5, 297: "Wild above rule or art; enormous bliss."

36. Pitter's own recollection is also favorable: "Lewis came with Owen Barfield to lunch in Chelsea with Kathleen O'Hara & myself. He is alluding to the end of the party, when I spread on the floor a number of painted trays & invited them to choose one each. . . . Yes, people did tend to stand the trays up as decorations and not to use them. The 'cornucopia' allusion—it was autumn, and I had taken some trouble to bring from the fruity Essex bower the richest specimens of grapes, pears, plums, & peaches: we arranged them on a large silver tray with sprays of vine-leaves, etc. The Blitzekatze was our cat, which we had found in the ruins after an air-raid." Pitter journal, MS. Eng. lett. c. 220/3, fol. 81. Later in this chapter I discuss a poem Pitter published about this cat.

37. These four poems are from *The Bridge*.

38. "Hen under Bay-Tree" appears in *The Ermine*, 43.

39. Apparently this was a private conference, perhaps arranged by Lewis. Other than Pitter's letter, no other information about the conference has survived.

40. Letter to Mary Cooley.

41. Letter to Rachel Cecil.

42. *On Cats* (London: Cresset Press, 1947).

43. T. S. Eliot says something similar in "The Ad-dressing of Cats" in *Old Possum's Book of Practical Cats* (London: Faber & Faber, 1939): "Now Dogs pretend they like to fight; / They often bark, more seldom bite; / But yet a Dog is, on the whole, / What you would call a simple soul" (55).

44. C. S. Lewis, *Narnia, Cambridge and Joy 1950–1963*, vol. 3 of *C. S. Lewis, Collected Letters*, ed. Walter Hooper (London: HarperCollins, 2006), 587. In other letters Lewis and his wife, Joy Gresham, make additional references to cats. On June 6, 1958, Gresham writes: "Is your pet a cat or dog? I've found that cats stand these changes and separations pretty well—one of mine when I was ill, took possession of a new home and mistress and had them completely under his thumb in a week. (If one can speak of a cat's thumb?)" (952). On February 24, 1961, Lewis writes: "I hope your vet is not a charlatan? Psychological diagnoses even about human patients seem to me pretty phoney. They must be even phonier when applied to animals. You can't put a cat on a couch and make it tell you its dreams or produce words by 'free association.' Also, I have a great respect for cats—they are very shrewd people and would probably see through the analyst a good deal better than he'd see through them" (1243). Still later on Mar. 7, 1962, he adds: "We are also both ruled by

cats. Joy's Siamese—my 'stepcat' as I call her—is the most terribly conversational animal I ever knew. She talks all the time and wants doors and windows to be opened for her 1000 times an hour" (1355–56). Lewis's anthropomorphic analyses of cats link him with Pitter and two contemporary writers who wrote slim collections of verse dedicated to cats: T. S. Eliot and Dorothy L. Sayers. I explore the relationship between the "cat" volumes of Pitter, Eliot, and Sayers in "Quorum Porum: The Literary Cats of T. S. Eliot, Ruth Pitter, and Dorothy L. Sayers." *Seven: An Anglo-American Literary Review* 18 (2001): 25–45.

45. First published in *Lilliput*, Dec. 1942:373. Reprinted in *On Cats*, 7; subsequent references in the text.

46. This poem elicited a number of favorable reactions from her readers. For example, J. A. Elliot sent Pitter the following letter:

> Dear Miss Pitter,
>   I write to tell you that my family and I have enjoyed "Quorum Porum" very much. We read it first in *Lilliput*, and it is a fact, incredible as you may think it, that my son, who is fifteen, has a copy in his pocketbook. Or, to be correct, he had a copy. I got your Cresset Press volume recently and was deeply aggrieved to find "Quorum Porum" a bit different. My boy's school just had a Founder's Day, and I visited him there. Among other things I told him about this. I think you would have enjoyed the resulting discussion. It was decidedly like the intemperate fury of two Shakespeareans on discovering some crime in a new edition, or, at any rate, some departure from tradition. Someone had been tampering with the Original Text. So my son produced the First Edition from his pocketbook and we studied it. We prefer "save *for* the involuntary caudal thrill" to the same line without the word "for." We prefer this line to come *after* "the horror was that they should sit so still," not before it. And lastly, we prefer "wearing negation like an oracle" to the Cresset volume line. I should say that I have enjoyed the Cresset volume enormously. I think the rest of it is just as good as "Quorum Porum." Especially "Musa Translated." Therefore, I thank you on behalf of this family for the fun we have had from learning Q. P. and for the fun we are going to have with your last volume. (July 2, 1947)

47. On the title page of the copy of *On Cats* she sent Lewis, she inscribed: "'In the morning he leaps up to catch the Musk, which is the blessing of God upon his labours' C. Smart. To C. S. Lewis, with the greatest gratitude. From Ruth Pitter, May 1947."

48. May 25, 1947. Pitter journal, MS. Eng. lett. c. 220/3, fol. 48. Pitter's nephew, Mark Pitter, now a classics teacher at Oakham School and her literary executor, later offered a critique of Lewis's declension in a letter to his aunt of February 29(?), 1982:

> My dear Aunt Ruth,
>   If you are going to start with a noun whose nominative singular ends in "us(s)", you have a choice of three: a) 2nd decl. masc. noun in *us*, as you state . . . , b) 3rd decl. neuter in *us*, *-eris* . . . and this won't suit Quorum Porum, because I wager that none of the feline hierophants at that assembly were neuters, 3) 4th decl. masc. or fem. nouns in s, s. . . . Pace C. S. Lewis, the 5th decl. won't work for puss, because its nominative singular ends invariably in *es*, which banjaxes the whole shooting match, for it gives us pes, which means "foot," and which anyway is 3rd declension, which is quite enough to confuse all comers. . . . I reckon to vote with the indolent schoolboy and adopt the 2nd declension, ruderies included. Ruderies of this sort are innocent enough, anyway. I think you're right in saying that C. S. Lewis thus

avoided the object of the exercise: he should have read more Aristophanes, the perfect example of the Rude being transcendentally innocent.

49. Blitzkit is undoubtedly the same cat Lewis referred to in his letter of September 22, 1949, cited above.

50. First published as "The Neuter Cat's Fulfilment," *Lilliput*, Jan. 1943:50–51.

51. Versions of this poem first appeared in the *New English Weekly* 3, no. 1 (Apr. 1933): 22–23, and *A Mad Lady's Garland*, 28.

52. A reference to neutering.

53. Ralph E. Hone, ed., *The Poetry of Dorothy L. Sayers* (Trowbridge, Wiltshire: Dorothy L. Sayers Society, 1996), 145–48. Written in iambic tetrameter quatrains of alternate rhyme, this has been called "one of [Sayers's] most beautifully crafted poems." With its obvious allusions to Virgil's *Aeneid* (books 1, 3, and 4), Dante's *Inferno* (canto 2, 32; 4, 122; and 26, 93), and the ravages of World War II Europe, the poem is a tour de force, as it relates the story of a "lean, hard-bitten" Tom/Aeneas who is newly landed on English soil, his equivalent of Carthage. Utilizing a muted tone, Tom/Aeneas chronicles his struggles, wondering "what fierce wrath could urge / Heaven, or for what obscure offence, / Five years to vex us with the scourge / Of famine, fear, and pestilence." Allusions to how falling bombs devastated the cat population of his former land so that "huge starving hordes of mice and rats" overran his country are followed by the tale of his journey by sail to the shores of England. True to Virgil's account, the cat queen/Dido (though motivated less by lust than by admiration) invites Tom/Aeneas to stay with her: "We too have seen the vengeful brand / Strike from the sky; but yet we live / Favoured of Heaven, and what our land / Can offer you, we freely give." The poem ends with Tom/Aeneas musing on a theological puzzle:

> Cat's eyes may not avail
>   To pierce the awful pantry-door
> Where Justice in her iron scale
>   Weighs out the meed of less and more.
> Enough that some dark deed of shame
>   By cats has set all Heaven at odds;
> For these prodigious woes proclaim
>   That there is war among the gods.

Paralleling the human propensity to associate pain and suffering with God's wrath aroused because of human sin, Tom/Aeneas attributes the existential dilemma of suffering cats to feline deeds of darkness that have inflamed the human gods' anger against them. Still another Sayers cat poem is "For Timothy, in the Coinherence" (1973). Written in memory of a cat belonging to Sayers's longtime friend Muriel St. Clare Byrne, it is a prayer hoping for the resurrection of Timothy and carries allusions to Charles Williams (particularly the last word in the title), Dante (the epigraph is from *Paradiso*, canto 28, 129), and Genesis 1–3 and 6–9 (the Garden of Eden and the Ark). The poem is available in *The Poetry of Dorothy L. Sayers*, 157–58.

54. Sayers also had earlier sent a copy to Lewis, who writes her on December 18[?], 1945: "As for *Aeneas at the Court of Dido*, the sentiments are just and the numbers pleasing." Lewis, *Books, Broadcasts and War*, 686.

55. A copy of *A Cat's Christmas Carol* is available in Pitter's uncataloged papers.

56. Although born in Belgium, Sarton (1912–1995) grew up in Cambridge, Massachusetts. A prolific writer, Sarton wrote nineteen novels, seventeen volumes of poetry, and fifteen volumes of nonfiction, as well as children's stories and screenplays.

57. Pitter writes Palmer after his visit to Penns: "Dorothy liked you: and though such a wreck, she's still a shrewd judge. She's been very poorly since: today she phoned that she was trying to get into a home, and by the sound of her voice I think she ought to. Poor lovely dear! . . . If only she could be Xtian! but she hasn't the mental force and clarity now. We can only pray for her" (July 3, 1947).

58. Encouraged by the American government and especially the Marshall Plan, the postwar European recovery plan conceived by U.S. secretary of state George C. Marshall, Americans began to send individual packages of basic foodstuffs to England and the rest of Europe. Cooley, who hailed from Ann Arbor, Michigan, decided to befriend Pitter and began sending her regular food parcels. She and Pitter began a correspondence that started in Mar. 1947 and ended with Cooley's death in 1977. Cooley's incredible generosity is documented in the dozens and dozens of letters of thanks Pitter wrote. Cooley's first letter arrived on Mar. 21, 1947:

> For some time I have been wishing that I had some friend in England to whom I could send a food package in these days when we over here are more fortunate in the way of supplies than you over there. It occurred to me the other day that a poet whose work you have enjoyed is in a sense a friend, and I thought why not send a package to some poet? But I'm not sure whether such a gift might not be misplaced. Perhaps you have everything you need. I'd like to send you a package if it would be welcome. If not, perhaps you would be kind enough to send me the name and address of some other writer who would be pleased to get one.

59. Later that summer, Pitter is overjoyed at Cooley's latest: "I am still dizzy with the thought of possessing so much food: but to show how valuable it is, here are some of the items in terms of rations. Cooking fat 2 lbs = 32 weeks rations for 1 person. Sugar 2 lbs = 1 month. Flour about 6 lbs = 2 weeks bread. Tinned meat about 4 lbs = about 2–3 months' 'points', or quite 8 weeks' fresh meat ration. Dried fruit 2 lbs = 2 months' rations. So you see I am almost in a position to play power politics. But joking apart, what I really mean to do is to have a real baking-day and make some cakes & biscuits with enough fat in them, for the sheer pleasure of it" (mid-July 1947).

60. She goes on in the letter to add:

> The funny thing is that this should have happened just when my partner, Kathleen O'Hara, retired from the business, because I did much the same to the other eye a few weeks after we started, nearly 19 years ago. It was a tin of cellulose paint which burst on that occasion, and the injury was a good deal worse. I could see very little for a month. While laid up I composed the poem "Stormcock in Elder," which people have liked a lot. I remember how vivid was the visual memory of the kind, down to the last detail, when I was virtually blind. Now, the other day, just 18 hours after the recent mishap, I switched on the radio and out came the song of the same bird—they were doing a program on it!

7. Lurking in the Undergrowth, 1950–1953

1. Pitter's Mar. 14, 1950, letter to Blackshaw is especially vitriolic regarding Eliot: "I enjoy your banging away at Eliot. He got a good drubbing in our 'Sunday Times' last issue, when the critic (J. Russell) left 'The Cocktail Party' for dead. He (Eliot) is a traitor to poetry, & one day people will see it. The award of the Order of Merit to him was very wounding to

people of discernment here—in the past it has not been given except for real, proved worth: he is still far too much *sub judice* for such an award: the King was badly advised."

2. Ignatius Roy Dunnachie Campbell (1901–1957) was a South African poet. Among his many books of verse, *The Flaming Terrapin* (1924) and *Flowering Rifle: A Poem from the Battlefield of Spain* (1936) are notable. Several poets and critics rated him as one of the best poets writing between World War I and World War II. The poem he is referring to is "The Earwig's Complaint" in *A Mad Lady's Garland*.

3. Pitter, *Urania* (London: Cresset Press, 1950). At about this time Pitter writes Cresset Press with a proposal that they reissue an edition of *A Mad Lady's Garland* illustrated by Joan Hassall. While both Pitter and Hassall were enthusiastic about the idea, Cresset Press never showed any interest in the proposal.

4. David Cecil, "Rare Beauty," review of *Urania*, *Observer*, Apr. 8, 1951:7.

5. "Metaphysical Poets," review of *Urania*, *Times Literary Supplement*, May 4, 1951:278.

6. Lewis, *Narnia, Cambridge and Joy*, 65; subsequent references in the text.

7. In Pitter's December 30, 1950, journal recollection of this letter, she says:

What a good argument for everyone's having a smattering of the natural sciences in their vocabulary. In my own case, a mere peppering of Latin and whiff of Greek, a good deal of reading in Floras, etc., and great curiosity in the field, enables me to move easily in this matter between ancient and modern. Oh, the Theocritus! The beautiful Cambridge edition—the ever-hurried Sir R. Storrs showed it me in the train: less than an hour's delight, but I emerged with my nose covered with honey (it is interleaved with an English version) but quite raised above the cares of life by having recognized (in the Greek) the *helichrysos*, the everlasting flower: someone coming from the bath with his hair all in twinkling points like this. . . . The duchess in question, now quite neglected—think he would have liked some of her work, but I don't know whether he ever read it. (Pitter journal, MS. Eng. lett. c. 220/3, fol. 92)

8. In Pitter's Mar. 17, 1951, journal recollection, she says:

The vine-branch in the engraving [on the dust-jacket of *Urania*] was done from our own dear vines in Essex. "Tasting spiritually"—there is such a thing indeed. But I never forget the man in Dante who could not pass from Purgatory into Paradise, for he sat down at the parting of the ways, "by the laden fruit-tree and under the spray of the fountain." I wish I could express the real spirituality of fruit, felt all my life, but always obscured by the sensuous garments. The fruits in "Perelandra" get very close. I have dreamed more than once of finding a garden unknown, within my own garden, but forgotten until one wandered in and remembered. It is always full of fruit untainted by the Fall, but I can never get anywhere near expressing this. Lewis once said that my name should have been *Pomona*; but the name I have contents me: Ruth is, anciently, *compunction: Pitter* (Peter) is *rock:* Compunction Rock, no bad name, if one could live up to it. *Clive Staples Lewis*, is in my interpretation *Clive*=sundered (for him). *Staples*=holding-places (for us). *Lewis*=*Levi*, "who hath no part nor inheritance with his brethren: the Lord is his inheritance, according as the Lord his God promised him." I am well aware, of course, that these derivations are only poetical, but there! Aren't the blurs in the Authorized Version sometimes terribly evocative? (Pitter journal, MS. Eng. lett. c. 220/5, fols. 97–98)

9. In Pitter's Mar. 26, 1951, journal recollection, she writes: "I had expressed mild pain at the idea of the spectacle-case lurking so long undiscovered in the crease of the armchairs. Never cleaned—didn't know they had to be?!" Pitter journal, MS. Eng. lett. c. 220/3, fol. 100.

10. Bodleian Library, MS. Eng. lett. c. 220/5, fol. 102; this postcard was inadvertently left out of *Narnia, Cambridge and Joy.*

11. Bodleian Library, MS. Eng. lett. c. 220/5, fol. 103; this letter was inadvertently left out of *Narnia, Cambridge and Joy.*

12. R. A. Scott-James, *Fifty Years of English Literature, 1900–1950* (London: Longmans, 1951). Scott-James is complimentary and very perceptive regarding Pitter. He says, in part:

> She is not, in the sense in which the word has been used, a "modern" poet. She belongs to no clique. She follows no modern fashion. Some of her poems assume a form that was within the reach of poetry long ago, but of these many have a significance which differentiates them from poetry of the past. She is intensely alive in the contemporary world, and sees it through its own eyes. But she is not quite of it. She stands apart, inhabiting a region of her own; and if it has not been as extensively communicated to the reading public as it might have been, that is perhaps because she belongs to no recognizable school, has no trumpeter, and has not been at pains to assert herself. She has written some lovely poetry, authentic, unmistakable, which in her later work is distilled in experience and projected in language fashioned with fine tact and metrical skill. It has substance, and form; hardness, and fragility; grit, with tenderness and delicacy . . . In the years of war she knew and felt the war experience, yet went on writing poetry which, not excluding that experience, transcended it; she continued to be attentive to things of perennial import and express them in strong, simple, and beautiful verse. (231–33)

13. She recalls the details of giving this address in her January 2, 1953, journal entry:

> This venerable body occasionally goes very broadminded and asks someone who is not a scientist to give a lecture. The procedure is (or was then) very intimidating. There is a dinner and a symposium beforehand, at which the lecturer talks far too much and gets worn out. Then he is assigned an escort (really a guard, as on one occasion the lecturer panicked and ran away). Parked in a small room, with the guard outside, he nervously shuffles over his script until just on time, when he and his guard are lined up in front of a tall pair of folding doors: at a similar pair is assembled a procession consisting of the President & the governing body, all in faultless tails & white ties. The guard peeps through a crack at the lecture-room clock. At a few seconds before the hour, the doors are set open, the governing body file to their places before the demonstration-bench, the lecturer mounts the rostrum: the huge solemn clock gives, not a musical note, but one scientific ping, and the lecturer must at once plunge *in medias res* without introduction or other frivolity. On the hour, at the next scientific ping, he must cease. I was not really frightened—as a poet one meets many horrors—but the knowledge of what to expect had made me work on my matter like a beaver. It is a great cure for nerves to have done one's homework. (Pitter journal, MS. Eng. lett. c. 220/5, fols. 112–13)

14. A copy of this address is available in Pitter's uncataloged papers.

15. This is another view she shared with Lewis, who wrote extensively about this in his

well-known debate with E. M . W. Tillyard and published as *The Personal Heresy* (London: Oxford University Press, 1939).

16. Pitter journal, MS. Eng. lett. c. 220/5, fols. 109–10. The lecture was "Hero and Leander," the Warton Lecture on English Poetry, read to the British Academy on February 20, 1952, and published in the *Proceedings of the British Academy* 38 (1952). It is reprinted in C. S. Lewis, *Selected Literary Essays* (Cambridge: Cambridge University Press, 1969), 58–73.

17. Most of the poems published in *The Ermine* appear in Pitter's manuscript notebooks of the 1940s and 1950s.

18. *The Ermine*, 11–13; subsequent references in the text.

19. The sense that a wandering lamb will be guided aright, recalls "Help, Good Shepherd" in *A Trophy of Arms*. There Pitter prayed to God, and by implication to Christ, the Good Shepherd, to "sound with thy crook the darkling flood, / Still range the sides of shelvy hill / And call about in underwood" in order to save humanity from itself: "For on the hill are many strayed, / Some held in thickets plunge and cry, / And the deep waters make us afraid. / Come then and help us, or we die" (27).

20. Pitter also explored her interest in the bird of paradise in "Fowls Celestial and Terrestrial" in *A Mad Lady's Garland*. See chapter 3.

21. *The Bridge*, 44.

22. Although entitled "Five Dreams and a Vision," including a kind of preamble, there are actually eight poems in this sequence. As far as I have been able to determine, Pitter never explained this inconsistency.

23. "The kingdom of heaven is like unto a merchant man, seeking goodly pearls: Who, when he had found one pearl of great price, went and sold all that he had, and bought it" (Matt. 13:45–46).

24. Although there is no way to document this, Pitter may have read by this time C. S. Lewis's sermon "The Weight of Glory," preached in the university church of Oxford, the Church of St. Mary the Virgin, on June 8, 1941, and reprinted in *The Weight of Glory and Other Addresses* (New York: Macmillan, 1949), where he argues the same point:

> It may be possible for each to think too much of his own potential glory hereafter; it is hardly possible for him to think too often or too deeply about that of his neighbour. The load, or weight, or burden of my neighbour's glory should be laid daily on my back, a load so heavy that only humility can carry it, and the backs of the proud will be broken. It is a serious thing to live in a society of possible gods and goddesses, to remember that the dullest and most uninteresting person you talk to may one day be a creature which, if you saw it now, you would be strongly tempted to worship, or else a horror and a corruption such as you now meet, if at all, only in a nightmare. All day long we are, in some degree, helping each other to one or other of these destinations. It is in the light of these overwhelming possibilities, it is with the awe and the circumspection proper to them, that we should conduct all our dealings with one another, all friendships, all loves, all play, all politics. There are no *ordinary* people. You have never talked to a mere mortal. Nations, cultures, arts, civilization—these are mortal, and their life is to ours as the life of a gnat. But it is immortals whom we joke with, work with, marry, snub, and exploit—immortal horrors or everlasting splendours. (14–15)

25. "The Mortal Lot," review of *The Ermine*, *Times Literary Supplement*, Aug. 21, 1953, 537.

26. Pitter writes on the title page of the copy she sends Lewis: "To C. S. Lewis as in love & duty bound from Ruth Pitter, May 11, 1953."

27. In her May 12 and 15, 1953, journal recollection of Lewis's letter, she writes: "It may be imagined what this royally generous letter meant to me. . . . I suppose this was my first book after becoming a practising Xtian. Does the change spoil a poet? I do not try to write anything explicitly Xtian, rather believing that all work (if good) is to the glory of God: though some people find fault with this attitude. One very good friend of mine, a truly pious farmer, challenged me on this subject. I could have retorted, 'Well, why don't you sow "God is Love" in radishes across your wheatfields, so that it can be read from the air?'" Pitter journal, MS. Eng. lett. c. 220/5, fol. 117.

28. In the midst of all this, on July 16, 1953, Pitter heard the sad news of Belloc's death. Later she said: "The older I get the more grateful I feel to him. In those days 'established' people did a lot for the younger writer" (letter to Arthur Russell, Oct. 6, 1974).

29. Pitter journal, MS. Eng. lett. c. 220/5, fol. 119.

30. Pitter journal, MS. Eng. lett. c. 220/5, fol. 119.

31. She adds at the end of the letter: "We expect to move by Xmas, if we can arrange to get rid of this house. I have been working on that problem for 8 months and haven't solved it yet. There are 4 parties whose interests have to be coordinated. I hate and detest legal business of every sort, and yet I have to see to it continually. As a friend of mine who landed in Ireland without a passport, and was duly detained, said to me, 'It is at these times one so bitterly misses the husband who ought to be there to be nagged!'"

32. In her December 21, 1953, journal recollection, Pitter writes about this letter:

It was in reply to this very warm-hearted letter (and how right he is about the way to a child's heart, it is my way too) that for the only time in my life, so far, I waxed prophetic. Being enamoured of the classics without knowing them except by their shining traces in our common life, I had asked a more learned niece to write out for me one Greek chorus, to have the consolation of repeating it parrot-fashion: and this is all the Greek I know. I told Lewis I could read between the lines of his letter (two American-bred little boys in that bachelor household!) and that I saw an opportunity to quote from my one ewe lamb, the chorus from [Euripides's] "Alcestis" which my niece, not I, had chosen:
    Your grief deserves our tears
    I know you have entered into sorrow.
    Yet you bring no aid to the dead.
    Heavy shall it be for you
    Never to look again
    On the face of the woman you love. (Pitter journal, MS. Eng. lett. c. 220/5, fol. 121)

33. Eighteen years later during an August, 23, 1971, BBC radio broadcast of "My Timeless Moment" on *Woman's Hour,* Pitter offers a sustained reflection on moving into the Hawthorns:

I belong to a generation of Surplus Women. In my young days there were more girls about than boys. And alas, so many young men were killed in the First World War that there were more of us than ever. It seemed quite natural to be unmarried, though. . . . We took it for granted that we couldn't all marry, and we quite liked the prospect of a career, and independence, and a nice little home of our own in our old age, when our working days were over. . . . So my friend Kathleen and I agreed from the first that should we continue unmarried we would find a Dear Little Cottage when we retired, and settle down blissfully in the country. A garden of roses and honeysuckle for the summer, and a fine big hearth with a blazing fire of logs, and tea and buttered toast, for the winter. And dear cosy little bedrooms with dormer windows peeping out of the thatch. . . .

It had to be an old cottage, of course. Though at this time we weren't so sure about thatch. Thatched houses are usually rather dark, and we needed light for our painting. . . . Very well, an old cottage with a tiled roof. . . . You should have seen the unbelievable little old hovels we were offered, at the price we could afford. And the mad things that had been done to some of them—the do-it-yourself Walt Disney touch. People have their dreams about cottages, and some of them are nightmares.

One day we'd been to see two or three of these cramped, dark, damp, huddled little holes at the back of nowhere. At the last one, the owners had been only just able to bear showing us round, with their snobbish noses in the air, and crazy ideas about price. We were feeling very near despair. Then we noticed a sale-board, and standing back from the road a villa. Yes, a villa. We popped in and had a look all round and through the windows. Brick walls 16" thick, sound tiled roof. Large, light sash windows. . . . Level roof and floors, dry as a bone. Several good sheds, a new, handsome garage. Two and a half acres, mostly orchard and grass. On a hill, with peeps of other hills all round. . . . It appealed to me, because it was all so spacious. . . .

My timeless moment didn't come when we moved in. By that time I was so tired that I was working in a daze. No, the timeless moment was on one of the many occasions when I came down alone to see about this and that before the move. Kathleen had to stay to attend to things in London. I sat on the back step, under the good substantial verandah, and unpacked my hardboiled egg and bread-and-butter and apple, with a little flask of wine. It was very late autumn, cool, quiet, and misty.

I sat and ate, looking out at the blessed tangle of old rosebushes and bits of hedge and great big old trees, and knew it was home. The last of the wine was not for me. It was for the kindly spirits of the place. I poured it on the earth, with a little prayer of thanks. Our own country home at last, paid for with spot cash, our own hard earnings and hard savings. Silence and peace and kind neighbours. Crops to be gathered, friends to be received, a generous green environment enfolding us. Thankful? I could hardly believe it. I felt humbled, too. Had we really deserved it? I've never forgotten that moment, nearly eighteen years ago. (BBC Written Archives)

8. Unexpected Turns, 1954–1955

1. Lewis, *Narnia, Cambridge and Joy*, 403–4; subsequent references in the text.

2. Candice Fredrick and Sam McBride have published *Women among the Inklings: Gender, C. S. Lewis, J. R. R. Tolkien, and Charles Williams* (Westport, CT: Greenwood Press, 2001), a helpful though not entirely thorough perspective on Lewis's relationships with women. However, the wonderful evidence of Lewis's lively correspondence with a number of women, including Pitter, Mary Neylan, Sister Penelope Lawson, CSMV, and Dorothy L. Sayers.

3. Reading biography into or out of an author's literary work is risky business, opening one at a minimum to Lewis's charge of committing the "personal heresy." Nonetheless, and even though I was schooled in New Criticism and the maxim that a poem should be valued as a work of aesthetic beauty and artistic integrity *in and of itself*, not as a biographical artifact, I find the insights of such a biographical reading of Gresham's and Pitter's love poetry compelling. At a minimum I believe these insights inform a deeper understanding of Lewis's decision to marry Gresham rather than Pitter.

4. George Sayer, *Jack: C. S. Lewis and His Times* (San Francisco: Harper & Row, 1988), 211–12.

5. This February 14, 1975, letter from Walter Hooper to Pitter is available in her uncataloged papers.

6. This appears in Pitter's January 26, 1954, journal recollection. Pitter journal, MS. Eng. lett. c. 220/5, fol. 123.

7. While it will fall to future scholars to explore the exact nature of this correspondence, Pitter, motivated by an understandable but uncharitable bitterness, later convinced herself that Gresham used her illness (bone cancer) to manipulate Lewis into marrying her and caring for her two sons. Pitter writes about this in "The Alabaster Box, or This Awful Power," a document that I date to the mid-1970s (in Pitter's restricted papers in the Bodleian Library). While Pitter's claims against Gresham are perhaps ill-conceived sour grapes—after all, she had some twenty years to let this kind of thinking fester—this is also evidence of what she saw as her own greatest character flaw: a critical spirit. For instance, on January 12, 1964, Pitter writes her sister-in-law, Mary: "Often & often I can't speak as I should to some people because if I did I should *go* for them, say far too much, and do horrid destruction." Indeed, as Pitter herself notes in several other letters, it was her critical spirit and temptation to say too much and thus hurt people that led Pitter to live a life of relative solitude; but, of course, a life of solitude is also fertile ground for a poet. In a letter to Arthur Russell on August 1, 1956, she critiques herself:

> Do you know, I agree so passionately about common chit-chat that (as a Xtian) I often feel very guilty about the violence of my feelings! This goes also for the unreasonableness. I asked to be forgiven. I mean my towering prejudices, which are as vivid as nightmares and often (I am sure) quite as unreal, so that when some people's names are mentioned I either take refuge in noncommittal mumblings or foolish abuse, often knowing next to nothing about them—some chance hearing or reading has damned them forever for me, and spiritually it is a very bad thing, as well I know. This is one of the reasons why I tend to keep myself to myself. This quite subjective inability is of course a recognized feature of the poetic character (famous even in remote antiquity) but it represents arrested development and it *ain't right*.

In "Ruth Pitter Talks to Hallam Tennyson" she says that even with her great friend Kathleen O'Hara she always felt she was essentially a lonely person: "[Kathleen] knew me very well, but it was only to a certain extent. We worked very well in double harness. . . . But being alone is what I always liked. In fact, my most delightful moments have always been in solitude at a cottage in the forest. In my youth, why I know not, it was to weep with pure felicity in that place, and I don't think I should have ever have done that in the presence of anyone else."

8. In "Ruth Pitter Talks about Her Own Poems" Pitter says:

> There is a deep instinct, a biologically sound one, I think, in women's hearts—that in love they must be sought out. They have a right of veto, but they mustn't make advances, even if they are deeply in love. In fact, the proof of a true lover is that he knows this and will discover their feelings however well they hide them. If he isn't interested enough to find out their secrets, he cannot be accepted. In . . . "If You Came," the woman is saying that she will surrender completely, but only if the lover can find out her hidden heart, which she conceals as jealously as a bird hides its nest in the woods.

9. It is worth noting at this point that the heroine of Gresham's first novel, *Anya* (New York: Macmillan, 1940), is sexually active in and outside of marriage.

10. For more on her conversion, see her autobiographical essay, "The Longest Way Round," in David W. Soper, ed., *These Found the Way: Thirteen Converts to Protestant Christianity* (Philadelphia: Westminster Press, 1951). For more on her involvement in American communism, see my "Finding Joy: A Comprehensive Bibliography of the Works of Joy Davidman," *Seven: An Anglo-American Literary Review* 23 (2006): 69–80; and my "Joy Davidman and the *New Masses*: Communist Poet and Reviewer," *Chronicle of the Oxford University C. S. Lewis Society* 4, no. 1 (Feb. 2007): 18–44.

11. See Clyde S. Kilby and Marjorie Lamp Mead, eds., *Brothers and Friends: The Diaries of Major Warren Hamilton Lewis* (San Francisco: Harper & Row, 1982).

12. Lewis was overwhelmed by the visit. On December 19, 1952, he writes his godson, Laurence Harwood: "I am completely 'circumvented' by a guest, asked for one week but staying for three, who talks from morning till night. I hope you'll all have a nicer Christmas than I. I can't write (write? I can hardly think or breathe. I can't believe it's all real)." Lewis, *Narnia, Cambridge and Joy*, 268; see also 260, 269, 270, and 271.

13. Lyle W. Dorsett, *And God Came In* (New York: Ballantine Books, 1984), 86.

14. In addition to *Letters to a Comrade* and *Anya*, Gresham also published a second novel, *Weeping Bay* (New York: Macmillan, 1950). She also published the nonfiction book *Smoke on the Mountain: An Interpretation of the Ten Commandments* (Philadelphia: Westminster Press, 1953), with a foreword by C. S. Lewis. All these works were published under her maiden name, Joy Davidman.

15. Joy Gresham, *Letter to a Comrade* (New Haven, CT: Yale Univ. Press, 1938), 40; subsequent references in the text.

16. She also explores the crucifixion in "I the Philosopher," 32–33.

17. The point of view in this poem could be that of the empress, but the verbal cues in the poem argue for a male perspective. For instance, at one point the persona says: "Let no recollection / Of any time when you were a woman come / Grinning at you with mortality written on bare teeth." Also, the phrase "the way my strength came forth" almost certainly refers to ejaculation.

18. Immediately proceeding "Yet One More Spring" is a poem entitled "Prothalamion" (64). It too bears witness to Gresham's intimation that there may be a lover for her in the future who will fulfill her.

19. It will not have escaped some readers that when Lewis first met Gresham she was thirty-seven and he was fifty-four; on the other hand, Pitter was fifty-five. We can hardly accuse Lewis of clay feet if he was more attracted to the younger woman.

20. Well before she met Lewis, she writes Herbert Palmer: "Have kept out of love as much as possible, as my psychology is such a muck-heap that it takes all my skill to carry on, without jarring impacts, which would ruin all my careful improvements. I lurk, intensely observant, in the undergrowth" (Nov. 14, 1936).

21. It is also worth recalling the irony that Pitter's *Persephone in Hades* is a poem about passion that is largely passionless.

22. In Pitter's Apr. 22, 1954, journal recollection she writes:

[Palmer's] rage with writers, critics, editors and publishers was hard to bear; he had no mercy on his hearers. More than once I have sat and watched the fire go out while he raved: indeed it seemed to me that he put it out. But he had the gift. . . . And I shall always maintain that he was a shrewd and just critic of minor work: great reputations maddened him & distorted his view, perhaps owing to the neglect (as he felt) of his own work. (Pitter journal, MS. Eng. lett. c. 220/5, fol. 125)

23. This memo, dated Apr. 1973, is available in Pitter's uncataloged papers.

24. From 1960 to 1964 Russell was a producer in overseas talks and features. He published four volumes of poetry: *In Idleness of Air* (1960), *Ice on the Live Rail* (1962), *New and Vanishing Delight* (1975), and *River Jumping with Kids* (1986). He was also a freelance poetry reviewer for publications such as the *Daily Telegraph*.

25. After years laboring as a don at Oxford, Lewis was vigorously pursued by Cambridge. In fact a special chair, the Professorship of Medieval and Renaissance Literature at Magdalene College, was created for him. Although he was reluctant at first, eventually the arguments of his friends led him to accept the appointment in 1955. At the same time, he continued living at the Kilns in Oxford, during term traveling back and forth on weekends.

26. This appears in Pitter's Mar. 5, 1955 journal recollection. Pitter journal, MS. Eng. lett. c. 220/5, fol. 128.

27. This appears in Pitter's Mar. 19, 1955 journal recollection. Pitter journal, MS. Eng. lett. c. 220/5, fol. 130.

28. *Letters on Poetry from W. B. Yeats to Dorothy Wellesley* (London: Oxford University Press, 1940).

29. Theodore Huebner Roethke (1908–1963) was an important twentieth-century American poet. His volumes of verse are *Open House* (1941); *The Lost Son and Other Poems* (1948); *Praise to the End!* (1951); *The Waking: Poems 1933–1953* (1953), which won the Pulitzer Prize; *I Am! Says the Lamb* (1961); *Sequence, Sometimes Metaphysical, Poems* (1963); *The Far Field* (1964); and *The Collected Poems of Theodore Roethke* (1966).

30. Carolyn Kizer (b. 1925) was a pupil under Roethke and has published eight volumes of verse: *The Ungrateful Garden* (1961); *Knock Upon Silence* (1965); *Midnight Was My Cry: New and Selected Poems* (1971); *Mermaids in the Basement: Poems for Women* (1984); *Yin* (1984), which won the Pulitzer Prize; *The Nearness of You: Poems for Men* (1986); *Harping On: Poems 1985–1995* (1996); and *Cool, Calm and Collected: Poems, 1960–2000* (2000).

31. BBC Radio, "On Poetry," May 17, 1955. This broadcast includes a reading of several of her poems: "Urania," "The Strawberry Plant," "The Bridge," "Close, Mortal Eyes," "The End of Fear," "The Bird in the Tree," "But for Lust," "The Ermine," "The Cedar," and "Hen under Bay-Tree."

32. BBC Radio, "Ruth Pitter Talks with Stephen Black," June 24, 1955. This is the same interview noted earlier in which Pitter discusses how the radio broadcasts of C. S. Lewis helped move her toward Christianity. See chapter 5. At the end of the Black interview, Pitter reflects more on her conversion: "I see now [maturing in faith is] a long process. There's a great deal to be pulled down before it can be built up, and I started very late. Very late in life. And one has fixed habits. It's a dreadful thing to get religion in middle age because there's so much to be undone. And it is a case of 'Lord I believe—Help Thou mine unbelief!'" Then she adds: "Oh I think [my vanity is] very great, although I've got to the stage where I'm conscious of it now and can laugh at it. What the soul asks is perfectly inordinate. The soul is guaranteed the sum total of everything if she will but consent—and it is to consent that is the difficult part. To win oneself away from oneself. Then one inherits everything."

33. The Gold Medal was first given by George V at the suggestion of Masefield (poet laureate 1930–1967). As it is not an annual award, recipients are chosen solely on their poetic merits "by a committee of eminent men and women of letters, under the chairmanship of the Poet Laureate." Other winners have included W. H. Auden (1936), Edmund

Blunden (1956), Siegfried Sassoon (1957), John Betjeman (1960), Philip Larkin (1965), Stevie Smith (1969), Ted Hughes (1974), and Kathleen Raine (1992).

34. Pitter is using terms used by Lewis in his *English Literature in the Sixteenth Century, Excluding Drama* (Oxford: Oxford University Press, 1954). See 64–65.

35. Later published as "Lewis Appears (Apropos of C. S. Lewis's Move to Cambridge, and His Possible Effect on [F. R.] Leavis and the Logical Positivists)," in Pitter's *A Heaven to Find* (London: Enitharmon, 1987). In Pitter's August 5, 1955, journal recollection she writes:

[This was] an epigram of mine on Lewis's going to Cambridge—in his inaugural lecture he referred to himself as a Dinosaur, a rare survival. . . . The "ambivalence" suggests that under the guise of a harmless Professor (and with suspected connivance on the part of the authorities) he had been smuggled in to blow some people out of the water. The second rhyme is more respectable than the first. "Min" for "men" is pure Essex, and I am fond of it: in that still half-barbarous county we (the women with grievances) attribute all that goes wrong to *The Min*—"Blast the Min!" when mud is tracked in, soot shaken down one's tottering Tudor chimney by a jet-plane, airborne invasions stream overhead towing gliders by means of thick nylon ropes when we have no best stockings. "Blast the Min!" one repeats with gusto, when American camps, complete with transport, showers, doughnuts, ice cream, are set up overnight half a mile from one's well, earth-closet, and oil lamp, and all village girls under 20 turned into honey-babies and set against honest work. As one goes west, this attitude softens with the climate, until one arrives at "Oh-dear-oh-dear! Whatever shall us do, then?" I hope sufficient has been said to demonstrate that *The Min* collectively (not one's own men) constitute a body responsible for whatever troubles we feel we must blow off steam about. (Pitter journal, MS. Eng. lett. c. 220/5, fols. 132–33)

9. *Public Figure, 1956–1966*

1. A listing of Pitter's BBC radio and television appearances is in the bibliography.

2. BBC Radio, "A Friendly Day," Oct. 21, 1958.

3. BBC Radio, "Glory Is Real," June 17, 1960.

4. BBC Radio, "Personal Pleasure: Growing Vegetables," Mar. 22, 1961.

5. BBC Radio, "Hunting the Unicorn," Feb. 17, 1961.

6. Pitter wrote this on a copy of the transcript available in her uncataloged papers. The original title of "Hunting the Unicorn" was "We Can't Take Less."

7. Russell's letter is available at the BBC Written Archives.

8. Most often a dinner followed the broadcast, and Pitter related to Arthur Russell an amusing anecdote on one occasion:

Many thanks for the encouraging, prompt letter about the last Brains Trust. We were a happy team, and only felt that we hadn't disagreed enough, but the producer said we had. I liked them all, but was particularly touched and amused by Prof. Goodhart's account of how on setting out his wife said to him that he must be very careful not to say anything unkind to Miss Pitter, that she knew my work and liked it, and she could tell from people's work what they were like; Miss Pitter, he would find, was small, very quiet, and very sensitive and easily hurt, so he must take care. As I gaily galloped my way through a huge bit of the very prime melon at lunch, singing its praises all the time, he began to shake gently, and at last came out with the above. Of course, Mrs. Goodhart is right really, only the shrinking violet has evolved a crash helmet.

9. Letter from Gillian Thorburn, Sept. 23, 1958. Another correspondent, Helen Mickerson, wrote Pitter on Mar. 2, 1959: "I want to thank you for the great pleasure you have given me during your appearances on the T.V. Brains Trust Programme, & I hope you will be back on the team again very soon. The answer you & Mr. Alan Bullock gave, many months ago now, about forgiveness will always remain a lovely memory, & there are many other things you have said which have given me an almost unearthly pleasure." Bullock had said:

I feel the burden [to forgive] lies upon all of us [because of] the burden of self. The imprisonment [is] in our own egotism and in our own selfishness, and it seems to me that forgiveness is an act which calls for the highest qualities in man, because it means renouncing yourself. The natural reaction of the egotist, the natural reaction of the self to injury, is resentment [and feeding on it] . . . and you have to break out of that circle and rise above yourself. . . . Forgiveness, it seems to me, is a divine quality in man, because there are occasions when you can see those who have suffered really great wrong, and somehow with a selflessness . . . rise above it. (Transcript, BBC Written Archives)

10. "From now until the end of winter is the planting season," *Woman: World's Greatest Weekly for Women* 43, no. 1116 (Nov. 1, 1958): 51.

11. "There's one thing the keen gardener can always do, however bad the weather may be—get things in order," *Woman: World's Greatest Weekly for Women* 44, no. 1125 (Jan. 3, 1959): 35.

12. "St. Valentine's Day, and they're here! The snowdrops, I mean," *Woman: World's Greatest Weekly for Women* 44, no. 1131 (Feb. 14, 1959): 39.

13. "By now the soil should be dry enough to sow a great many seeds, and we begin to have a sense of hurry," *Woman: World's Greatest Weekly for Women* 44, no. 1135 (Mar. 21, 1959): 40.

14. "This is the most magical time of the whole year—midsummer, with its 'livelong summer days,' when there's hardly any night," *Woman: World's Greatest Weekly for Women* 44, no. 1150 (June 27, 1959): 46.

15. "It really is autumn now. However fine the weather may be, the days are shorter, and the evenings and early mornings chillier," *Woman: World's Greatest Weekly for Women* 45, no. 1164 (Oct. 3, 1959): 50.

16. "From now until the end of winter is the planting season," *Woman: World's Greatest Weekly for Women* 43, no. 1116 (Nov. 1, 1958): 51.

17. "Ears," *Nursing Mirror and Midwives Journal* 109, no. 2854 (Mar. 11, 1960): 2070.

18. "Eyes," *Nursing Mirror and Midwives Journal* 109, no. 2855 (Mar. 18, 1960): 2162.

19. "Noses," *Nursing Mirror and Midwives Journal* 109, no. 2856 (Mar. 25, 1960): 2250.

20. "Hands," *Nursing Mirror and Midwives Journal* 110, no. 2857 (Apr. 1, 1960): 56.

21. "Voices," *Nursing Mirror and Midwives Journal* 110, no. 2858 (Apr. 8, 1960): 166.

22. On another occasion she writes Russell: "I found it passing strange that on the same day I should spend a good part of the morning having a fine elucidation of C. S. Lewis, pass on to a conference on Orwell, and find my Bengali interlocutor quoting Dorothy Wellesley. . . . The three people who have most impressed, disturbed, altered me (in my adult life) of all the numbers I have known!" (Oct. 3, 1959). Still later she adds: "Oh, about D. Wellesley's impact; yes, it did make a difference. She knocked down so much of

my cardboard scenery. . . . Not that it was altogether negative. She was a keen critic and often a farsighted one, she had a superb ear (at times); she knew the mysterium of poetry, and occasionally, in her presence, the mirror would form (that's the way I put it) and the mystery would be incarnate. Conversely, all might be horrible dislocation and destruction. It was as though bits of heaven and hell had been mixed. But I think the romantic heaven and hell; it was all on a much smaller canvas than Dante's! And, let me not forget, she was a gardener of the best kind, at least mentally. She gave me a new vision of flowering shrubs and species roses" (Oct. 9, 1959). Later Pitter published an essay titled "Dorothy Wellesley, 1889–1956" in *The Wind and the Rain: An Easter Book for 1962*, ed. Neville Braybrooke (London: Secker & Warburg, 1962), 201–8.

23. About the nature of the illness, Pitter later writes Mary Cooley:

As you will have heard, I have been unlucky this year: in hospital 4 months. It was gall bladder trouble, and I should have been out in a month, but the first incision was infected. Result, drainage tubes galore, a thrombosed leg & arm, and a large abscess in the back. And on the ambulance journey from the big hospital at Oxford to the local cottage hospital to convalesce, I had rather a rough ride & got a strained l[eft] shoulder tendon, which inflamed: and I expect to have to go in & out of Oxford for treatment for perhaps some months. Add to this a couple of bad colds and an alimentary infection, nearly all my hair coming out, nails like greaseproof paper, and you will see I have been paying life's glad arrears with a vengeance. But the goodness of people! The use of cars, presents of flowers, etc., visitors galore, a little ward all to myself for free (because of my germs), etc! I hardly knew I was seriously ill, though there were some nasty times. The mental experiences were extraordinary, and I quite thought I was permanently changed for the better morally: but this is not so. (Dec. 29, 1965)

24. At about this time Eugene Walter petitioned her to permit him to publish portions of *Persephone in Hades* in *Botteghe Oscure*. Both surprised and delighted, Pitter readily agreed in a series of letters: "Well, what a surprise. . . . I shall be honoured if [you] print a passage from the poem, and I suggest that you should make the choice as you have read it so thoroughly—you will choose better than I" (Apr. 7, 1957); "Thank you very much for your nice letter with the excerpts. Yes, these are quite representative from my point of view, and they do give the feeling of the whole poem very well. My only misgiving is that it may be a mere belly laugh to most readers, as it could hardly be more unfashionable, but you know about this better than I . . . [and] I am delighted to give permission for these selections to be printed in *Botteghe Oscure*" (May 3, 1956); and "I am so glad about Persephone & *Botteghe Oscure*. Strange after all these years, too—I mean one can never foresee what will happen to one's work" (Aug. 20, 1956). Pitter's uncataloged papers. Bodleian Library.

25. Stephen James Napier Tennant (1906–1987) was a British illustrator, poet, and writer. This letter is privately held by Ann Soutter.

26. This letter is privately held by Ann Soutter.

27. This letter is privately held by Ann Soutter.

28. *Narnia, Cambridge and Joy*, 700; subsequent references in the text.

29. *The Screwtape Letters* (London: Geoffrey Bles, 1942).

30. *Out of the Silent Planet* (London: Bodley Head, 1938), *Perelandra* (London: Bodley Head, 1943), and *That Hideous Strength: A Modern Fairy-Tale for Grown-Ups* (London: Bodley Head, 1945).

31. *The Allegory of Love: A Study in Medieval Tradition* (Oxford: Oxford Univ. Press,

1936) and *English Literature in the Sixteenth Century, Excluding Drama*. The Oxford History of English Literature, vol. 3 (Oxford: Clarendon Press, 1954).

32. *The Problem of Pain* (London: Centenary Press, 1940).

33. In her lectures on the trilogy, given July 9–13, 1956, as a part of the annual Worship and Arts conference she attended in Oxford, she says: "I want to tell you, speaking as an ordinary sinner and as a poet, how these strange and wonderful books have helped me to worship better, by making me more aware of myself, of my own mind, and my relationship to God, to His creation in general, and to other immortal beings in particular." After summarizing the books, she offers a fine assessment:

In these books God is given an unfamiliar name, Maleldil, and our Lord is referred to as Maleldil the Young. These are not pleasing names to me, but they have the great merit of cutting loose from the great mass of associations the Holy Names have in our minds. Much of this mass is lumber, and with unfamiliar names we can often become much more aware. *Eldil* is used for all great spirits, [and] it is roughly equivalent to *angel*, again a word with a lot of dead wood about it. Like the new names he opines for the planets, these names enable us to start with a clean sheet, and this I think is invaluable. The old dead mechanical notions, the false assumptions, the ideas gathered in infancy and not looked at again, tend to dissolve—the scales drop from our eyes, and some notion of the living God in his terrible and unknowable glory, in his love and humility so intimately appearing to us, does take shape. Professor Lewis has an unusually vivid notion of the supernatural, and he refuses to separate it from the natural by any watertight division. One might say that there is not a page which does not practice the presence of God. So pervading is this sense of divine immanence that I will merely suggest it as the permanent medium of all three books. . . . These books take a good deal of facing. To any honest person, the contemplation of his own sinful nature is always painful, but it is necessary, and here we are persuaded to take a good look at our own dirty littleness, and to make up our minds that . . . we have not a leg to stand on, except God's promises. There, and there alone, we are potentially creatures of infinite glory, only because he makes us, he loves us, and he dies for us. Heaven or hell—there is the naked choice, and it lives with us to make it. (Pitter's uncataloged papers)

34. For more on this, see Walter Hooper's *C. S. Lewis: A Companion and Guide* (London: HarperCollins, 1996), 57–107.

35. MS. Eng. lett. c. 220/5, fol. 141; this letter was inadvertently left out of *Narnia, Cambridge and Joy*. In her January 28, 1957, journal recollection of this letter, Pitter says:

I had of course seen the announcement of his marriage and (so tragically soon after) the news of his wife's illness. Not being near enough to help practically (supposing this would have been acceptable) I thought it best not to bother him, except for an occasional brief message requiring no reply. I had been taught in youth that a woman's friendship with a married man must be by grace and favour of his wife, and as Joy recovered and lived on so amazingly, I did from time to time write to her: but there was never any reply, so I decided to be thankful for this correspondence and friendship with so rare a creature as Lewis, and to leave it at that. (Pitter journal, MS. Eng. lett. c. 220/5, fol. 142)

36. Letter to Mary Pitter.

37. In her August 20, 1962, journal recollection of this letter, Pitter writes:

I was glad of the salutary observation about drug-visions. During a long illness in 1965 I was to have my fill of them: curiously strange & memorable, many of them, but for what I can see, pointless (the mysterious seaweed-eating creatures towards the end of "Perelandra." "Merely *other*."). Sensibility much enhanced, judgment much impaired: no moral content. There is one exception: I found that during that time a new dimension was given to one's feeling about the great books one knew—only some of them, not all—and that this has persisted as valid. (Pitter journal, MS. Eng. lett. c. 220/5, fol. 148)

38. After the appearance of Lewis's *Poems* (London: Geoffrey Bles, 1964), she writes Walter Hooper: "May I thank you for so well presenting the 'Poems' of C. S. Lewis, which one is so glad to have! They embody so many virtues, not least the brilliance of technique—he is matchless there. You will have earned much gratitude" (Nov. 17, 1964).

39. Pitter, "New Light on An Old Question: Review of *Letters to Malcolm, Chiefly on Prayer*," *Sunday Telegraph*, Jan. 26, 1964, 20.

40. Ruth Pitter letters to Walter Hooper in the Walter McGehee Hooper Papers #4236, Southern Historical Collection, Wilson Library, University of North Carolina at Chapel Hill.

41. Pitter notes her spiritual debt to Lewis in many places. To correspondent Andrew Nye on May 18, 1985, she writes: "As to my faith, I owe it to C. S. Lewis. For much of my life I lived more or less as a Bohemian, but when the second war broke out, Lewis broadcast several times, and also published some little books (notably "The Screwtape Letters"), and I was fairly hooked. I came to know him personally, and he came here several times. Lewis's stories, so very entertaining but always about the war between good and evil, became a permanent part of my mental and spiritual equipment."

42. Worth noting here is that a review of Lewis's letters shows that typically he was writing others, offering counsel, advice, and spiritual comfort. With Pitter the reverse was more typical—that is, when he wrote her he was seeking her advice about poetry or expressing his great admiration for her verse.

43. On July 23, 1985, Lyle Dorsett, then director of the Marion E. Wade Center at Wheaton College in Wheaton, Illinois, taped an interview with Ruth Pitter at the Hawthorns. In the written transcript of the interview Dorsett writes: "From [the] interview it was apparent that this woman once loved C. S. Lewis. It is sad that the expressions on her face when she talked of him cannot be seen by others." In the interview, the question of Lewis marrying Pitter came up:

D: Someone said that if C. S. Lewis was ever going to marry, that he would marry Miss Ruth Pitter.

P: Oh. Think of that! Did he say that?

D: That is what I've read somewhere that he said to one of his friends.

P: You can't be—

D: No, no, I take that back. I want to correct that. That one of his friends surmised that was what said, that if he were to marry, he would marry Miss Ruth Pitter.

P: Well, it's slender, isn't it? All the same it's very gratifying to the feelings. I'm glad to have heard it.

D: Yes, yes, it's a nice thing to have said, isn't it? . . . Well, do you think it would be fair to say that if Miss Ruth Pitter had ever married, maybe she would have married C. S. Lewis?

P: Don't put it to me like that, because honestly I don't know. I think on the whole, I've never been the marrying sort. I think it may be the case, it was just as well I were not called upon to make that decision. Well, I—I'm left with the hope that we shall meet again in heaven.

44. *Still by Choice* (London: Cresset Press, 1966).

45. That Pitter was writing verse during this time is illustrated by the fact that Carolyn Kizer, who became editor of *Poetry Northwest,* urged Pitter to send her some new poems. Eventually Pitter complied, and the following poems appeared in *Poetry Northwest* 1, no. 3 (Winter 1960): "Moths and Mercury-Vapour Lamp," "Exercise in the Pathetic Fallacy," "Tawny Owl in Fir-Tree," "One Right Kind of Music," "Old Nelly's Birthday," "Three Feminine Things," and "Sweet Other Flesh." Pitter sent Cecil a copy of the *Poetry Northwest* issue and said: "I thought you might like to have this for the sake of the new poems—I daresay you won't have seen it in the usual way of business. The editress is a perfect furnace of energy & enthusiasm—one feels a bit guilty at not being able to play up with equal ardor" (Mar. 27, 1960).

46. Indeed, a check of her manuscript notebooks from these years bears this out. As compared to earlier notebooks, the ones from these years contain fewer poems, and many of them appear in multiple drafts, suggesting both that she was finding it harder to write and that she was working harder at revision.

47. *Still by Choice,* 1; subsequent references in the text.

48. As predicted by this poem, the Hawthorns has in fact vanished. After Pitter's death, the Hawthorns was purchased and pulled down; in its place today is a small building estate (subdivision). The only hint that Pitter ever lived nearby is the name of the road leading into the building estate: Pitter's Piece.

49. C. S. Lewis, "The Weight of Glory" in *The Weight of Glory and Other Addresses* (New York: Macmillan, 1949), 1–2.

50. She offers additional insights on the poem in her comments before reading the poem for the Library of Congress recording: "[This poem] is called 'Exercise in the Pathetic Fallacy' and that is what it is, but I find people will persist in thinking that it has some depth, some revelation and perhaps it has. It may reveal something about my personality that I did not intend to reveal, but for myself I simply intended it as a construction of what could be made emotional out of a very simple arbitrary pattern."

51. Pitter is alluding to Hebrews 13:2: "Be not forgetful to entertain strangers: for thereby some have entertained angels unawares."

52. In *Perelandra* the narrator describes an *eldil* as "a very faint rod or pillar of light. I don't think it made a circle of light either on the floor or the ceiling, but I am not sure of this. . . . [And] it was not at right angles to the floor. But as soon as I have said this, I hasten to add that this way of putting it is a later reconstruction. What one actually felt at the moment was that the column of light was vertical but the floor was not horizontal—the whole room seemed to have heeled over as if it were on board ship. The impression, however produced, was that this creature had reference to some horizontal, to some whole system of directions, based outside the Earth, and that its mere presence imposed that alien system on me and abolished the terrestrial horizontal" (10–11).

53. Richard Kell, "Extension and Structure," review of *Still by Choice, Guardian,* Feb. 18, 1966:8.

54. Maurice Wiggin, "Poetry or Punch-Up?" review of *Still by Choice, Sunday Times,* Apr. 3, 1966:34.

55. "Personal Poets," review of *Still by Choice, Times Literary Supplement,* May 19, 1966:424.

10. Flickering Fires, 1967–1992

1. Cecil published the book as *Visionary and Dreamer: Two Poetic Painters, Samuel Palmer and Edward Burne-Jones* (London: Constable, 1969).

2. Although Mark Pitter gave these recordings to the British Library sometime in the 1970s, as of now they have not been located.

3. Unless otherwise noted, Pitter's letters to Tennant are available at Washington State University Libraries.

4. Almost a year later she also writes Cooley about Mark Pitter: [Mark], "now 17, is good looking and gifted, and is more interested in me and my work than anyone has ever been; he is keen to get as much recorded as he can while there is time, and is coming in the vacation to work at it. . . . I am particularly glad that coming as he does of highly irritable people on both sides, and at an age not remarkable for patience or tolerance, he is patient, amenable, and judicious; I love to talk with him" (June 11, 1968).

5. This letter is privately held by Ann Soutter.

6. *Poems 1926–1966* (London: Barrie and Rockcliff / Cresset Press, 1968); subsequent references in the text.

7. "Damp in the Country," review of *Poems 1926–1966*, *Times Literary Supplement*, Dec. 12, 1968:1407.

8. John Wain, "A Note on Ruth Pitter's Poetry," *Listener*, Feb. 20, 1969:239–40.

9. Her reference to having "seen something" links this preface to her BBC broadcast "Hunting the Unicorn," discussed earlier.

10. BBC Radio, "Ruth Pitter Talks to John Wain," Oct. 31, 1968.

11. Arthur Russell, ed., *Ruth Pitter: Homage to a Poet* (London: Rapp & Whiting, 1969), 13; subsequent references in the text.

12. "So Good of Their Kind," "So I Thought She Must Have Been Forgiven (A Dream)," "To a Lady in a Wartime Queue," and "Bad Child Left Behind," *Southern Review* 7, no. 2 (Spring 1971): 579–85.

13. BBC Radio, "The Pleasures of Old Age," Oct. 1, 1971.

14. Copies of these scripts are available in Pitter's uncataloged papers.

15. Later she writes Cooley:

I think I told you our mediaeval play (part of the York Cycle) was very successful, and we are going to repeat it. I have just finished making modern revisions (not too modern) of the six episodes involved, and thought I'd earned a rest: but now, blest if they don't want to do one more episode, on a float, for our village festival week. I suppose I shall have to do that too. The idea is to have the float, drawn by two very big handsome horses, stop in front of each pub (we have 6, I think), and the horses go into the yard and the driver into the pub, while the scene is enacted. I hope they won't want to do anything with angels in it, as all the fat old women hurl themselves at the parts of Angels, and look awful. You want fierce young men; only of course fierce young men have fierce young girlfriends who won't let them do anything without them. (Nov. 17, 1972)

Several years later she tells Arthur Russell:

We have just finished the run of our "mystery" plays; I have been trying to get to as many rehearsals as possible in order to catch faults due to not quite understanding the old texts, etc., and also I was nabbed to take the part of a neighbour who died. It

was quite respectable in the end, and the music was A1, being all mediaeval (due to
musically learned vicar), but a number of the leading parts were nabbed at the very
outset three seasons ago by amateur actors, all conceit and no talents; I am afraid
nothing but death will shift them, and they kill their parts stone dead. The way to
cast these   ~~h the village for the right types, then persecute them until
they agree   ·~~ld be so childishly vain and blind. At
least one

16. To a   ribe the inertia that has
overtaken   )ccupied in caring for her
that I have   )wells, May 9, 1973; BBC
Written A

Mysel   d since K's death: nearly
54 ye: eries for most of her life,
and   d & affectionate at the
last. Just 88: on..   I hope to be able to stay
here, and don't really doubt that   ntil her affairs are settled,
I shan't know my exact position. I have most affecti... : friends, really wonderful,
an excellent doctor, and our Vicar is the most delightful there could be—learned,
charming, most assiduous in his duties, *well-bred!!* (for a wonder) and he has known
& liked my work all along: also my health is good, for my age, so that really my last
state is better than my first. (July 15, 1973)

To Russell she says: "She was just 88, and did it beautifully in 3 d~~
years (almost a lifetime) of such numerous infirmities, for ν
done, this was a mercy. At first I felt tremendously relieved,
sense of bereavement & disorientation grows on me. I think
I wish, but of course her affairs are not settled yet, and my
this" (Sept 21, 1973).
   However, Pitter's most detailed account of O'Hara's last d

First I must tell you that K. has gone. She died on the
88. After almost a lifetime of various ailments, her death
could be imagined. She had a very happy birthday on the
with plenty of flowers, presents, etc., and a surprise visit
next day was quite nice and cheerful too. She took her   .. rather early,
having filled her own hot [water] bottle. But when I we   up later, she couldn't get
her tablets right. Every night she would set them all out, such an array, against all
contingencies, but now she was whimpering a bit (most unlike her) and I noticed
her speech was not quite clear. And then she swayed a bit. I helped her into bed, and
then she said she was afraid of going to sleep for fear she should not wake up (what
an Irish thing to mind!) and if she didn't feel safe, might she come to me? Of course I
said yes. No sooner had I got into bed than there she was, with all her pillows (about
6). She dumped them down, and got into bed beside me. She put her poor right
arm, very much wasted, round me, and with her left arm pulled up the bedclothes
and tucked them in round me, patting me as if I had been an infant. Then we both
slept—slept for some hours, quite peacefully. Very early I got up and made tea, and
she drank half a cup, holding cup and saucer normally. Then she actually got up for

a few minutes and paid the usual visit, pulling the flush and all. But an hour or two afterwards, when I took her a little porridge, she could neither swallow nor speak in the least articulately, but she very cleverly asked me if it was a stroke, pointing to her head and raising her eyebrows. Of course I got the doctor and a neighbour at once. By midday she was pretty well unconscious. I watched by her the next night, but she never moved. The next morning they took her to our nice little Cottage Hospital, and she died in the small hours of the next day. Her funeral was so loving and cheerful, too. I thought I could not mourn for her, but one cannot part with the companion of over half a century without feeling it. The lamp of life somehow burns low. It will brighten again when the full year is past. I shall end my days here if I can afford to, but I think it will be all right when her estate is cleared up. (Nov. 1973)

17. About Cruickshank Pitter later writes Russell: "[She is] my fellow-poetess and neighbour . . . very intellectual and much neglected; she has published several books, her own poems, translation of Rilke's 'Life of Mary' (lovely) and a Life of Rilke. She is dark, and Scottish, and has poor health, and I think my ambience here tends to overshadow and depress her, who is so much better a Christian than I, full of work and help and charity. But like a true Scot, she argues to win rather than to elucidate, and makes me bristle in an obscure way. However, in a certain sense each is all the other has in this place; you might say we are marooned on the same island" (Nov. 6, 1976).

18. This letter is privately held by Ann Soutter.

19. In early February of 1974, Pitter had learned of the award through a letter from the Rt. Hon. the Lord Butler KG, CH, president of the Royal Society of Literature. In part, he wrote: "In 1961 the Royal Society of Literature created a new honour, with the title of Companion of Literature (C.Lit.), to be conferred upon a few writers who have given exceptional distinction to the English literature of their day. . . . The number of Companions of Literature are limited to ten, who must be elected by vote of the [Royal Society]. Your name has just received this unanimous vote."

20. *End of Drought*, 3; subsequent references in the text.

21. BBC Radio, "Ruth Pitter Talks to Hallam Tennyson," Nov. 7, 1977.

22. Or "Be opened." This comes from an incident in Mark 7:32–37.

And they bring unto him one that was deaf, and had an impediment in his speech; and they beseech him to put his hand upon him. And he took him aside from the multitude, and put his fingers into his ears, and he spit, and touched his tongue; And looking up to heaven, he sighed, and saith unto him, Ephphatha, that is, Be opened. And straightway his ears were opened, and the string of his tongue was loosed, and he spake plain. And he charged them that they should tell no man: but the more he charged them, so much the more a great deal they published it; And were beyond measure astonished, saying, He hath done all things well: he maketh both the deaf to hear, and the dumb to speak.

23. Letter from Kenneth Stowe. On June 4, 1917, King George created an order of chivalry, the Most Excellent Order of the British Empire. The order consists of five classes in civil and military divisions: knight grand cross or dame grand cross (GBE), knight commander or dame commander (KBE or DBE), commander (CBE), officer (OBE), and member (MBE).

24. Cruickshank reports this as an excerpt from her diary and records it in an essay entitled "Remembering Ruth Pitter." It is available in Pitter's uncataloged papers.

25. "Brambleberries, Blackberries" first appeared in *Harpers & Queen* in Mar. 1986.

26. *A Heaven to Find* (London: Enitharmon, 1987). There is no pagination.

27. In the manuscript there is an alternate conclusion: "For broken hearts derided, / For weary flesh hither and thither driven, / For ardent loves divided, / Only one sovereign Remedy is given: / Happy such lovers when they turn to Heaven."

28. First published in *Ten Oxford Poets* (Oxford: Charles Brand, 1978), 3.

29. "Good Enthroned" is a shortened and better version of "Happy Christmas," first published in *End of Drought*.

30. Selena Hastings, "Lurking in the Thorny Undergrowth," *Sunday Telegraph*, Feb. 17, 1991:12.

31. In a review of a revision of the 1990 *Collected Poems*, Jane Dowson adds: "One benchmark of her poetry is undoubtedly a sensitivity to suffering, allied to an almost absurdist detachment." See Dowson, "Otherworldly yet Clay-Footed," review of *Collected Poems*, *Poetry Review* (Winter 1996–1997): 89–90.

32. Pitter, "Call Not to Me," *A Trophy of Arms*, 21.

33. "Ruth Pitter," obituary, *Daily Telegraph*, Mar. 2, 1992, 21.

34. "Ruth Pitter Obituary," *Times*, Mar. 3, 1992, 15.

35. Ann Margaret Ridler, "Capturing the Dance in Stillness," *Guardian*, Mar. 3, 1992, 35. Ann Ridler is now Ann Soutter.

36. Carolyn Kizer, "The Book of Ruth," *Writer's Chronicle* 32 (Oct.–Nov. 1999): 29–31, 34.

37. Mario A. Di Cesare, ed., *George Herbert and the Seventeenth-Century Poets* (New York: W. W. Norton, 1978), 30.

38. *End of Drought*, 25.

39. Di Cesare, *George Herbert and the Seventeenth-Century Poets*, 185.

40. *A Trophy of Arms*, 51.

41. *Collected Poems*, rev. ed. (Petersfield, UK: Enitharmon, 1996), 15.

42. *The Oxford Book of Twentieth-Century English Verse* (Oxford: Oxford Univ. Press, 1973). The poems he includes are "The Eternal Image," "Time's Fool," "But for Lust," and "Hen under Bay-Tree."

43. Letter to Judy Egerton, Mar. 16, 1969, in Anthony Thwaite, ed., *Selected Letters of Philip Larkin: 1949–1985* (London: Faber & Faber, 1992), 412–13.

Bibliography

The central repository of Ruth Pitter's papers—including letters to her, manuscript note-books, unpublished poems, financial records, photographs, and related materials—is the thirty-nine boxes of uncataloged material held in the Modern Papers and John Johnson Reading Room, New Bodleian Library, University of Oxford.

Works by Ruth Pitter

Poetry Publications

"Against the Winter." *New Age* 26, no. 5 (Dec. 4, 1919): 84.

"Alone." *New Age* 26, no. 16 (Feb. 19, 1920): 260.

"Andante." *New Age* 26, no. 12 (Jan. 22, 1920): 196.

"Apology." *New English Weekly* 1, no. 18 (Aug. 18, 1932): 425.

"Appraisement." *New Age* 26, no. 23 (Apr. 8, 1920): 363.

"Arise, Dead Beauties." *New Age* 28, no. 7 (Dec. 16, 1920): 84.

"An Autumn Morning." *Coburn Magazine*, Feb. 1912, n.p.

"Bad Child Left Behind." *Southern Review* 7, no. 2 (Spring 1971): 584.

"The Beautiful Negress." *New English Weekly* 8, no. 10 (Dec. 19, 1935): 188.

"Be Dim, O Sanctuary." *New Age* 27, no. 7 (June 17, 1920): 109.

"Better than Love." *Poetry Review* 32, no. 2 (Mar.–Apr., 1941): 75–76.

"The Birds Mourning." *Illustrated Review* 1, no. 2 (July 1923): 74.

"Brambleberries, Blackberries." *Harpers & Queen*, Mar. 1986.

The Bridge: Poems 1939–1944. London: Cresset Press, 1945.

"Burning the Bee-Tree." *London Mercury* 35 (Feb. 1937): 358–59.

"Caged Lion." *New English Weekly* 7, no. 10 (June 20, 1935): 196.

"Call Not to Me." *New English Weekly* 1, no. 7 (June 2, 1932): 169.

"The Captive Bird of Paradise." *Poetry Review* 42, no. 2 (Mar.–Apr. 1951): 72.

"The Careless Spirit." *New Age* 24, no. 2 (Nov. 14, 1918): 32.

"Childe Edward His Treasure (Fragment)." *New Age* 31, no. 22 (Sept. 28, 1922): 274.

"The Chimney Piece." *Virginia Quarterly Review* 15 (1939): 246.

"Chinese Poem (1920)." *Poetry Review* 40, no. 5 (Nov.–Dec. 1949): 326.

"Choice of Death." *New Age* 32, no. 20 (Mar. 15, 1923): 323.

"Clear Eve." *New Age* 23, no. 12 (July 18, 1918): 190.

"Cockroach." *New English Weekly* 4, no. 10 (Dec. 21, 1933): 236–37.

"The Coffin-Worme Which Consider." *New English Weekly* 5, no. 11 (June 28, 1934): 252.

Collected Poems. Introduction by Elizabeth Jennings. Rev. ed. 1990. Petersfield, UK: Enitharmon, 1996.

"The Companion of Youth." *New Age* 22, no. 6 (Dec. 6, 1917): 117.

"The Consummation." *New Age* 23, no. 18 (Aug. 29, 1918): 289.

"Crumbs for the Bird." *Poetry Review* 52, no. 2 (Apr.–June 1961): 72.

"Dark." *New Age* 29, no. 14 (Aug. 4, 1921): 168.

"The Dark Harvest." *New Age* 31, no. 20 (Sept. 14, 1922): 247.

"The Dead Fay." *New Age* 18, no. 7 (Dec. 16, 1915): 163.

"The Debtor." *New Age* 25, no. 6 (June 5, 1919): 101.

"The Desert Loves." *New Age* 28, no. 12 (Jan. 20, 1921): 144.

"Digdog." *New English Weekly* 3, no. 18 (Aug. 17, 1933): 426.

"Downward Pointing Muse." *London Mercury* 35 (Feb. 1937): 359–60.

"The Earth and the Heaven, in the Evening." *New Age* 21, no. 21 (Sept. 20, 1917): 454.

"The Earwig's Complaint." *New English Weekly* 2, no. 13 (Jan. 12, 1933): 308–9.

"Ecclesiasticella: Or the Church Mouse." *New English Weekly* 3, no. 24 (Sept. 28, 1933): 573.

"Elfeshill." *New Age* 23, no. 14 (Aug. 1, 1918): 228.

"The Elfin Heart." *New Age* 23, no. 13 (July 25, 1918): 199.

"Enchanted." *New Age* 20, no. 7 (Dec. 14, 1916): 165.

End of Drought. London: Barrie and Jenkins, 1975.

"Enthroned." *New Age* 27, no. 22 (Sept. 30, 1920): 324.

The Ermine: Poems 1942–1952. London: Cresset Press, 1953.

"Errant." *New Age* 29, no. 9 (June 30, 1921): 108.

"The Eternal Image." *New English Weekly* 7, no. 9 (June 13, 1935): 173.

"Euclidean Merely; Yet O Leave It Me!" *London Mercury* 32 (June 1935): 114.

"Exercise in the Pathetic Fallacy." *Poetry Northwest* 1, no. 3 (Winter 1960): 5–6.

"Fairy Denied Heaven." *New Age* 26, no. 14 (Feb. 5, 1920): 215.

"Fairy-Gold." *New Age* 11, no. 8 (June 20, 1912): 184.

"Fairy Tale." *New Age* 30, no. 21 (Mar. 23, 1922): 280.

"Farewell to Beauty." *New English Weekly* 4, no. 5 (Nov. 16, 1933): 119.

"Farewell to Life." *New Age* 18, no. 12 (Jan. 20, 1916): 283.

"Felicity Seen from Afar." *New Age* 25, no. 11 (July 10, 1919): 188.

"Fie, Innocents." *New Age* 30, no. 22 (Mar. 30, 1922): 292.

"Field Grasses." *New Age* 9, no. 2 (May 11, 1911): 29.

First and Second Poems: 1912–1925. Preface by Hilaire Belloc. London: Sheed and Ward, 1927.

First Poems. London: Cecil Palmer, 1920.

"The Flower-Piece." *New English Weekly* 1, no. 18 (Aug. 18, 1932): 425.

"Fons Nympharum." *New Age* 32, no. 11 (Jan. 11, 1923): 163.

"The Friends." *New Age* 22, no. 24 (Apr. 11, 1918): 475.

"The Frog in the Well: A True History, and Image of the State." *New English Weekly* 5, no. 6 (May 24, 1934): 132–33.

"Fugitive Beauty." *New Age* 34, no. 6 (Dec. 6, 1923): 72.

"The God." *New Age* 25, no. 7 (June 12, 1919): 124.

"Harmony." *New Age* 23, no. 15 (Aug. 8, 1918): 231.

"The Heavenly Love." *New Age* 26, no. 11 (Jan 15, 1920): 180.

A Heaven to Find. London: Enitharmon, 1987.

"A Hero." *Dial* 86 (Jan. 1929): 27–28.

"Homage to Ivan Mestrovic." *New English Weekly* 9, no. 5 (May 14, 1936): 90.

"Hospitality (From the French of Fabre d'Eglantine, 1750–1794)." *New Age* 17, no. 4 (May 27, 1915): 93–94.

"Humble Simile." *Commonweal* 20 (July 13, 1934): 282.

"I Fear the Gentle Forest Folk." *New Age* 28, no. 6 (Dec. 9, 1920): 72.

"I Gather Acorns." *New English Weekly* 1, no. 1 (Apr. 21, 1932): 18.

"I Have Taken Earth." *New Age* 28, no. 10 (Jan. 6, 1921): 120.

"An Impatience." *New English Weekly* 4, no. 12 (Jan. 4, 1934): 275.

"In the Open." *Poetry Book Society Bulletin* No. 48 (Apr. 1966): 2.

"The Kitoun's Eclogue." [Under pseudonym B. Forester] *New English Weekly* 2, no. 10 (Dec. 22, 1932): 237.

"The Knightly Damoiseau." *New Age* 24, no. 9 (Jan. 2, 1919): 148.

"The Knight's Doom." *New Age* 26, no. 21 (Mar. 25, 1920): 344.

"Lament for the Landless." *London Mercury* 39 (Mar. 1939): 512–13.

"Leal." *New Age* 30, no. 20 (Mar. 16, 1922): 267.

"Let Us Repent." *Forum and Century* 102 (Aug. 1939): 96.

"A Little Cloud." *New Age* 9, no. 4 (May 25, 1911): 92.

"Lo, Here That Mystery." *New Age* 26, no. 10 (Jan. 8, 1920): 151.

"The Lost Hermitage." *New English Weekly* 1, no. 12 (July 7, 1932): 279.

"Love's Martyrs or The Bee Turned Anchorite." *New English Weekly* 2, no. 19 (Feb. 23, 1933): 452–53.

A Mad Lady's Garland. Preface by Hilaire Belloc. London: Cresset Press, 1934.

"The Maid's Burial." *New Age* 22, no. 21 (Mar. 21, 1918): 423.

"Mar. and the Children." *New Age* 30, no. 17 (Feb. 23, 1922): 224.

"Markelin." *New Age* 25, no. 3 (May 15, 1919): 41.

"Maternall Love Tryumphant, or, Song of the Vertuous Femayle Spyder." *New English Weekly* 2, no. 18 (Feb. 16, 1933): 429.

"The Matron-Catts Song." *New English Weekly* 3, no. 1 (Apr. 1933): 22–23.

"Melancholy." *New Age* 28, no. 11 (Jan. 13, 1921): 132.

"Melilote." *New Age* 21, no. 7 (June 14, 1917): 148.

"Merry Death." *New Age* 30, no. 15 (Feb. 9, 1922): 199.

"The Military Harpist." *New English Weekly* 12, no. 20 (Feb. 24, 1938): 390.

"The Missal." *New Age* 23, no. 12 (July 18, 1918): 189.

"Moths and Mercury-Vapour Lamp." *Poetry Northwest* 1, no. 3 (Winter 1960): 4–5.

"My Love's Cold." *New Age* 27, no. 26 (Oct. 28, 1920): 372.

"The Neuter Cat's Fulfilment." *Lilliput*, Jan. 1943:50–51.

"Now I Make Death My Treasure." *New Age* 27, no. 20 (Sept. 16, 1920): 300.

"The Oak Tree." *New Age* 23, no. 14 (Aug. 1, 1918): 221.

"O Come Out of the Lily." *Virginia Quarterly Review* 15 (1939): 248.

"Of the Damned." *New Age* 27, no. 8 (June 24, 1920): 120.

"Old Clockwork Time." *Poetry Review* 43, no. 2 (Mar.–Apr. 1952): 76.

"Old Nelly's Birthday." *Poetry Northwest* 1, no. 3 (Winter 1960): 8.

"An Old Song." *New Age* 27, no. 19 (Sept. 9, 1920): 284.

"The Old Woman." *New English Weekly* 4, no. 12 (Jan. 4, 1934): 275.

"On a Passage from the 'Metamorphoses' of Ovid." *New English Weekly* 6, no. 23 (Mar. 21, 1935): 480.

On Cats. London: Cresset Press, 1946.

"One Right Kind of Music." *Poetry Northwest* 1, no. 3 (Winter 1960): 8.

"O Sweet Fidelity." *New Age* 26, no. 24 (Apr. 15, 1920): 392.

"The Outlaw." *New Age* 9, no. 5 (June 1, 1911): 108.

"Overture." *New Age* 26, no. 26 (Apr. 29, 1920): 424.

"Pageant." *New Age* 31, no. 19 (Sept. 7, 1922): 235.

"The Paradox." *New English Weekly* 8, no. 3 (Oct. 31, 1935): 51.

"Pastiche: High Summer." *New Age* 27, no. 18 (Sept. 2, 1920): 276.

"Pastiche: In Praise." *New Age* 27, no. 1 (May 6, 1920): 16.

"Pastiche: On 'Tristion En Romance,'" *New Age* 27, no. 2 (May 13, 1920): 32.

"Pastiche: The Fays to the Man." *New Age* 27, no. 12 (July 22, 1920): 192.

"Pastoral with Artifice." *New Age* 31, no. 12 (July 20, 1922): 152.

"Penitence." *Virginia Quarterly Review* 26 (1950): 62.

Persephone in Hades. Auch, France: A. Sauriac, 1931.

"The Pipe of Glass." *New Age* 25, no. 8 (June 19, 1919): 140.

"The Plain Facts by a Plain but Amiable Cat." Garland Chapbook No. 1.

Poem. Southampton: Shirley Press, 1943.

Poems 1926–1966. London: Barrie and Rockliff / Cresset Press, 1968.

"The Poor Poet." *New Age* 21, no. 22 (Sept. 27, 1917): 462.

"The Portrait." *New Age* 28, no. 19 (Mar. 10, 1921): 224.

"Portrait of a Gentleman." *New English Weekly* 3, no. 16 (Aug. 3, 1933): 381.

"Poverty Malcontent." *New Age* 32, no. 25 (Apr. 19, 1923): 403.

"Prayer for a Fair People." *New Age* 21, no. 23 (Oct. 4, 1917): 488.

"The Primordial Cell." *New English Weekly* 11, no. 15 (July 22, 1937): 290.

"The Promised Rest." *New Age* 24, no. 10 (Jan. 9, 1919): 168.

"Quorum Porum." *Lilliput*, Dec. 1942:373.

"The Realm." *New Age* 18, no. 19 (Mar. 9, 1916): 452–53.

"The Rejected Fair." *New Age* 32, no. 13 (Jan. 25, 1923): 201.

"Resurgam: Or the Glorious and Pitifull Historie of the Hereticall Catterpiller." *New English Weekly* 2, no. 20 (Mar. 2, 1933): 477–79.

"Retrospect." *Virginia Quarterly Review* 16 (1940): 380–81.

"Romford Market." In G. Rostrevor Hamilton and John Arlott, eds. *Landmarks: A Book of Topographical Verse for England and Wales.* Cambridge: Cambridge University Press, 3.

"Royal Psyche." *New Age* 27, no. 24 (Oct. 14, 1920): 348.

The Rude Potato. London: Cresset Press, 1941.

"A Sadd Lament of a Performing Flea." *New English Weekly* 4, no. 23 (Mar. 22, 1934): 546.

"The Satten Cloke." *New Age* 28, no. 1 (Nov. 4, 1920): 12.

"Saturn's Counsel." *New English Weekly* 4, no. 12 (Jan. 4, 1934): 275.

"Sea-Herb." *New Age* 26, no. 25 (Apr. 22, 1920): 408.

"Seek the Wide Solace." *New Age* 24, no. 13 (Jan. 30, 1919): 216.

"September Night." *New Age* 24, no. 14 (Feb. 6, 1919): 232.

"The Ship-Book." *New English Weekly* 6, no. 16 (Jan. 31, 1935): 341.

"Silence Shall Cover Thee." *New Age* 27, no. 6 (June 10, 1920): 83.

"Sing, Gentle Joy." *New English Weekly* 4, no. 12 (Jan. 4, 1934): 276.

"The Singer." *New Age* 23, no. 11 (July 11, 1918): 176.

"Sleep." *New Age* 29, no. 19 (Sept. 8, 1921): 228.

"So Good of Their Kind." *Southern Review* 7, no. 2 (Spring 1971): 579–81.

"So I Thought She Must Have Been Forgiven (A Dream)." *Southern Review* 7, no. 2 (Spring 1971): 581–83.

"The Solitary." *New English Weekly* 9, no. 4 (May 7, 1936): 70.

"The Solitary Thought." *New Age* 32, no. 18 (Mar. 1, 1923): 292.

"Song, Grieve No More." *New Age* 23, no. 15 (Aug. 8, 1918): 241.

"Song (The End of True Love Is to Sit and Mourn)." *New Age* 23, no. 7 (June 13, 1918): 112.

"Song (When I Die)." *New Age* 11, no. 4 (May 23, 1912): 88.

"Song (When That Thy Spirit)." *New Age* 26, no. 7 (Dec. 18, 1919): 116.

"A Song for the Leaders." *New Age* 18, no. 18 (Mar. 2, 1916): 429.

"A Song of a Child's Happiness." *New Age* 10, no. 12 (Jan. 18, 1912): 268.

"The Sorrow of Truth." *New Age* 23, no. 16 (Aug. 15, 1918): 260.

The Spirit Watches. London: Cresset Press, 1939.

"The Spirit Watches." *Virginia Quarterly Review* 15 (1939): 247.

"Spring (Rondeau)." *New Age* 15, no. 4 (May 28, 1914): 92.

"The Spring Flood Shineth." *New Age* 30, no. 5 (Dec. 1, 1921): 51.

"Sprite Alone." *New Age* 24, no. 6 (Dec. 12, 1918): 96.

Still by Choice. London: Cresset Press, 1966.

"Stockdove." *London Mercury* 37 (Nov. 1937): 8.

"Sturdy Thieves." *New Age* 25, no. 26 (Oct. 23, 1919): 432.

"The Swan." *New Age* 23, no. 15 (Aug. 8, 1918): 244.

"The Swan Bathing." *Virginia Quarterly Review* 16 (1940): 381–82.

"Sweet Buds." *New Age* 30, no. 18 (Mar. 2, 1922): 230.

"Sweet Other Flesh." *Poetry Northwest* 1, no. 3 (Winter 1960): 10–11.

"Sweet They May Sing Thee." *New Age* 32, no. 23 (Apr. 5, 1923): 365.

"Tace I and II." *New Age* 25, no. 13 (July 24, 1919): 220.

"The Task." *London Mercury* 32 (June 1935): 113.

"Tawny Owl in Fir-Tree." *Poetry Northwest* 1, no. 3 (Winter 1960): 7.

"Thanksgiving for a Fair Summer." *New English Weekly* 1, no. 12 (July 7, 1932): 279.

"Thou Sawest Thy Star." *New Age* 31, no. 4 (May 25, 1922): 39.

"Three Feminine Things." *Poetry Northwest* 1, no. 3 (Winter 1960): 9–10.

"The Three Poplars." *London Mercury* 32 (June 1935): 113–14.

"The Thorn." *New Age* 19, no. 4 (May 25, 1916): 87.

"Thy Song Is Like a Lemon Tree." *New Age* 21, no. 19 (Sept. 6, 1917): 414.

"To a Lady in a Wartime Queue." *Southern Review* 7, no. 2 (Spring 1971): 583–84.

"To Nymphes That They Would Confess the Pre-eminent Beauties of Pyrrha." *New English Weekly* 4, no. 13 (Jan. 11, 1934): 309–10.

"Too Light and Merrily." *New Age* 32, no. 17 (Feb. 22, 1923): 263.

"To Prodigal of Pity." *New Age* 28, no. 22 (Mar. 31, 1921): 264.

"To Righteousness Outcast and Disguised." *New Age* 21, no. 4 (May 24, 1917): 94.

"To the Beloved." *New Age* 27, no. 14 (Aug. 5, 1920): 220.

"To the Dead." *New Age* 27, no. 17 (Aug. 26, 1920): 264.

"To the People." *New Age* 9, no. 14 (Aug. 3, 1911): 332.

"To the Poets." *New English Weekly* 8, no. 18 (Feb. 13, 1936): 352.

"To the Shade of Sir Philip Sidney." *New English Weekly* 6, no. 10 (Dec. 20, 1934): 221.

"To the Soul: That She Would Cease From Troubling." *New English Weekly* 1, no. 18 (Aug. 18, 1932): 425.

"To the Unknown Art." *New Age* 33, no. 3 (May 17, 1923): 47.

"A Tree in Heaven." *New Age* 30, no. 10 (Jan. 5, 1922): 120.

A Trophy of Arms: Poems 1926–1935. Preface by James Stephens. London: Cresset Press, 1936.

"Unknown Glory." *New Age* 30, no. 19 (Mar. 9, 1922): 248.

"Unregretted." *New Age* 28, no. 3 (Nov. 18, 1920): 36.

"Urania." *New English Weekly* 4, no. 12 (Jan. 4, 1934): 276.

Urania. Selections from *A Trophy of Arms, The Spirit Watches,* and *The Bridge.* London: Cresset Press, 1950.

"Villanette." *New Age* 28, no. 18 (Mar. 3, 1921): 216.

"The Viper." *New English Weekly* 4, no. 12 (Jan. 4, 1934): 276.

"Virginal." *Dial* 84 (May 1928): 384–85.

"The Waters of Paradise." *New Age* 23, no. 6 (June 6, 1918): 96.

"Weeping Water, Leaping Fire." *New English Weekly* 1, no. 12 (July 7, 1932): 279.

"Well Beloved." *New Age* 22, no. 23 (Apr. 4, 1918): 459.

"Where Didst Thou Learn." *New Age* 34, no. 7 (Dec. 13, 1923): 84.

"White and Red." *New Age* 27, no. 23 (Oct. 7, 1920): 336.

"Whom We Have Buried." *New Age* 25, no. 1 (May 1, 1919): 16.

"Willow." *New Age* 26, no. 9 (Jan. 1, 1920): 135.

"The Winnower to the Winds." *New Age* 32, no. 12 (Jan. 18, 1923): 182.

"Winter Mourned." *New Age* 31, no. 2 (May 11, 1922): 24.

"A Worn Theme." *Virginia Quarterly Review* 26 (1950): 61.

"Young Loves." *Illustrated Review* 1, no. 6 (Nov. 1923): 304.

BBC Radio Broadcasts

Unless otherwise noted, the transcripts of her BBC radio and television appearances are held at the BBC Written Archives, Caversham Park, Reading.

"Alexander Pope." Jan. 26, 1946.

"As I See It [Autumn in the Country]." Oct. 30, 1960. Transcript available in Pitter's uncataloged papers. Bodleian Library.

"As I See It [Having a Home]." Nov. 27, 1960.

"As I See It [Memory of an Old Character]." Jan. 8, 1961.

"As I See It [Potterer's Dreams]." Oct. 2, 1960.

"As You Like It." May 31, 1947.

"At Home with a Poetess." Apr. 25, 1969.

"Attitudes toward Children." Mar. 6, 1961.

"Beauty." May 16, 1957.

"Colour Supplement: Poetic Impressions of Colour." Mar. 8, 1966. No transcript available.

"Comments on Listeners' Letters." June 29, 1964.

"Contemporary Women Writers." Nov. 26, 1946. No transcript available.

"Dorothy Wordsworth." Jan. 30, 1946.

"First Meeting: Ruth Pitter and David Patterson." July 8, 1959. Transcript available in Pitter's uncataloged papers. Bodleian Library.

"First Meeting: Ruth Pitter and Sir William Haley." Sept. 2, 1959. Transcript available in Pitter's uncataloged papers. Bodleian Library.

"A Friendly Day." Oct. 21, 1958.

"Glory Is Real." June 17, 1960.

"Harvest Time." Sept. 4, 1960.

"Heroes of Our Time, Charles Williams." July 18, 1961.

"How I Go About It." Sept. 27, 1961.

"Hunting the Unicorn." Feb. 17, 1961.

"The Hut." Oct. 27, 1961.

"I Know That My Redeemer Liveth." Apr. 8, 1971.

"In Praise of Aunts." Jan. 13, 1972.

"In Praise of Virtues, Frugality." Sept. 28, 1960.

"Judging Poetry." Oct. 8, 1956.

"June in Their Gardens, Discussion with Jim Middleton." June 9, 1961. No transcript available.

"Keep Beauty in Your Life." July 15, 1963.

"A Lifelong Dream Come True." May 4, 1972.

"The Most Important Thing I Have Learned in Life." July 10, 1948

"The Mystery of Holy Week." Apr. 8, 1971. Transcript available in Pitter's uncataloged papers. Bodleian Library.

"On Poetry." May 17, 1955. Transcript available in Pitter's uncataloged papers. Bodleian Library.

"Pause for Thought." Oct. 23, 1970. No transcript available.

"Pause for Thought, Happiness." May 11, 1971. Transcript available in Pitter's uncataloged papers. Bodleian Library.

"Personal Philosophy: Interview with J. Ryder-Smith." Sept. 28, 1970. Transcript available in Pitter's uncataloged papers. Bodleian Library.

"Personal Pleasure: Growing Vegetables." Mar. 22, 1961.

"A Piece of My Mind." Sept. 6, 1960.

"A Pinch of Philosophy." Oct. 1, 1956.

"The Pleasures of Old Age." Oct. 1, 1971.

"Poems by Ruth Pitter." May 17, 1958.

"Poetry Readings, Book of Verse: Virginia Sackville-West and Ruth Pitter." Nov. 30, 1946.

"Points from the Postbag." Feb. 6, 1961. No transcript available.

"Public Image and Reality on Nuns." Sept. 6, 1961. No transcript available.

"Public Image and Reality on Painters." Nov. 8, 1961.

"Romance." Sept. 4, 1963.

"Ruth Pitter Lyrics." Sept. 14, 1956. Transcript available in Pitter's uncataloged papers. Bodleian Library.

"Ruth Pitter's Personal Memories of George Orwell." Jan. 3, 1956.

"Ruth Pitter Talks about Her Own Poems." July 19, 1955.

"Ruth Pitter Talks to Hallam Tennyson." Nov. 7, 1977. Audio recording available at the British Library, Sound Archives. NP3012W

"Ruth Pitter Talks to John Wain." Oct. 31, 1968. Audio recording available at the British Library, Sound Archives. NP1220W.

"Ruth Pitter Talks to Stephen Black." June 24, 1955.

"The Summer Road." Aug. 15, 1961.

"Thinking of the Incarnation." Oct. 30, 1960. Transcript available in Pitter's uncataloged papers. Bodleian Library.

"Think on These Things." Apr. 10, 1966. No transcript available.

"Timeless Moments." Aug. 23, 1971.

"Town Walk." May 17, 1962. No transcript available.

"Visit to Savill Gardens." June 9, 1964. No transcript available.

"What Is a Poet?" Oct. 26, 1955.

"Where Do We Go from Here?" Jan. 28, 1974.

"Where We Live." Oct. 30, 1964.

"Whither the Church." Jan. 1, 1959.

"William Collins." June 15, 1946.

"A Word in Edgeways." Mar. 4, 1972. No transcript available.

"You Ask For It: Persons and Personalities." Jan. 23, 1958.

BBC *The Brains Trust Appearances*

No. 90. Sunday, May 26, 1957. Bernard Braden, question master. Guests: Dr. Julian Huxley, Professor A. J. Ayer, Ruth Pitter, and John Betjeman.

No. 93. Sunday, June 16, 1957. Bernard Braden, question master. Guests: Ruth Pitter, Marghanita Laski, Sir Ifor Evans, and Professor Alexander Kennedy.

No. 99. Sunday, July 28, 1957. Bernard Braden, question master. Guests: Ruth Pitter, Sir Eric James, Sir John Maud, and Professor A. L. Goodhart.

No. 106. Sunday, Sept. 15, 1957. Bernard Braden, question master. Guests: Ruth Pitter; Alan Bullock; Sir John Maud; and the Most Reverend Joost de Blank, archbishop elect of Cape Town.

No. 129. Sunday, Mar. 2, 1958. Norman Fisher, question master. Guests: Professor D. W. Smathers, Lady Violet Bonham Carter, Ruth Pitter, and Dr. J. Bronowski. No copy of the transcript for this broadcast is available.

No. 134. Sunday, Apr. 6, 1958. Michael Flanders, question master. Guests: Ruth Pitter, Lord David Cecil, Sir Miles Thomas, and Sir Ifor Evans.

No. 141. Sunday, May 25, 1958. Norman Fisher, question master. Guests: James Fisher, Ruth Pitter, Margery Fisher, and Rupert Hart-Davis.

No. 150. Sunday, Aug. 3, 1958. Michael Flanders, question master. Guests: Reg Butler, Ruth Pitter, James Laver, and John Newsom.

No. 173. Sunday, Jan. 11, 1959. Norman Fisher, question master. Guests: James Fisher, Ruth Pitter, Noel Annan, and Lord David Cecil.

No. 188. Sunday, Apr. 26, 1959. Norman Fisher, question master. Guests: Dr. Leslie Weatherhead, Ruth Pitter, Professor Alexander Kennedy, and Lord Halsbury.

No. 236. Sunday, Apr. 28, 1960. Norman Fisher, question master. Guests: Wolf Mankowitz, Ruth Pitter, and Lord David Cecil.

Essays

From *Woman: World's Greatest Weekly for Women*

The following ran under the head "The Flower of Peace: A Countrywoman's Diary" by Ruth Pitter. There are no individual essay titles. I identify them here in chronological order by the first line of each essay. Oddly, the series was never formally introduced nor concluded. It just started abruptly on October 25, 1958, and ended just as abruptly on December 5, 1959.

"Often there is such lovely weather at this time of year." 43, no. 1115 (Oct. 25, 1958): 47.

"From now until the end of winter is the planting season." 43, no. 1116 (Nov. 1, 1958): 51.

"While it's raining I try to catch up with some jobs under cover—the sort of jobs I'm apt to leave on one side as long as it's dry enough to be out!" 43, no. 1117 (Nov. 8, 1958): 48.

"I wish you could see a particular tree in my garden just now." 43, no. 1118 (Nov. 15, 1958): 48.

"Gathering sticks! What a magic sound it has." 43, no. 1119 (Nov. 22, 1958): 47.

"Only a few days more, and we shall be in December." 43, no. 1120 (Nov. 29, 1958): 45.

"I am very lucky. I have a work room, a fairly large, light room with windows on three sides." 43, no. 1121 (Dec. 6, 1958): 47.

"How I dislike it when the wind blows!" 43, no. 1122 (Dec. 13, 1958): 48.

"Now we are reaping the reward of hard work in the garden, as its many contributions come in to help with the Christmas preparations." 43, no. 1123 (Dec. 20, 1958): 43.

"The typical wife and mother has been kept at her busiest for weeks past." 43, no. 1124 (Dec. 27, 1958): 37.

"There's one thing the keen gardener can always do, however bad the weather may be—get things in order." 44, no. 1125 (Jan. 3, 1959): 35.

"Have you ever looked closely at an old rotting tree stump?" 44, no. 1126 (Jan. 10, 1959): 47.

"Winter is digging season." 44, no. 1127 (Jan. 17, 1959): 41.

"If cutting wind, and frosts, and even a certain amount of snow, turn up just now, they may not succeed in driving me indoors for the whole day." 44, no. 1128 (Jan. 24, 1959): 48.

"In this climate we never know what to expect." 44, no. 1129 (Jan. 31, 1959): 39.

"No outdoor work today. It's just too horrid." 44, no. 1130 (Feb. 7, 1959): 47.

"St. Valentine's Day, and they're here! The snowdrops, I mean." 44, no. 1131 (Feb. 14, 1959): 39.

"By now the daylight has increased so much that it's still light at six o'clock in the evening." 44, no. 1132 (Feb. 21, 1959): 47.

"The best things about the garden about this time are surely the later-flowering hellebores—the family of plants the well-loved Christmas Rose belongs to." 44, no. 1133 (Feb. 28, 1959): 47.

"The garden is not the most alluring place when cold winds are blowing." 44, no. 1134 (Mar. 7, 1959): 43.

"Mar. weather, in our unreliable climate, may be almost the worst of the year." 44, no. 1135 (Mar. 14, 1959): 40.

"By now the soil should be dry enough to sow a great many seeds, and we begin to have a sense of hurry." 44, no. 1136 (Mar. 21, 1959): 48.

"The glorious Eastertide is here once more. It's time to put the winter really behind us, even if there's no settled fine weather yet." 44, no. 1137 (Mar. 28, 1959): 40.

"What a help it is to have grass-plots round the house!" 44, no. 1138 (Apr. 4, 1959): 41.

"The old-fashioned poets used to have a great time with Apr.." 44, no. 1139 (Apr. 11, 1959): 39.

"What a pleasant place the orchard is now!" 44, no. 1140 (Apr. 18, 1959): 41.

"If you have a garden pool, you'll know what a lot of pleasure it can give." 44, no. 1141 (Apr. 25, 1959): 41.

"One of the great things about living in an old country like ours is the number of our traditions." 44, no. 1142 (May 2, 1959): 41.

"We're nearly all so much better off nowadays that it's strange to read about the poverty of past times." 44, no. 1143 (May 9, 1959): 41.

"I wonder how many households are having guests this weekend, and how many thousands of people are going to stay with friends and relatives, or in hotels and boarding-houses." 44, no. 1144 (May 16, 1959): 45.

"Of all our British birds, I think the handsomest is the big spotted missel-thrush." 44, no. 1145 (May 23, 1959): 42.

"Looking out of the window—what a fascinating pastime it is!" 44, no. 1146 (May 30, 1959): 35.

"Here's June, and in spite of its usual associations with lovers' moonlight and roses, it may prove to be wet." 44, no. 1147 (June 6, 1959): 35.

"The festive time of the garden is just beginning." 44, no. 1148 (June 13, 1959): 38.

"In the fields and orchards, and all along the hedges, the grasses and weeds are at their tall-
est." 44, no. 1149 (June 20, 1959): 45.

"This is the most magical time of the whole year—midsummer, with its 'livelong summer
days,' when there's hardly any night." 44, no. 1150 (June 27, 1959): 46.

"I wish I could share the liking many people have for keeping poultry." 45, no. 1151 (July
4, 1959): 37.

"Early in the year I was being very thankful for a roof over my head to shelter me from the
cold and wet and darkness of winter." 45, no. 1152–1159 (July 4–Aug. 29, 1959): 34.

"It seems that fine weather in this country scarcely ever lasts for more than a certain time."
45, no. 1160 (Sept. 5, 1959): 39.

"What do you think of when you read the words, 'Out on the common'?" 45, no. 1161
(Sept. 12, 1959): 43.

"The sage and thyme have been good this year." 45, no. 1162 (Sept. 19, 1959): 48.

"It doesn't often happen that I'm alone in the house, but when it does, I try to get down to
some neglected jobs." 45, no. 1163 (Sept. 26, 1959): 47.

"It really is autumn now. However fine the weather may be, the days are shorter, and the
evenings and early mornings chillier." 45, no. 1164 (Oct. 3, 1959): 50.

"'How time does fly!' Busy people are always saying it, aren't they?" 45, no. 1165 (Oct. 10,
1959): 45.

"I once heard of an old lady who never went away for a holiday because, 'she couldn't leave
Pussy; and she had a plant in a pot, too.'" 45, no. 1166 (Oct. 17, 1959): 57.

"There are so many grand gardens; public gardens in cities; splendid private gardens—but
the small ones are often just as perfect in their way." 45, no. 1167 (Oct. 24, 1959): 47.

"Are you fond of nooks—little secret places where you can sit alone, hidden away from the
world?" 45, no. 1168 (Oct. 31, 1959): 48.

"Round comes bonfire night again, with its own particular enchantment." 45, no. 1169
(Nov. 7, 1959): 45.

"Once a week, there's a bus from our village to the city, sixteen miles away." 45, no. 1170
(Nov. 14, 1959): 45.

"After a lovely hot summer, the ground is very warm, and it stays warm for months." 45,
no. 1171 (Nov. 21, 1959): 42.

"In spring, we plan for open-air and fine weather—longer days and increasing activity for
many weeks ahead." 45, no. 1172 (Nov. 28, 1959): 42.

"A leafless, silent winter wood, under a pale sun or a dull December sky; to me, this has
always been a thing of beauty and magic." 45, no. 1173 (Dec. 5, 1959): 48.

Other Essays

"The Art of Reading in Ignorance." *Essays and Poems Presented to Lord David Cecil.* London: Constable, 1970.

"Dorothy Wellesley, 1889–1956." In *The Wind and the Rain: An Easter Book for 1962.* Edited by Neville Braybrooke. London: Secker & Warburg, 1962. 201–8.

"Ears." *Nursing Mirror and Midwives Journal* 109, no. 2854 (Mar. 11, 1960): 2070.

"Eyes." *Nursing Mirror and Midwives Journal* 109, no. 2855 (Mar. 18, 1960): 2162.

"God Be in Mine Eyes." *London Mercury* 38 (Aug. 1938): 345–47.

"Hands." *Nursing Mirror and Midwives Journal* 110, no. 2857 (Apr. 1, 1960): 56.

Introduction. *Ends of Verse.* By Norman S. Power. London: Mowbrays, 1971.

"New Light on an Old Question: Review of *Letters to Malcolm, Chiefly on Prayer.*" *Sunday
Telegraph*, Jan. 26, 1964, 20.

"Noses." *Nursing Mirror and Midwives Journal* 109, no. 2856 (Mar. 25, 1960): 2250.
"Poetry Today." *Poetry Review* 29, no. 3 (May–June 1938): 185–87.
"A Return to Poetic Law." The Royal Institute of Great Britain, Ulysses Catalogue No. 9, 1952.
"Voices." *Nursing Mirror and Midwives Journal* 110, no. 2858 (Apr. 8, 1960): 166.

Interviews

"The Poet Speaks." Ruth Pitter interviewed by Hilary Smith. Mar. 24, 1964. Audio recording available at the British Library, Sound Archives. C144, Tape 682.
Ruth Pitter Talks to Lyle Dorsett. July 23, 1985. Audio recording and transcript available at the Marion E. Wade Center, Wheaton College, Wheaton, Illinois.

Letters and Journals

Pitter's letters and journals not already acknowledged may be found in her uncataloged papers or as indicated in the following:

Letters to John Adams. Privately held by John Adams.
Letter to C. S. Lewis. July 17, 1946. CSL /L-Pitter/ 1a, the Marion E. Wade Center, Wheaton College, Wheaton, Illinois.
Letters to Thomas McKean. Privately held by Thomas McKean.
Letter to Andrew Nye. Privately held by Andrew Nye.
Letters to Mary Pitter. Privately held by Mark Pitter.

Audio Recordings

"Pitter Reading Her Poetry." British Library, Sound Archives. British Council Tapes. C144/682–83. Mar. 24, 1964.
"Ruth Pitter Reading Her Poetry." Recorded by Lee Anderson for Yale University. Apr. 26, 1960.
"Ruth Pitter Reading Her Poetry." Recorded by Louis Untermeyer for the Library of Congress. Dec. 20, 1960.

Critical Reviews, Essays, and Books

Adcock, Fleur, ed. *The Faber Book of 20th Century Women's Poetry*. London: Faber & Faber, 1987.
Belloc, Hilaire. Preface. *First and Second Poems*. By Ruth Pitter. London: Sheed and Ward, 1927.
———. Preface. *A Mad Lady's Garland*. By Ruth Pitter. London: Cresset Press, 1934.
———. "Two Poets." Review of *A Trophy of Arms* and A. E. Housman's *More Poems*. *G. K.'s Weekly*, Oct. 26, 1936:146.
Benét, William. Review of *A Mad Lady's Garland*. *Saturday Review of Literature* 13 (Nov. 30, 1935): 16.
Bogan, Louise. Review of *The Spirit Watches*. *New Yorker* 16 (Apr. 20, 1940): 92.
———. "A Singular Talent." Review of *A Trophy of Arms*. *Poetry: A Magazine of Verse* 49 (Oct. 1937): 43–45.
Brantley, Frederick. "Sparrow's Skull." Review of *The Bridge*. *New York Times*, May 5, 1946:8.
Bridson, D. G. "An English Eccentric." Review of *A Mad Lady's Garland*. *Poetry: A Magazine of Verse* 47 (Nov. 1935): 103.
Cecil, David. "Rare Beauty." Review of *Urania*. *Observer*, Apr. 8, 1951:7.

Church, Richard. "A Disciple of Aesop." Review of *A Mad Lady's Garland. Christian Science Monitor,* Nov. 21, 1934:12.

———. "Gold in the River Sands." Review of *First and Second Poems: 1912–1925. Spectator* 144 (Apr. 5, 1930): 562.

"A Classical Poet." Review of *First and Second Poems: 1912–1925. Times Literary Supplement,* May 5, 1927, 316.

Cuneo, Andrew P. "Selected Literary Letters of C. S. Lewis." Diss., University of Oxford, 2001.

"Damp in the Country." Review of *Poems 1926–1966. Times Literary Supplement,* Dec. 12, 1968:1407.

Davidman, Joy. *Anya.* New York: Macmillan, 1940.

———. *Letter to a Comrade.* New Haven, CT: Yale University Press, 1938.

———. "The Longest Way Round." *These Found the Way: Thirteen Converts to Protestant Christianity.* Ed. David W. Soper. Philadelphia: Westminster Press, 1951.

———. *Smoke on the Mountain: An Interpretation of the Ten Commandments.* Philadelphia: Westminster Press, 1953.

Davidson, Eugene. Review of *The Bridge. Yale Review* 36 (Autumn 1946): 152.

de la Mare, Walter. *Behold, This Dreamer!* London: Faber & Faber, 1939.

Deutsch, Babette. "Delight and Dismay." Review of *The Bridge. Poetry: A Magazine of Verse* 68 (May 1946): 103.

Di Cesare, Mario A., ed. *George Herbert and the Seventeenth-Century Religious Poets.* New York: W. W. Norton, 1978.

Dickinson, Peter. "Ruth Pitter." *Canadian C. S. Lewis Journal* 79 (Summer 1992): 1–3.

Dorsett, Lyle W. *And God Came In.* New York: Ballantine, 1984.

Dowson, Jane. "Otherworldly yet Clay-Footed." Review of *Collected Poems. Poetry Review* (Winter 1996–1997): 89–90.

Eliot, T. S. *Old Possum's Book of Practical Cats.* London: Faber & Faber, 1939.

Emerson, Dorothy. "Ruth Pitter." Review of *A Trophy of Arms. Scholastic* 33 (Nov. 12, 1938): 23E.

Emerson, Oliver F. "Originality in Old English Poetry," *Review of English Studies* 2 (Jan. 1926): 18–31.

"*First Poems:* A Review." *Daily Telegraph,* Apr. 21, 1920.

Forbes-Boyd, Eric. "Two English Poets." Review of *The Spirit Watches. Christian Science Monitor,* Feb. 24, 1940:11.

Frederick, Candice and Sam McBride, eds. *Women Among the Inklings: Gender, C. S. Lewis, J. R. R. Tolkien, and Charles Williams.* Westport, CT: Greenwood Press, 2001.

"From Death to Life." Review of *The Bridge. Times Literary Supplement,* Apr. 7, 1945:164.

Gawsworth, John. Review of *A Trophy of Arms. New English Weekly,* Sept. 24, 1936.

Gibson, Wilfrid. Review of *The Bridge. Manchester Guardian,* May 23, 1945:3.

Gilbert, Rudolph. *Four Living Poets.* Santa Barbara, CA: Unicorn Press, 1944.

Gilbert, Sandra M. and Susan Gubar, eds. *The Norton Anthology of Literature by Women: The Traditions in English,* 2nd ed. New York: W. W. Norton, 1996.

Hamilton, George. *The Tell-Tale Article: A Critical Approach to Modern Poetry.* Oxford: Oxford University Press, 1949.

Hamilton, George Rostrevor, and John Arlott, eds. *Landmarks: A Book of Topographical Verse for England and Wales.* Cambridge: Cambridge University Press, 1943.

Hastings, Selena. "Lurking in the Thorny Undergrowth." *Sunday Telegraph,* Feb. 17, 1991:12.

Hawkins, Desmond. "Recent Verse." Review of *The Spirit Watches. Spectator* 163 (Dec. 15, 1939): 876.

Hone, Ralph E., ed. *The Poetry of Dorothy L. Sayers*. Trowbridge, Wiltshire: Dorothy L. Sayers Society, 1996.

Hooper, Walter. *C. S. Lewis: A Companion and Guide*. London: HarperCollins, 1996.

Hutchison, Percy. Review of *A Mad Lady's Garland*. *New York Times Book Review*, Dec. 1, 1935:35.

Jarrell, Randall. Review of *The Bridge*. *Nation*, 162 (May 25, 1946): 633.

Jennings, Elizabeth. Introduction. *Collected Poems*. By Ruth Pitter. Rev. ed. Petersfield, UK: Enitharmon, 1996.

Johnson, Thomas H., ed. *Final Harvest: Emily Dickinson's Poems*. New York: Little, Brown, 1961.

Kaplan, Cora, ed. *Salt and Bitter and Good: Three Centuries of English and American Women Poets*. New York: Paddington Press, 1975.

Keegan, Paul, ed. *The New Penguin Book of English Verse*. London: Allen Lane, Penguin Press, 2000.

Kell, Richard. "Extension and Structure." Review of *Still by Choice*. *Guardian*, Feb. 18, 1966:8.

Kenmare, Dallas. "The Triumph of 'Pure Poetry.'" *Poetry Review* (1937): 373–80.

King, Don. "The Anatomy of a Friendship: The Correspondence of Ruth Pitter and C. S. Lewis, 1946–1962." *Mythlore* 24 (Summer 2003): 2–24.

———. *C. S. Lewis, Poet: The Legacy of His Poetic Impulse*. Kent, OH: Kent State University Press, 2001.

———. "Finding Joy: A Comprehensive Bibliography of the Works of Joy Davidman." *Seven: An Anglo-American Literary Review* 23 (2006): 69–80.

———."Fire and Ice: C. S. Lewis and the Love Poetry of Joy Davidman and Ruth Pitter." *Seven: An Anglo-American Literary Review* 22 (2005): 60–88.

———. "Joy Davidman and the *New Masses*: Communist Poet and Reviewer." *Chronicle of the Oxford University C. S. Lewis Society* 4, no. 1 (Feb. 2007): 18–44.

———. "The Poetry of Prose: C. S. Lewis, Ruth Pitter, and *Perelandra*." *Christianity and Literature* 49 (Spring 2000): 331–56.

———. "Quorum Porum: The Literary Cats of T. S. Eliot, Ruth Pitter, and Dorothy L. Sayers." *Seven: An Anglo-American Literary Review* 18 (2001): 25–45.

———."The Religious Poetry of Ruth Pitter." *Christianity and Literature* 54 (Summer 2005): 521–62.

———. "Silent Music: The Letters of Ruth Pitter." *Bulletin of the New York C. S. Lewis Society* 35 (Spring 2004): 1–15.

Kizer, Carolyn. "The Book of Ruth." *Writer's Chronicle* 32 (Oct.–Nov. 1999): 29–31, 34.

Landreneau, Francine Muffoletto. "Ruth Pitter." *British Poets, 1914–1945*. Edited by Donald E. Stanford. Detroit, MI: Gale, 1983.

Larkin, Philip, ed. *The Oxford Book of Twentieth-Century Verse*. Oxford: Oxford University Press, 1973.

Lee, Lawrence. "The Extension of Poetry in Time." *Virginia Quarterly Review* 16 (Summer 1940): 481–84.

Letters on Poetry from W. B. Yeats to Dorothy Wellesley. London: Oxford University Press, 1940.

Lewis, C. S. *The Allegory of Love: A Study in Medieval Tradition*. Oxford: Oxford University Press, 1936.

———. *Books, Broadcasts and the War, 1931–1949*. Vol. 2 of *The Collected Letters of C. S. Lewis*. Edited by Walter Hooper. London: HarperCollins, 2004.

———. *English Literature in the Sixteenth Century, Excluding Drama*. The Oxford History of English Literature, vol. 3. Oxford: Clarendon Press, 1954.

———. *Narnia, Cambridge and Joy 1950–1963*. Vol. 3 of *The Collected Letters of C. S. Lewis*. Edited by Walter Hooper. London: HarperCollins, 2006.

————. *Out of the Silent Planet*. London: Bodley Head, 1938.

————. *Perelandra*. New York: Macmillan, 1944.

————. *Poems*. Ed. Walter Hooper. New York: Harcourt Brace Jovanovich, 1964.

————. *The Problem of Pain*. London: Centenary Press, 1940.

————. *The Screwtape Letters*. London: Geoffrey Bles, 1942.

————. *Selected Literary Essays*. Cambridge: Cambridge University Press, 1969.

————. *That Hideous Strength: A Modern Fairy-Tale for Grown-Ups*. London: Bodley Head, 1945.

————. *The Weight of Glory and Other Addresses*. New York: Macmillan, 1949.

Lewis, Warren. *Brother and Friends: The Diaries of Major Warren Hamilton Lewis*. Edited by Clyde S. Kilby and Marjorie Lamp Mead. San Francisco: Harper & Row, 1982.

Lith, Neo. "Upon Reading 'Love's Martyrs' by Ruth Pitter." *New English Weekly* 2, no. 22 (Mar. 16, 1933): 516.

Mairet, Philip. *A. R. Orage: A Memoir*. London: Dent, 1936; New York, University Books, 1966.

Masefield, John. Introduction. *A Mad Lady's Garland*, by Ruth Pitter. New York: Macmillan, 1935.

Maynard, Theodore. Review of *The Bridge*. *Catholic World* 163 (July 1946): 373.

"Metaphysical Poets." Review of *Urania*. *Times Literary Supplement*, May 4, 1951:278.

Monro, Alida, ed. *Recent Poetry, 1923–1933*. London: Gerald Howe and the Poetry Bookshop, 1933.

More Poetry Please! 100 Popular Poems from the BBC Radio 4 Programme. London: Everyman, 1988.

Morley, Christopher. "Testament against Terror." Review of *The Bridge*. *Saturday Review of Literature* 29 (Mar. 23, 1946): 12.

"The Mortal Lot." Review of *The Ermine*. *Times Literary Supplement*, Aug. 21, 1953:537.

Munson, Gorham B. "Concerning Ruth Pitter." *Commonweal* 10 (Sept. 11, 1929): 472–75.

Norton Anthology of English Literature, 8th ed. New York: W. W. Norton, 2006.

Nott, C. S. *Teachings of Gurdjieff: The Journal of a Pupil; An Account of Some Years with G. I. Gurdjieff and A. R. Orage in New York and at Fontainebleau-Avon*. London: Routledge & Kegan Paul, 1969.

Palgrave, Francis T. *The Golden Treasury: Selected from the Best Songs and Lyrical Poems in the English Language*. London: Oxford University Press, 1964.

Palmer, Herbert. *Post-Victorian Poetry*. London: Dent, 1938.

Peake, M. "Portrait." *London Mercury* 36 (July 1937): 236a.

"Personal Poets." Review of *Still by Choice*. *Times Literary Supplement*, May 19, 1966:424.

"Portrait." *Illustrated London News* 227 (Oct. 29, 1955): 745.

Powell, Dilys. "Ruth Pitter's New Poems." *London Mercury* 34 (Oct. 1936): 558–59.

"Recent Verse." *New Age* 26, no. 14 (Feb. 5, 1920): 225.

Review of *The Bridge*. *Kirkus* 13 (Dec. 15, 1945): 552.

Review of *The Bridge*. *New Yorker* 22 (Feb. 23, 1946): 91.

Review of *The Bridge*. *Wisconsin Library Bulletin* 42 (May 1946): 72.

Review of *The Spirit Watches*. *Catholic World* 151 (Aug. 1940): 630.

Review of *The Spirit Watches*. *Christian Century* 57 (Apr. 24, 1940): 547.

Ridler, Ann Margaret. "Capturing the Dance in Stillness." *Guardian*, Mar. 3, 1992:35.

Roberts, Michael. "The Eternal Fog." *Spectator*, 157 (Oct. 16, 1936): 652.

————. "Satire Stays at Home." *Spectator* 154 (Jan. 25, 1935): 132.

"Ruth Pitter." Obituary. *Daily Telegraph*, Mar. 3, 1992:21.

"Ruth Pitter." Obituary. *Times*, Mar. 3, 1992:15.

Russell, Arthur, ed. *Ruth Pitter: Homage to a Poet*. London: Rapp & Whiting, 1969.

Russell, George William. *Letters from AE*. Edited by Alan Denson. Forward by Monk Gibbon. London: Abelard-Schuman, 1961.

Sarton, May. "Two Poets: W. B. Yeats and Ruth Pitter." *University Review (Kansas City)*, Oct. 1940:63–65.

Sassoon, Siegfried. "Two Poets." Review of *A Trophy of Arms*. *New Statesman & Nation* 12 (Dec. 19, 1936): 1034.

Sayer, George. *Jack: C. S. Lewis and His Times*. San Francisco: Harper & Row, 1988.

Schlueter, Paul. "Ruth Pitter." *An Encyclopedia of British Women Writers*. Edited by June Schlueter and Paul Schlueter. New Brunswick, NJ: Rutgers University Press, 1999.

Schultz, Jeffrey and John West, eds. *The C. S. Lewis Readers' Encyclopedia*. Grand Rapids, MI: Zondervan, 1998.

Scott-James, R. A. *Fifty Years of English Literature, 1900–1950*. London: Longmans, 1951.

Short, R. W. Review of *The Spirit Watches*. *Yale Review* 30 (Autumn 1940): 214.

Speaight, Robert. *The Life of Hilaire Belloc*. New York: Farrar, Straus & Cudahy, 1957.

Spender, Stephen. Review of *The Spirit Watches*. *New Statesman & Nation* 18 (Dec. 9, 1939): 834.

Stansky, Peter, and William Abrahams. *The Unknown Orwell*. New York: Alfred A. Knopf, 1972.

Stephens, James. *Letters of James Stephens*. Edited Richard Finneran. New York: Macmillan, 1974.

Stonier, G. W. Review of *The Bridge*. *New Statesman & Nation* 29 (Apr. 28, 1945): 276.

Suryanarayn, Indu. *A Parallel Study of Two British Women Poets: Ruth Pitter and Elizabeth Jennings*. Diss. University of Rhode Island, 1980. Ann Arbor, MI: UMI. 8102342.

Swartz, Roberta T. Review of *The Spirit Watches*. *Poetry: A Magazine of Verse* 56 (Sept. 1940): 334–37.

Ten Oxford Poets. Oxford: Charles Brand, 1978.

Thwaite, Anthony, ed. *Selected Letters of Philip Larkin: 1949–1985*. London: Faber & Faber, 1992.

"Two Contemporary British Poets Who Build Bridges." Review of *The Bridge*. *Christian Science Monitor Weekly Magazine Section*, July 7, 1945:15.

Untermeyer, Louis. "Exquisite and Stern." Review of *The Spirit Watches*. *Saturday Review of Literature* 22, July 20, 1940:10.

Wain, John. "A Note on Ruth Pitter's Poetry." *Listener*, Feb. 20, 1969:239–40.

Wall, Michael. "The Story of the 'Brain Trust.'" *Listener*, May 5, 1960:791–93.

Walton, Eda. "The Distinguished Poetry of Ruth Pitter." Review of *A Trophy of Arms*. *New York Times*, Jan. 10, 1937.

———. "A Seventeenth-Century Mind." *Nation 131* (Oct. 8, 1930): 383.

"The Watching Spirit." Review of *The Spirit Watches*. *Times Literary Supplement*, Dec. 23, 1939:876.

Watkin, E. I. "*Urania*: The Poetry of Miss Ruth Pitter." In *Poets and Mystics*. London: Sheed and Ward, 1953.

Welch, Louise. *Orage with Gurdjieff in America*. Boston: Routledge & Kegan Paul, 1982.

White, Mark. "Logos." *London Mercury* 39 (Feb. 1939): 385.

Wiggin, Maurice. "Poetry or Punch-Up?" Review of *Still by Choice*. *Sunday Times*, Apr. 3, 1966:34.

"Wit-Melancholy." Review of *A Mad Lady's Garland*. *Times Literary Supplement*, Oct. 4, 1934:670.

Wordsworth, William. *William Wordsworth*. Edited by Stephen Gill (Oxford: Oxford University Press, 1984), 565.

Index

Abraham, 184–85
Adams, John, 262–63
AE (George William Russell), 22, 63, 65–67, 69, 80, 83, 143, 198
Aeneas at the Court of Dido, 158
"After Apple Picking," 128
"Againrising," 200
"Aged Cupid," 145
Allegory of Love, The, 103, 143, 236
"Alone," 22
"Ancient Mariner, The," 115
And God Came In, 196, 199
"Angels," 240, 247–48
Anglican, 142, 161, 194
Annan, Noel, 227
Aristotle, 170
Arlott, John, 253
Army Education, 115
Arnold, Matthew, 149
Ascension, The, 255
Ascension Day, 268
"As Silly Child," 30
"As When the Faithful Return," 74, 198
As You Like It, 159
Auden, W. H., xiii, 251
Austen, Jane, 140, 219
"Autumn 1944," 117–18
Ayer, A. J., 226–27, 235

"Bad Child Left Behind," 260–61
Baddeley, Clinton, 140
Baptism, 124
Barfield, Owen, xv, 146, 150–53, 161, 169, 192, 238

Barnett, Raymond, 218, 231–32
Barrie and Jenkins, 258
"Bat, The," 129, 145, 259
Battersea Bridge, xiii, 116, 118, 121
BBC, xiv, xv, xvi, xvii, 84, 114, 116, 138–40, 141, 146, 159, 161, 194, 210, 213–14, 219–28, 231, 235, 250, 252–53, 257, 262
Belloc, Hilaire, xv, 22, 27–30, 32, 40–41, 44–45, 52, 54–55, 62, 64–68, 70, 80, 83, 152, 213, 217, 222, 266
Benét, Stephen Vincent, 199
Benét, William, 64
Betjeman, John, 191, 226, 235, 253, 256, 270
"Better than Love," 133–34
Bible, The, 76, 126, 175
"Bible and the Imagination, The," 231
"Bird in the Tree, The," 94–95, 180
"Birds Mourning, The," 137
Black, Stephen, 213
Blackshaw, Richard, 163, 167, 210–11, 220
Blair, Eric, 25, 162
Blake, William, 23, 81, 95, 169, 177
Blitz, xvi, 100, 119–20, 122
Blondel, 97
"Bloweth Where It Listeth," 89–90
Blunden, Edmund, 253
Boer War, 1
Bogan, Louise, 98
Book of Verse, 159
Botteghe Oscure, 173–74
Braden, Bernard, 235
Brains Trust, The, xiii, xvi, 214, 226–28, 234–35
"Brambleberries, Blackberries," 269

Brantley, Fredrick, 136

"Bridge, The," xiii, 22, 114, 121–22, 137, 145

Bridge, The, xiii, xvi, 22, 43, 118, 120–38, 151–53, 163–64, 178, 180, 185, 198, 259

Bridges, Robert, 136

Bridson, D. G., 64

Bullock, Alan, 227

"Burning the Bee-Tree," 91, 129, 246

"Bush-Baby, The," 96, 244

"But for Lust," 43, 131–32, 137, 145, 198

Butler, Reg, 227

"But My Neighbour Is My Treasure," 187

"Call Not to Me," 22, 80, 270

Calvinism, 235

Cambridge, 211–12, 217

Campbell, Roy, 163–64

"Captive Bird of Paradise, The," 180, 190, 259

Carter, Violet Bonham, 227

Cat's Christmas Carol, A, 158

"Cedar, The," 177

Cecil, David, xv, xvi, 82–83, 86–87, 99–100, 102–5, 113–14, 116–19, 134–35, 140, 146, 148, 158–60, 162, 164–65, 172–73, 177, 190–93, 195, 207–9, 227, 231, 238, 250, 253–55, 257, 263–64, 266

Cecil, Jonathan, 86–87

Cecil, Rachel, 86–87, 105, 140, 160, 173–74, 190–91, 207, 254

"Charity and Its Object," 246

Chaucer, Geoffrey, 155, 169, 199

Chelsea, xiv, xv, 34–35, 37, 71, 83, 87, 102, 108, 116, 120–22, 127, 137, 151, 161–62, 172–73, 178, 187, 191, 193–94, 207–8, 217–18, 232, 257

Chesterton, G. K., 22

"Chimney Piece, The," 86

Christianity, xvi, 77, 118, 124, 126–27, 133–34, 141–42, 161, 168, 182–83, 185, 187–88, 198–99, 228, 263, 271

Christ, Jesus, 78–79, 134, 175, 188, 199, 200, 230–31, 272, 274

Chronicles of Narnia, 165

Church, Richard, 30, 52, 64, 140, 253–54

Churchill, Winston, 232

"Cider in the Potting Shed," 107

"Clean Woman, The," 84

"Close, Mortal Eyes," 267

Coburn School for Girls, 6–7

Cockney, 108–9, 168

"Cockroach," 61

"Coffin-Worme Which Consider, The," 56–57, 63

Collected Poems, 269–70, 274

Colles, Dudley, 215

Collins, William, 138, 159

"Coloured Glass, The," 134

Commander of the British Empire, xiii, 264

Companion of Literature, xiii, 258

Comus, 144, 172, 207

"Concerning God," 231

Confirmation, 141–42, 161

"Consummation, The," 16

Cooley, Mary, 159–62, 164, 166–68, 174, 191–92, 195–96, 208–12, 218, 221, 231–32, 250, 255–58, 262

"Corinna's Going A-Maying," 5

Cottage in Hainault Forest, xiv, xv, 7–13, 24, 32–34, 38, 40, 70–73, 88–90, 96, 127–28, 175, 194

"Cottage, The," 32, 130

Crabtree Hill, 10

Crashaw, Richard, 163

Cresset Press, 88, 106, 164, 235

"Cricket Match, 1908," 267

"Crow, The," 130

"Crownèd A, A" 260

Crowther, Barbara, 226

Cruickshank, Norah, 231, 235, 257, 266, 269–70

C. S. Lewis: Apostle to the Skeptics, 199

C. S. Lewis, Poet: The Impulse of His Poetic Legacy, ix

Culham College, 2, 16

"Cygnet, The," 122–26, 130, 134, 137, 165

Davies, W. H., 83, 98

Deane and Forester, xv, 35, 44–45, 53, 66–67, 83–87, 101, 104, 112–13, 115, 120, 161, 163

"Death of a Beauty," 135

"Debtor, The," 21

de Blank, Joost, 227

de la Mare, Walter, 53, 85, 87, 98, 136, 163

Deutsch, Babette, 136–37

Dickinson, Emily, 73

Dickinson, Muriel, 265, 269–70

Dickinson, Peter, 269

Dido, 58

"Diehards, The," 108

"Difference, The," 43, 95

"Division," 203–5
Donegal, 65–66
"Donkey's Delight," 148
Donne, John, 163, 251
Dorestt, Lyle, 196, 199
Doubting Thomas, 255
Downshall Elementary School, 6
"Downward-Pointing Muse, The," 97, 100
"Dream, A," 245–46
Dymer, 143
Dyson, Hugo, 146

"Early Rising," 43, 73, 198
"Ears," 230
"Earwig's Complaynt, The," 55–56, 163
Eastgate Hotel, 196–97, 199
"Ecclesiasticella: Or the Church Mouse," 60, 63
Eliot, T. S., xiii, 83, 112–13, 135, 152, 159, 163, 166–67, 169, 171, 181, 217–18, 233, 251
"Empress Changes Lovers, The," 202–3
"End of Drought," 261
End of Drought, xvi, 258–61, 272
"End of Fear, The," 145
Enitharmon Press, 269
English Literature in the Sixteenth Century, Excluding Drama, 211, 236
"Ermine, The," 182–83
Ermine, The, xiii, 43, 134, 161, 163, 174, 175–90, 194, 198, 209, 213, 241, 259
"Eros with Chilblains," 35
Essex, xiv, 1, 11, 34, 102, 104–5, 108, 162, 173–74, 232, 252
"Estuary, The," 134
Evan, Ifor, 227
"Exercise in the Pathetic Fallacy," 244
"Eyes," 230

"Fair Is the Water," 74, 198
"Fairy-Gold," 18
Fairies, 19, 22–23, 72
Fascism, 77
"Father Questioned, The," 176–77, 190
"February Walk," 260
"Field Grasses," 16–17
Fifty Years of English Literature, 1900–1950, 167, 270
Finland, 101
First and Second Poems, xv, 27–32, 55, 152, 163
First Poems, xv, 22, 29, 30

Fisher, James, 227
Fisher, Margery, 227
"Five Dreams and a Vision," 184, 190
"Flower of Peace: A Countrywoman's Diary, The," 228–30
"Flowers in the Factory," 126–27
Forbes-Boyd, Eric, 98
Forester, B., 54
"Forms with Infinite Meaning," 185–86
"For Sleep, or Death," 22
"For the Little Cat Murphy," 153–54
"For Unhappy Lovers," 267
"For Us All," 110
For Whom the Bell Tolls, 204
"Fowls Celestial and Terrestrial," 57–60, 82, 144, 150
"Frog in the Well, The," 61–62
"Freemasons of the Air," 130, 259
"Friendly Day, A," 222–23
Frost, Robert, 128, 163, 199
"Fruit-Fly and Drop of Honey," 259
Fuller, Roy, 253
"Funeral Wreaths," 126–27
Furse, Roger, 107

Galsworthy, John, 22
"Gardeners All," 108
Gawsworth, John, 80, 112–13
"Gentle Joy," 75
Georgian Verse, 18, 21
Gibson, Wilfrid, 135
G. K.'s Weekly, 70
"Glory is Real,"
"Good Enthroned," 268–69
Goodheart, A. L., 227
Golden Treasury, The, 5, 18, 23, 270
"Gosling," 260
Graves, Robert, 163
"Great and Terrible Dream, The," 187–88
Great Depression, 34
Great Divorce, The, 143
"Great Winter, 1946–47, The," 190
Gresham, David, 197
Gresham, Douglas, 197
Gresham, Joy Davidman, xvi, 192–93, 196–207, 210–11, 237–38, 240
Gresham, William, 198–99
Grief Observed, A, 206
Grieve, Mary, 228–30, 253
Gunn, Thom, 253

Hainault Forest, xiv, xv, 4, 7–13, 21–22, 24, 31–34, 38–41, 43, 70–71, 73–74, 76, 88, 90, 96, 103, 127–28, 175, 194–95, 211, 222–23, 245, 254, 261
"Half-Remembered Tune, The," 268
Halsbury, Lord, 227
Hamilton, Clive, 143
Hamilton, George, 151, 163, 169
Hamlet, 125
"Hands," 230–31
"Hap," 110
"Happy Christmas—Love to all, A," 260
Hardie, Christian, 197
Hardie, Colin, 197
Hardy, Thomas, xiii, 110, 169
Harrowing of Hell, The, 255
Hart-Davis, Rupert, 227
Hassall, Christopher, 83
Hassall, Joan, 164
Hastings, Stella, 270
Hawthorns, The, 191, 193, 195, 208–13, 231, 241, 259, 265, 269
Hawthornden Prize for Poetry, xiii, xvi, 82–83, 88, 164, 209, 214–15
Hawkins, Desmond, 98
"Heart's Desire Is Full of Sleep, The," 43, 243–44, 264
Heaven to Find, A, xvi, 266–69
Heinemann Award, William E., xiii, 209, 213–15
"Help, Good Shepherd," 78–79
Hemingway, Ernest, 204
"Hen under Bay-Tree," 43, 153, 180–81
Herbert, George, 163, 189, 272–73
"Herding Lambs," 176, 190
"Heroic Couplets," 150
"Hermitage, The," 31
Herrick, Robert, 5, 64, 200
Hesper, 79
"High Summer," 267, 269
"Hill and Valley," 177–78, 190
"Hill of the Kindred, The," 128
"Holiday in Heaven," 260
Holmes, Winifred, 116
Hooper, Walter, 197, 239, 251, 253
House of Commons, 105
Housman, A. E., xiii, 169
"Hoverfly on Poppy," 134
"Hunting the Unicorn," xvii, 224–26, 238
"Hut, The," 89

Hutchison, Percy, 64
Huxley, Julian, 226–27, 235

"If You Came," 42–43, 93, 137, 192, 198
"I Know That My Redeemer Liveth," 254
Ilford, 1, 2, 6, 232
"Il pleure dans mons Coeur," 201
"Impatience, An," 76
"Innocence," 273
"Interesting People," 231
"In the Open," 242
"In the Service of God," 230–31

James, Eric, 227
Jarrell, Randall, 136–37
Jennings, Elizabeth, 253, 269, 274
Jennings, Frank, 13
Jennings, Marie-Rose, 13, 24
Jennings, Mildred, 13, 15, 24, 26, 34
Johnson, Lyndon, 232
"Joy and Grief," 75
Jude the Obscure, 146

Karl, Dorothy, 210
Keats, John, 23, 58, 169, 239, 270
Kell, Richard, 248
Kenmare, Dallas, 81–82
Kennedy, Alexander, 227
Kennedy, John, 232, 238
Kilns, The, 199
King David, 97
King Saul, 97
"Kitoun's Eclogue, The," 54–55, 62
Kizer, Carolyn, 212–13, 253, 271–72
Korean War, 167

"Lake Isle of Innisfree, The," 72
"Lame Arm," 260
"Lament for One's Self," 43, 131–32, 198
"Lament for the Landless," 90, 179
"Lammastide Flower, The," 181–82
Larkin, Philip, xiii, 270, 274
Laski, Marghanita, 227
Last Poems, 99
Laver, James, 227
Lawrence, D. H., 203
"Leafcutter Bees," 246–47
"Let Me Not Live," 31
Letter to a Comrade, 199–207
Letters to Malcolm, 238

"Lewis Appears," 267

Lewis, C. Day, 140, 256

Lewis, C. S., xv, xvi, 82, 103, 114, 118, 140, 141–55, 158–59, 161, 164–67, 169, 172–74, 189–93, 195–99, 200, 206–12, 217, 231, 236–40, 243–44, 251, 266

Lewis, Warren, 192, 199, 207, 209–10, 212

Library of Congress, 235

"Lilies and Wine," 134, 137, 141

"Line Engaged," 260

Lion, the Witch and the Wardrobe, The, 165, 209

"Little Verse," 201

Loines Memorial Award, 199

London, 24, 34, 38, 66, 83, 85, 87, 100, 105–6, 122, 162, 167, 173, 207, 217, 232

London Calling Asia, 210, 221

London County Council, 2, 174

London Mercury, 28, 44–45, 84, 88

London University, 13

Long Crendon, xv, xvi, 191–94, 208–10, 221, 231, 235, 241, 265, 271–72

Longinus, 170

"Lost Hermitage, The," 71

"Lost Tribe, The," 132, 180, 185

"Love and the Child," 145

Lowell, Robert, 251

Lyndsay, David, 146

Macbeth, 154–55

McKean, Thomas, 266, 269

Mad Lady's Garland, A, xv, 27, 44, 52–68, 71, 82–83, 85, 95, 107, 144–45, 150, 241, 269, 272

Magdalen College, 145–46, 153, 164, 199

"Main-Road Lighting," 267–69

"Man Accuses Man," 132

Mankowitz, Wolf, 227

Mansfield, Katherine, 22

Marriage of Heaven and Hell, The, 177

Marsh, Ngaio, 253

Marvell, Andrew, 163

Mary Magdalen at the Sepulchre, 255

Masefield, John, 52, 83, 214–15, 218

"Maternall Love Tryumphant," 55

"Matron-Cat's Song, The," 157–58

Maud, John, 227

Mayfair Wingfield Hospital, 237

Maynard, Theodore, 136–37, 146, 175

McCrossan, Mary, 34

"Melancholy," 31

Mere Christianity, 118

Metamorphoses, 7

"Military Harpist, The," 96–97, 100

Milne, Marjorie, 150, 152–53

Milton, John, 6, 164, 168–69, 207, 239, 267, 270

"Mister the Blitzkit (for K.)," 155–56

"Money Is Not Everything," 231

Monroe, Alida, 140

Morland, Catherine, 140

Morgen's Crucible Factory, 116–20, 126

"Morals of Pruning, The," 109–10

Morley, Christopher, 136–37

"Morning Glory," 245

Morrell, Lady Ottoline, 82

"Moths and Mercury-Vapour Lamp," 242–43

"Mountainous Country, The," 84

Munson, Gorham, 30

Murrell, Kitty, 3, 14

"My Favourite Virtue, Frugality," 231

"My Life as a Poet," 231

"My Love's Cold," 16

"My Name Is Peace," 31

Narrative Verse, xv

"Narrow Fellow in the Grass, A," 73

National Institute of Arts and Letters, 199

National Register, 105, 116

"Nativity Ode, The," 168

"Natural Sorrow, A," 93

Nazism, 87–88, 126

"Neophyte, The," 183

Nesbit, Edith, 22

"Neuter-Cat's Apotheosis, The," 156–57

New Age, xv, 16, 18, 22, 27–28, 31, 70, 188, 217

New English Weekly, 53–55, 71, 84, 88

"New House, The," 241–42

Newsom, John, 227

New Yorker, 136

"Night-Piece," 201–2

"1938," 92–93

Noah, 92

Northanger Abbey, 140

Norway, 84–85

"Noses," 230

"Nun's Priest's Tale, The," 155

Nursing Mirror and Midwives Journal, 230–31

Oak Cottage, 34, 69–70, 86, 90, 102, 108, 116, 120, 162, 173–74, 178–79, 224, 252

"Oak Tree, The," 21
"O Come Out of the Lily," 86, 94
"Ode on a Nightingale," 58
"Of the Damned," 20–21
"Of Silence and the Air," 79
O'Hara, Kathleen, xv, 24, 26–27, 34, 37–38,
    45, 53, 84, 101, 103–4, 112–13, 116, 120,
    160–63, 172–74, 187, 190–91, 193, 195,
    197, 208, 211, 214–15, 217, 231, 235,
    237–38, 250, 254–57, 265
"Old, Childless, Husbandless," 97
"Old Clockwork Time," 181–82
"Old Fashioned Song, An" 145
"Old Woman Speaks of the Moon, The," 97
On Cats, xvi, 64, 114, 153–59, 259
"One Does Get Old at Last," 261
"One Tree to the North," 135, 153
Orage, A. R., xv, 16–18, 22, 27, 32, 40–41, 53–
    55, 63, 67–69, 83, 198, 213, 217, 222, 266
Orwell, George, 25–26, 35–37, 114–15, 162–
    63, 198, 208, 220, 222, 240, 266
O'Shaughnessy, Eileen, 114–15
"Other, The," 189
"Other People's Glasshouses," 108
"Our Best Stoker," 259
Out of the Silent Planet, 144, 236–37, 239
Ovid, 7
Owen, Wilfred, 21
"O Where Is the Dwelling?" 72
Oxford, xv, 114, 145–46, 151–53, 161–62,
    164, 166, 172–74, 177–78, 190–91, 193,
    195–96, 199, 211, 234, 237–38, 254
Oxford Book of Twentieth-Century Verse, The,
    274

Palgrave, Francis, 5, 270
Palmer, Herbert, 82, 85–86, 102, 106, 112,
    115, 117, 119, 142–48, 159, 208
Palmer, Nettie, 53, 63, 68–69, 84, 120, 135,
    138–40, 142, 145, 159, 164, 168–69
"Paradox, The," 79
Parnassus, 63
"Passion and Peace," 43
"Pastiche: In Praise," 32
Patmore, Coventry, 238
Patterson, John, 209
"Penitence," 183, 190
Penns in the Rock, 120, 140, 159, 177
"Penny Chick, The," 260
Perelandra, ix, 144, 146–47, 149, 153,
    236–37, 239

Persephone, 7
Persephone in Hades, xv, 7, 27, 44–51, 52–53,
    83, 147, 150–51, 164, 173
Personal Call, 213
Philoctetes, 150
Philomel, 58
Pilgrim's Regress, The, 142–43
Pitter, Geoffrey, xiv, 2–5, 9–11, 222–23, 257
Pitter, George, 2–8, 10–12, 14–18, 26, 32–34,
    107, 130
Pitter, Louisa Rosamund Murrell, 2, 3, 5,
    7–15, 34, 38, 65, 102–4, 106, 108
Pitter, Mark, 238, 240, 250–51
Pitter, Mary, 238, 250, 256–57
Pitter, Olive, xiv, 2–6, 9–11, 14, 176, 222–23
Pitter, Ruth: as an artisan, 13, 24, 26–27,
    34–35, 37–38, 53–55, 83–84, 87–88,
    100–102, 104–6, 112, 115–16, 119–22,
    160–62, 168, 193–95, 222, 226–27; birth,
    1; death, 270–71; early days at the cot-
    tage in Hainault Forest, 4, 7–12, 222–26;
    poems inspired by Hainault Forest, 38–41,
    71–73, 88–90, 127–29, 176–77, 245–46;
    romantic love, 15–16, 35–38, 41–44,
    55–57, 66, 73–75, 130–33, 148, 192,
    196–98, 202–3, 206–7, 238–40; spiri-
    tual life, 76–79, 91–95, 97–98, 118–19,
    121, 124–27, 133–34, 141–42, 146–47,
    175, 178–80, 182–89, 227–31, 242–45,
    247–48, 263–65, 268–69, 273–74; writing
    poetry, 22–23, 27–28, 30–32, 38–41, 44–
    45, 51–53, 57–60, 66–67, 70–71, 82–83,
    85–87, 95, 100, 106–7, 109–10, 112–14,
    134–35, 137–38, 148–53, 164–65,
    167–68, 169–72, 190, 212–20, 233–36,
    251–53, 258, 261, 266, 271–74
"Plain Facts, The," 259
"Planting Mistletoe," 258–59
"Pleasures of Old Age, The," 253–54
"Ploughboy's Plea, The," 267
Poems 1926–1966, 251
Poetic Diction, 146, 150
"Poetry in Various Moods," 231
Poetry Northwest, 213
Poetry Society of London, 269
"Poet Speaks, The," 41
Poet's Club, 140
"Polymorph Pervers," 133, 178
Pope, Alexander, 138, 159, 169
"Poor Poet, The," 15
Post-Victorian Poetry, 143

"Pot-Bound," 259–60
"Potting Shed Tutti-Frutti," 269
Pound, Ezra, xiii, 22, 152, 167, 251
Powell, Dilys, 80
"Prayer for a Fair People," 20
Prelude, The, 41
"Primordial Cell, The," 97, 99
Problem of Pain, The, 236
"Promised Rest, The," 21

"Quality," 231
Queen Elizabeth II, 214–15, 218–20, 236,
    262, 264
Queen Victoria, 1
Queen's Gold Medal for Poetry, ix, xiii, xvi,
    214–15, 217–21, 236
"Quorum Porum," 154–55

Radcliffe Infirmary, 234
Raine, Kathleen, 232, 253
"Rainy Summer," 128, 135, 152
"Raspberry Nectar," 259
"Reading of Poetry, The," 231
"Red Boy," 261
"Reflection after Victory," 190
Resurrection, 57, 59–60, 124–25, 134, 200
Resurrection, The, 255
"Retrospect," 127–28, 135, 145
"Return to Poetic Law, A," 169–72, 174
"Return, The," 72
"Rhubarb, Rhubarb," 259
Richard the Lionheart, 97
Ridler, Ann Margaret, 271
Rixon, Ellen, 265, 270
Rixon, John, 265
Rixon, Rachel, 265, 270–71
Road to Emmaus, The, 255
Roberts, Michael, 64, 81
Roethke, Theodore, 212, 251
"Rogation Hymn," 268–69
"Romance," 226
"Romford Market," 9
Royal Institution of Great Britain, 169
Royal Society of Literature, xiii, 85, 209, 258
"Rubarb Pie," 109
"Rude Potato, The," 107–8, 113
Rude Potato, The, xvi, 64, 104, 106, 107–11,
    145, 148, 259
Russell, Arthur, 210, 217–20, 222, 231, 233–
    36, 241, 253, 258, 262–63, 266, 270
Russell, Bertrand, 166

Ruth Pitter: Homage to a Poet, 253
"Ruth Pitter Talks about Her Own Poems,"
    215–17, 219

"Saboteuse, The," 149
Sackville-West, Virginia, 140, 159
"Sadd Lament of a Performing Flea, A," 60
Samson Agonistes, 150
Sands, Mary Ann, 213, 219
Sarton, May, 99, 159, 166, 211
Sassoon, Siegfried, 21, 22, 81
Sauriac, A., 45
Sayer, George, 196–98, 217, 240
Sayers, Dorothy, 158
Schweitzer, Albert, 219
Scott-James, R. A., 167, 270
Screwtape Letters, The, 114, 236, 239
"Seagulls in London," 100–101
"Sea-Herb," 32
"Serious Child, The," 132–33
Shakespeare, William, 6, 118, 159, 169, 267,
    270
Sheed and Ward, 28
Shelley, Percy, 169
"Silence Shall Cover Thee," 20
"Sinking," 165
Sirens, 57
Skelton, Robin, 253
Smathers, D. W., 227
Smith, Hilary, 119
"Snow in Madrid," 199
"So Good of Their Kind," 259
Sohrab and Rustum, 149
"Solemn Meditation, A," 77, 144, 212–13
"Solitary, The," 99
"Song, Grieve No More," 20
"Song of a Child's Happiness, A," 18–19
"Sorceress Eclogue," 201
"Sparrow's Skull, The," 125–26, 130, 137,
    145, 153, 165
Spectator, The, 146
"Spectrum," 272
Spender, Stephen, 98
Spenser, Edmund, 64, 147, 153, 272
"Spirit Watches, The," 86, 93–94, 99, 124
Spirit Watches, The, xvi, 43, 84, 87, 88–100,
    110, 121, 127, 129, 137, 145, 152, 159,
    164, 179–80, 192, 198, 244, 246
Spot in time, xv, 41, 71, 178
"Spring (Rondeau)," 18–19
"Spring, The," 92–93

Stuart-Smith, Stephen, 269
Stephens, James, 80, 266
Still by Choice, xvi, 43, 221, 235–36, 240,
    241–49, 250
"Stockdove, The," 91–92
"Stolen Babe, The," 175–76
Stonier, G. W., 136
"Storm," 75, 144
"Stormcock in Elder," 38–40, 71, 128
Storrs, Ronald, 147–48
"Stranger and a Sojourner, A," 184–85
"Strawberry Plant, The," 11, 73
Stricken Deer, The, 82
Strong, L. A. G., 140
"Strongest in Spring," 247
"Struggling Wheat," 91
Studio, 13
"Sudden Heaven," 75, 92, 133, 178, 273–74
Suffolk, 13, 26
"Swan, The," 21, 137
"Swan Bathing, The," 130–31, 134, 135, 198,
    207, 213
"Sweet Other Flesh," 244–45
"Swifts," 259
Sydney, Philip, 170

"Tall Fruit-Trees, The," 128, 153
Taylor, Ian, 266
Tell-Tale Article, The, 151, 163, 169
Tennant, Stephen, 235–36, 250–51, 256, 258
Tennyson, Alfred, 6, 270
Tennyson, Hallam, 119, 253, 262
"Thanksgiving for a Fair Summer," 77
That Hideous Strength, 143, 236–37, 239
"There Is a Spirit," 251–52
"They Have Murdered My Village," 260
Thomas, Dylan, 140, 207–8, 251
Thomas, Mary, 264–66, 270
Thomas, Miles, 227
"Tigress, The," 95–96
"Time's Fool," 88–89
Times Literary Supplement, 29, 63, 98, 165, 188
Tolkien, J. R. R., 193, 197
"To the People," 18
"To a Lady in a Wartime Queue," 260
"To the Soul," 76
"To the Virgins," 200
"To the Virgins, to Make Much of Time," 200
Traherne, Thomas, 179, 272–74
"Transparent Earth, The," 186–87
"Tree, The," 186

"Tree at Dawn, The," 178–80, 189–90
"Trophy of Arms, A," 79
Trophy of Arms, A, xiii, xvi, 22, 43, 70–83,
    86–88, 90, 92, 97–99, 121, 127, 129, 133,
    135, 138, 144–45, 150, 152, 164, 175,
    178, 198, 207, 259, 267, 270, 273
"True Love's not Told," 43, 73, 198
"Tuft of Violets, The," 178, 190
"Twa Corbies," 56
"Two Kinds of Memory," 146–47
"Tyger, The," 95
Tyler, Dorothy, 166

Ulysses, 57
Unicorn, The, 150
Untermeyer, Louis, 22, 98–99, 235
Urania, 97, 126
Urania, 164–65, 167, 251

"Valediction (for Milton's Tercentenary)," 267
Valéry, Paul, 170
Vaughan, Henry, 163, 178
Venus, 94, 97
"Victory Bonfire," 259
"Vine in Bloom, The," 90–91, 100
"Viper, The," 73, 129, 259
Virginia Quarterly Review, 84, 86–88
Visionary and Dreamer, 254
"Vision of the Cuckoo," 132, 135, 198
"Vitraea Circe," 148
"Voices," 231
Voyage to Arcturus, 146

Wain, John, 119, 251–53
Walberswick, 13, 14
Walberswick Peasant Pottery Company, 13,
    24, 34
Walsh, Chad, 199
Walter, Eugene, 140, 159, 173–74
Walton, Eda, 30, 80
War Office, 13
Warrender, Alice, 82
Weatherhead, Leslie, 227
"We Cannot Take Less," xvi–xvii
"Weed, The," 108–9
"Weeping Water, Leaping Fire," 43, 74, 198
Wellesley, Dorothy, 117, 120, 140, 159, 161,
    165, 177, 212, 233
"What of These?" 145
"Wherefore Lament," 133
Whistler, Laurence, 83, 140, 148

"Whom We Have Buried," 20
Wiggin, Maurice, 248
"Wild Honey," 129
"Windows, The," 272
Winter's Tale, The, 150
"Women Are Magic," 231
Woman's Hour, xvi, 159, 219, 222–23, 234
"Woman, the Good Peasant, the Good Lady, and the Good Queen," 231
"Woman, This," 200–201
"Women in the Priesthood," 153
Woman: World's Greatest Weekly for Women, 228–30, 232
Woodland Trust, xiv
Wordsworth, Dorothy, 138, 159
Wordsworth, William, 6, 40–41, 169, 189, 270

"World is Hollow, The," 151, 183–84, 189–90
World War I, xv, 1, 13, 14, 20, 26, 118, 128, 197
World War II, xiii, xv, xvi, 38, 87, 100, 112, 120–27, 133, 137, 161, 210, 240
"Worn Theme, A," 181, 190

Yeats, W. B, xiii, 72, 80, 99, 117, 120, 163, 190, 212, 251
"Yet One More Spring," 205–6
"Yorkshire Wife's Saga," 246
Young, Andrew, 253
Young, Stanley, 255, 262, 265, 270–71
"Young King Cole," 148
"Young Loves," 31
"Youth Has Been Storm," 31